Strategies of
Educational Research:
Qualitative Methods

Social Research and Educational Studies Series

Series Editor
Robert G. Burgess,
Senior Lecturer in Sociology,
University of Warwick.

1. Strategies of Educational Research: Qualitative Methods
   Edited by *Robert G. Burgess.*

By the same author:
Experiencing Comprehensive Education (1983)
In the Field: An Introduction to Field Research (1984)

Further edited volumes:
Field Research: A Sourcebook and Field Manual (1982)
Exploring Society (1982)
The Research Process in Educational Settings: The Case Studies
(Falmer Press, 1984)
Field Methods in the Study of Education (Falmer Press, 1984)

Social Research and Educational Studies Series: 1

Strategies of Educational Research:
QUALITATIVE METHODS

Edited by

Robert G. Burgess

 The Falmer Press

(A member of the Taylor & Francis Group)
London and Philadelphia

UK   The Falmer Press, Falmer House, Barcombe, Lewes, East Sussex, BN8 5DL

USA   The Falmer Press, Taylor & Francis Inc., 242 Cherry Street, Philadelphia, PA 19106-1906

First published 1985

Library of Congress Cataloging in Publication Data

Main entry under title:

Strategies of educational research.

   (Social research and educational studies series; 1)
   Bibliography: p.
   Includes index.
   1. Education—Research—Great Britain—Addresses, essays, lectures. 2. Educational statistics—Great Britain—Addresses, essays, lectures. I. Burgess, Robert G. II. Series.
   LB1028.S844 1985   370′.7′8041   85-4584
   ISBN 1-85000-033-6
   ISBN 1-85000-034-4 (pbk.)

Typeset in 11/13 Garamond by Imago Publishing Ltd, Thame, Oxon.

Printed in Great Britain by Taylor & Francis (Printers) Ltd, Basingstoke

Contents

Series Editor's Preface

The purpose of the *Social Research and Educational Studies* series is to provide authoritative guides to key issues in educational research. The series includes overviews of fields, guidance on good practice and discussions of the practical implications of social and educational research. In particular, the series deals with a variety of approaches to conducting social and educational research. Contributors to this series review recent work, raise critical concerns that are particular to the field of education, and reflect on the implications of research for educational policy and practice.

Each volume in the series draws on material that will be relevant for an international audience. The contributors to this series all have wide experience of teaching, conducting and using educational research. The volumes are written so that they will appeal to a wide audience of students, teachers and researchers. Altogether, the volumes in the *Social Research and Educational Studies* series provide a comprehensive guide for anyone concerned with contemporary educational research.

The series will include individually authored books and edited volumes on a range of themes in education including: qualitative research, survey research, the interpretation of data, self-evaluation, research and social policy, analyzing data, action research, the politics and ethics of research.

The contributors to this volume demonstrate how qualitative methods include a broad range of research strategies that can be used to conduct contemporary and historical research in the field of education. Together this collection of essays points to some of the processes, problems and procedures of doing research that have been encountered by practising researchers and the ways in which they can be handled in the study of educational settings.

Robert Burgess
University of Warwick

Preface

This collection of essays is designed for individuals who are interested in conducting qualitative research in educational settings. This approach has increased in popularity in the last decade as many research reports on educational projects now indicate that researchers have used participant observation, unstructured interviews and written and oral documents in the course of their research. Yet, it is relatively rare for research reports to contain detailed discussions of research methodology.

When researchers do provide reflections on the conduct of their research projects much space is often devoted to theoretical frameworks or perspectives and to descriptions of informal social processes that surround the collection and analysis of data. However, social anthropologists and sociologists who have used this approach have to some extent omitted to discuss the detailed strategies and tactics that have been used to collect data. As a consequence, the conduct of research using qualitative methods is surrounded in mystery.

Accordingly, this set of essays sets out to focus directly on the strategies and tactics that have been used by social and educational researchers to collect data using a range of qualitative methods. In the essays that follow the focus is upon the characteristics of qualitative research and the procedures that have been adopted when using particular methods while collecting educational research data. As a result the authors take as a central theme those strategies and tactics they have found most effective. In turn, they also point out some of the problems involved in using these methods and the ways in which they have attempted to overcome them. Finally, some of the essays point to ways in which researchers may extend their repertoire of qualitative methods and develop this approach in the conduct of educational research.

All the essays that are included in this volume were specially commissioned from individuals who were known to have had considerable experience in using a particular method on a recent educational project. The contributors were therefore able to draw on their experiences to illustrate the ways in which they have used qualitative methods in the study of educational settings. It is therefore to be hoped that the material contained in these essays will help to give undergraduates, postgraduates and researchers some insight into the conduct of qualitative research which will assist in developing their own practice. In turn it is also to be hoped that the strategies which are discussed in these papers will contribute to ongoing debates about the ways in which qualitative methods can be specifically developed in the study of education.

Most of the papers in this volume were originally prepared for a three-day workshop entitled 'Qualitative Methodology and the Study of Education' that was held at Whitelands College, London in July 1983. This workshop focused discussion on the collection, analysis and use of qualitative data. All the papers that were prepared for this workshop were pre-circulated so that the initial drafts could be the subject of extensive discussion and debate. All the workshop sessions were tape-recorded which provided further material for authors to use in recasting and restructuring their papers for publication. In addition to the paper-givers, contributions were also made to our discussions by Clem Adelman, Martin Bulmer, Carol Cummings, Sara Delamont, Dave Ebbutt, Lee Enright, Janet Finch, Tony Green, Gordon Griffiths, Martyn Hammersley, Andy Hargreaves, Alan James, Alison Kelly, Saville Kushner, Colin Lacey, Andrew Pollard, John Scarth, Sue Scott, Marten Shipman, Pat Sikes, Helen Simons, Marie Stowell, Margaret Threadgold, Rob Walker, Sue Webb, Mary Willes and Peter Woods.

This workshop was made possible by a grant that I was awarded by the Social Science Research Council. I would, therefore, like to thank the members of the Education and Human Development Committee who supported my proposal for this workshop to examine issues of qualitative method in the study of education. My thanks are also due to the Research Resources and Methods Committee of the Social Science Research Council who provided an additional grant so that the session at which original versions of the papers by Stephen Ball, Lynda Measor and myself were given could be video-taped. Copies of the video may be hired free of charge from the editor at the Department of Sociology, University of Warwick. I would also like to thank all the workshop participants; especially the paper-givers who have provided help, advice and encouragement in the course of preparing these papers for publication. In turn, we are all indebted to the domestic staff at Whitelands College and to the technical staff of the Roehampton Institute who contributed to the success of the workshop. I am also indebted to Hilary Burgess who has provided support, encouragement and constructive criticism throughout this project. Finally, I have been fortunate to have the secretarial services of Sue Turner on this project. She has worked efficiently and effectively in typing and retyping the papers and has taken great care over the appearance of this manuscript. As always, however, any errors or omissions are, of course, my own.

Robert Burgess
University of Warwick

Introduction

Robert G. Burgess

The last decade has witnessed several changes in the scale, substance, style and strategy of social and educational research. In a field that was at one time dominated by talk of indicators, variables, and measurements, by the use of surveys and quantitative techniques, some space has been cleared for qualitative research. Nevertheless, the term 'qualitative methods' has been used to cover approaches that are claimed to be 'soft' and 'non-rigorous' compared with the 'hard', 'objective', 'rigorous' approaches that are referred to as quantitative methods. As a consequence even those who use qualitative approaches have highlighted some of the differences between these styles of research and taken on some of the terminology that has been used to make abusive remarks about their methodology. In reporting on a symposium concerned with the analysis of qualitative data[1], Halfpenny (1979) kept a record of the terms that were used to distinguish between qualitative and quantitative approaches. He found that the participants at the symposium used the following terms to describe their own activities and those of others:

Qualitative	*Quantitative*
soft	hard
dry	wet
flexible/fluid	fixed
grounded	abstract
descriptive/exploratory	explanatory
pre-scientific	scientific
subjective	objective
inductive	deductive
speculative/illustrative	hypothesis testing
political	value-free
non-rigorous	rigorous

idiographic	nomothetic
holistic	atomistic
interpretivist	positivist
exposes actors' meanings	imposes sociological theory
phenomenological	empiricist/behaviourist
relativistic	universalistic
case-study	survey
good	bad
bad	good
	(Halfpenny, 1979, p. 799).

Such a range of terms indicates the necessity to specify carefully what is meant by 'qualitative research' and 'qualitative methods'. In many texts that are devoted to this style of investigation the content consists of discussions about participant observation and in-depth, unstructured or semi-structured interviews which allow the researcher to learn first hand about the social world (cf. Filstead, 1970; Bogdan and Taylor, 1975; Bogdan and Biklen, 1982). While such methods allow the researcher to get close to the data and to understand the definitions, concepts and meanings that participants attribute to social situations, it is often the case that these methods are narrowly defined and used at the expense of other approaches. Indeed, some methodologists have gone so far as to suggest that qualitative methods should be used to the exclusion of other approaches. For example, Filstead introduces his volume on qualitative methodology by stating:

> The assets of qualitative methodology in sociology need to be stressed and the shortcomings of quantitative methodology need to be exposed in their boldest relief. (Filstead, 1970, p. 8)

Such an approach is very narrow and places an unnecessary straightjacket on research as a brief glance at empirical studies reveals a series of situations where researchers utilize a variety of approaches in the course of learning about the social world. For example, some commentators such as McCall and Simmons (1969) have indicated that it is misleading to regard even participant observation as a single method as they consider it:

> refers to a characteristic blend or combination of methods and techniques ... (it) involves some amount of genuinely social interaction in the field with the subjects of the study, some direct observation of relevant events, some formal and a great

deal of informal interviewing, some systematic counting, some collection of documents, and artifacts, and open-endedness in the direction the study takes. (McCall and Simmons, 1969, p. 1)

While this has the advantage of encouraging researchers to consider the repertoire of research methods that can be used, it is vital that some consideration be given to the kinds of methods that are appropriate for particular research problems and the ways in which different research techniques may be used alongside each other to obtain different types of data. In particular, Zelditch (1962) has indicated that researchers need to ask themselves: What kinds of methods are relevant for the particular topic under investigation? What kinds of information are relevant? How can the methods used be evaluated? Zelditch suggests that these questions can be addressed by considering the 'efficiency' and 'informational adequacy' of particular methods in gathering data which he summarizes in table form:

Table 1:   Types of Information by Methods of Obtaining Information

Information Types	Methods of Obtaining Information		
	Enumerations and Samples	**Participant Observation**	**Interviewing Informants**
Frequency distributions	Prototype and best form	Usually inadequate and inefficient	Often, but not always, inadequate; if adequate it is efficient
Incidents, histories	Not adequate by itself; not efficient	Prototype and best form	Adequate with precautions, and efficient
Institutionalized norms and statuses	Adequate but inefficient	Adequate but inefficient, except for unverbalized norms	Most efficient and hence best form

Source: Zelditch, 1962, p. 576.

However, some commentators such as Sieber (1973) have indicated that they would want to take this argument a stage further. The result is that Sieber claims that methods should not merely be used alongside each other but should be integrated in the course of a research project. Indeed, Sieber indicates how qualitative and quantitative methods may be used together by providing a specific discussion of fieldwork and surveys. In writing about the contribution of fieldwork to survey research design when studying suburban schools he comments:

> the initial fieldwork sharpened the focus of the investigation on a specific educational problem by directing attention to the contrast between pre- and post-suburbanized systems, necessitating the inclusion of a second system. A survey was then conducted to gain fuller knowledge of the impact of suburbanization on the schools. Fieldwork, in sum, dictated the design of the survey investigation. (Sieber, 1973, p. 1342)

Furthermore, he considers that fieldwork can assist in the analysis and interpretation of survey data by providing a theoretical structure, by validating survey results, by helping to interpret statistical relationships, by providing the framework for the construction of indices, and by clarifying questionnaire data. Overall, such an approach suggests that the researcher who has a flexible research design and who utilizes a range of research methods can bring distinct advantages to a project.

However, it is one thing for commentators to suggest how qualitative methods might be used and quite another when it comes to research practice. It is, therefore, appropriate at this point to turn to examples of studies that have used qualitative methods. As reviews of studies of schools and classrooms in Britain and the USA[2] have indicated, there are now numerous accounts that have been based on qualitative research. We turn, therefore, to three projects that have used participant observation, interviews and life history methods in the study of aspects of English education.

In the course of studying a Roman Catholic co-educational comprehensive school I wanted to examine the ways in which teachers and pupils defined and redefined situations and attributed meanings in different social settings (Burgess, 1983). Accordingly I took the role of a part-time teacher in the school which provided me with the opportunity to collect data using participant observation, unstructured interviews and documentary materials (cf. Hargreaves, 1967; Lacey, 1970; Ball, 1981). My attention focused on what teachers and pupils experience in classrooms, on public occasions such as school assembly, in the staff common room and in meetings. Such observations could, in turn, be followed up through informal interviews with teachers and pupils and by examining some of the notes, circulars and memoranda that were circulated. This approach was characteristically in the ethnographic tradition that had been developed by Gluckman (cf. Gluckman, 1964) in the study of different aspects of British society utilizing observational methods.[3]

While this approach puts observation at the centre of the investigation other researchers have utilized interviews. For example, in studying classroom rules and the ways in which teachers use these rules to impute deviance to pupils, Hargreaves, Hester and Mellor (1975) used observational methods and interviews as they state:

> Our principal method was to observe a lesson and from these observations to extract those teacher statements and/or actions which consisted of a reaction to a deviant act ... We then reported the reaction back to the teacher at a later stage, asking for his commentary upon what he did ... we often merely quoted what the teacher had said, and the teacher was willing to make a commentary upon his action without any direct question from us. On other occasions we reported the teacher's statement back and then asked why the teacher had said or done something. (Hargreaves, Hester and Mellor, 1975, p. 219)

In this sense, the researchers attempted to develop a non-directive way of examining classroom events with teachers based on conversations as they remark:

> As far as possible we tried to minimize the evaluative overtones to these conversations, by suggesting that we ourselves were not making evaluative judgements on the teachers and were not making personal judgements about whether or not the teacher had said or done the 'right' thing. (Hargreaves, Hester and Mellor, 1975, p. 220)

In this study the interviews were used to complement observational work that was done by the researchers (cf. Woods, 1979). However, some investigators have used individual and group interviews as the main methods in their research.[4]

A third strategy that has regained some popularity in recent years has been the life history method.[5] Among those researchers engaged in the study of education, it has been Ivor Goodson who has consistently advanced arguments about the advantages of this approach (cf. Goodson, 1983). In conducting his study *School Subjects and Curriculum Change* (Goodson, 1982) the main aim was to examine the development of environmental studies as a new school subject. Here, Goodson decided that the life history method was most appropriate as he writes:

> The research method employed was to begin by collecting the life histories of the major participants in the promotion of this new subject. The patterns of decision, the changes of direction and the stated rationales given by these promoters of the subject were echoed in the evolutionary profile of the subject which was later reconstructed. In a real sense the life histories of these key personnel constituted the life history of the subject in question (Goodson, 1983, p. 148).

However, life history material was not the only data that Goodson used as his study reveals how letters, minutes of meetings, the syllabus for various examinations and other sets of documentary materials were also used to establish a case study of curriculum subjects (cf. Goodson, 1982).

These are just three examples of the ways in which different researchers have used qualitative methods in the conduct of educational research projects. Here our examples have focused on the main qualitative methods that social and educational researchers have used, although this is by no means an exclusive list. For example, some researchers have utilized photographic evidence as a means of studying the activities that occur in schools and classrooms (cf. Collier, 1973; Walker and Wiedel, 1985), while others have utilized audio and audio-visual recordings of classroom activity either with tape-slide or video recordings of classrooms.[6] In addition, some sociologists who have utilized the theoretical perspective known as ethnomethodology consider that conventional forms of qualitative data (observation, interviews and documents) produce data that are too anecdotal with the result that they have collected audio and video-tape material in order to have a record of participants' speech, acts and gestures that can be used in the conduct of conversation analysis.[7]

The term 'qualitative methods' is therefore used to refer to a range of research and writing. Some writers have used other terms to refer to some aspect of qualitative methods. Among the most common terms to refer to particular strategies are fieldwork, field research, ethnography, case study and interpretive procedures. Each of these terms covers an element of qualitative method and indeed there is some overlap involved. However, these terms indicate different kinds of emphasis that are given to qualitative research projects. For example, fieldwork is a term that is commonly used by social anthropologists to signify the collection of observational material, while among sociologists it might include survey research as well as observational work. Field research tends to refer to those methods that are known as participant observation, unstructured interviews and documentary materials. Meanwhile, ethnography is a term that many social anthropologists (cf. Wolcott, 1975) reserve for the study of culture, although among many British investigators in schools and classrooms the term has been used to refer to investigations that principally use observational methods (cf. Hammersley, 1980; 1982). However, some investigators such as Stenhouse (1984) consider that ethnography is tainted with the spirit of colonialism and as a consequence is distant from the 'subjects' of study. For this reason, Stenhouse indicates that his work should be described as 'case study' where an intense relationship is developed with teachers in projects that utilize observation, tape-recorded interviews and the study of documents (Stenhouse, 1984; 1985). While the approach advocated by Stenhouse keeps to the concepts and categories of the participants' other studies, especially those conducted by sociologists work within a particular theoretical framework. Among the most common theoretical perspective used is that which is loosely known as symbolic interactionism (cf. Rock, 1979). It is research that leans heavily on this perspective that Williams (1981) has referred to as 'interpretive procedures'.[8] Yet all these approaches highlight one element of qualitative work against another which in some cases results in a narrow definition of the field of vision. Accordingly, this collection of essays is concerned with 'qualitative methods', a term that is used to signify that we are not dealing with any particular method but a variety of activities which may be used to collect qualitative data. But, we might ask, what are the characteristics of qualitative research?

The Characteristics of Qualitative Research

We have already indicated that the term 'qualitative method' refers to a range of activities with the result that researchers engaged in educational studies who utilize this approach might sit at the back of classrooms with notebook and pencil, might interview teachers and pupils, might collect documents that are held in a school office or might produce a video recording of classroom activities. Nevertheless, all these investigations have much in common and to a greater or lesser degree share the following features:

1   The Researcher Works in a Natural Setting

For many qualitative researchers the main objective involves studying individuals in their natural settings to see the way in which they attribute meanings in social situations. In this context the main research instrument is the researcher who attempts to obtain a participant's account of the situation under study. Even when tape-recorders and cameras are used the researcher cannot leave it all to the machine as a written record has to be maintained about the location in which events are photographed and interviews tape-recorded. Indeed, even when documents are collected it is the researcher who has to consider the circumstances in which documents were produced. In short, much of the investigation is devoted to obtaining some understanding of the social, cultural and historical setting.

2   Studies may be Designed and Redesigned

All the methods associated with qualitative research are characterized by their flexibility. As a consequence researchers can turn this to their advantage as a rigid framework in which to operate is not required. Researchers can, therefore, formulate and reformulate their work, may be less committed to perspectives which may have been misconceptualized at the beginning of a project and may modify concepts as the collection and analysis of data proceeds. The advantage to this approach is that the researcher has little reason to terminate a study through lack of commitment to a set of standardized methods of data collection.

3   The Research is Concerned with Social Processes and With Meaning

Many qualitative studies are conducted within a theoretical framework that focuses upon social processes and the meanings which participants attribute to social situations. For those researchers who work from a sociological perspective the theoretical orientation is principally derived from symbolic interactionism whereby studies are conducted with a view to understanding the way in which participants perceive situations. As Blumer remarks:

> One would have to take the role of the actor and see his world
> from his standpoint. This methodological approach stands in
> contrast to the so-called objective approach so dominant
> today, namely, that of viewing the actor and his action from
> the perspective of an outside, detached observer ... the actor
> acts towards his world on the basis of how he sees it and
> not on the basis of how that would appears to the outside
> observer. (Blumer, 1966, p. 542)

The kinds of studies that are conducted using this perspective
involve focusing on how definitions are established by teachers and
pupils (cf. King, 1978 and 1984; Burgess, 1983) and how teacher and
pupil perspectives have particular implications for patterns of schooling
(cf. Woods, 1980a and 1980b).

4   Data Collection and Data Analysis Occur Simultaneously

Just as researchers are able to formulate and reformulate their studies
on the basis of a flexible research design, so this element of flexibility
occurs throughout the collection and analysis of data. These elements
of the research project are not part of a linear process but occur
alongside each other. Indeed, data are not usually collected to support
or to refute hypotheses but categories and concepts are developed
during the course of data collection. The theory is therefore not
superimposed upon the data but emerges from the data that are
collected. It is this style of work that has been advocated by Glaser
and Strauss (1967) but many researchers have indicated that there are
real difficulties involved in developing theories from data (cf. Brown,
1973; Williams, 1976). As a result, researchers who have used this
approach have highlighted some of the problems involved (cf. Porter,
1984).
   Qualitative research is, therefore, not based upon a fixed set of
rigid procedures, but nevertheless the researcher does need to develop
a set of strategies and tactics in order to organize, manage and
evaluate. Such strategies involve the researcher in considering how to
plan, organize, collect and analyze data. In writing about field
research Schatzman and Strauss (1973) have considered all the major
strategies and tactics associated with the field research process among
which are some relatively brief discussions about the strategies

associated with particular methods. Accordingly, the main contributions to this book are concerned with a detailed discussion of the strategies that are associated with qualitative methods and techniques which can be used in the study of education. It is therefore to the major themes of this volume and the contents of the papers that we now turn with a view to setting them within a broader context.

Some Issues, Themes and Questions Concerning Qualitative Methods

All the papers in this volume examine the specific issues that arise when researchers use qualitative methods to study education. The papers cover four major issues:

1 Those methods that have traditionally been associated with anthropological studies: participant observation, interviewing and the use of key informants. In this context, we need to consider what particular problems are involved in using these approaches to study an aspect of our own society (cf. Burgess, 1984a, pp. 11–30) and when studying pupils and teachers.

2 The use of documentary and historical records: the case record, the life history, the written document and archival material. In these circumstances, questions concerning the use of historical methods (cf. Lipset and Hofstadter, 1968) need to be considered in the context of education.

3 The use of ethnomethodology and conversation analysis as a more systematic approach to qualitative research. In this context, it is essential to consider what advantages are gained by using these methods over more 'conventional' qualitative approaches.

4 Finally, there are questions concerning the extent to which qualitative methods may be used alongside each other: observations with interviews, interviews with historical material and so on. While this issue is specifically dealt with in the final paper it is also handled in an incidental fashion in many of the earlier papers. In this context we might consider the extent to which methods may be used to complement each other or whether integration is ever possible.

The first three papers in the volume deal with methods that are traditionally associated with ethnography (cf. Hammersley and

Atkinson, 1983) but in this instance Ball, Measor and Burgess respectively are not only concerned with general methodological issues that relate to participant observation, interviewing and the use of key informants.

We begin by turning to the most commonly-used qualitative method, namely participant observation. This method is usually reviewed in relation to the participant, participant-as-observer, observer-as-participant and observer typology of research roles that was established by Gold (1958). While this typology may provide a useful analytic distinction it does not address the major issues that a participant observer will confront while doing research in educational settings. Among the issues involved are: Can adults do participant observation with children? Should researchers take teacher roles? For some researchers such as Spindler (Spindler and Spindler, 1982) the question of doing research with children can be answered in the affirmative as he has shown how he has taken his place in a desk alongside pupils. Similarly Mandy Llewellyn's accounts of the classroom are seen from a pupil perspective (Llewellyn, 1980). Meanwhile, Birksted (1976) and Corrigan (1979) have discussed the problems involved of taking a pupil perspective, and, for that matter, taking a teacher perspective. It is these issues that Stephen Ball turns to in his paper on participant observation with pupils. Drawing not only on his own experiences but also those of several colleagues, Ball raises questions not only about the applicability of the research technique (in terms of ascribed roles and achieved roles) but also aspects of the research process (gaining access, selecting informants or being selected by them, as well as issues of confidentiality). It is on this latter issue that Ball advances a proposal for a research archive that would contain recordings (such as those that he has made) where researchers would reflect on the processes associated with the conduct of social and educational research. In this sense, this proposal has the potential to extend the current interest of many researchers who write short autobiographical accounts of their research experience.[9]

The paper that follows from Lynda Measor focuses on research experience in relation to strategies of interviewing that she has used on two educational research projects. Measor begins by drawing attention to the fact that she intends to talk about issues that she regards to be nothing more than 'intuition'. However, her analysis takes us towards an account of the research process and the strategies that can be used to bring about a successful interview. Her account diverges somewhat from the image of a 'standard interview' that is portrayed in many textbooks but converges with the interview experience of other researchers engaged in qualitative work (cf. Oakley, 1981; Stenhouse, 1984; Burgess, 1984a; Finch, 1984). Among the issues that Lynda Measor raises is the extent to which interviewing in qualitative research builds on relationships and the art of conversation that is developed in everyday life. In this respect, Measor's paper has much in common with the discussion provided by Stephen Ball and also the account provided by Robert Burgess.

In qualitative research much is said about the importance of the relationship between the researcher and the researched. But we might ask: What form do these relationships take? How may these relationships be used in qualitative research? It is to an analysis of such issues that Burgess turns in discussing his use of key informants in an ethnographic study of a comprehensive school (cf. Burgess, 1983). Apart from work reported by social anthropologists (Casagrande, 1960) there has been relatively little discussion by sociologists and others about the role of informants in their research. The paper by Burgess looks at the role of informants in projects based on participant observation and interviewing and suggests ways in which they not only contribute to data collection but also to data analysis.

It is to issues of data collection and analysis that Jean Rudduck takes us in her paper on case records. The 'case record' was a term devized by Lawrence Stenhouse to describe an archive of raw data that could be worked on by other researchers in the course of writing case studies and producing multi-site case study generalizations. In her paper, Rudduck begins by reviewing Stenhouse's work including his call for the establishment of case records (cf. Stenhouse, 1978) and his use of case records in the library access, library use and user education in academic sixth forms (LASS) project that is partly reported in Stenhouse (1984). In particular, Rudduck discusses the way in which she has used such case records in the course of producing a research report (cf. Rudduck, *et al*, 1983). She also raises issues concerned with preparing material for the archive, the importance of referencing and indexing and the use of the archive in handling data and writing up. In this sense Rudduck is setting out a way in which we might establish a data archive which could complement Ball's notion of a research archive. However, she indicates that a number of problems still remain to be worked upon including issues concerned with the use of field notes, interview transcripts and found or unsolicited documents that are collected by researchers in qualitative projects. In this sense, Rudduck indicates that documentary evidence which takes many forms and which is produced by both the researcher and the researched is a central feature of qualitative research (cf. Burgess, 1982 and 1984a).

The importance of documentary evidence in qualitative research has been well illustrated by Thernstrom (1965) among many others who has shown how documents can help to provide context in qualitative projects; a feature that has also been emphasized in qualitative educational projects by Woods (1983). It is therefore a consideration of documentary materials to which we turn in the following four papers from Ivor Goodson, Alison Andrew, June Purvis and Rene Saran. Each of these researchers have different disciplinary allegiances, utilize different theoretical perspectives in their projects and a range of written and oral evidence. In all these papers the researchers draw on detailed evidence from their own experiences of conducting educational research.

We begin with a paper from Ivor Goodson who argues the case for including life history data in qualitative investigations. In particular, he indicates how the use of historical and documentary methods may help to overcome some of the inadequacies associated with research methods in general and with studies that are interactionist and ethnographic. Goodson focuses on the strategies that can be used for building up case studies using life history data. In particular, he illustrates that the collection of life stories from teachers who were key participants in the development of rural studies helped to provide insights for him on aspects of curriculum change. In this sense, his key participants who are used to reconstruct historical material are very similar to the key informants that Burgess has discussed in relation to ethnographic work. In turn, Goodson also discusses further strategies associated with life history material including the ways in which they might be combined with other methods of investigation, their resemblance to oral history (cf. Thompson, 1978) and their value in historical studies. The paper by Goodson is, therefore, a challenge to researchers to consider how historical sources and historical methods may be used in their studies. But we might ask, how are such sources and methods used in historical studies?

Alison Andrew picks up some of the themes that have been developed by Goodson; especially the issue concerning the poverty of sociology which is devoid of an historical perspective.[10] A key issue that Andrew raises concerns the identification and use of primary and secondary sources. However, she utilizes this discussion to examine aspects of sampling and selection. Furthermore, she discusses the way in which researchers pose questions and use concepts in studying historical sources (cf. Thompson, 1972 and 1976). Her account reveals that researchers who use written historical materials are engaged in a form of interaction with their sources and are concerned with selection and sampling.[11] However, as far as data analysis is concerned she indicates that a central question is: whose account counts?

While Alison Andrew takes up the question of accounts in relation to the working class and the middle class, June Purvis turns our attention to accounts about men and women and to power relations between the sexes. In many ways, she takes up similar issues to those that have been discussed by Andrew: the use of sources, questions, concepts and categories. However, she also raises the issue: how does a researcher evaluate the documentary evidence that he or she obtains and uses? It is in addressing this issue that we are brought towards examining authenticity, selection and bias (cf. Platt, 1981a and 1981b; Burgess, 1984a). Finally, Purvis also considers the way in which texts may be classified (cf. Purvis, 1984); an issue that brings us back to looking at the sources that are used.

It is to a consideration of sources and their use in an educational research project that Rene Saran turns. In particular she examines the ways in which archival data can be used alongside interview data. As well as considering the way in which different sources may be combined, Saran also raises such issues as the value position of the researcher and the way in which this influences what is to be researched, and also the way in which evidence is matched from different sources. In this paper we are brought back to considering some of the practicalities of interviewing but in this case the interviews are being used in relation to sets of historical data. Accordingly the paper brings us full circle and raises not only some of the issues that were raised by Measor but also those that were raised by Goodson. In this sense, the papers that are devoted to historical material examine the way in which such data and such methods may overcome some of the deficiencies in observational and interview material.

In a similar way, the papers by Stephen Hester and by David Hustler and George Payne indicate that there are other styles of qualitative research that will overcome the problems of 'conventional approaches'. Hester begins by looking at the value of ethnomethodology in studying deviance in classrooms, while Hustler and Payne focus on the use of conversation analysis whose techniques can be used to give rigour to other qualitative approaches (cf. Shone and Atkinson, 1983). Hester indicates that if researchers are to come to terms with such problems as the partiality of much qualitative data, the production of sociological accounts and the observability of interpretative procedures it is essential to reorientate towards ethnomethodology and conversation analysis. In particular, he discusses the importance of using an approach that overcomes the problems associated not only with conventional ethnography but also with ethnomethodological ethnography (cf. Atkinson and Drew, 1979) with the result that he favours conversation analysis with its emphasis on transcripts of naturally occurring talk as the preferred methodological strategy. In a similar way Hustler and Payne also highlight the advantage of using conversation analysis whereby naturally occurring talk can be used for the purposes of analysis. However, they raise such issues as: What constitutes data? How may these data be analyzed? How may the data be located in a broader context? In addressing these questions the researchers indicate not only how they have adopted other approaches but how they have adapted this style of investigation in relation to the problems that they are examining.

Such issues are raised in several of the papers which indicate how a flexible research design in qualitative investigations results in a situation where researchers modify the methods that are used and utilize them in a variety of different combinations. It is to this issue that Brian Davies and his colleagues bring us back to consider in the final paper. They indicate that the key questions that have to be posed about any research strategy are: Is it reliable? Is it valid? Davies and his colleagues outline the ways in which the selection of methods is embedded within the problems and processes associated with the natural history of a particular project. Furthermore they indicate that for them methods can only be used alongside each other; juxtaposition has advantages but integration is hardly possible given the difficulties involved in putting together various theoretical perspectives (cf. Archer, 1981). In this sense, Davies and his colleagues remind us that methods, techniques, strategies and processes should not be isolated from one another as they can each influence the other in the course of an investigation.

The focus of all the papers in this volume is upon the development of strategies and styles of investigation in qualitative research and the ways in which particular methods can be developed and used in relation to particular problems in the conduct of educational research. While the researchers have come from different projects and different disciplines they all indicate that their work shares a common set of issues that recur in the papers in this volume and include:

(i)   the strategies that can be used in qualitative research;
(ii) the methods and the ways in which they may be combined with each other;
(iii) the ways in which the strategies adopted by a researcher relate to:
    (a)   the research problem;
    (b)   the research design;
    (c)   the research process;
(iv) the importance of selection strategies in social investigation;
(v)   the relationship between the researcher and the research;
(vi) the ways in which different strategies may overcome some of the deficiencies of conventional approaches.

These are some of the issues that are raised by the various contributors to this volume. While many of the contributors have indicated how they have handled these issues in their own projects, they have not advanced a set of universal solutions that can be used by any researcher in any project. Instead their contributions have contributed to the debate about the use of qualitative methods in social science in general and educational projects in particular. Nevertheless there are still numerous issues for researchers to continue to consider which include:

(a)   the status of qualitative research;
(b)   the problem of bias in qualitative investigations;
(c)   the influence of the researcher upon the research;
(d)   the relationship between problem, theory and method;
(e)   the relationship between qualitative and quantitative research.

While these papers do not provide instant solutions to these problems, it is nevertheless hoped that they will contribute to the debate that continues among researchers who utilize qualitative methods in the study of educational settings.

Notes

1 For a complete report of this symposium see BLAXTER (1979).
2 See for example ATKINSON and DELAMONT (1980) on British studies, and WILCOX (1982) on studies in the USA.
3 For further discussion of this approach in studying schools see LACEY (1982) LAMBART (1982) and for its use in the study of other areas of British life and culture see FRANKENBERG (1982). For a detailed metho-

dological discussion of the school study that has briefly been discussed here see Burgess (1984a).

4 For further discussion of interviews in educational studies see Burgess (1984a), Simons (1981) and Hammersley and Atkinson (1983). On interview strategy in qualitative projects see, for example, Spradley (1979).

5 For discussions of life history methods see, for example, the papers in Bertaux (1981) and the introductory text by Plummer (1983).

6 Such approaches have not only been pioneered by social scientists but also documentary film makers. See, for example, Roger Graef's film *School* in the *Space Between Words* series and the narrative documentaries produced by Richard Denton (see, for example, *Public School* and *Kingswood*). Meanwhile, in the USA there is Frederick Wiseman's film *High School*. For analysis of ethnographic films see the regular features that appear in each issue of *The American Anthropologist* and on films about education see Graef (1980).

7 For a discussion of the relevance of this approach in the study of schools see Mehan (1978 and 1979). Most of the developments that have occurred in this field have taken place over the last fifteen years. As a consequence there is a vast number of published and unpublished studies and commentaries. For an introduction see Benson and Hughes (1984) and for a detailed review of this material since 1975 see, for example, Heritage (1984) which contains an excellent bibliography.

8 For a more detailed guide to these different perspectives see Burgess (1984a), especially the introduction.

9 For examples of this approach in social and educational research in Britain see Shipman (1976) and Burgess (1984b), and in the USA see some of the papers in Popkewitz and Tabachnick (1981) and Spindler (1982), especially part one. For other collections (mainly by sociologists and social anthropologists) see, for example, Hammond (1964), Spindler (1970), Bell and Newby (1977), Bell and Encel (1978), Shaffir, Stebbins and Turowetz (1980), Roberts (1981), Bell and Roberts (1984).

10 For discussions of the relationship between history and sociology see, for example, Lipset and Hofstadter (1968) and the articles in the special issue of the *British Journal of Sociology* (1976).

11 In her discussion Alison Andrew indicates that there is some similarity between her approach and that of Glaser and Strauss (1967) as far as selection, sampling, saturating categories and knowing when to stop collecting further data are concerned.

References

Archer, M.S. (1981) 'Educational systems', *International Social Science Journal*, 33, 2, pp. 261–84.

Atkinson, J.M. and Drew, P. (1979) *Order in Court*, London, Macmillan.

Atkinson, P. and Delamont, S. (1980) 'The two traditions in educational ethnography: sociology and anthropology compared', *British Journal of Sociology of Education*, 1, 2, pp. 139–52.

BALL, S.J. (1981) *Beachside Comprehensive: A Case Study of Secondary Schooling*, Cambridge, Cambridge University Press.

BELL, C. and ENCEL, S. (Eds.) (1978) *Inside the Whale*, Oxford, Pergamon Press.

BELL, C. and NEWBY, H. (Eds.) (1977) *Doing Sociological Research*, London, Allen and Unwin.

BELL, C. and ROBERTS, H. (Eds.) (1984) *Social Researching: Politics, Problems*, and *Practice*, London, Routledge and Kegan Paul.

BENSON, D. and HUGHES, J.A. (1984) *The Perspective of Ethnomethodology*, London, Longman.

BERTAUX, D. (Ed.) (1981) *Biography and Society: The Life History Approach in the Social Sciences*, London, Sage.

BIRKSTED, I.K. (1976) 'School performance viewed from the boys', *Sociological Review*, 24, 1, pp. 63–77.

BLAXTER, M. (Ed.) (1979) 'The analysis of qualitative data: a symposium', special issue of *Sociological Review*, 27, 4, pp. 649–827.

BLUMER, H. (1966) 'Sociological implications of the thought of George Herbert Mead', *American Journal of Sociology*, 71, 5, pp. 535–44.

BOGDAN, R. and BIKLEN, S.K. (1982) *Qualitative Research for Education: An Introduction to Theory and Methods*, Boston, Allyn and Bacon.

BOGDAN, R. and TAYLOR, S.J. (1975) *Introduction to Qualitative Research Methods*, New York, Wiley.

BRITISH JOURNAL OF SOCIOLOGY, (1976) *Special Issue on History and Sociology*, 27, 3, September.

BROWN, G.W. (1973) 'Some thoughts on grounded theory', *Sociology*, 7, 1, pp. 1–16.

BURGESS, R.G. (Ed.) (1982) *Field Research: A Sourcebook and Field Manual*, London, Allen and Unwin.

BURGESS, R.G. (1983) *Experiencing Comprehensive Education: A Study of Bishop McGregor School*, London, Methuen.

BURGESS, R.G. (1984a) *In the Field: An Introduction to Field Research*, London, Allen and Unwin.

BURGESS, R.G. (Ed.) (1984b) *The Research Process in Educational Settings: Ten Case Studies*, Lewes, Falmer Press.

CASAGRANDE, J. (Ed.) (1960) *In the Company of Man*, New York, Harper and Row.

COLLIER, J. (1973) *Alaskan Eskimo Education: A Film Analysis of Cultural Confrontation in the Schools*, New York, Holt, Rinehart and Winston.

CORRIGAN, P. (1979) *Schooling the Smash Street Kids*, London, Macmillan.

FILSTEAD, W.J. (Ed.) (1970) *Qualitative Methodology*, New York, Markham.

FINCH, J. (1984) ' "It's great to have someone to talk to": the ethics and politics of interviewing women', in BELL, C. and ROBERTS, H. (Eds.) *Social Research: Politics, Problems and Practice*, London, Routledge and Kegan Paul.

FRANKENBERG, R. (Ed.) (1982) *Custom and Conflict in British Society*, Manchester, Manchester University Press.

GLASER, B. and STRAUSS, A.L. (1967) *The Discovery of Grounded Theory*, London, Weidenfeld and Nicolson.

GLUCKMAN, M. (Ed.) (1964) *Closed Systems and Open Minds: The Limits of Naivete in Social Anthropology*, Edinburgh, Oliver and Boyd.

GOLD, R. (1958) 'Roles in sociological field observation', *Social Forces*, 36, pp. 217–23.

GOODSON, I.F. (1982) *School Subjects and Curriculum Change*, London, Croom Helm.

GOODSON, I.F. (1983) 'The use of life histories in the study of teaching', in HAMMERSLEY, M. (Ed.) *The Ethnography of Schooling*, Driffield, Nafferton.

GRAEF, R. (1980) 'The case study as Pandora's box', in SIMONS, H. (Ed.) *Towards a Science of the Singular*, Norwich, Centre for Applied Research in Education, Occasional Publication, No. 10.

HALFPENNY, P. (1979) 'The analysis of qualitative data', *Sociological Review*, 27, 4, pp. 799–825.

HAMMERSLEY, M. (1980) 'Classroom ethnography', *Educational Analysis*, 2, 2, pp. 47–74.

HAMMERSLEY, M. (1982) 'The sociology of classrooms', in HARTNETT, A. (Ed.) *The Social Sciences in Educational Studies: A Selective Guide to the Literature*, London, Heinemann.

HAMMERSLEY, M. and ATKINSON, P. (1983) *Ethnography: Principles in Practice*, London, Tavistock.

HAMMOND, P.E. (Ed.) (1964) *Sociologists at Work*, New York, Basic Books.

HARGREAVES, D.H. (1967) *Social Relations in a Secondary School*, London, Routledge and Kegan Paul.

HARGREAVES, D.H., HESTER, S. and MELLOR, F. (1975) *Deviance in Classrooms*, London, Routledge and Kegan Paul.

HERITAGE, J. (1984) 'Recent developments in conversation analysis', *Warwick Working Papers in Sociology No. 1*.

KING, R. (1978) *All Things Bright and Beautiful? A Sociological Study of Infants' Classrooms*, London, Wiley.

KING, R. (1984) 'The man in the wendy house: researching infants' schools', in BURGESS, R.G. (Ed.) *The Research Process in Educational Settings: Ten Case Studies*, Lewes, Falmer Press.

LACEY, C. (1970) *Hightown Grammar: The School as a Social System*, Manchester, Manchester University Press.

LACEY, C. (1982) 'Freedom and constraints in British education', in FRANKENBERG, R. (Ed.) *Custom and Conflict in British Society*, Manchester, Manchester University Press.

LAMBART, A.M. (1982) 'Expulsion in context: a school as a system in action', in FRANKENBERG, R. (Ed.) *Custom and Conflict in British Society*, Manchester, Manchester University Press.

LIPSET, S.M. and HOFSTADTER, R. (Eds.) (1968) *Sociology and History: Methods*, New York, Basic Books.

LLEWELLYN, M. (1980) 'Studying girls at school: the implications of confusion' in DEEM, R. (Ed.) *Schooling for Women's Work*, London, Routledge and Kegan Paul.

MCCALL, G.J. and SIMMONS, J.L. (Eds.) (1969) *Issues in Participant*

Observation: A Text and Reader, Reading, Mass., Addison Wesley.

MEHAN, H. (1978) 'Structuring school structure', *Harvard Educational Review*, 48, pp. 32–64.

MEHAN, H. (1979) *Learning Lessons: Social Organisation in the Classroom*, Cambridge, Mass., Harvard University Press.

OAKLEY, A. (1981) 'Interviewing women: a contradiction in terms', in ROBERTS, H. (Ed.) *Doing Feminist Research*, London, Routledge and Kegan Paul.

PLATT, J. (1981a) 'Evidence and proof in documentary research: some specific problems of documentary research', *Sociological Review*, 29, 1, pp. 31–52.

PLATT, J. (1981b) 'Evidence and proof in documentary research: some shared problems of documentary research', *Sociological Review*, 29, 1, pp. 53–66.

PLUMMER, K. (1983) *Documents of Life: An Introduction to the Problems and Literature of a Humanistic Method*, London, Allen and Unwin.

POPKEWITZ, T.S. and TABACHNICK, B.R. (Eds.) (1981) *The Study of Schooling: Field-Based Methodologies in Educational Research and Evaluation*, New York, Praeger.

PORTER, M.A. (1984) 'The modification of method in researching postgraduate education', in BURGESS, R.G. (Ed.) *The Research Process in Educational Settings: Ten Case Studies*, Lewes, Falmer Press.

PURVIS, J. (1984) *Understanding Texts*, Course E205 Unit 15, Milton Keynes, Open University Press.

ROBERTS, H. (Ed.) (1981) *Doing Feminist Research*, London, Routledge and Kegan Paul.

ROCK, P. (1979) *The Making of Symbolic Interactionism*, London, Macmillan.

RUDDUCK, J., HOPKINS, D., GROUNDWATER-SMITH, S. and LABETT, B. (1983) *Library Access and Sixth Form Study*, report to the British Library Research and Development Department.

SCHATZMAN, L. and STRAUSS, A.L. (1973) *Field Research: Strategies for a Natural Sociology*, Englewood Cliffs, N.J., Prentice Hall.

SHAFFIR, W.B., STEBBINS, R.A. and TUROWETZ, A. (Eds.) (1980) *Fieldwork Experience: Qualitative Approaches to Social Research*, New York, St. Martin's Press.

SHIPMAN, M. (Ed.) (1976) *The Organization and Impact of Social Research*, London, Routledge and Kegan Paul.

SHONE, D. and ATKINSON, P. (1983) 'Ethnography and conversational analysis', in HAMMERSLEY, M. (Ed.) *The Ethnography of Schooling*, Driffield, Nafferton.

SIEBER, S.D. (1973) 'The integration of fieldwork and survey methods', *American Journal of Sociology*, 78, pp. 1335–59, reprinted in BURGESS, R.G. (Ed.) (1982) *Field Research: A Sourcebook and Field Manual*, London, Allen and Unwin.

SIMONS, H. (1981) 'Conversation piece: the practice of interviewing in case study research', in ADELMAN, C. (Ed.) *Uttering, Muttering: Collecting, Using and Reporting Talk for Social and Educational Research*, London, Grant McIntyre.

SPINDLER, G.D. (Ed.) (1970) *Being an Anthropologist: Fieldwork in Eleven Cultures*, New York, Holt, Rinehart and Winston.

SPINDLER, G.D. (Ed.) (1982) *Doing the Ethnography of Schooling: Educational Anthropology in Action*, New York, Holt, Rinehart and Winston.

SPINDLER, G. and SPINDLER, L. (1982) 'Roger Harker and Schönhausen: From the familiar to the strange and back again', in SPINDLER, G.D. (Ed.) *Doing the Ethnography of Schooling: Educational Anthropology in Action*, New York, Holt, Rinehart and Winston.

SPRADLEY, J.P. (1979) *The Ethnographic Interview*, New York, Holt, Rinehart and Winston.

STENHOUSE, L. (1978) 'Case study and case records: towards a contemporary history of education', *British Educational Research Journal*, 4, 2, pp. 21–39.

STENHOUSE, L. (1984) 'Library access, library use and user education in academic sixth forms: an autobiographical account', in BURGESS, R.G. (Ed.) *The Research Process in Educational Settings: Ten Case Studies*, Lewes, Falmer Press.

STENHOUSE, L. (1985) 'A note on case study and educational practice', in BURGESS, R.G. (Ed.) *Field Methods in the Study of Education*, Lewes, Falmer Press.

THERNSTROM, S. (1965) 'Yankee City revisited: the perils of historical naivete', *American Sociological Review*, 30, pp. 234–42.

THERNSTROM, S. (1968) 'Quantitative methods in history: some notes', in LIPSET, S.M. and HOFSTADTER, R. (Eds.) *Sociology and History: Methods*, New York, Basic Books.

THOMPSON, E.P. (1972) 'Anthropology and the discipline of historical context', *Midland History*, 1 (3) pp. 41–55, reprinted in BURGESS, R.G. (Ed.) (1982) *Field Research: A Sourcebook and Field Manual*, London, Allen and Unwin.

THOMPSON, E.P. (1976) 'On history, sociology and historical relevance', (Review article) *British Journal of Sociology*, 27, pp. 387–402.

THOMPSON, P. (1978) *The Voice of the Past: Oral History*, Oxford, Oxford University Press.

WALKER, R. and WIEDEL, J. (1985) 'Using pictures in a discipline of words', in BURGESS, R.G. (Ed.) *Field Methods in the Study of Education*, Lewes, Falmer Press.

WILCOX, K. (1982) 'Ethnography as a methodology and its application to the study of schooling', in SPINDLER, G.D. (Ed.) *Doing the Ethnography of Schooling: Educational Anthropology in Action*, New York, Holt, Rinehart and Winston.

WILLIAMS, R. (1976) 'Symbolic interactionism: the fusion of theory and research?', in THORNS, D.C. (Ed.) *New Directions in Sociology*, Newton Abbott, David and Charles.

WILLIAMS, R. (1981) 'Learning to do field research: intimacy and inquiry in social life', *Sociology*, 15, 4, pp. 557–64.

WOLCOTT, H. (1975) 'Criteria for an ethnographic approach to research in schools', *Human Organization*, 34, 2, pp. 111–27.

WOODS, P. (1979) *The Divided School*, London, Routledge and Kegan Paul.

WOODS, P. (Ed.) (1980a) *Teacher Strategies*, London, Croom Helm.

WOODS, P. (Ed.) (1980b) *Pupil Strategies*, London, Croom Helm.
WOODS, P. (1983) *Sociology and the School: An Interactionist Viewpoint*, London, Routledge and Kegan Paul.
ZELDITCH, M. (1962) 'Some methodological problems of field studies', *American Journal of Sociology*, 67, pp. 566–76, reprinted in BURGESS, R.G. (Ed.) (1982) *Field Research: A Sourcebook and Field Manual*, London, Allen and Unwin.

1   Participant Observation with Pupils

Stephen J. Ball

In this paper I hope to examine some of the peculiar and hitherto almost totally neglected problems of doing participant observation with school pupils. This exercise, I believe, serves not only to draw attention to some of the weaknesses in our current understanding of the school experiences of pupils but also raises some significant questions about the variety of activities that pass for 'doing participant observation'.

The paper draws upon three main sources: (i) my own experience of fieldwork in schools; (ii) taped interviews with other researchers who have been particularly concerned with the way in which pupils experience and make sense of their school lives; and (iii) published accounts of 'doing participant observation with pupils'. The sample, if it may be called that, of research experiences was selected to provide a degree of variation (a) in the age of the pupils involved; (b) in the mode of engagement employed by the researchers; (c) in the nature of the research relationship that was developed; (d) in the nature of the institutions referred to (primary, middle, comprehensive and approved schools); and (e) in the mix of gender relations (male-male, female-male, female-female, and so on). In addition, the work of Andrew Pollard, as teacher-researcher, provides an interesting point of comparison with that of the externally-based researchers. And Lynda Measor (discussing the fieldwork of Measor and Woods, 1984) describes experiences with pupils involved in the transition from middle school to comprehensive school, and from childhood to adolescence.

The informal taped discussions with Lynda Measor, Lynn Davies and Andrew Pollard, which I quote extensively in the text, were particularly valuable I think, both to me personally as a practising researcher, able to learn from and share detailed experiences with colleagues, and in identifying and pursuing a set of general themes and issues for this paper. The researchers provide an insider's view of the research process and their accounts offer important insights into aspects of working with school pupils which are simply not touched upon in most of the published research biographies. I tried as far as possible to treat these tape-recordings as data in the normal way. I listened to the tapes and identified certain categories and issues which seemed to highlight points of contrast or consensus between the respondents. I used my own experiences as a further point of reference. What I have been able to include in the paper is only a small selection of the range of topics dealt with in the tape-recordings and the 'analysis' must be seen as my responsibility. It would be unfair to identify the respondents with the weaknesses and inaccuracies which I am sure remain in the discussion presented below. I would want to recommend that as a research community we make more effort to collect and preserve the research experiences of colleagues; recent published work (Burgess, 1984) has begun to do this but publication is not the only means we have available. I now have a valuable archive, be it only three tapes at the moment, of oral testimony from educational researchers who have studied pupils in schools. Perhaps more could be collected in a more systematic fashion.

In order to proceed I intend to make, for purposes of discussion, what is perhaps a controversial distinction. A distinction between, on the one hand, children, and, on the other, teenagers. A distinction between those pupils who inhabit a world which revolves around home, school and playing with friends, as against those who have entered the semi-autonomous social world of adolescence: the latter being more likely to have developed social horizons which extend beyond the immediate neighbourhood and the social life of the family into those spheres where adult supervision no longer runs — the disco, the coffee bar, the football terrace, and so on. However, I am not suggesting a hard-and-fast break point between these two cultural spheres nor do I envisage the movement from one to the other being made by all pupils at the same point in time. (Although I would tentatively suggest that the shift comes for the majority of pupils sometime between the beginning of their last year in primary (or middle) school and the end of their first year in the secondary school.) It may be that the social arrangements of schooling actually affect the transition (see Measor and Woods, 1984). And I readily recognize that the categories 'child' and 'teenager' are themselves not unitary, they are riven with gender, race and class divisions.

Nonetheless, I hope that the usefulness of such a distinction will become more apparent as the paper develops.

School Life and Social Life

I want to begin with the 'teenage' group and some reflections on my own experience of 'doing participant observation with pupils' at Beachside Comprehensive. And perhaps the first question I would want to ask of my own work is whether 'doing participant observation' is an adequate or accurate way of referring to my involvement with pupils. Definitions of participant observation abound in the literature of research methods but they can perhaps be divided very roughly into what might be called hard-line and soft-line positions. The former stress the need to share in the activities of the researched in a direct and complete way, to do what they do, while the latter emphasize the necessity of the observer's presence but without specifying the need to do what the researched do. The latter definitions obviously open up a wider range of possibilities for study by participant observation methods than the former. Indeed, according to the hard-line position participant observation with pupils is, except under exceptional circumstances, extremely difficult to bring off. Znaniecki (1934) provides an example of the hard-line.

> When I wish to ascertain at first hand what a certain activity is, just as when I wish to obtain first hand information about a certain object, I try to experience it . . . There is only one way of experiencing an activity, it is to perform it personally.

Kluckhohn (1940) offers another when she suggests that 'participant observation is a conscious and systematic sharing; in so far as the circumstances permit, in the life-activities, and on occasion, in the interests and affects of a group of persons' (p. 331). Even here though we have the get-out clause provided by 'in so far as circumstances permit'. Becker *et al.* (1968) are a good example of the soft-line position, here:

> The participant observer follows those he studies through their daily round of life, seeing what they do, when, with whom, under what circumstances, and querying them about the meaning of their actions. (p. 13)

One general way around this problem of how much sharing and

experiencing is required of the participant observer is the classification, as done by Gold (1958), of different modes of participant observation (complete participant, participant-as-observer, observer-as-participant, and complete observer).

My own work with pupils at Beachside must be placed on the soft-line side of the definition and probably in some ways fits with Gold's category of 'observer-as-participant', at least that is as far as the younger pupils are concerned; I will say something about my relationships with the sixth-form later on. The vast bulk of my observation work was done *at school* and, as far as the pupils were concerned, the vast bulk of my observation of them at school was done in classrooms. In this sense at least Becker *et al.*'s definition above describes exactly what I was doing. But obviously, the daily round of life for pupils does not only consist of their activities,formal or informal, in the classroom. Nonetheless, observation of, and involvement with, pupils in other settings was minimal. And my observation of them out of school was virtually non-existent. (Some of the decision-making involved in this process of selection and focusing down is discussed in Ball, 1984.) I did watch and interact with pupils on occasions in the playground and the corridors of Beachside, I did on occasions prowl around the school buildings searching for and occasionally finding those 'backstage' areas where, in the folklore of schools, rules are broken and venial sins against the teachers' code of behaviour are committed. But my cursory, and often embarrassing, presence in these places could hardly be described as any kind of participant observation. My work was, of necessity I would want to say, concerned with the school lives of the pupils, and perhaps even more narrowly with their classroom lives. It seems to me that I share this focus with the vast majority of participant observation studies of pupils.

But what of the exceptions? Ian Birksted (1976), a cognitive anthropologist, provides one example of a rather different mode of work with pupils, as he explains of his study of a group of six comprehensive school boys: 'I was interested less in seeing how they fitted into the structure of the school than in how the school fitted into the structure of their lives' (p. 65). Birksted's contact with pupils began not in the classroom but by 'regular attendance at a youth and community centre' and once having entered the school after two months of attendance at the youth centre Birksted organized his participant observation around the boys' version of life at school, not the teachers' version. Thus, in his account it is out of lesson time that assumes greatest importance.

The boys would spend school breaks in a terrapin behind the school. There they quickly assembled and soon had the room organized to their liking. Chairs and tables were disposed in a suitable way for a game of cards, windows opened to get rid of smoke and to allow quick disposal of incriminating cigarettes in case of an emergency, cigarettes were lit, cassette or radio brought out, and Steve would deal out the cards. (p. 68)

Indeed, this reversal of the usual emphasis of observation produced a reversal in the portrayal of school life. 'School breaks did not seem to be gaps between classes, but classes seemed to be interruptions in the gathering. After these blanks, normal life had to be picked up again and continued' (p. 68).

It could be said that all we have here is a different kind of research project and a different kind of researcher's concern. But Birksted's account suggests more than that. His work with these boys places school within a wider context. His participation, of necessity, extended outside of the school itself. And he met with them frequently on their own ground.

Over the summer holiday, the boys would meet at each others' houses in the morning, smoke, have a coffee, listen to music while playing cards, or sit in the shelter in the local park, or lie around on the grass in the sun. They would meet again after dinner, though Ken often stayed home and Frank always went over to his girlfriend's house in the evening. (p. 68)

Birksted argues that sociologists of education have tended to present a distorted picture of pupils' views of school by assuming in the first place that school, positively or negatively, was of prime importance in their lives. He suggests that it may be for some pupils that school is *in toto*, as a formal institutional experience, peripheral. The boys with whom he worked 'did not see school as an organizational principle of their lives' (p. 74).

Birksted clearly made considerable progress in penetrating the social lives of these boys but he does not suggest in his work that participant observation of this kind is necessarily easy. In a second paper based on his relationship with Andrew, another boy from the same school, he describes a situation where:

More than any other of the pupils I met, Andrew's relationship to me throughout the research was very ambivalent

> ... He both sees me as a person with whom he deals in a cooperative way and as a person to be avoided and to be suspicious of. I was once interviewing Andrew in his home in the absence of his parents, when he told me that he didn't mind being interviewed because I was 'so obviously involved in my work. At first, my dad told me to be careful in case you were just somebody trying to find out about things'. (Birksted, 1974, p. 4)

Here again we must note that Birksted is in Andrew's territory, in his home. Indeed a great deal of the material that Birksted presents was elicited during visits to Andrew's home, and from this vantage point a more rounded view of Andrew's social life is captured than would ever have been possible for a school-based researcher. Thus:

> School, for Andrew, is caught up in the adolescent problem of transition to adulthood. What the experience of school is to Andrew does not depend only upon how the school is organized, but on the complex of conflicts and perceptions that Andrew brings to the situation. (p. 13)

Institutional Studies and Cultural Studies

It might be possible then to differentiate in a crude way between *institutional studies* of pupils from what might be termed *cultural studies*. That is to say, studies which concern themselves with the school lives of pupils as pupils, as against those which concern themselves with pupils' social lives as teenagers or children inside but also beyond school itself. I would not want to suggest that the former are in some way deficient or inadequate but we must be willing to admit that the landscape looks different depending on the particular hill you happen to choose to stand on.

Lynn Davies (1978, 1979, 1980, 1983 and 1985) conducted an institutional study, examining the 'differences in deviance between boys and girls' in a West Midlands comprehensive, and 'bringing the girls back in'. Thus, she says 'my research was to act as a counter to all the male oriented research on pupil deviance'. Davies' methods included various forms of observation of and interviewing of pupils, focusing primarily upon groups of deviant girls. She sought in effect both to observe 'the action' and to understand the 'interests and affects' of the particular girls with whom she was concerned. She described her relationship with the girls as follows:

My role, I think, with them, was very much that of the cultural stranger. There was no way I was going to become part of the group, ever going to get very much into their confidence. My origins, although working class, were of a very different type and geographical locality to the culture of the West Midlands area where I was doing the research. My own experience of school was a middle/upper class single sex girls' school, compared with this mixed, predominantly working class intake in the research school. My age, my accent, precluded me 'passing' as a pupil, which some researchers have apparently managed with girls ... I don't think I lost out entirely. The strangeness has the advantage of the unfamiliarity of the anthropologist. I wasn't part of the girls' or the schools' taken for granted world and therefore I could frame all sorts of stupid questions with impunity. And sometimes it worked the other way, they were almost over anxious to expose me to what they saw as the covert operations of school life; they would take me to the smokers' corner and the places where the action was happening in an attempt to help my journalistic aims. I think they knew I could be trusted not to reveal confidences and activities to staff. They had no hesitation in saying what they thought, recording things, admitting various sorts of misdemeanors. I think that sort of trust was very quickly built up. They would have known very swiftly if what they had said had got back. But they always addressed me as Mrs. Davies or 'Miss'. For some reason I never insisted on the use of my christian name, it would have seemed a little inappropriate or artificial. But I think 'my girls', as I referred to them, were almost quite proud of my attachment to them, they were singled out as special, perhaps for the first time in their school career. And they would remark to other people 'she's our mate', they appropriated me in some ways and attached me to them. If I was going out with them, for example, on a school trip. And apparently they would ask teachers when I was coming in again, probably if I was honest, because they could escape lessons to talk to me. They treated me as a sort of pet gerbil really.

The last remark is one that I recognize personally from my own work, being enthusiastically 'adopted' by some by the classes I worked with. Lynda Measor also found this, but Lynn Davies' account of her research role raises a number of other very important points.

First is the question raised earlier about the nature of adult participation in a teenage group, although, as we shall see, there have been attempts made by participant observers to join teenage groups and even to 'pass' as teenagers. But Davies not only points to the problems created by differences in age but also differences in background — region of origin and school experiences. Viewing this optimistically she sees all these factors combining to create a situation of anthropological strangeness for the researcher.

For Lynn Davies interviewing was the most appropriate technique in these circumstances, although the girls were willing to offer her at least honorary membership of their group. The second point relates to this, that is the strangeness for the girls of Davies' adaption of the typical adult/teacher role. Again this is an experience which I recognize very strongly. Davies clearly occupied an anomalous position vis-a-vis the girls, being both 'Miss' and 'mate', and having real but benign interest in their interests and activities, especially the illicit ones. It is on the basis of such a peculiar role that trust is established. Revelation can actually tie the researcher to his or her informants. By entrusting the researcher with 'guilty knowledge' the researcher becomes implicated as an accessory after the fact, if you like. This can be, as William Foote Whyte discovered, a source of uncomfortable ethical problems (I shall return to ethics later).

Thirdly, Davies' point about regional differences is worth underlining. Corrigan (1979) makes a similar point about being an outsider in his research in Sunderland but he goes on to say that 'what I have got to say below does NOT relate purely to Sunderland; the schools, police and youth in Sunderland are not, in *respect of this piece of writing*, very different from those of London or Coventry' (p. 9). The final important point here is clear if we consider Birksted's and Davies' work together, that is the question of the affects of gender on the relationships between researcher and researched. These examples are of matched gender.

It seems likely, at least in commonsense terms, that shared gender is likely to increase the degree of intimacy in the research relationship and therefore the depth and quality of data obtained. Some feminist researchers have indeed argued that not only is 'shared femininity' a distinct advantage for women researchers working with female respondents but that research done on women by male researchers is by definition inadequate and probably undesirable. This is an issue which is fully explored elsewhere (Roberts, 1981 and

Spender, 1980) but two general points may be worth making. Morgan (1981, p. 91), following Lynn Davies' optimistic line, stresses that gender differences can actually serve to heighten awareness of gender as an issue in fieldwork:

> Gender differences in fieldwork are not simply a source of difficulties, such as exclusion from important central rituals, or, in my case, exclusion from all-important interactions in the toilets, but are also a source of knowledge about the particular field. The 'participant observer', in short, has a gender identity.

Certainly I did not find gender differences to be a handicap in my own fieldwork in a mixed school. Indeed, among the pupils, girls tended to be overall more forthcoming and easier to work with than boys, with the exception perhaps of the first year girls, some of whom I found to be initially shy and giggly. But after the first year girls quickly seemed to become more confident and articulate than the boys when talking in one to one, or small group, situations, although there were, of course, exceptions on both sides. It is probably possible to begin to relate this to gender differences in socialization and experience at school. For instance, while at break and lunchtimes many of the boys were engaged in hectic games of football in the playground or were marauding in large groups, the girls, for the most part, sat and talked. This also meant that the girls were often more accessible to me at times like these. My longer interviews were also always done with girls; probably the longest and most personal interviews I obtained were with a group of 'deviant' fifth years, some of whom I actually taught in my sociology class. Nonetheless, a number of researchers have found that in mixed-sexed talk women experience 'restrictions in style' and that 'in single-sex groups women are more likely to use cooperative verbal strategies' (Spender, 1980, p. 129). My interview transcripts might very well bear closer scrutiny on these points. But it is significant that I have retreated into a discussion once again of interviewing; participation with the girls was almost entirely limited to classroom activities.

The sort of data to which I had, or was given, access is clearly likely to be different from that available, potentially at least, to a woman researcher. For example, Lynda Measor's fieldwork gave her access to a whole range of intimate details.

> I'm talking about who's lost their virginity, and who's just started their periods for the first time and what it felt like,

who's mum beat hell out of them last night, who's dad's about to leave who's mum, and stuff like that.

Even so the data provided to me by girls was often broader than that obtained from the boys. Almost all the material I collected on family relationships came from the girls; they were willing and able to talk about relationships with their parents in a way that the boys were not. Spender (1980) draws attention to the idea that:

> It is often believed that males have difficulty in expressing emotion and disclosing their personal selves — partly as a product of their conditioning — and that they need some encouragement and assistance to begin to talk about their feelings and therefore participate in the sort of discussion with which women are familiar. (p. 47)

Measor's *key informants* (see Burgess' paper in this volume) were almost all girls, except for some 'ace' deviant boys and one conformist boy with whom she had built up a relationship in the middle school. Even then the girls who took on the key informant roles were not fully representative:

> I think it was people I happened to get on with, in terms of the girls, girls who were quite like me in personality. Some girls who were quite quiet and retiring, I never got on with them as well.

Research relationships with the boys in the secondary school carried other difficulties:

> At the end of the first year I discovered that there were all sorts of sexual commentaries being made. And I took one kid, Philip, who I had known at the middle school. He was one of my key informants, and I had always interviewed him on his own, because it always seemed best that way, and all the other boys started making all these sexual innuendos about it ... people would say things like 'are you going off with your girlfriend again'. So that is part of what was going on with the boys ... Their concerns at that point in their life are so much with sexual development and I think I just fitted in with that.

The other point I would want to make about shared gender is that it is sometimes easy to over-estimate the primacy of gender in research relationships. Lynn Davies underlines this with her comments on age, region and school background. In highlighting the particular significance of gender in research relationships it is important not to lose sight of the cross-cutting impact of social class, regional and personality factors. Gender sharing is not a magic key to unlock good data, Davies again:

> Sometimes, of course, neither of them were very willing to talk, not I think because of the presence of the tape-recorder, none of them seemed to mind that, but I think they simply weren't used to having their opinions asked about some of the questions I was asking . . . Some days they were simply more willing to let me eavesdrop onto what they were talking about, other days were hard work . . . a couple of Asian girls rarely said anything, just nodded or shook their heads, which was difficult . . .

The 'invisibility' of girls in accounts of teenage culture has been commented on frequently in recent reviews. Brake (1980, p. 137), for example, notes that if 'subcultures are solutions to collectively experienced problems, then youth culture is highly concerned with the problems of masculinity'. And McRobbie and Gerber (1976, p. 211) argue that 'they may be marginal to the sub-cultures, not simply because girls are pushed by the dominance of males to the margin of each social activity, but because they are centrally into a different, necessarily subordinate set or range of activities'. McRobbie and Gerber go on, in a discussion of 'teeny bopper culture', to make the important point that primary aspects of the teenage 'culture of femininity' may be played out in the private confines of the girls' bedrooms.

> Teeny bopper culture can easily be accommodated, for ten to fifteen year old girls, in the home, requiring only a bedroom and a record player and permission to invite friends; but in this capacity it might offer an opportunity for girls to take part in a quasi-sexual ritual (it is important to remember that girls have no access to the masturbatory rituals common amongst boys). The culture also offers a chance for both private and public manifestations — the postered bedroom or the rock concert. (p. 220)

My own data from Beachside, drawing on the diaries that pupils kept for me, suggests that the 'culture of the bedroom' is a general and important basis for friendship meetings between girls. This being so the would-be participant observer has a major problem of access.

There are normally no gangs or large social groups available on street corner locations: 'girls' culture, from our preliminary investigations, is so well insulated as to operate to effectively exclude not only other "undesirable" girls — but also boys, adults, teachers and researchers' (McRobbie and Gerber, p. 222). One possibility for the researcher faced with such problems is to take the hard-line versions of participant observation seriously and attempt to 'pass' as a pupil.

Participation and 'Passing'

I never attempted to 'pass' as a pupil at any time during my field-work, although I regularly made attempts and sometimes succeeded in 'passing' as a teacher. There were, however, situations in which I was able to participate in a full sense in pupil activities, almost exclusively with the sixth-formers. I attended sixth-form parties, drank with them in local pubs, some visited my house to eat and I went on a camping trip with a sixth-form group, several became my friends. But to a great extent I did not treat the sixth formers as a specific source of data. In general terms though, the older the pupils and the closer they are in age to the researcher then the greater the possibilities of some sort of active participation and even 'passing'.

James Patrick (1973) provides an example of 'passing' as a member of a juvenile Glasgow gang while he was working in an approved school. Tim, a gang member, whose older brother was serving a life sentence for murder, acted as coach and collaborator and indeed was instigator of Patrick's spending time with the gang in the 'repetitive monotony' of hanging around street corners and indulging in petty acts of deviance. Tim coached Patrick in the appropriate dress 'a midnight-blue suit, with a light blue handkerchief with a white polka dot (to match my tie) in the top pocket' (p. 325) and helped out with dialect problems and a cover story. Patrick's accounts of his time with the gang show some of the strain he was under, not simply because of the difficulties of maintaining his 'cover', although he made a number of mistakes in this respect, or the 'unending boredom' but particularly as a result of the imminent violence and continual petty delinquency which were a part of gang life.

Mandy Llewellyn's (1980) exploration of the commitment to school and involvement in school of adolescent girls is the only example I am aware of, of a serious attempt to take on a participant pupil role inside of school. Her work in two secondary schools, concentrating upon the fourth and fifth year, is based on what she calls 'intensive participant observation'.

> I wanted to enter the field as 'one of the girls' ... I spent five days a week (two or three days at each) for the entire school year September 1975 to July 1976, and two or three days a week regularly throughout the subsequent academic year. I was involved in every aspect of school life with the girls from quick fags in the lavvies to inter-form hockey tournaments and being humiliated in French lessons for only getting three out of twenty for my test. Although the girls were aware that I was undertaking some sort of project on girls in school, I spent so much time with them that they tended to forget this, and they did not relate their personal contact with me to trying to find out and question them about aspects of their lives. Throughout the two years I maintained this contact with the entire range of girls both from the various cliques of friends in the three grammar school forms and the seven streamed classes in the secondary modern. I was thus able to gain access to almost the entire range of activities available to and engaged in by the girls: from reading magazines, listening to records and chatting in bedrooms; to evangelical church services and coffee evenings; and hanging around the streets of the estate, and the occasional fair. (p. 44)

Llewellyn then did achieve access to the private spheres that are so central to the social lives of adolescent girls, but she points out in her discussion of data collected that access does not automatically provide a basis for understanding adolescent culture.

> Once I had entered the field I encountered a mass of problems and dilemmas, some of them generally related to this style of research, others more specifically concerned with the focus of my study. These latter involved the difficulties of gaining some sort of purchase on the privatized, fairly excluding spheres inhabited by adolescent girls. (p. 44)

Llewellyn also makes the important point that:

> Crucially, girls' and women's experiences are structured in response to male definitions, and therefore data relating to the previous invisibility of females cannot simply be 'filled in' because it raised crucial questions as to how the previous work had been understood. (p. 45)

Angela McRobbie (1978) suggests similar problems and worries about interpretation in relation to her 'participant observation' with girls in a Birmingham youth club.

> It was necessary to be as reflexive as possible methodologically; this meant continually questioning the means by which the data was collected and checking every possible instance to make sure that what the girls actually said and meant was being clearly understood. (p. 97)

These comments highlight the complexity and variety of the data gleaned from participant observation with teenagers and the impossibility or dangers of simply 'reading off' an interpretation. This is discussed further below.

Lynda Measor's fieldwork with thirteen-year-olds throws up further problems about the possibilities of passing and in some ways adds further complications to the neatness of the child-teenager dichotomy.

> I never tried to pretend I was them and the only time I did try to pretend by going to *The Stranglers* concert, they told me I wasn't allowed to pretend, I had to stay who I was. I couldn't throw myself into their social world, I could perhaps with sixteen year olds, but not with thirteen year olds. It is something to do with their intense consciousness of the point they are at, half way, young pretenders, between child and adult. So that all I could do was hand a bridge out to them and say 'if you want to sometimes come across the bridge and talk, the gate's always open at my end' but that doesn't mean to say that there isn't a gulf and that doesn't mean that we don't have to genuinely try to make a bridge.

Fine and Glassner (1979, p. 167) make a similar point when they comment that 'children seem to have a sense of whether a researcher looks like a good bet as a friend and will spot those who attempt to be something other than what they are'. What this suggests perhaps is an important relationship between participation and *acceptability*; 'passing' is the ultimate acceptability but anyone who aspires to some kind of participant observer role must strive for acceptance. Measor's work suggests several of the elements involved in being acceptable. Moving away from the established adult roles was important, 'not seeming like a *proper adult*'.

> I wasn't a teacher, I wasn't a parent, I didn't have any kind of

authority hassles with them. I wasn't trying to make them do anything. Kids of that age, someone's always trying to make them do something, their parents are becoming a bit of an enemy.

What is going on is fraternization and in relation to this Measor found that presentation of self, especially in terms of *dress*, was of major importance.

My clothes got commented on every single day and things like wearing very large earrings, I got referred to as 'the woman with the chandeliers in her ears'. Straight jeans had just come in instead of bell-bottoms and some of the teachers in the school, even the more hip ones, were still wearing bell-bottoms and I never did, and stuff like that mattered and I used to play around with appearance a bit ... but there was always a tightrope between pleasing the kids and keeping my nose clean with the teachers. But the way I dressed, the kids made it clear to me that I was acceptable, in youth culture terms.

Also a fundamental test of acceptability, as other extracts have indicated, is *trust*.

The first couple of times I interviewed them they were quite restrained in what they said and I said 'look I won't tell anybody else what you've said, I certainly won't tell teachers'. But they didn't know that at first, it was only when I interviewed them a second time, or in some cases the third time, they discovered that it was actually true I wouldn't tell anybody, they really could say what they wanted. They tested me out.

What is at the heart of this process of gaining acceptability, of gaining access, of being given privileged insight into the pupils' lives and beliefs and fears, is the making of a research relationship. Measor makes the point that after a time the pupils' understanding of the research enterprise 'stopped mattering'.

What happened was they developed a relationship with me and I think they were genuinely pleased to see me when I came to school and if I ever missed a day they objected ... They enjoyed discussions and talks and being sociable with me and I think that that was what their conception of me was all about. The relationship was everything.

All of this raises critical questions about the other form of 'passing' that is available to the would-be participant observer in school — passing as a teacher. A lot has been written about the 'to teach or not to teach' dilemma that faces many researchers but I do not want to rehearse those issues again in any detail. The essential point is whether by taking on a teacher role the researcher inhibits or precludes the development of other types of relationships with the pupils. Can the researcher act in a disciplinary capacity and at the same time be an interested friend to pupils? Probably not (see Hargreaves, 1967, pp. 201–4, Woods, 1979, pp. 260–3 and Fine and Glassner, 1979, pp. 156–9 for further discussion). In my own case I carefully separated the teacher role and the researcher role as much as possible; I never taught the pupils or classes I had chosen to focus my direct data collection work on. However, I did find that one class I was teaching became of greater and greater research interest to me as time went on. I began to collect research materials from the pupils in this class in the form of essays, diaries, and later, interviews. These pupils, fifth-formers, seemed to be able to manage the switch from one kind of relationship in the classroom, to another in my paper store cum interview room. This was even true of the three 'deviant' girls in the class with whom I had had considerable discipline problems. They were willing in interviews to reflect on and talk about our clashes in the classroom and to divulge information about their escapades out of school that would have been very damaging to them if it had been known to the other staff. Thus a complex playing off of common knowledge and shared experiences actually became possible with *some* of the pupils in this class. I had direct experience of the problems of control and the differences in their participation and cooperation in the classroom. We were able to discuss these *shared* events and the structure of the class itself, it was 'our' sociology class, a unique option grouping drawing pupils from across the whole of the fifth year. In some senses, for a short period, the lessons with this class provided a laboratory within which I was able to test out and experience first-hand the processes and structures I was observing in other areas of the school. For me this served as a powerful confirmatory experience, not necessarily in a strict methodological sense, but in a personal sense that was related to my own commitment to my analysis. I do not, however, offer this as a model that can necessarily be replicated. I cannot imagine this kind of relationship being possible with the other classes I taught.

It might be more useful to consider the situation of the teacher as researcher, although accounts of research of this kind are few and far between. Andrew Pollard (1985) provides one; he describes the strategy of using a group of children as surrogate researchers, both to collect useful data and as a way of overcoming the problems of the teacher role. Again the goal is to establish *trust*.

> The groups of friends who were invited to talk were invited by other children, children operated the cassette recorders, children set the scene and children initiated the discussions. The message being conveyed was that going to the interviewed was 'safe' and 'could be fun'. This trust became increasingly secure during the year and my degree of intervention grew with it. (Pollard, 1985; p. 229)

Pollard (on tape this time) does suggest that there are advantages to being known to the pupils as a teacher of a particular type.

> I think I had a reasonable identity in the school. The fact that I'd taught those kids before, that we'd had a few sets of experiences, and I think I measured up reasonably well on their own criteria of a teacher who is fun to be with, is liked. I'd had the advantage of doing various kinds of things which don't do one any harm if one wants to talk to kids like that. I was the one who threw custard pies at the Headteacher in the school pantomime during this year. I had something of a reputation through my work in the playground as somebody who could play marbles and I spent a lot of time in the playground playing games, chatting to them, talking to them. So I think I had an identity which was open and they trusted me, and particularly in a way I was being sponsored by certain of the children ...

Perhaps what Polland (1979, 1980, 1981 and 1982) is telling us is that in a similar way to Measor he was not a proper adult, not a proper teacher, as far as the pupils are concerned.

The Ethics of Participant Observation with Pupils

When researchers are negotiating entry into schools it is normally the case that it is the headteacher who makes the crucial gatekeeping decisions, sometimes but certainly not always in consultation with teachers. No one consults the pupils. Similarly, once in the school access to classrooms must normally be negotiated with the teachers; pupils are rarely asked whether they want to have a researcher in their lessons. They are told, or find a stranger sitting unannounced at the back of their classroom one Monday morning. Furthermore, teachers will commonly offer the pupils' cooperation to the researcher: 'I'm sure they will be willing to help you'. This is a taken-for-granted aspect of the 'politics of childhood' that researchers regularly trade upon. Lynda Measor reports that:

> I asked that no introduction be made about me, I didn't want teachers telling kids what I was, and some of the kids in this form, I think four of them, knew me from the middle school already, so they already had a relationship with me, which helped. And what I used to do, I'd sit in the back of the class and kids would turn round and look at me, girls, almost exclusively girls, certainly at first, and I would make a point of smiling and being friendly ... Girls, they would just come across and say 'What are you doing here?' and I would say 'I'm writing a book', which was a lie at the time, but I thought that was something that they would understand, 'about the problems and things that happen to people when they transfer from the middle to the secondary school'. I said the idea was maybe to help other kids in the future, and that was something that seemed acceptable to them.

Despite the absence of consultation with pupils over entry it is clear from the reports I obtained and written accounts of fieldwork that the response of the majority of pupils to the prospect of being researched is in fact an eager willingness to cooperate and be involved. Lynn Davies found that:

> The girls themselves never seemed to mind. I don't think I found any pupils uncooperative, some were more articulate clearly than others and a few objected I think to the questionnaire and therefore I had a few spoiled or uncompleted papers. But always they were interested in what I wanted it all *for*, why was I doing it, why did I want their points of view, was I going to show the teachers, where was it all going? And I had to answer these questions as honestly and as fully as I could.

Andrew Pollard reports a very similar situation with his middle school pupils.

> There were one or two children who had to be persuaded in and that might have affected the type of data they produced,

there were sometimes other types of activity going on that made people simply not want to come in but the bulk of people were very interested ... I found that kids were really flattered in a way to have somebody take an interest in this aspect of their view on school or whatever. I don't remember a child who was reluctant to come in and talk with the exception of those bound up in some other sort of activity, but that was more a case of putting it off, they would come in some other time when it was raining or something.

However, it is easy to concentrate on the willingness and interest of the majority and discount the uncooperative and the inarticulate, the 'reluctants'. Each of the researchers with whom I have talked has mentioned such pupils; one can only assume that certain 'types' of pupil are systematically missing from our accounts of school life. Denzin (1977, p. 59) makes the general point that:

> Most sociological methods work best in the study of persons most like the sociologist. These methods typically assume articulate respondents. They work least well with those persons who do not share the sociologist's perspective, and sociologists confront real problems when those studied are inarticulate. Children do not make good sociological subjects. Their speech patterns are often slurred and idiosyncratic. They may speak a private language that only a few other persons can understand. They often refuse to show proper deference to self or other.

We should perhaps consider that Denzin is reflecting on his work as observer of pre-school groups, and that his general comments certainly do not reflect the overall experiences of the researchers reported here. It is dangerous to generalize from one age group to another. But the problems that he raises do apply to particular pupils. Lynn Davies found:

> It would appear that some girls were simply used to conversing in monosyllables, that sounds patronizing, but the shrug and the 'don't know' is a clear response to anything which requires a lot of thought or putting oneself on the line.

I have already noted Measor's point about key informants being those pupils with whom she got on best and she readily admits that the 'quieter and more withdrawn pupils' would be underrepresented in her analysis. I would have to admit the same thing in my own work. Clearly one makes efforts, but as Measor says:

> I really did try and cover them and I think in the end got somewhere. But you'll never know whether their perceptions are genuinely different from the others or whether you just haven't got at their perception. I can't see any way out of that.

It is perhaps easy to assume that the majority of pupils, the eager and cooperative, by their natural curiosity and gregariousness, are opening themselves up to 'exploitation by research'.

But researchers do not act simply as blank voyeurs in their involvements with pupils; it is clear that as in anthropological fieldwork (Wax, 1952) there is a degree of personal reciprocity in the researcher-pupil relationship. Lynda Measor recalled that 'they also said, particularly the girls, that they thought I was someone that they could talk to, and I think I ended up playing a role that I can only describe as counselling'. Lynn Davies took on similar responsibilities, as well as providing a valid reason to escape from lessons.

> The difficult girls as I said enjoyed getting out of lessons and I think they got some mileage out of having some kind of personal biographer, I became drawn into their script, which was also part of the interpretation difficulties. To start with I was sort of first bystander. I had to referee events and disputes, 'You saw that didn't you Miss'. Then I think I became a sort of springboard, a sounding board for their ideas.

In moving between a secondary school and a middle school in her fieldwork Lynda Measor was also able to offer a particular kind of reciprocity to the middle school pupils.

> I also think it's to do with the fact that in the Middle School I was a person who actually had something that they wanted, and that is I had information about the Secondary School, I came from the Secondary School and could tell them things about it.

On the other hand, we must not see the pupils as naive respondents providing data for the researcher irrespective of their own best interests, nor, as noted already, were all the pupils willing and cooperative respondents. While the pupils have little say in whether the researcher should sit in their lessons, they do of course have some option whether or not to cooperate any further with the process of data collection. And it is certainly worth underlining the difference in aim between those studies which are concerned with coming to grips with the 'public' classroom life of the pupils, the *institutional studies*, and those which seek to explore the 'private' out of school lives of the pupils, the *cultural studies*. The pupils certainly do have an effective right of veto, of exclusion, in the latter case. I asked Lynda Measor whether she was attempting to research in this 'private' sphere.

> I took the view that I had no right in it, I would go to the school disco but it wasn't comfortable, they didn't want me there. I didn't go often. You know that's about kissing somebody in the corner and you feel guilty enough about it already ... I think it was because I respected certain areas of their privacy that they were prepared to talk to me, I think children are incredibly private.

Again, Fine and Glassner (1979, p. 167) had similar experiences: 'children frequently guard their privacy; by preadolescence their sense of presentation of self is highly developed, particularly as it relates to adults. Thus any intimate, sharing relationships will take time to develop and may never develop if pressured'.

I have already referred to some of the problems that Ian Birksted reported in his attempts to initiate a research relationship with Andrew. Birksted's concerns were much more with the out-of-school social worlds of pupils. He describes an early encounter with Andrew in the following way:

> In subsequent registration sessions I was formally introduced to Andrew by the teacher. Andrew and I chatted in a polite and guarded manner. Later, it was suggested to me that I might like to take some children in a discussion group during the PE lesson as these children were regularly avoiding having to do PE either by not bringing their equipment or by using medical certificates. I was told where the pupils would be waiting for me: in a coffee area of the sports hall. They had been told that they were to spend the hour talking to me. When I walked into the coffee-area, I immediately recognized Andrew ... He also recognized me: 'Oh! Not you again! What have we got to talk about this time?' I answered that we could talk about anything they wanted, and I kept quiet, to let them react. Silence followed. Following upon this silence, Andrew turned towards his friends and they started talking about Friday's forthcoming disco. (p. 3)

Lynn Davies found among her girls that:

> they were cooperative, but clearly this varied from individual to individual, some girls, without being rude, were nevertheless not going to give any information about themselves or their out of school life at all and I had to infer all sorts of things from the remarks of other girls, as to their particular views.

Clearly the pupils are able to exclude the researcher from certain areas, to draw lines, to keep certain issues or topics private. However, aside from the Andrews, if we consider only the public areas of the school, one of the points made by all the researchers I have quoted is the willingness of pupils to talk, to cooperate, to be open and frank. Perhaps we need to be concerned therefore about the extent to which pupils are unwittingly revealing themselves to the researcher, out of ignorance of the researcher's treatment of their words as data. But Lynda Measor certainly thinks not.

> I think one of the strongest things in kids' culture is knowing who you don't tell certain things to, it's one of the things that kids have very clear in their minds and I think kids don't make mistakes about that. Of course therefore there were limits to what they could tell me.

Bronwyn Davies (1982) found a comparable situation in her conversations with younger pupils:

> There is a momentary hitch when what they have to say is something they would prefer to keep from the teachers ...
> As *adult* my membership of the adult team may lead me to betray confidences given me by the children in the interview (team situation). (p. 54)

Again it would seem the pupils are in control of the flow of information that they vouchsafe to the researcher. I quote later Lynn Davies' comments about the unwillingness of her girls to gossip about each other. As it happens this was not a restraint felt by Measor's pupils. 'They gossiped about each other all the time, I'm sure that's what doing this kind of research is all about, it's one of those things that I've always felt guilty about, having people talking about other people behind their back and then you call it triangulation'. And pupils seem only too willing to talk *about* their teachers. Lynda Measor says that 'teachers are the first things that pupils are willing to talk about, that's no great breakthrough'. Bronwyn Davies found a similar ease. 'They talk for instance, about their problems with their various teachers, their parents and each other' (p. 54). And Andrew Pollard, as a teacher himself, sometimes had problems with this.

> Lots of time where the children were very rude about the Headteacher would have been a problem if the Headteacher had ever got hold of the data. I remember once that there were some kids who were really tearing into the Headteacher and he actually walked in and I turned off the tape and we kind of bluffed our way through it. I felt as guilty as the children ... I reckoned that my role in this situation was not as a teaching one, it was in my own time, I reckoned that the priority was legitimately on trying to understand the perspectives of these kids about school. Now that puts you in an ethical dilemma vis-a-vis your professional teaching role. But I took a position on that to suspend the conventional priorities and substituted a different set.

Despite the limits operated by the pupils (there are more examples below) it is certainly true to say that the researchers themselves occasionally worried about the information they obtained as data. I was certainly landed with information about the pupils which I felt I could not include in the write-up of my study (stealing by one boy and sexual behaviour of two girls which were discussed openly with me) and other material which would have damaged the school reputation of the pupils concerned. Andrew Pollard was in an even more difficult position as teacher-researcher.

> One particular situation arose when I was told about 'Nicking sweets' and the theft of a five pound note from a local shop. This was a test case of my credibility and I did nothing, thus perhaps condoning the activity. This, apart from the rights and wrongs of the case, would have been extremely awkward to explain to the Headteacher had my knowledge of the culprit come to light and it might have threatened my relationship with the staff.

While pupils may control what they do offer to the researcher as data they do not have control over the use made of their words and actions. And it is unlikely that many pupils have a clear idea at all of the process they are participating in (see Lynn Davies, 1985 and Burgess, 1985b). It is normal to promise confidentiality in research with pupils as with other respondents but confidences once passed on have to be protected, sometimes from teachers. Lynda Measor reported that teachers sometimes tried to 'abuse' her relationship with pupils 'and ask me for information, but I would never give it. The pastoral staff would sometimes ask for quite personal information, if I knew what was going on. And I'd sometimes give veiled hints, very veiled, if I thought it could be useful.' In published accounts the standard procedures of anonymization and pseudonymization come into play. Although Lynn Davies found that this did not necessarily satisfy her 'girls'.

> They were told by the Head of Upper School that I was writing a book. This wasn't on my instigation but that's what he told them, but in fact I was happy to go along with that and it wasn't untrue as it turns out. They were very interested, the pupils, to have their opinions elicited. And they wanted all their own names to go in the book and they wanted to know they were going to appear and they were quite disappointed when I said the names would have to be changed and they would remain anonymous, but they liked the idea of there being published material emerging from the research.

In one sense this is amusing and probably recognizable to any participant observer who has worked with school pupils, but it underlines the weight of responsibility that lies on the researchers' shoulders. While it may seem glamorous to have one's name in print the researcher must be very aware of any revelations that might have untoward consequences for pupils in the longer term. Anonymity is the best policy. It is not usual to find anyone in the field who will look out for the interests of the pupils, and no-one keeping in close touch with the research process, by design. For reasons of confidentiality the teachers do not know the sort of data that the researcher is eliciting. While researchers do not share their data with teachers, teachers can normally be persuaded to share theirs (school records and so on) with the researcher. Ultimately, in these circumstances, one can probably do no better than consider the arguments put forward in Becker's (1964) paper on 'Problems in the Publication of Field Studies' and his conclusion that 'with respect to the question of *what to publish*, I think there is no general solution except one as may be dictated by the individual's conscience' (p. 280).

Understanding the World of Childhood

> If there is any scepticism about the existence of children's
> culture, it is a reflection of our own adult ideological commit-
> ment which has all but obscured the fact of its existence ...
> (Speier, 1976, p. 99).

While some kind of 'passing' or authentic participation for the
researcher may seem possible in the teenage world, it is difficult to
imagine circumstances where this would be possible among children,
other than by taking on existing adult roles — teacher, auxiliary,
parent, and so on (Fine and Glassner, 1979). On the whole, researchers
committed to participant observation methods have shied away from
work with young children and research in this area has been
dominated by psychologists, who from their positivist stance share
none of the participant observer's worries about making culturally
invalid interpretations of the world of those being studied. As
Bronwyn Davies (1982) notes, 'children have been written about from
many perspectives, and for a multitude of purposes. Rarely have they
been asked to speak for themselves' (p. 1). But there is an increasing
number of studies which have extended the interactionist project into
primary and middle schooling. Bronwyn Davies begins her own
study of primary school children by taking on board the assumption
that such children interpret the world in ways different and distinct
from adults. These differences are embedded not in some kind of
developmental deficiency, later to be remedied by growing up, but in
the independent and authentic *culture of childhood*. Bronwyn Davies'
concern was to understand this culture in terms of its most important
features and its rules. Active participant observation of the children's
play and interactions seemed untenable and once again interviewing
provided a second best alternative. But Davies argues that 'the
interviews were, in an important sense, not separate from life as the
children knew it; they were life, brought into the interview room
from the classroom and the playground' (p. 2). Woods (1979, p. 265)
makes the same point; he found that in talking to groups of pupils
'Many of the conversations became ... part of their experience rather
than a commentary on it'. The use of group interviews, Davies
suggests, actually provided for a re-creation of the relationships,
cultural meanings, standards, roles and beliefs that constituted the
active, living culture of childhood. These were being played out in a
way which allowed her both to observe and participate in a first-hand
way. Perhaps Lynn Davies is making a similar point when she

describes her group meetings with 'her girls' and actually contrasts 'merely wanting to record the girls' views and conversations and everyday comments on life', their accounts of action, with 'the difficulty of intervention of actually generating chat, the worry that the whole thing each time would turn into an interview instead of a spontaneous account of what was going on'. And she goes on to describe some of these meetings where 'they would tease each other about boyfriends, about teachers, about relationships'. The problem is to find some way of tapping into the private and autonomous social world of childhood in order to come to grips with the forms and practices of this world which 'are reproduced from one generation of children to another and are apparently relatively unaffected by and immune from adult influences' (Morgan, O'Neill and Harre, 1979, p. 2). Once a method is arrived at the second problem exists of achieving a valid and meaningful interpretation of data. This Bronwyn Davies suggests was the most challenging aspect of her own research, 'understanding those aspects of the children's world to which I am not privy and yet which, I feel, are central to their construction of the world' (p. 3). She goes on to say that 'though adults may assume a reciprocity of perspectives when they interact with children, it is clear if one listens to children that this is a somewhat fallacious assumption' (p. 3). Bronwyn Davies' struggle was to attain a 'we-relationship' with the children with whom she worked; her basic strategy was to establish a collaborative and interactive style of interviewing, seeing the children regularly over a period of several months. The children were recruited in effect as informants in an anthropological sense, and Davies mobilized their interest in the process of the research to develop cross-checking procedures. The pupils were keen

> that I get it right. They were interested in the process of recording their conversations, and of replaying these conversations so that they could, amongst other things, draw my attention to those aspects of the conversation which they thought were noteworthy: so that they could teach me to interpret social scenes from their point of view. (p. 21)

Andrew Pollard was able to use his pupil collaborators in a similar sort of way.

> The fact that as I went along I was able to talk to a group of children who were on the inside of the project. I mean not far inside maybe, but I could certainly say to them, that it seems

to me that you are broadly concerned with these sorts of issues . . . and they would check it out. So in a way I was able to feed it back and get it checked.

In several senses Bronwyn Davies' research strategy can be seen as a realistic surrogate for participant observation and as significantly different from normal interviewing (coming closer to clinical or life history interviewing techniques). The pupils were interviewed in groups, the interviewing was based on the establishment over time of a personal interactive relationship between adult-researcher and children. The children were reflexively involved in the research process, the groups were encouraged to interact through the interview, to elaborate, amend, contradict, exemplify and control their colleagues' contributions. However, as noted by the other researchers above, Davies is clear that there were limits drawn by the children to the range of discussion and disclosure in which they would partake. In particular, 'the children rarely talked about their romances and they especially carefully skated around the topic of sex when it was mentioned' (p. 100). She suggests that this may have been a result of the children's awareness of adult uneasiness about sex as an issue. Lynn Davies mentions a similar self-censorship among her teenage girls.

> They did have certain sorts of codes of ethics about talking about each other. They would respect each others' confidences, this is the thing. Donna said on one occasion, 'I don't think Lorraine would like it if I brought it up, like if I talk about Julie, I don't think it's right to say it if Julie ain't here'. So if the group were incomplete there were all sorts of things going on which the others would rightly respect, they wouldn't gossip about each other in my presence and all sorts of events had to be inferred rather than having 'authentic' accounts.

Bronwyn Davies is, however, very aware of the fundamental point that there is a discontinuity of form between the talk of the interview and the action of 'real events' in the world of childhood. In some circumstances this can lead to action being distorted through words.

> The relationship between the words spoken and the experience described or analyzed is an extraordinarily complex one. Sometimes the words create the experiences by bringing together isolated fragments of experience which had no coherence in their original form, and on other occasions words can appear to destroy the original experience by

construing it in ways too different from the original experience. (p. 189)

Davies is careful, rightly I think, to stress the difficulty of reading or
making sense of the pupils' culture; she underlines the problems of
arriving at an authentic interpretation of their world. And her
analysis attempts to reflect the complexity and idiosyncracy of their
social construction of reality — Willis (1977) is also careful to
preserve and work through the complex and contradictory aspects of
the social world of the teenage 'lads'. Other writers seem to have had
few problems in this respect, or do not reveal the problems involved
in interpretation. However, as far as the school age child is concerned, investigators do agree on the possibility of understanding the
social worlds of childhood. And participant observation strategies
would appear to provide a powerful means toward this end.

Discussion

Considering this review of research experiences in general terms there
are several points to be made. First, it emerges that in practice
participant observation with pupils presents a range of difficulties for
the adult researcher both as regards data collection and the analysis of
data (and gender, social class, regional and personality factors serve to
compound the generational problems). Entry into the lives of pupils
is constrained by a whole range of practical and ethical problems (and
neither of these areas has received due attention in the literature on
participant observation). As Bronwyn Davies notes, as adults researchers are identified, whether they like it or not, with the adult 'team'.
The adult-pupil relationship is a political one, set within a considerable inequality of power. In many respects the interactions between
adults and pupils are marked by attempts at coercion and resistance.
Set against this is the fact that all the researchers quoted here found
that a genuine interest in pupils' lives, within certain limits, was
received by most pupils with enthusiasm and cooperation. However,
it is equally clear that a number of pupils were unwilling or unable to
act as 'good' respondents. The researcher in this area is reliant for the
most part on outgoing and articulate pupils to provide 'good' data.
One can only speculate as to the possible distortions of this in the
accounts that are being generated. Second, the comparison between
and interrogation of the research experiences of a number of investigators working with school pupils has thrown up a number of crucial

tensions and differences in this field of research. For example, I have found it necessary to contrast the social worlds of childhood and adolescence as qualitatively distinct 'lived forms' and as posing very different kinds of methodological difficulty for the researcher. I have also suggested a separation between institutional studies of the pupil role and cultural studies of the child or adolescent outside or beyond school. And I point to the existence of 'hard-line' and 'soft-line' definitions of participant observation and the concomitant division between participation and 'passing'. Third, moving away from the substance of the paper, I hope to have demonstrated the value of a systematic analysis of research experiences in a particular field. The comparison of the experiences of a number of researchers has uncovered and highlighted several significant issues (trust, privacy, access, control of data, interpretation, and so on) which should prove valuable both to readers of the research and others embarking upon fieldwork in similar situations. Most writing on research methods relies either on abstract prescription or recounts, in the form of a research biography, the reflections of an individual fieldworker. There is little opportunity to question in detail experienced researchers and learn from their mistakes or to engage in the systematic comparison of fieldwork done by different researchers.

If this current exercise is a useful one, and I certainly think it is, then perhaps more careful thought needs to be given to extending and developing the idea of an archive of interviews on research experience. The cultivation of methodological rigour in qualitative research requires exactly this kind of interrogation of experience, as against the development of sets of abstract rules of procedure. Procedures must be derived from involvement in the field and be founded upon the actions and reactions of the researched. The creation of such an archive and the work of contrast and comparison of the experience of different researchers would be a significant contribution to the development of qualitative research methods and the acceptance of these methods as valid basis for the analysis of the social world.

References

BALL, S.J. (1984) 'Beachside reconsidered: reflections on a methodological apprenticeship', in BURGESS, R.G. (Ed.) *The Research Process in Educational Settings: Ten Case Studies*, Lewes, Falmer Press.

BECKER, H.S. (1964) 'Problems in the publication of field studies', in VIDICH, A.J., BENSMAN, J. and STEIN, M.R. (Eds.) *Reflections on Community Studies*, New York, Harper and Row.

BECKER, H.S., GEER, B. and HUGHES, E.C. (1968) *Making the Grade*, New York, John Wiley.

BIRKSTED, I. (1974) 'Growing up: another view of school', Staff/Research Student Seminar, Education Area, University of Sussex, unpublished paper.

BIRKSTED, I. (1976) 'School performance: viewed from the boys', *Sociological Review*, 24, 1, pp. 63–77.

BRAKE, M. (1980) *The Sociology of Youth Culture and Youth Sub-Cultures*, London, Routledge and Kegan Paul.

BURGESS, R.G. (Ed.) (1984a) *The Research Process in Educational Settings: Ten Case Studies*, Lewes, Falmer Press.

BURGESS, R.G. (ED.) (1985a) *Field Methods in the Study of Education*, Lewes, Falmer Press.

BURGESS, R.G. (1985b) 'The whole truth?' in BURGESS, R.G. (Ed.) *Field Methods in the Study of Education*, Lewes, Falmer Press.

CORRIGAN, P. (1979) *Schooling the Smash Street Kids*, London, Macmillan.

DAVIES, B. (1982) *Life in the Classroom and Playground: The Accounts of Primary School Children*, London, Routledge and Kegan Paul.

DAVIES, L. (1978) 'The view from the girls', *Educational Review*, 30, 2.

DAVIES, L. (1979) 'Deadlier than the male' in BARTON, L. and MEIGHAN, R. (Eds.) *Schools, Pupils and Deviance*, Driffield, Nafferton.

DAVIES, L. (1980) *Deviance and Sex Roles in School*, unpublished PhD thesis, University of Birmingham.

DAVIES, L. (1983) 'Gender, resistance and power', in WALKER, S. and BARTON, L. (Eds.) *Gender, Class and Education*, Lewes, Falmer Press.

DAVIES, L. (1985) 'Ethnography and status: focussing on gender in education research' in BURGESS, R.G. (Ed.) *Field Methods in the Study of Education*, Lewes, Falmer Press.

DENZIN, N.K. (1972) 'The genesis of self in early childhood', *Sociological Quarterly*, Vol. 13, pp. 291–314.

DENZIN, N.K. (1977) *Childhood and Socialization*, New York, Jossey-Bass.

FINE, G.A. and GLASSNER, B. (1979) 'Participant observation with children: promise and problems', *Urban Life*, 8, 2, pp. 153–74.

GOLD, R.L. (1958) 'Roles in sociological field observations', *Social Forces*, 36, pp. 217–23.

HARGREAVES, D.H. (1967), *Social Relations in a Secondary School*, London, Routledge and Kegan Paul.

HARRE, R. (1974) 'The conditions for a social psychology of childhood', in RICHARDS, M.P.M. (Ed.) *The Integration of a Child into a Social World*, Cambridge, Cambridge University Press.

KLUCKHOHN, F. (1940) 'The participant observation technique in small communities', *American Journal of Sociology*, 46, 3, pp. 331–43.

LLEWELLYN, M. (1980) 'Studying girls at school: the implications of a confusion', in DEEM, R. (Ed.) *Schooling for Women's Work*, London, Routledge and Kegan Paul.

McROBBIE, A. (1978) 'Working class girls and the culture of femininity', in CENTRE FOR CONTEMPORARY CULTURAL STUDIES *Women Take Issue*, London, Hutchinson.

McROBBIE, A. and GERBER, J. (1976) 'Girls and subcultures: an exploration', in HALL, S. and JEFFERSON, T. (Eds.) *Resistance Through Rituals*, London, Hutchinson.

MEASOR, L. and WOODS, P. (1984) *Changing Schools. The Pupils Experience of Transfer*, Milton Keynes, Open University Press.

MORGAN, D. (1981) 'Men, masculinity and the process of sociological enquiry' in ROBERTS, H. (Ed.) *Doing Feminist Research*, London, Routledge and Kegan Paul.

MORGAN, J., O'NEILL, G., and HARRÉ, R. (1979) *Nicknames*, London, Routledge and Kegan Paul.

PATRICK, J. (1973) *A Glasgow Gang Observed*, London, Eyre-Methuen.

POLLARD, A. (1979) 'Negotiating deviance and "getting done" in primary school classrooms' in BARTON, L. and MEIGHAN, R. (Eds.) *Schools, Pupils and Deviance*, Driffield, Nafferton.

POLLARD, A. (1980) 'Teacher interests and changing situations of survival threat in primary school classrooms' in WOODS, P. (Ed.) *Teacher Strategies*, London, Croom Helm.

POLLARD, A. (1981) *Coping With Deviance, School Processes and Their Implications for Social Reproduction: A Middle School Case Study*, Unpublished PhD thesis, University of Sheffield.

POLLARD, A. (1982) 'A model of coping strategies', *British Journal of Sociology of Education*, 3, 1.

POLLARD, A. (1985) 'Opportunities and difficulties of a teacher-ethnographer', in BURGESS, R.G. (Ed.) *Field Methods in the Study of Education*, Lewes, Falmer Press.

ROBERTS, H. (Ed.) (1981) *Doing Feminist Research*, London, Routledge and Kegan Paul.

SPEIER, M. (1976) 'The child as a conversationalist: some culture contact features of conversational interactions between adults and children' in HAMMERSLEY, M. and WOODS, P. (Eds.) *The Process of Schooling*, London, Routledge and Kegan Paul.

SPENDER, D. (1980) *Man Made Language*, London, Routledge and Kegan Paul.

WAX, R. (1952) 'Reciprocity in fieldwork', *Human Organization*, 11, 3, pp. 34–41.

WILLIS, P. (1977) *Learning to Labour*, Farnborough, Saxon House.

WOODS, P. (1979) *The Divided School*, London, Routledge and Kegan Paul.

ZNANIECKI, F. (1934) *The Method of Sociology*, New York, Farrar and Rinehart.

2 Interviewing: a Strategy in Qualitative Research

Lynda Measor

This paper looks reflexively at my own interviewing practices, as they developed during my work on two separate educational projects. Both projects were set in a qualitative research framework and unstructured, in-depth interviewing was an important strategy for data collection in both. The paper is not intended as a theoretical approach to the methodology of interviewing, but as an account of some of my own experiences in doing research. In this spirit, it is important to record my initial reaction, when I was asked to write such a paper. It was a strongly negative one, to the idea of having to analyze what it is I do, when interviewing. My reluctance was caused by having to examine rationally a set of practices which I had developed intuitively and without methodological rigour. A number of issues emerged as important. Access was the first, and the strategies that researchers use to build relationships with those they are interviewing. Secondly, strategies for retaining a critical awareness about the respondent's replies in the interview. The third issue involves an analysis of the context of the interview as it is an artificially arranged and set piece of interaction; and qualitative research places much emphasis on observation of the natural context. The fourth issue concerns validating the data that one gathers through interviewing strategies, together with questions of objectivity and bias.

All the data in this paper are taken from two studies. The first (with Peter Woods) looked at the transfer from middle school to comprehensive. The pupils were contacted in their last year at middle school, and observed through their first secondary school year. The research concentrated on 'pupil worlds' and on the pupils' experience of the transfer, and on how it felt to adapt to secondary school. The two main data gathering tools were participant observation and interviewing. (The research has now been completed and is reported in Measor and Woods, 1984). The second study (with Pat Sikes and Peter Woods) looked at teachers' careers. We interviewed art and science teachers in secondary schools. There were three groups of teachers: retired, mid-career and young (with five years teaching experience). We interviewed forty-eight teachers in all, half in South Yorkshire and half in South East England. We used a 'life history' method (Bertaux, 1981) as an extension of ethnographic techniques. It involved repeated sets of interviews with the same teacher; we aimed for six with each, but it could be more with key informants (see Burgess' paper in this volume, page 79) and less with teachers who were short of time or the inclination to participate in the project. In both research projects I worked with two quite different sets of clients: pupils and teachers; and would therefore hope in this paper to look at some of the effects that clients can have upon the practice of interviewing.

Access

Access is the first major issue involved in interviewing. There is an initial problem, which is real enough, of finding informants and getting them to agree to be interviewed and give up their time; especially if they are a busy Head of Department in a comprehensive school and it's a 'flu-ridden February of a long spring term. Access is also a problem with pupils. My experience was that teachers were most reluctant to allow 'time out' of lessons for my research. It was interesting that teachers of some subjects like mathematics and English were never prepared to allow pupils to leave lessons to be interviewed, while in other subjects like art and humanities, this was more often possible. Those teachers frequently made distinctions between the pupils they would allow out, and those they would not. Janet, a 'conformist' pupil was released easily, as the teacher considered, 'She will easily make up the work'. Christine who was viewed in an opposite way was also released, as the teacher remarked, 'She is so far behind, it doesn't matter'.

This left lunch times, when pupils had sports practices and other interests to divert them; and there was always a problem of a place to do interviews. I resorted to a large draughty lecture hall, or a tiny, smelly laboratory technician's preparation room, where I found myself interrupted constantly, often at crucial points in the pupils' account.

The second problem is the process of building relationships with people you want to interview, and hence getting access to their life and view of the world. Questions arise about how you get people to accept you as a reasonable person to talk about personal areas of their lives. There are three issues: building a relationship — especially when there is a time constraint; personal appearance and the 'how' of building rapport.

Building Relationships

In our research, we operated with the idea that the quality of the data is dependent on the quality of the relationships you build with the people being interviewed. This raises enormous questions of data validation, bias and 'scientific' standpoints. It is an idea which has no credence at all within positivist sociology, which is full of warnings against 'over rapport' with interviewees, and recommends maintaining a proper distance to avoid 'bias' (Goode and Hatt, 1952; Moser, 1958).

Qualitative research has taken a different line, but often discussion of the issue has used terms that are somehow very distanced. Hammersley and Atkinson, for example, point out that, 'the objects studied are in fact subjects and such subjects produce accounts of the world' (1983, p. 179). However, some of Bertaux's authors are prepared to go much further, in their accounts of using life history methodology. For example, Catani asserts that interviewing for life history, 'is above all the product of an encounter. The story recounts the development of an intense affective relationship whose exchange exists on a purely oral basis' (1981, p. 212). While Ferrarotti discusses the issue in even stronger terms, where the affective element is stressed. In the search for sociological data, he insists:

> Knowledge does not have 'the other' as its object, instead it should have inextricable and absolutely reciprocal interaction between the observer and the observed. It will then become a mutually shared knowledge, rooted in the intersubjectivity of the interaction, a knowledge all the more profound and objective, as it becomes integrally and profoundly subjective. The price to be paid, for a thorough and more pointedly scientific knowledge of his object, will to be reciprocally known, just as thoroughly by the latter. Knowledge thus becomes what sociological method has always wished to avoid — a risk. (1981, p. 20)

But how does one go about building these affective ties with interviewees, and getting the access, inside people's lives? On the research team, we have identified a number of strategies that are important, and yet rarely talked about.

Appearance

Appearance is one strategy that should be featured. In the teacher careers project, we have a joke about researchers needing a clothes allowance. This would enable us to manage the appearance part of our 'front' properly. My experience is that appearance and particularly clothes has been an important issue in researching both pupils and teachers, but there are different aspects to each. Each group had different requirements in a sense, but the issue mattered to them all. Certainly, when interviewing retired teachers, I felt it important to be extremely careful of my appearance. My intuition led me to dress very conservatively, I never wore jeans or even trousers, and wore neat little blouses and tidy, classic skirts. It led me to patronize clothes shops that I had never ventured into before. I felt it was important to have my shoes polished, and keep my tape recorder dusted, and to search for missing buttons. My intuitive reaction was right, given the data I received. All the older teachers, with only one exception, made a point about their strenuous objections to the appearance of young people in general, and young teachers in particular.

> *Mr King*   Young art teachers, clueless wonders, some of them, drab girls, who came looking as though they were selling off jewellery and wiggly hair, and long woollen things, and skirts that came down to their ankles, and toenails that could have been cleaned.

The older teachers considered the young to be scruffy and messy, and, moreover, felt that such an appearance demeaned their professional ethos.

> *Mr Shoe*   I think you have got to be prepared to set standards, and I think the way in which you dress, the way in which you appear is crucial, if you are sloppy in any way, kids will quickly catch on to it. I do think the standards I set are going. They want

a more free and easy kind of association, which I could never go along with.

The older teachers were prepared to discuss this matter with me, which suggests they saw me as being in agreement with them on the issue. In fact, I do not share these opinions at all, I am very negative to them. However, my appearance suggested I appreciated the issues, and presumably I would have missed these data had my appearance been wrong.

Appearance management is important, it needs some thought, it is easy to get it wrong and find problems as a result. The 'neat little teacher' image can be a mistake. This has been the case specifically with younger art teachers and some science teachers. They, as an essential part of their identity and orientation to teaching, have refused to accept what they consider to be a 'teacher uniform'.

> *Mr Tucks* I've never worn teacher uniform, I teach in what I am wearing now (cord trousers, casual shirt, no tie, desert boots) ... often criticized by colleagues.

Mr Tucks went on to describe 'teacher uniform' in its extreme form:

> *Mr Tucks* Suits, or tweed jackets with leather elbows, cherry blossom boots and cavalry twills (laughs). I have to say that few colleagues of mine have ever fallen into that category, but they were essentially tie wearers, and I was essentially not a tie wearer.

I interviewed one art teacher, in a private school, (the data are from my field notes) who I described as follows:

> I met Mrs. Think at her house, she was wearing tight blue jeans, a roll neck black jumper, fluorescent pink socks and white lace up shoes. She has long peroxided blonde hair and enormous gold earrings. At the end of the interview she offers me a lift to the station and puts on a leopard skin (artificial) short coat. She makes a point of her appearance, she indicates the coat and says in an imitation cockney accent, 'It's a bit of alright this, isn't it? Really attention seeking in'it?'. On the ride to the station, she explains that she has six versions of the same outfit, and they are all she ever wears.

My own appearance in a neat little skirt was therefore wrong, very wrong, and the interview was stilted and unadventurous. The next interview I went in my own clothes and things improved. Other studies have pointed out the need for the interviewers to monitor their personal characteristics, comments, gestures and actions, since they can influence the interview (Bogdan and Taylor, 1975; Burgess, 1984). In addition, it seems interviewers need to consider and monitor their appearance and image.

This material is important, because appearance has emerged as a central issue in teacher worlds. Appearance is certainly one of the key factors in 'Becoming a proper teacher' (for a more detailed discussion see Measor, forthcoming). It is one of the more important signals in defining the teachers' orientation towards school life. In teacher culture, appearance matters enormously; had my own appearance been wrong, I could have missed out on the data completely. My own appearance was an important factor in determining the data I obtained.

Appearance was also tremendously important with pupils in school. As Delamont (1980) pointed out, adolescents are obsessed with the clothes and appearance of those around them in school, especially if they themselves are in school uniform. My own experience was that pupils were very aware of every detail of my appearance, from the beginning, right through to the very end of the research. Before the kids knew me well, I was named as 'the woman with the chandeliers in her ears' because of a prediliction for very large earrings. A day hardly passed without my appearance being commented on by pupils. Very fine gradations in detail were made, and I had to try and tune into them. One woman, a science teacher, was totally unacceptable to the girls. Mrs. Lines, for example, was unpopular with the girls, she was strongly disapproved of, and appearance was one factor.

> Amy   Mrs. Lines — she's too posh.
> Ros   Did you know she's a judo expert, Mrs. Lines.
> Rebecca   Oh, God, I didn't know that.
> Ros   That's why she must wear trousers isn't it.
> Amy   Yes, she's horrible.
> (For a full discussion of all the implications see Measor, 1983.)

My own appearance in jeans was by contrast fine, because jeans are acceptable in youth culture and because they were 'straights'. I think my appearance was crucial in gaining acceptance from the girls, and hence in gaining access to some of the personal areas of their lives, for example, adolescent sexuality. Nevertheless, I had to employ careful 'knife edge' strategies (Measor and Woods, 1984). Pupils responded well when I wore fashionable items of clothing, but I had to keep my peace with teachers in the school as well, and they could have very different notions of what was appropriate. Teachers acted as a real constraint in this matter. Researchers facing a new situation probably need to give careful consideration to their appearance and clothes. Appearance does need to be managed, and one's image manipulated to some extent in this kind of research.

'Access' to people involves being accepted by them, and ultimately getting their trust. The strategies are the usual human ones we all employ in building a new relationship. Nevertheless they are employed in a somewhat unnatural context. Participant observation means 'hanging about' at the back of other people's classrooms, writing notes, only some of which are entirely public. Both teachers and pupils are intensely aware of a stranger in the classroom, and acted accordingly. Pupils would turn to look curiously at me, and I would smile back, which is something teachers do not normally do. The next stage was conversational; pupils would ask questions about the research, and then about me, the researcher. This process is one that Burgess (1984) has described when he comments 'To have avoided these questions would have provided the "sanitized" interviews demanded by the textbook writers, but would have ruined my relationships with the teachers and pupils' (p. 105). (See also Oakley, 1981.)

At this point another strategy becomes important, and it is that of shared interests. I made sure I was properly clued up on the sorts of things I thought would interest pupils. They were rock music, football and fashion. Basically, I was aware of whether Liverpool or Manchester United had reached the top of the table in a particular week, and I went to a number of rock music concerts. There is, I discovered, an important issue, the interests need to be genuinely mutual, otherwise pupils object. When I went to see a 'Who' concert, the pupils were enthusiastic and interested, as I was too. On another occasion I went to see a 'Stranglers' concert, not out of my own interest and volition, but because I knew it was music which appealed to thirteen-year-olds. The pupils sensed this, and were cool and withdrawn about this concert. I found it equally important to have shared interests with the teachers I was interviewing. Many of the retired teachers were very interested in gardening, as I was. The fact that I knew precisely when my daffodils were about to bloom was useful. My interest in orchid growing broke the ice very quickly with another teacher, whose room was full of plants of this type. I was glad

I knew something about classical music, but I could have done with knowing more about bird watching. Humour was certainly crucial; I suspect that having been a teacher was important too.

Sharing interests and talking about them with interviewees is an important element in building a rapport, so that people will talk to you. I find this a very uncomfortable area to analyze, partly because it is asking questions about the strategies that you as a person use to go about starting and running relationships in your life. Nevertheless, the building of 'research relationships' is different from social and personal ones and that highlights again the fact that the interview situation is an unnatural one. In a 'research relationship', one presents a particular 'front' or a particular self. My own view is that it is important to 'come over' as very sweet and trustworthy, but ultimately rather bland. The blandness needs further discussion and will be examined later.

The interviewer needs strategies to ease the access. I always reassure people that they, their school, even their town, will remain anonymous. We decided that the teachers in the second project should be offered transcripts of their interviews and the right to change things in it. I emphasize, from the very beginning, that the research is about what concerns teachers, it is an opportunity to air their grievances and interests publicly. I also offer the idea, that their experiences as older, successful teachers, can be helpful to younger teachers 'learning the ropes'. In part, this is an attempt to offer the interviewee more control over the interview, and over the research generally. This has been a useful tactic and Mr. King's response was typical: 'If I can put back a bit into teaching, I'm happy to do it because teaching gave me so much'.

However much of the access is gained through non-verbal signals, eye contact, smiles, a projection of concern. These are a number of tactics one employs. People do need reassurance when they are being interviewed. You do have to listen, but you also have to look as if you are listening. It reminds me of the advice that driving instructors give you before you do your test, about making sure the examiner notices you are looking into the mirror, before you signal, or turn a corner. You have to make the gesture larger than life. In interviewing, looking as if you are listening, means, I think, nodding at the client at frequent intervals, making a range of appropriate incoherent 'uhm's!' 'aah-ha's' and 'yes's', and God forbid you should miss laughing at someone's joke. It is important to agree with people's interests and show a willingness to enter into the way they see the world. It is all part of building confidence and trust (Oakley,

1981; Finch, 1984). In another way, however, it feels rather as if the interviewer is manipulating other people, and may be partially responsible for the reluctance I felt when asked to analyze my own interviewing practices.

The amount of time you have available for the research can be a real constraint in building relationships. The first research project involved my spending eighteen months with the same group of pupils. I would claim that I got to know at least some of the pupils very well, and that was reflected in the data. Pupils, or rather female pupils, were willing to talk about their own patterns of adolescent sexuality, for example. A long period of research time is conducive to getting at the things that are most significant to people, but also most sensitive.

By contrast, the second teacher-based research project had no such time dimension over a long period. Again, the research is based on the quality of relationships, but there is only a very short time in which to build them; the teacher is interviewed, at the most, five or six times. Strategies are needed to compensate for this; for example, I always plan the interview with a period of time for 'just a chat' at the beginning and end of the session. I never turn on the tape recorder immediately I arrive. I also try to provide some information about myself for the teacher, so it feels less a one-way information flow.

Interviewing — Listening Beyond

The interviewer has to stay 'critically aware' during the interview, and I find this places a constraint on the length of the interviews. The teacher can usually talk on, but after an hour-and-a-half I find myself incapable of that critical listening. I stop the interview and explain why I am stopping to the interviewee. There is a more theoretical point involved in this term 'critically aware'. So far I have emphasized the importance of rapport, building relationships, trust and confidence. This is all well and good, but at the same time the researcher's job is also to remain critical and aware of what the interviewer is saying. It involves entering another person's world, and their perspective, but remaining alert to its configurations at the same time. Interviewers need to keep their antennae up for pointers, which lead into the meaning of what is being said; and for data which fit the themes of the research.

There is a contradiction, in aiming for intimate rapport and yet treating the person's account both critically and sociologically. A partial solution comes through strategies of respondent validation, and notions of teacher as researcher that we have worked towards. We take data and make a first stage sociological analysis of it; that analysis is then returned to the teacher for his or her comments and use. One example of this is the data on appearance and teacher uniform that I have already discussed. Mr. Tucks identified himself as not wearing a teacher uniform. He later discussed the importance of appearance to other teachers in the school. He then went on to discuss the way that a teacher's appearance seemed to be connected with a number of other attitudes and beliefs; about pupil deviance, for example.

> *Mr Tucks* The school has always been fairly easy going about the dress of pupils. I like to cherish my relationship with pupils, so I would think twice about threatening it by pointing out that pupils had yellow socks on or something.

Pedagogy and teacher style was also crucial:

> *Mr Tucks* I think an informal teaching style has to go along with that kind of teacher culture. I've worked on some of the new schemes that are around for teaching maths and science. I actively want to debunk the academic pretensions of some scientists, and especially some science teachers.

As Mr. Tucks talked, I began to build up a notion from him of a 'proper teacher', which he was determined never to be. I took the idea and tried it out on other teachers, who laughed and recognized the idea, and fleshed it out in a number of ways. Mrs. Castle embroidered the importance of appearance:

> *Mrs Castle* I never succumbed. The way we went about it mainly, the younger ones, was with what we wore. The head did comment once about, something about open sandals. So we all went to great pains, the younger ones, to wear our sandals as minimal as we could, with the most violent scarlet nail polish on our toe nails.

Mr King testified about his notions of pedagogy, what he thought he was doing when he taught art:

> *Mr King* I was after one thing, what was my job, it was er

> ... to stimulate, to open eyes, to er ... make
> them think as well, to live in an art room, to be
> alive, think, make, do, use, feel, touch, it's a
> beautiful sense, I was nearly arrested in Spain,
> for putting my fingers on a Goya painting, but
> the paint was ... so ... and I had to.

Once I had a full picture, I took the analysis, of teacher socialization
and teacher adaptations, and an ideal type notion of being a proper
teacher, back to Mr Tucks. He took up the idea, and added a number
of other factors, which he identified as being important in becoming a
proper teacher, like attitude to promotion, and unions, and the
analysis was extended and elaborated as a result.

We also need strategies which cope with picking up a contradiction in what an interviewee is saying. The difficulty arises, because by
commenting on the contradiction, the interviewer breaks the
empathic stance. One example was Mrs. Castle, a retired art teacher in
her sixties. I have already discussed her view of teachers' appearance
when she was young. She described a 'dissolute' youth as a Commu-
nist Party member with a fashionable hairstyle, and a lot of clothes
consciousness.

> *Mrs Castle*   I think my clothes were a wee bit strange, a wee
> bit different, I don't think they were quite as
> conformist. In fashion, when skirts were
> straight, we wore black, straight, slimline skirts,
> with slits up the side, longer or shorter, accord-
> ing to how you were feeling, and how much you
> wanted to shock. I was very blonde, and kept up
> with fashion quite a bit.

Her politics came into it too:

> *Mrs Castle*   They knew I was the left wing kind. I did join
> the Communist Party, while I was in Wales. I
> got told off by the Deputy Head for selling the
> 'Daily Worker' outside the market.

Two interviews later, Mrs. Castle criticized young teachers for *their
appearance*:

> *Mrs Castle*   I occasionally used to see teachers drifting
> around, looking most peculiar, and I used to
> think 'My God, what do the children think of
> teachers who dress like that', and I don't know,

> I think probably teachers ought to look a bit old fashioned.

She also disapproved of minor deviances, like being late for lessons:

> *Mrs Castle*   You see, younger teachers, being a bit irresponsible, feckless, and not pulling their weight, seeing them sort of 'scamping their duties' and being late to do registration.

Earlier on Mrs. Castle had admitted this was one of her faults when young. I asked her directly about the contradiction in her opinions. This teacher did not object to being confronted in this way, and gave an explanation that was important for the whole analysis:

> *Mrs Castle*   As you go on teaching, and get older, I mean, you do adopt different attitudes. Certainly as I went on I think I became a lot more committed, and I accepted myself as a teacher.

Mrs. Castle discussed the way that the quality of commitment one has to a profession changes as one gets older, and invests more in it. It was data that was important in terms of making an analysis of life cycle and generational change throughout a career. (For a full discussion of this analysis see Measor, Sikes and Woods, forthcoming.) Nevertheless, other teachers with different personalities and different early biographies might well have minded this kind of questioning.

In looking at transcripts of the interviews I realized a series of phrases and questions were frequently being repeated by all the teachers interviewed, although they were not present in pupil interviews. I include three examples here.

> *Mr Quilley*   You ask me the questions you want, because I can ramble on to no consequence.
>
> *LM*   No, no, it's great, it's exactly what we want.

> *Mr Redford*   As you've discovered, I can talk about anything ad infinitum, so do stop me.

> *Mr Shoe*   No, I prefer it if you ask me direct questions, there's a time element for you, keep me on the track you want.

Respondents constantly asked, 'Is this what you want, stop me talking, if it's not'. They prefaced statements with phrases like, 'This is tangential'. The frequency with which these phrases cropped up made me consider their implications. People seem to feel that being interviewed is somehow very self-indulgent. Many teachers said they had really enjoyed the opportunity to talk about their work and to air their grievances about their work situation. It may be that such research has a counselling function (Measor and Woods 1984).

The interview is, after all, an unnatural social situation. The set-up is that a stranger arrives, sets up a tape recorder, asks questions, but most importantly is prepared to sit and listen to you, talking about yourself for an hour and a half, then they disappear. The unnaturalness of the interview situation sets something off in people, it makes them a little uncomfortable. I want to suggest that this is because it goes against a cultural value, which we hold strongly — one about not talking too much about oneself. We learn not to do so, and we have stereotyped images of very boring figures who do talk about themselves too much. This emotional reaction from people interviewed is important. Qualitative methodology is based upon an attempt to observe people and events as they are and happen; and in their natural setting. It stands in opposition to methodologies which create artificial conditions for experiments and observations, claiming that artificial results will be gained. Nevertheless we have to note that those interviewed did not experience the interview as a natural setting, but one that was artificial and contrived (Brunswick, 1956).

Order in the Interview

Structured interviews are avoided in qualitative research (Stenhouse, 1984); it is one of the key elements of the methodology. On the other hand the researcher does need a set of thematic areas which he or she wants to cover. Inevitably the interviewee will 'ramble' and move away from the designated areas in the researcher's mind. 'Rambling' is nevertheless important and needs some investigation. The interviewee in rambling is moving onto areas which most interest him or her. The interviewer is losing some control over the interview, and yielding it to the client, but the pay-off is that the researcher reaches the data that is central to the client. I always go along with rambling at least for a while, but try to make a note about what is missed and cover it in the next interview (Burgess, 1984, discusses this issue further).

One example was a teacher of rural science, doing an MEd course. I began the interview with a general question.

LM	This research is looking at teachers' careers and the issues that most concern teachers.
Mr Shaw	Well, I know what most concerns me, it's being a rural science teacher, a head of department for all these years, all the exhibitions I've done, I went out and did an Open University course, then a diploma, but still it's this wellington boots image. They won't let me up from a scale 3. I've been to the Headmaster, I've told him, I've applied for deputy headships all over the place, no luck, nothing, it's the straw in the mouth and the mud on the boots image, but look at what we do really. Finally I've come on this course, maybe that will change something.

Mr. Shaw spent forty-five minutes of the interview discussing this matter; it was a burning issue for him, and the dominating concern of his life. He was in his mid-forties, and felt he had no hope of getting promotion, because of his unfashionable subject specialism. At the interview, it was this he wanted to talk about, it was his consuming interest. My general tactic with other teachers was to put questions to them, to get an ordered chronological account of their biography. This would have been a useless tactic with Mr. Shaw, I would simply have got polite, non-involved data. Instead he talked freely, we built an empathetic relationship, and in the second interview I filled in the parts that were missing. (For a full discussion of order in interviews see Burgess (1984).)

There are difficulties with people rambling, however. This is perhaps particularly true of older teachers. I made a decision that I would not interview anyone older than sixty-eight on this project. I had interviewed very old people on a number of social and labour history projects, and it is very hard work. The problem basically is keeping older folk on the point; there is a tendency for them to take off at a tangent, and discuss matters about which they have a 'bee in their bonnet', like striking miners for example. The interviewer needs strategies to guide them tactfully back to the point, which with teachers is not always very easy; they are used to doing a lot of talking, even all the talking. Many researchers tell a similar tale, about interviewing headmasters. My own experience was that I managed to ask three short questions in a one-and-a-half-hour tape, the head filled in the rest. Finally, when the tape ran out, I allowed him to talk on.

'Topography' of an Interview

I recognize a kind of topography to an interview, and grade my questions on the basis of 'danger zones'. Some questions deal with more sensitive issues than others, they probe areas which are important to people, and they go in 'close to the bone'. In practice this means I never begin an interview with a 'danger zone' question, I start with innocuous things. It refers back to the point about building a relationship, as the interview progresses, and a kind of conversational intimacy gets going, when I feel it is more appropriate to ask more personal questions. One example was with pupils. I found that they were ready to discuss their teachers quite early on; discussing other pupils seemed much more dangerous, and they asked for reassurance, 'You won't tell her will you' or 'If this gets back to her she'll kill me', before they were prepared to do it. Another example concerned a retired chemistry teacher. I first asked him a simple question about how he had organized the chemistry timetable which he answered with a flood of precise detail. Later I slid into other areas, which asked about strategies for getting sympathetic timetabling from the headmaster, and priority over resources.

> *Mr Ladyhill* During the time I served with that headmaster there was a building-up period. It has been our policy, among the science staff, and particularly the head of department to fight and fight and fight again for more money, and this is what we have done.

This data led into an analysis of the relative status of school subjects in boys' and girls' schools, and a gender and curriculum argument (for a full discussion see Measor, Sikes and Woods, forthcoming).

People will sometimes offer a cue that they are going to 'come out' and open up with something quite personal. On rare occasions, interviewees tell you directly that they are entering danger zone data. One young science teacher one day apologized for his lack of coherence throughout an interview. He was discussing his relationship, which was very fraught, with the head of department. He explained that it represented 'baring his soul' and he was not finding it easy. There are other less direct signals; people frequently lower their voices, sometimes they use phrases like 'Maybe I shouldn't be saying this ... but'. Often, too, people will tell you things after the tape is turned off. For example, I interviewed a teacher who had that morning learned that she had not got promotion that year. She very much wanted to discuss it, but not when the tape was turned on. One of the counselling staff at the school insisted I turned off the tape before telling me the gory details of an assault on one of the first year girls who had the reputation of a 'tart' at the school!

> *Mrs Bridges* Turn that thing off.

[Pause while I do so.]

> *Mrs Bridges* Roy and some of the others — it's big trouble, assaulting little girls by the tennis courts — yes Shirley — who else! A whole group of them said they'd meet her, by the tennis courts after school — there's never anybody around, right down there. They got her trapped in, by a big circle of lads, they all stood round, and made her take off most of her clothes!

Mrs Bridges went on to describe the range of teasing, threatening, and touching that had gone on, with Shirley in her underwear, before a teacher had happened to pass by and intervene.

By contrast some teachers were prepared to pass comments while the tape was on although they recognized it as a constraint.

> *Miss Nott* Are we on the air, because I don't mind if I do say it. I think one thing that is true, since they have started so many mixed comprehensive schools, there have been fewer and fewer chances for women to be headteachers, and in my experience the women were always the better headteachers.

Obviously there are things that people will not tell you; sometimes you can gain oblique insights into what they are. In group interviews it is possible to touch on material that one or two members of the group consider 'too sensitive'. The others may not agree, conflict arises in the group as a result. An example occurred with a group of boys who were 'good mates'. I interviewed three of them; the missing boy, Roy, had just been placed in the bottom stream for mathematics. The pupils were in their first year at the school; this was their first encounter with streaming.

> *Andy* Dy'e know where Roy got put ...
> *Pete* Shut up!
> *Andy* He's been put in the maths ...
> *Pete* Shut it, Andy.

Andy   In the maths group with the dummies.
Pete   Just shut it Andy. [growled threateningly]

Pete would not let Andy discuss the matter, the information was not for my consumption. The reason soon became apparent, it was too damaging to Roy's reputation. Roy was an ace deviant, but within two weeks he had worked hard enough to get out of the bottom stream, out of contact with the 'dummies'. Then Pete told me the news, immediately I arrived in school one morning. 'Roy's got out of that group, he was too good for the "thickies"'. (A full account is in Measor and Woods, 1983.)

In one particular context, I was given some specialized verbal cues about information. This was in relation to the myths I collected from pupils, which arose around their transfer from middle to secondary school. When discussing the myths pupils typically prefaced their accounts with phrases like, 'There's all these rumours that', or 'There's stories about', or 'I have heard that', all of which were a signal that a particular kind of information was about to be given, information which had a different character from more general comments. The most frequently repeated myth concerned how 'You get yer 'ead flushed down the loo on yer birthday', in the secondary school. One version is given:

Phillip   They say you get your head flushed down the loo on your birthday an' that.
LM   Do you believe that?
Phillip   And that you get thrown in the shower with your clothes on on your birthday.
LM   Do you believe it?
Phillip   [Laughs loudly] No! [laughs again then says] I won't tell them when my birthday is.

(For a full analysis see Measor and Woods, 1983.)

I have discovered the importance of the things people say when they first meet you, or when you contact them about the interview. The problem is, that in all the confusion of arriving, taking off your coat, working out where to sit, and where the tape recorder can best go to obtain a decent recording, you fail to record people's first comments. One example occurred with a mid-career woman art teacher. I arrived at her house a little late and a little flustered, and in a taxi. The train had been delayed. I complained about the taxi-driver, who had spent the journey graphically describing the way he nearly 'got beaten up' all the time. Her response was 'Ah, welcome to

Withington-on-Sea'; she repeated her comment several times, and always in sarcastic tones. This teacher has remained radical through-out her career. Her whole stance is oppositional to the prevailing norms of society and school, and her sense of identity is fuelled by her image of negativity. She agreed with this analysis when it was presented to her. She takes a position of distanced opposition to her environment, it is a key point in building her identity. It is therefore interesting that this distanced opposition should be in evidence from the very first statement she made.

Strategies for Validating Data

In 1980 and in 1983 I gave a paper at two conferences on educational research. Both papers provoked discussion on the validity of data drawn from interviews, and on the validity of analysis made from that data. The argument on both occasions was that in the interviews the respondents had been 'putting me off' and avoiding giving real answers. A number of questions arise.

Firstly, are there any strategies that deal with being put off? I think not. If respondents have decided they do not want to tell you why they never married, failed to get promotion, or left their boyfriend last week, they have a right to privacy. It is unethical to poke around the issue, trying to pressure them for the data you want. The best strategy is to build good relationships in the first place, so people feel free to talk to the interviewer. Sometimes, just waiting is the best strategy, people may choose to tell a researcher things, when they feel they know them better. One older, unmarried woman art teacher was a good example. At the first meeting I followed my usual policy of trying to get the basic chronological structure of her career. She made no mention of the fact that she had not married. During the second interview, Miss Nott said: 'At that stage, 1938, I was engaged, and making things for my bottom drawer, but the war upset that'. The implication was that perhaps the man involved was killed in the war. By the fifth interview, Miss Nott wanted to tell the whole story.

Miss Nott	My mother wanted to cling to me, and his mother, I realized, wanted to cling on to him, and the battle got to the state where I couldn't stand the strain any longer. The best thing of course would have been if we had buzzed off and got married. Instead of that, I was very nice, and said

> perhaps we can be friends until we can see our
> way to getting married, and then the war came. I
> am sorry about that. I think if we had torn free
> and gone up to London ... but, I thought, if you
> push someone into it, and that mother commits
> suicide, how do you start life together?

Miss Nott had carried a bitterness about her mother's actions in
general throughout her whole life. I would suggest that asking
questions about marriage at the first interview would have been
fruitless, it was important to wait until the teacher chose to talk.

The second issue is the validation of data. A number of strategies
for validation of qualitative data have been put forward (Hammersley, 1979). Triangulation is one of the most frequently cited tactics. In
the research on pupil transfer it was possible to collect data from a
number of different sources, using a variety of methods. Participant
observation and interviews were used. It was possible to observe and
interview pupils, teachers and parents. For example when I was
collecting data on pupil myths, a number of vantage points were
available. I was first alerted to the existence of the myths, by middle
school pupils talking about themselves. When I interviewed pupils
specifically on the matter, they gave fuller, more elaborate versions. I
then discovered that pupils at the secondary school knew the myths,
as did the teachers, although not in their fullest versions. Finally
when parents were interviewed they also knew about the myths. It is
much more difficult with life history methodology, where there is
one respondent, discussing his or her own life and his or her
perspective. Taking the data in context, like archaeologists do, is
probably one of the best. We have tried to get 'grounded' life history
data, by a number of methods. For example, I interviewed both
science and art teachers in the same school. I interviewed teachers of
both art and science who were retired, but who had worked in that
school. In one grammar school, Valley, there was a separate boys' and
girls' school. I interviewed both art and science teachers from the
separate sections. In addition, I interviewed people who had been
pupils at that school, about the teachers.

This discussion avoids one major issue. When I was challenged
about the validity of data, my own reaction was really that I *felt* the
data was valid. My intuitive reaction was that the responses were real,
and that I had not been 'put off'. Such an emotive statement of course
has no validity in social science terms, and it has no ornamentation of
scientific rigour. Nevertheless, I felt that after spending eighteen

months with a group of pupils, I did have a sense of what was accurate, the data were based on a well-established relationship. It may be that we have to come to terms with the intuitive, subjective elements in our work, because the work is with people. Catani pointed out, it is this factor which 'presents the researcher with difficulties, when drawing his analysis. They must first objectify and translate into scientific terms, what is in the first instance a human encounter'. (Catani, 1981; p. 213)

Images of the Researcher

What the interviewer is influences and maybe determines the kind of data he or she receives. There are a number of factors; age, gender, and ethnicity are probably the most significant (cf. Pryce, 1979). It occurs to me that being a woman is an enormous advantage if the research involves interviews which attempt to reach in depth areas of personal life (cf. Finch, 1984). In our society, the emotions are cast as women's territory, and therefore people find it easier, more acceptable, more 'proper' to talk about subjective aspects of their life with a woman. The gender of the interviewer has an impact in pupil-based research too. I always felt that the data I received from the girls was far superior to that from the boys. A man in that research might have done better than I could with the boys, but all researchers seem to find that girls are more willing to talk than boys (see Ball's paper in this volume, page 23). Nevertheless, I am certain that had I been male, I would not have received data from the girls on issues like menstruation and puberty; and these were central issues in research on adolescence.

There is, in my view, a need to 'stay bland' during research; the problems arise over how much of one's self to reveal. Building rapport and then relationships necessarily entails giving information about one's own life and interests. Things work relatively easily, if you get on well with the client and if you have enough basic viewpoints in common. My own approach is to be 'neutral but nice', for there have been occasions when letting my own opinions show was a block to data collection. Some of the senior teachers at the school, where the transfer research was based, avidly read the 'Sun'. One day I was 'unresearcherly' enough to let a comment slip about page three of that newspaper. Word got about that I was very, very feminist. It meant that there were certain topics that I could not collect data on with these teachers. I spent each lunch time in their company, and their behaviour, for example, towards girls, may well have been constrained by their knowledge of my views.

In other situations, however, giving information about oneself is useful. One retired art teacher was a member of the Labour Party, and saw himself as a 'lefty'.

> *Mr Quilley*   In my first job, in Yorkshire, the moment you said you were Labour, you were in, you were the bright-eyed boy. But down here, in the South, the moment they knew I was Labour I was in trouble.

I also am a member, and it gave us an immediate point of contact. At the beginning of the second interview with the 'punk' art teacher, the conversation turned to the fact that I had a baby. This provoked her into a long intense reflection about having children and keeping a full-time interest in a career. She explained her reasons for her choice not to have children, which were her commitment to research and teaching. It was excellent data in life history terms, but I could not have directly asked her in an interview why she had not had children.

With pupils too, details of my own biography provoked data of an interesting kind. At the time of working on the pupil transfer research, I was married, but had no children, and I had retained my maiden name. After a year's quiet questioning pupils had established all of this information. Knowing the full picture, and knowing me provoked an outburst of fury from many of the girls. The ferocity of their outburst shocked me:

> *Amy*   You're just really selfish you, aren't you!
> *Ros*   You only care about yourself, no-one else!
> *Rebecca*   It's important, having children, it keeps a family together!

In fact, I was, in their eyes, wrong not to have a child. For them it emerged children were a kind of dream, a symbol of what they wanted out of life.

> *Mandy*   I want two little children, to stay at home with me, and cuddle.
> *Jacquie*   Yes, and make jam tarts for.

One of the themes of the transfer research was gender codes, and the ways they are laid down at this age and stage of life. Their outbursts were very pertinent data, about what they considered properly 'feminine' behaviour.

The central issue in interviewing is probably that of keeping a critical alertness about the interview, and also about yourself and your own performance. It is difficult always to monitor your own reactions and input to the interview, and to retain your own predispositions and bias. This was brought home to me quite forcibly, by the experience of doing team research. Pat Sikes noted teachers discussing the importance of tradition and a community ethos in schools. Once she had alerted me to this, I realized I also had been getting data on the issue, but had been ignoring it, because of my own negative reactions to the matter, based probably on my negative reactions to my schooling where tradition was strongly emphasized. Warnings about staying alert are probably not enough, we need tactics so we can sort out our biases. There are a range of options:

(i) Interviewing fellow researchers as in team research, where members of the team could interview each other.

(ii) Writing an educational biography like the University of Sussex PGCE students, who write their own educational biography to alert them to their own opinions, and to trace how they arrived at them.

(iii) Critical reflexive thought.

(iv) Writing papers on 'doing research'.

(v) Keeping an account of images of self you receive from people you interview.

(vi) Using other research experiences. I also have to count a period of time I spent doing participant observation at a mental hospital, run on group therapy principles, that alerted me to some of the techniques of observation used in family therapy analysis; and also the need to take account of unconscious factors in an interviewee's account.

In a paper which focuses on the practice of interviews, a number of strategies emerge as important. In qualitative research, the interviewer needs ways of easing access to respondents, and strategies which help build research relationships. Appearance, conversation, areas of interest and non-verbal signals are all important in this context. Time can act as a real constraint in building research relationships, but there are strategies which can help, and allow space for rapport to build. The interviewer also needs ways of staying critically aware, while being able to enter into the participants' world; to gain a strong picture of it, while remaining aware of which aspects of it are particular and special. It is a particular stance, but also a particular cast of mind.

References

BERTAUX, D. (Ed.) (1981) *Biography and Society*, London, Sage.

BOGDAN, R. and TAYLOR, S. (1975) *Introduction to Qualitative Research Methods*, New York, Wiley.

BRUNSWICK, E. (1956) *Perception and the Representative Design of Experiments*, California, University of California Press.

BURGESS, R.G. (1984) *In the Field: An Introduction to Field Research*, London, Allen and Unwin.

CATANI, M. (1981) 'Social-life history as ritualized oral exchange', in BERTAUX, D. (Ed.) *Biography and Society*, London, Sage.

DELAMONT, S. (1980) *Sex Roles and the School*, London, Methuen.

FERRAROTTI, F. (1981) 'On the autonomy of the biographical method' in BERTAUX, D. (Ed.) *Biography and Society*, London, Sage.

FINCH, J. (1984) '"It's great to have someone to talk to": the ethics and politics of interviewing women' in BELL, C. and ROBERTS, H. (Eds.) *Social Researching: Politics, Problems and Practice*, London, Routledge and Kegan Paul.

GOODE, W. and HATT, P. (1952) *Methods of Social Research*, London, McGraw-Hill.

HAMMERSLEY, M. (1979) 'Data collection in ethnographic research', Block 4, Part 3, DE 304, *Research Methods in Education and the Social Sciences*, Milton Keynes, Open University Press.

HAMMERSLEY, M. and ATKINSON, P. (1983) *Ethnography: Principles in Practice*, London, Tavistock.

MEASOR, L. (1983) 'Gender and the sciences' in HAMMERSLEY, M. and HARGREAVES, A. (Eds.) *Curriculum Practice: Some Sociological Case Studies*, Lewes, Falmer Press.

MEASOR, L. (forthcoming) 'Becoming a proper teacher' in MEASOR, L., SIKES, P. and WOODS, P. *Teachers' Careers*, Lewes, Falmer Press.

MEASOR, L. and WOODS, P. (1983) 'An interpretation of pupil myths' in HAMMERSLEY, M. (Ed.) *The Ethnography of Schooling*, Driffield, Nafferton.

MEASOR, L. and WOODS, P. (1984) *Changing Schools*, Milton Keynes, Open University Press.

MOSER, C.A. (1958) *Survey Methods in Social Investigation*, London, Heinemann.

OAKLEY, A. (1981) 'Interviewing women; a contradiction in terms' in ROBERTS, H. (Ed.) *Doing Feminist Research*, London, Routledge and Kegan Paul.

PRYCE, K. (1979) *Endless Pressure*, Harmondsworth, Penguin.

STENHOUSE, L. (1984) 'Library access, library use and user education in academic sixth forms: an autobiographical account' in BURGESS, R.G. (Ed.) *The Research Process in Educational Settings: Ten Case Studies*, Lewes, Falmer Press.

3   In the Company of Teachers: Key Informants and the Study of a Comprehensive School

Robert G. Burgess

Ethnographic research is characterized by the intense nature of relationships that are established between researcher and researched. Accordingly, many of the basic sociological texts devoted to this style of social investigation discuss elements of the personal relationships involved in this work: establishing relationships, developing trust and the presentation of self (cf. Lofland, 1971; Schatzman and Strauss, 1973; Johnson, 1975). While such accounts touch the heart of ethnographic research that involves describing and understanding the lives of particular groups of people, they do, nevertheless, spend little time on key informants and their role within the ethnographic enterprise.

This omission is somewhat surprising on at least three counts. First, ethnography relies for its basic data on the testimony of individual informants (cf. Conklin, 1968). Secondly, some ethnographic accounts are focused upon the relationship between the researcher and a key informant. For example, the data that were collected in Whyte's classic study *Street Corner Society* (Whyte, 1981) and in Liebow's *Tally's Corner* (Liebow, 1967) relied heavily upon the key informants: Doc and Tally respectively. Indeed, it is the key informants who are synonymous with these studies.[1] Finally, if we turn to anthropological accounts of ethnographic work (cf. Agar, 1981) the informant and the informant's role is seen as a central part of ethnographic research. Indeed, Casagrande (1960) considers that the anthropologist who engages in fieldwork is involved in a collaborative enterprise with a group of informants, for he argues that

> the successful outcome of field research depends not only on
> the anthropologist's own skills, but also on the capabilities

and interests of those who teach him their ways. (Casagrande, 1960, p. x)

For Casagrande considers that the anthropologist-informant relationship will result in informants inviting the researcher to participate in their activities as well as teaching the researcher about events they feel will be of interest. It is in this way that the researcher becomes conversant with everything from routine activities to momentous events together with the role that gossip plays in the everyday lives of the people who are studied.

Nevertheless, when we turn to major educational studies that have utilized an ethnographic style of investigation we find that informants are not mentioned (cf. Hargreaves, 1967; Lacey, 1970). Even when they are discussed it is often in the context of other work, yet their role does appear to have had some significance. For example, Woods (1981) in discussing the role of talk in ethnographic work comments upon key informants. However, his remarks suggest that they played an important role in developing his methodology for he states:

> I was fortunate in finding some key informants. They helped give perspective to the entire methodological front from the very beginning, for example by identifying the nature of other people's talk and behaviour. (Woods, 1981, p. 16)

Indeed, he points to the value of informants in providing knowledge on different social contexts, in providing explanations of situations that have been observed, and in giving the researcher some sense of the historical events in which observational work needs to be located.[2] Similarly, Ball (1984) commenting upon his study *Beachside Comprehensive* (Ball, 1981) indicates that teacher informants did play an important role. In particular, he discusses the role of five teachers who he argues could not be described as typical or untypical or representative of all teachers in the school. They were individuals who he got to know well and who could adopt a reflexive stance towards the school. They could also discuss and evaluate some of the situations that he had observed.[3]

Certainly, when I conducted an ethnographic study of a purpose built co-educational comprehensive school that I called Bishop McGregor (Burgess, 1983) I found that much of my fieldwork was done in collaboration with teacher and pupil informants (cf. Burgess, 1983, especially chapters 2, 4, 7 and 8). Yet when we turn to many methodological accounts of ethnographic work in educational settings we find little attention given to informants.[4] Accordingly, in an attempt to begin to fill this gap in our knowledge, this paper focuses upon a selection of teachers who became key informants in the course of my Bishop McGregor study. Among the issues that we shall address are: initial contacts, establishing and developing a group of informants, selection issues, informant roles and some ethical problems involved in the researcher-informant relationship.

Initial Contacts

As the authors of the celebrated anthropological guide to fieldwork, *Notes and Queries* (Royal Anthropological Institution, 1951) state, there is a sense in which every member of the group that is studied is a potential informant as all individuals may be observed in the course of an investigation. However, it is usual for the researcher to focus on particular individuals during the period of study but we might ask: are they purposely selected by the researcher? Do they select the researcher? Are they representative of broader groups that are studied?

My initial contact at Bishop McGregor School was the headmaster (Burgess, 1985a) but having agreed to allow me to conduct research within the school he passed me on down the staff hierarchy to a teacher called Sylvia Robinson who at that time was Head of Careers and in charge of the Newsom Department[5]; the department that I intended to study. It was Sylvia Robinson who was to become a key informant and who was to play a major role in my study.

Numerous anthropologists (cf. Williams, 1967; Harrell-Bond, 1976) have warned that some individuals who attach themselves to the researcher may well be marginal to the group or institution that is studied. At the time, I did not consider the extent to which Sylvia might or might not be representative of other teachers for she appeared to me to be an ideal guide for a research novice. She was willing to introduce me to a variety of teachers, to take me into groups to which she belonged and to facilitate my presence in various areas of the school. On the first day of term she made it her business to meet me in the early morning and to take me to the House to which I had been allocated where she introduced me to all the staff. Similarly, in terms of the department she busied herself introducing me to other teachers and to groups of pupils who I was to teach. Furthermore, during morning breaks she took me to the staff common room where I was introduced to the group with whom she regularly sat. This group consisted predominantly of Heads of House (the most senior teachers in the school). During my early days in the common room I kept a systematic record of the teachers who sat in this group and on this basis I found that not only was I marginal to this group in terms of status but so was Sylvia. Indeed, I later learned that it was widely rumoured that Sylvia Robinson sat with this group in an attempt to become involved in the day-to-day activities of those teachers who ran the school.

Sylvia Robinson was marginal to this informal group in the staff common room and to several groups in various departments (Newsom, biology and religious education) where she taught. However, she used her marginal position to engage individuals in conversation. She was a collector of gossip in the school and would relay whatever information she had acquired to other teachers. In this sense, she was widely regarded by teachers as the staff gossip-monger. Her role as collector and transmitter of gossip among the staff was of great value to me as a researcher as I acquired a working knowledge of different areas of the school, rapidly became acquainted with knowledge about members of the school (which needed subsequently to be checked with other informants) and was introduced to a wide variety of teachers.

However, it did not stop there. Sylvia was a fund of knowledge about individual pupils and could provide a potted history of their school lives, their misdemeanours and their relationships with other teachers. For just as she engaged staff in conversation so were many of her classes devoted to gossip with pupils, so much so that pupils regularly declared that 'Miss Robinson's been trying to find out all our business again'. Yet in research terms, it was gossip that provided a good start for my research as Sylvia gave me leads to follow, information that could subsequently be checked and ideas about documents that I should ask to see. Often when I wanted to hear about specific events in the past or to find out about a situation I had not witnessed or a meeting I had not attended, it was to Sylvia I turned as I could be sure that she would have a version of what had occurred or, if she did not, she would make it her business to find out what had transpired.

Sylvia Robinson worked with me throughout the whole period of my research and provided a constant supply of data about teachers, pupils, departments and various other areas of the school. Meanwhile, Maggie Rolls (a Head of House) provided guidance on the House system during my first term in the school. Maggie Rolls had joined the school as an assistant teacher when it had first opened four years before my research began. She had been a member of many of the initial planning meetings in departments and had been the first of several teachers to be promoted internally from the position of assistant teacher in a department to Head of House. However, among the Head of Houses she was the most junior in terms of chronological age and years of teaching experience. In the early days of my research she was willing to explain school routines, answer numerous questions and queries, dig out specific documents and pupil files which she thought would be of interest to me and give access to the whole filing system within her House that provided sets of minutes and logs of decisions on most activities that had been planned in the early development of the school.

In the case of this teacher I found her knowledge of the school and the background she could provide on the development of school routines invaluable. Indeed, many of her remarks could be followed up through the documents that were located in the detailed filing system she had established. Indeed, when documents were missing from her files she was able to indicate the kind of material that I should request from the school secretary. Just as Sylvia Robinson was a guide to the departmental system, so Maggie Rolls was a guide to the House system as she taught me what for her was involved in being a Head of House.

As far as Maggie Rolls was concerned, being a Head of House meant being the equivalent of a head of a small junior school. However, she did indicate that other House Heads saw the position in different terms. Furthermore, she indicated that for her, being a Head of House meant finding out about pupils' home backgrounds, following up situations when they were in trouble, handling court appearances and dealing out punishment in her House. She explained to me her policy on punishment and on corporal punishment which in some instances was different from other House Heads. For example, she indicated a number of offences, including truancy, for which she would always administer corporal punishment. By the time we discussed this matter I was already aware of the 'heavy' caning policy in her House as I often witnessed pupils waiting to be caned, heard caning taking place and saw corporal punishment being administered. However, when I asked if she entered each offence in the school punishment book she laughed and said that neither she nor her deputy could afford the time to enter everything in the book. Yet even in these circumstances I found that according to the records in the punishment book more pupils were caned in her House compared with other Houses and the offences as listed were different from those that were catalogued by other House Heads.

My initial contact with Maggie Rolls provided me with guidance on a different aspect of school organization to that provided by Sylvia Robinson. Maggie Rolls introduced me to the way in which she operated as a House Head. While it could not be claimed that her actions and activities were 'typical' of House Heads I did find that following her method of working gave me insights into this aspect of school organization, which helped me to orientate my questions on the House system and to make comparisons between her House and the other five Houses in the school. Certainly, when I moved to another House at the beginning of the next academic year I began to make comparisons between the rules and routines in the two Houses, to the ways in which the House Heads defined their activities and to the ways in which school routines were reinterpreted within the Houses. In this sense, this key informant not only helped to focus my data collection but also to orientate aspects of data analysis. However, at the beginning of the new academic year several new staff appointments were made, including some teachers who were to take Newsom classes for less able pupils that I had already been working with. It was this experience that helped me to establish a working relationship with some of these teachers and to broaden the group of individuals who were my key informants.

Establishing and Developing a Group of Informants

Among the teachers who were appointed to the staff in the autumn term 1973 were several probationary teachers, two of whom were required to teach their subjects to bottom sets in the fifth year that were heavily populated with Newsom pupils. As these two teachers were allocated to the same House as I was in, we came into frequent contact with each other. They were eager to talk to me about the problems associated with teaching Newsom classes and for that matter about some of the routine difficulties that they encountered in their first few weeks of full time teaching. As a former teacher who was now doing research in the school and who was teaching Newsom classes it appeared that I could be used as a source of advice and support. Any admission of difficulty to me could be discussed without anything 'counting against them' in the formal assessment of probationary teachers, for although I was part of the school I was also an 'outsider'.

The two teachers belonged to the English and religious education departments. Of the two, I came to know Paul Klee in the

English department best of all. He had recently completed a degree course in English and sociology and was acquainted with ethnographic research, having taken a special option on this subject in his final year at university. Without any prompting from me, he was able to ask searching questions about my research, my research focus, my methodology and the key aspects of my analysis. To begin with I found it somewhat unnerving to be confronted by someone who knew about participant observation. However, he was amused by what staff thought ethnographic research was about and what participant observation involved compared with what it *actually* involved. Without prompting from me, I found that he began to act as an honorary research assistant on my project.

For the purpose of research I was a part-time teacher in the school. Accordingly, I was only in the school for two days each week and could, as a lone researcher, only participate in a limited number of activities and meetings. Paul Klee would, therefore, spend time each day I was in the school updating me on the activities that had taken place in my absence. He was also willing to provide an eye witness account of meetings that he attended which gave me access to further dimensions of the school which could be checked out against my own observations. For example, he provided details of what occurred in the probationary teachers' meetings which gave me comparative data on the role of the head and heads of departments as well as data on activities that occurred in another sector of the school.

In turn, Paul Klee introduced me to members of the English department with the result that I used this department as a means of coming to terms with the 'academic' system in the school. Indeed, it was through Paul Klee that I became acquainted with the head of department and several English teachers, including those who taught Newsom classes. As well as introducing me to a wider range of teachers and helping to promote my work among them, Paul also talked about pupils and about classes. Indeed, it was Paul who would regularly update me on the latest round of activities that occurred in his English lessons and who informed me which pupils were absent and who was 'on form' on a particular day; a term that he reserved for pupils who were set on a course of maximum distraction and disruption in his lessons. Often Paul would join a group (including myself) in the staff common room where he would turn the conversation towards Newsom classes and Newsom pupils. This generated further material for me.

Of all the teachers with whom I worked, it was with Paul that I discussed my methodology in some depth. Indeed, it was on the basis

of encouragement from Paul that I finally decided to invite teachers
to keep diaries after which I conducted diary interviews with them
(cf. Burgess, 1981; Burgess, 1984b, pp. 128–35). However, it was not
merely at the level of talking about methods that Paul was helpful for
he also assisted with data collection and analysis. On occasions when
I indicated that I did not know the details about some activity, or that
I did not know about an individual's involvement in a situation, Paul
would agree to find out the information by entering into conversation
with particular teachers. However, Paul was also eager to contribute
to the way in which I might interpret my data and spent several
evenings talking to me about his interpretation of situations and the
sociological concepts that he would use in order to begin to organize
the data and analyze it.

Paul Klee provided me with a new probationary teacher's
perspective of the school and in turn fed me into a number of social
networks to which he belonged in the English department and among
young male teachers in the staff common room. In him I found that I
had an informant who could provide a different perspective on the
school and its members. However, I also appreciated that this junior
teacher's perspective needed to be complemented by an account from
a senior teacher. Here I was fortunate as in the spring term a new
House Head was appointed to the House to which I belonged. The
new House Head was a man called Ron Ward who had previously
been a House Head in another Catholic comprehensive school. As a
House Head Ron was responsible for discipline and order in the
school and was a member of the House Heads' meeting which was
part of the senior management team. On this basis, Ron was an ideal
informant who complemented my other informants. His teaching
duties included an assortment of subjects and some Newsom classes.

In common with other teachers Ron Ward found difficulty in
teaching Newsom classes. Accordingly, he spent some considerable
time talking to me about the Newsom pupils, the Newsom Department and the curriculum that was on offer. It was evident from Ron's
remarks that he was not convinced by the approach that was being
taken towards these pupils in Bishop McGregor School. He devoted
some time with me trying to find out my ideas about Newsom
teaching and about the way that Newsom teaching operated in the
school, as well as testing out his ideas on me. Furthermore, he
proceeded on several occasions to mount a critique of the way in
which the school was organized and to offer suggestions about ways
in which the headmaster's ideas about patterns of work and school
routines could be redefined (cf. Burgess, 1983, pp. 52–83).

It was in these different ways that Ron provided me with a further perspective on the way in which the school operated. His remarks helped me to engage in further comparative analysis of the House system and the way in which it operated. However, he also gave me access to two other areas of school life. When I had negotiated access to the school I was given permission to examine all logs of decisions that came from the House Heads' meetings but I was not allowed to attend the meetings. Accordingly, much of my material on these meetings involved reconstruction of what had occurred on the basis of notes that were kept by the headmaster. Now with Ron's arrival I was given a participant's account as without prompting from me he was prepared to talk about the business that was transacted within the House Heads' meetings and the positions that were taken by individual House Heads over particular issues.

In the latter part of the spring term Ron indicated that he was finding particular difficulty with one of the Newsom groups that he taught. He suggested that because I was timetabled at the same time as he was and because I also had a small group we might combine our groups in order to engage in a team teaching activity. I considered this was a good opportunity not only to discover another teacher's conception of Newsom teaching but also to observe another teacher without having the label 'observer' attached to me. Accordingly, I agreed to co-operate in this activity as it provided further ethnographic data on teaching and on the relationships between teachers and pupils. In these terms, I used Ron's team teaching suggestion not only as a teaching venture but also as a further dimension to my research activities for it complemented the work that I had done with other teachers, and my own experience of teaching Newsom classes. On this basis it facilitated further comparative analysis. However, it might be argued that such activities were covert as far as my informant and his classes were concerned and that any researcher contemplating similar activities should consider whether the ends justify the means (Bulmer, 1982; Burgess, 1985a).

While Ron Ward gave me access to various dimensions of the school, the House system and the Newsom Department, he also, in common with many other teachers, indicated the importance of the headmaster in all the activities that were established in the school. It was evident from my research experience that the head should be one of my key informants yet there were few opportunities outside the formal school timetable when I could engage in conversation with him. All my contacts with the head on a one-to-one basis were fleeting encounters. I had an opportunity to meet him briefly when he came into the staff common room each morning break that he was in the school or during the course of many of his innumerable walks across the school site. On such occasions I found that, like other teachers, I would be the subject of a quick comment or question before he moved on to talk in a similar fashion to other teachers. While such encounters were the experience of many teachers they could not be used to provide detailed ethnographic material on the headteacher and on headship. Yet I also had further formal encounters with the head: when he took morning assembly, when he chaired meetings of the Newsom Department and when he chaired full staff meetings. In addition, much of the documentary material on routines and procedures in the school had been written by the head.

In these circumstances, I decided that I would need to conduct a series of informant interviews with him if I was to obtain his life history, his educational experience, his educational philosophy and details of the way in which his ideas were put into operation in Bishop McGregor School. Originally, I had planned for two sessions in which to interview the head, but we mutually agreed to a series of discussions that resulted in eight one-and-a-half-hour tape-recorded conversations. These interviews not only generated conversational data but also resulted in further documents being provided about the school and school activities. These eight encounters that took place over a three-month period were not merely 'interviews' but also chart the consolidation of a relationship. Here, I was tested with confidential information, used as a confidant, and as a 'sounding board' about further ideas for the school. Furthermore, just as I was attempting to get the head to talk about his conception of the school, so in turn he attempted (but in my view with relatively little success) to get me to talk about the views that particular teachers held of the school. At the end of this period of interviewing I negotiated permission to spend several days with him, rather in the style in which Wolcott (1973) had done with an elementary school principal in the United States. Accordingly, the study of the school has included a chapter on the headmaster where a detailed account could be provided about his activities and relationships with other teachers (cf. Burgess, 1983, pp. 26–51).

Finally, the head has, as a key informant, provided comments on all the materials that I have written about the school. All the material that he has read has always been in a pseudonymized form. Here, he has provided a check on the 'accuracy' of my material (at least from his perspective) and on occasion has provided alternative explanations to my accounts. Some of these I have not accepted as, for example, on one occasion when he indicated that a chapter was 'fine' apart from some repetition for which he gave me the page references and which he thought I could delete without further discussion. On checking I found that my 'repetition' included a critical passage on the head himself and I have, therefore, kept this material within the final study. However, there have been situations in which he has provided alternative explanations which I have entered in footnotes for the benefit of readers. In addition, he has also provided new perspectives on 'old' problems and generated further questions and further data that could be used for this study and subsequent projects. Accordingly, he has, for me, been an informant *par excellence*.

For the purpose of this discussion I have presented five people who I considered were key informants in my study. These informants included men and women, senior and junior teachers, teachers drawn from the pastoral, as well as the departmental side of the school and a range of people who although at different stages of their teaching careers all taught in the Newsom Department. As informants they provided different services for me and in turn introduced me to different dimensions of the school and raised different issues about key informants in ethnographic research to which we now turn.

Issues on Key Informants

(i) *Selection Strategies*

Many researchers have indicated that their encounters with individuals who became key informants occurred by 'chance' and or that they were people who they got to know particularly well or with whom they became friends. While I would not deny that these are dimensions of my research encounters I would also argue that some account has to be taken of who becomes a key informant, their sex, status and role, if the researcher is to exercise some control over the collection of data. At Bishop McGregor School I kept a record of my informants and of my key informants in order that I could examine the pattern that emerged.

As table 1 indicates there were twelve teachers who I regarded as regular informants, five of whom became key informants; that is teachers with whom I had a more intense relationship. All of these teachers provided a high level of co-operation with my research. However, I draw a distinction between informants and key informants on the basis of my contact with them, their commitment to my

Table 1: *Key Informants and Informants at Bishop McGregor School*

Name	Sex	Status/teaching experience	Post in school	House/department
Key Informants				
Sylvia Robinson	Female	Teacher of ten years experience with head of department status	Head of Careers in charge of Newsom Scale III	Careers/Newsom
Maggie Rolls	Female	Head of House (a senior teacher but junior in terms of age)	Head of House Scale V	House
Paul Klee	Male	Probationer (new to the school)	Scale I	English
Ron Ward	Male	New Head of House	Head of House Scale V	House
Geoff Goddard	Male		Headmaster	A variety of teaching duties
Informants				
Jane Adams	Female	Deputy head of department	Scale III	English
George Jackson	Male	Head of department	Scale V	English
Keith Dryden	Male	Junior assistant teacher in departments	Scale II	Art/Newsom
Tony Davis	Male	Junior assistant teacher in departments	Scale II	Craft/Newsom
Terry Goodwin	Female	Junior assistant teacher in departments	Scale II	Home Economics/Newsom
Gerry Cochrane	Male	Probationer (new to the school)	Scale I	Religious Education
Michael O'Donoghue	Male	Assistant teacher in charge of a subject	Scale III	Science

Note: Teacher posts were graded one to five at the time of the study.

work and assistance with the project on a regular basis. It was the key informants whom I got to know best and who helped me to orientate my research questions, and my observations. In working with both informants and key informants I attempted to ensure that I had a cross-section of teaching staff in terms of age, sex, level of seniority, teaching experience, post of responsibility and areas of the school from which they were drawn. In these terms, I attempted to maintain some balance between the individuals with whom I worked. Furthermore, I tried to take into account the areas of the school to which they would give access. Of the informants with whom I worked there were individuals who represented academic subject departments, practical subjects and the Newsom Department. While I would argue that I obtained a cross-section of teachers on this basis, I think those teachers whom I got to know best tended to be concentrated more towards the arts subjects than the sciences. However, among these teachers I did have people with a range of teaching experiences which included probationary teachers, junior teachers, middle ranking teachers (who were deputy heads of departments) and a head of department. Meanwhile, beyond them in the teaching hierarchy my key informants included Heads of Houses and the headmaster.

On this basis I would argue that my informants, including key informants, constituted a cross-section of the teaching staff. Yet I cannot argue that they were purposely selected, for in some cases they included teachers who had attached themselves to me when I joined the school or when they joined the school. However, I monitored the kinds of people with whom I talked throughout the research period in order to take account of the different perspectives and different versions of the school to which I was exposed by my key informants.

(ii) *The Role of Key Informants*

As with many aspects of ethnographic work and research involving participant observation, discussions about the roles played by key informants have resulted in typologies (cf. Dean *et al*, 1967) consisting of informants who are especially sensitive to the area of concern and informants who are willing to discuss situations. While this may pinpoint the kind of person who is selected as an informant it does not highlight the role that an informant plays in an investigation. For example, in my own study I found that key informants acted as guides, assistants, interpreters, providers of historical narrative, and contributed to my preliminary data analysis. In particular I found individuals who fulfilled one or more of these aspects of the key informant role. Indeed, on the basis of my five key informants I was able to distinguish four major roles:

(a) *The guide*

It is often assumed that key informants are guides to fields of study. However, it is essential that researchers make some critical appraisal of the extent to which informants provide only partial guidance to the institutions in which they are located. Accordingly, in Bishop McGregor School some account had to be taken of the areas to which individuals had access, the areas which they wanted to advance or promote and those that they wanted to suppress. Furthermore, it was essential to consider those areas in which a key informant was welcome and those areas which the individual was unable to penetrate by virtue of his or her own social location within the school.

For example, of my key informants it was Sylvia Robinson who could provide me with access to the Newsom Department and to Newsom classes but I had to compare her conception of Newsom work with conceptions that were held by other teachers. Similarly, when she advanced a jaundiced view of the House system and the Heads of Houses I had to consider this in relation to the knowledge that she had on two occasions unsuccessfully attempted to gain an appointment as a Head of House and was critical of many of their activities. However, her claim that there was a division between the Houses and departments and especially between House Heads and heads of departments resulted in me following up this line of enquiry which I found could be substantiated on the basis of the actions and activities of other teachers (cf. Burgess, 1983, especially pp. 52–119).

Among probationary teachers I found that Paul Klee alerted me to areas of school organization that more senior teachers assumed were 'obvious' or 'self-evident'. Accordingly, Paul Klee pointed me towards examining the contradictions in the 'rules' that existed in different Houses and in different departments. Furthermore, he was able to provide me with a portrait of the activities at the probationary teachers' meeting to which my other key informants (apart from the head) did not have access.

(b) *The assistant*

While informants may act as guides to the field of research they may also become informal or unpaid research assistants. Certainly, in my project Paul Klee performed this role. When I was not in the school

Paul would collect any circulars that were issued to staff in order to ensure that I did not 'miss out' on any material that he considered important for my research. When meetings were held in my absence or when he attended meetings that I was unable to attend he relayed to me an account of the discussions and the positions that had been adoped by various members of the teaching staff. Finally, when activities occurred in which particular teachers were involved, Paul would make it his business to engage them in conversation in order to report back to me what had transpired.

While such a service by an informant is of great value to a researcher, it is essential to evaluate all the data that are provided. For the position of the key informant who takes on this role may result in only a selection of data about certain situations, events and activities being presented to the researcher.

(c)   *The interpreter*

In one sense, all key informants are interpreters as they sift and select the information that they relay to researchers and as they include and exclude areas on which the researcher might focus. However, some key informants provide interpretations of the words and the behaviour of other individuals. For example, Sylvia Robinson provided accounts of the behaviour of many of her Newsom pupils and gave her version of the reasons for their activities and actions with Newsom and non-Newsom teachers. Meanwhile, in the extensive interviews that I arranged with the headmaster I found that he spent some time not only reporting and interpreting the actions of members of his staff, but also providing a self-analysis by interpreting his own activities within the school. In these circumstances, the interpretations that were given by these key informants could subsequently be checked out with my own observations and the observations that were provided by other members of the teaching staff and by pupils. Such an approach highlights the importance of using multiple methods in an investigation and to cross checks occurring within a study (cf. Denzin, 1970; Burgess, 1982, pp. 163–99; Burgess, 1984b, pp. 143–65).

Another dimension to interpretation which I found came close to data analysis involved one informant who was prepared to offer suggestions about concepts that could be used to examine events and situations in which we had participated. Paul Klee spent some time with me trying out various sociological concepts that he considered would be appropriate to analyze particular aspects of school life. When I borrowed concepts from his analyses I have indicated where this occurs within the study. Furthermore, in situations where my analysis employs different concepts or differs from the analysis provided by Paul Klee I have discussed this within the notes and references provided in the study.

(d)   *The historian*

While the researcher who engages in ethnographic research may complement first-hand observations in the field with the analysis of historical documents (cf. Thernstrom, 1965 and 1968; Burgess, 1982, pp. 131–60), another way in which the historical context of a study can be established is by interviewing key informants.

Bishop McGregor School had opened four years before the beginning of my research; a period during which many school routines had been established. While many of these routines were discussed in various documents I also needed to obtain some first hand accounts about the ways in which these routines originated and how they were implemented and modified. By whom had they been formulated? How were they implemented? To what extent were they modified? Here, I relied particularly on two of my key informants the headmaster and Maggie Rolls to provide me with their versions of the ways in which school organization, rules and routines had been established. Both these teachers had been key participants but they had been involved from different perspectives. Accordingly, I obtained their accounts of situations which could be cross checked against each other and subsequently followed up with other teachers. In addition, these two teachers could not only provide data on the historical context, but they could also indicate further documents that I should consult and the areas in which I might locate this material.

On the basis of examining the roles which my key informants fulfilled I was able to identify four major roles which they performed. Not all these roles were played by each person, as different teachers provided a different range of services. In this sense, some of my informants played all these roles while others highlighted one or more of these dimensions to their role. Nevertheless, no matter which role or combination of roles that informants play, they do present a number of problems for the researcher to which we now turn.

Problems of Using Key Informants

Among the problems that I encountered while working with key informants I found that the majority focused on the ethical, political and moral dimensions of the research process to which we briefly turn.

(i)   *Manipulating the Researcher*

Key informants are in a position of some considerable power as they can define those activities to which the researcher will have access or which they would like the researcher to have access. Furthermore, key informants are in a position to point the researcher towards certain areas of enquiry. Within my study I found that Sylvia Robinson in particular attempted to get me to talk about issues on which she required information. On several occasions she engaged me in conversation about the ways in which the headmaster used scale posts in the school. She enquired whether I knew if he had used all the points that the local education authority had allocated to him, as she found that whenever she went to see him to ask for promotion he always indicated that he had no further points to offer staff. At the time that she discussed this with me I had recently been given access to the head's confidential document on the distribution of points and posts within the school but I felt obliged not to divulge the contents of this document. Yet I did consider whether I should give her some idea about the contents of the document as she was providing me with a range of information and teacher contacts.

As well as attempting to seek information from me Sylvia also provided suggestions about what I might investigate and what I might say to the head. As she was critical of the basic organizational framework of the school she often suggested that I should communicate her views to the headmaster. Furthermore, she was also keen for me to suggest that she might play a more senior role in the school. However, I did not act on either of these suggestions as I thought this went well beyond my role as a researcher within the school.

(ii)   *Protecting informants*

As I have indicated, informants provided me with a range of services including giving me access to documentary evidence some of which was supposedly 'secret' and 'confidential'. On one occasion Ron Ward had shown me a 'secret document', that is a document which no Head of House was supposed to show to any assistant teachers. As a consequence I had asked the secretary for a copy of this document which was my usual practice when material was issued to teachers. However, when I asked the secretary for this document she refused to discuss it and went straight to report the fact that I knew about this material to the deputy head (cf. Burgess, 1983, pp. 101–14). While the deputy head explained that I could not have a copy of the document at that particular time, but that I could get a copy later, he did not enquire how I had come to know about this material. However, the school secretary had several questions: Who told you about this document? Who else has seen the document? While I told her how I had seen the document I was not prepared to let her know that Ron Ward had not only shown it to me but also to another teacher and had put the document in a place where other members of his House staff could consult it if they so wished.

Just as I felt that I had a moral obligation to protect Ron Ward so I felt obliged to let Paul Klee know what had happened, for I had spent the whole of a 'free' lesson discussing the contents of the document with him and considering different ways in which it could be interpreted. Accordingly, I did not want to put him in a difficult position if he discussed the document in public. As a result I went to find him at the end of the lesson in which this situation had occurred in order to warn him about the circumstances surrounding the 'secret document'.

When my informants told me about the ways in which they worked I kept this confidential. Indeed, the headmaster claimed that he only discovered that pupils smoked in front of Newsom teachers when he read drafts of my study some six years after the fieldwork was completed and several years after the teachers concerned had taken up posts in other schools. He argued that I should have told him what had occurred within these classes as the pupils involved and those that had followed them in later years had gained very little from the experience. However, I maintained that it was my duty to use this material only for the purpose of sociological study rather than to act as an informer for the head. My research role and my obligations to the teachers outweighed my obligations to the head in this context.

(iii) *Exploiting Key Informants*

While conducting my study I got to know five teachers who became key informants. While I saw them as informants I never told them of their special role in my research. Indeed, for some who read this paper it might well come as a surprise to learn of the way in which I used them and the services which I consider they provided. In these circumstances one might ask: did I exploit them? Did these teachers expect to be written about in this way? Did they expect to become the principal subjects of my research?

At this point we might turn to some of the ethical problems that have been discussed by commentators such as Becker (1964) and Douglas (1976) on reporting field studies. I would argue that I did not deceive any of these teachers for the research was conducted openly and they were all informed that I was intending to write a study of their school. But here we come directly up against the meaning of 'informed consent' and whether these teachers really did not know what they were involved in when they agreed to co-operate with my investigation. Furthermore, it could be asked: what did they get for participating in my research? Unlike the informants used by social anthropologists no payment was involved but for some I provided assistance with Open University and higher degree courses, for others I loaned books and in one case I wrote a reference for the teacher to gain admission to a university. But was this just their equivalent of 'thirty pieces of silver' for their role in my research?

Conclusion

This paper has addressed an area that is relatively under-examined in ethnographic research on educational settings, namely the use of key informants. In particular I have focused on five teachers with whom I became acquainted. They were not 'special teachers' but were merely individuals who I got to know during the course of my research at Bishop McGregor School and who influenced the collection and analysis of data. Certainly, we have come some distance from the time when the anthropologist's informants were summoned to the verandah of the local missionary or government official and questioned by the researcher, but have we yet thought through how we 'use' key informants and the ethical, social and political problems which that poses for them and for us in our attempts to understand social situations? It is to be hoped that researchers will, in future, consider the status of key informants in their studies and acknowledge the extent to which they play a major role in the collection and analysis of data.

Notes

1 For the use of key informants in British studies see, for example, Tim in PATRICK (1973).
2 In this sense, informants, especially in work conducted from an interactionist perspective, may help to give an historical perspective which will benefit the studies (cf. WOODS, 1983, p. 182 and GOODSON in this volume, page 121).
3 For further accounts of informants in other settings who, while not representative, nevertheless help to shed light on patterns of social relations see PONS (1969) and NICHOLS and BEYNON (1977, pp. 78–103).
4 See, for example, the papers in SIMONS (1980); POPKEWITZ and TABACHNICK (1981); SPINDLER (1982); HAMMERSLEY (1983) and BURGESS (1984a and 1985b).
5 The Newsom Department provided courses for pupils for whom the maximum expectation of success in public examinations seemed likely to be three CSE grade fives or less.

References

AGAR, M. (1981) *The Professional Stranger*, New York, Academic Press.
BALL, S.J. (1981) *Beachside Comprehensive: A Case Study of Secondary Schooling*, Cambridge, Cambridge University Press.
BALL, S.J. (1984) 'Beachside reconsidered: reflections on a methodological apprenticeship', in BURGESS, R.G. (Ed.) *The Research Process in Educational Settings: Ten Case Studies*, Lewes, Falmer Press.
BECKER, H.S. (1964) 'Problems in the publication of field studies' in VIDICH, A.J., BENSMAN, J. and STEIN, M. (Eds.) *Reflections on Community Studies*, New York, Harper and Row.
BULMER, M. (Ed.) (1982) *Social Research Ethics*, London, Macmillan.
BURGESS, R.G. (1981) 'Keeping a research diary', *Cambridge Journal of Education*, 11, 1, pp. 75–83.
BURGESS, R.G. (Ed.) (1982) *Field Research: A Sourcebook and Field Manual*, London, Allen and Unwin.
BURGESS, R.G. (1983) *Experiencing Comprehensive Education: A Study of Bishop McGregor School*, London, Methuen.
BURGESS, R.G. (Ed.) (1984a) *The Research Process in Educational Settings: Ten Case Studies*, Lewes, Falmer Press.
BURGESS, R.G. (1984b) *In the Field: An Introduction to Field Research*, London, Allen and Unwin.
BURGESS, R.G. (1985a) 'The whole truth? Some ethical problems in studying a comprehensive school' in BURGESS, R.G. (Ed.) *Field Methods in the Study of Education*, Lewes, Falmer Press.
BURGESS, R.G. (Ed.) (1985b) *Field Methods in the Study of Education*, Lewes, Falmer Press.
CASAGRANDE, J. (Ed.) (1960) *In the Company of Man*, New York, Harper and Row.

CONKLIN, H. (1968) 'Ethnography', in SILLS, D.H. (Ed.) *International Encyclopaedia of the Social Sciences*, 5, New York, Free Press.

DEAN, J.P., EICHORN, R.L. and DEAN, L.R. (1967) 'Fruitful informants for intensive interviewing', in DOBY, J.T. (Ed.) *An Introduction to Social Research*, (2nd edn), New York, Appleton-Century-Crofts.

DENZIN, N. (1970) *The Research Act*, Chicago, Aldine (2nd edn published in 1978 by McGraw Hill).

DOUGLAS, J. (1976) *Investigative Social Research*, Beverly Hills, CA, Sage.

HAMMERSLEY, M. (Ed.) (1983) *The Ethnography of Schooling*, Driffield, Nafferton.

HARGREAVES, D.H. (1967) *Social Relations in a Secondary School*, London, Routledge and Kegan Paul.

HARRELL-BOND, B. (1976) 'Studying elites: some special problems', in RYNKIEWICH, M.A. and SPRADLEY, J.P. (Eds.) *Ethics and Anthropology: Dilemmas in Fieldwork*, New York, Wiley.

JOHNSON, J. (1975) *Doing Field Research*, New York, Free Press.

LACEY, C. (1970) *Hightown Grammar*, Manchester, Manchester University Press.

LIEBOW, E. (1967) *Tally's Corner*, Boston, Mass., Little Brown.

LOFLAND, J. (1971) *Analysing Social Settings*, New York, Wadsworth.

NICHOLS, T. and BEYNON, H. (1977) *Living With Capitalism*, London, Routledge and Kegan Paul.

PATRICK, J. (1973) *A Glasgow Gang Observed*, London, Eyre Methuen.

PONS, V. (1969) *Stanleyville: An African Urban Area Under Belgian Administration*, Oxford, OUP.

POPKEWITZ, T.S. and TABACHNICK, B.R. (Eds.) (1981) *The Study of Schooling: Field Based Methodologies in Educational Research and Evaluation*, New York, Praeger.

ROYAL ANTHROPOLOGICAL INSTITUTION OF GREAT BRITAIN AND IRELAND (1951) *Notes and Queries in Anthropology* (6th edn), London, Routledge and Kegan Paul.

SCHATZMAN, L. and STRAUSS, A.L. (1973) *Field Research: Strategies for a Natural Sociology*, Englewood Cliffs, N.J., Prentice Hall.

SIMONS, H. (Ed.) (1980) *Towards a Science of the Singular*, Norwich, Centre for Applied Research in Education, University of East Anglia.

SPINDLER, G. (Ed.) (1982) *Doing the Ethnography of Schooling*, New York, Holt, Rinehart and Winston.

THERNSTROM, S. (1965) 'Yankee City revisited: the perils of historical naivete', *American Sociological Review*, 30, 2, pp. 234–42.

THERNSTROM, S. (1968) 'Quantitative methods in history: some notes', in LIPSET, S.M. and HOFSTADTER, R. (Eds.) *Sociology and History: Methods*, New York, Basic Books, pp. 59–78.

WHYTE, W.F. (1981) *Street Corner Society* (3rd edn), Chicago, University of Chicago Press.

WILLIAMS, T.R. (1967) *Field Methods in the Study of Culture*, New York, Holt, Rinehart and Winston.

WOLCOTT, H. (1973) *The Man in the Principal's Office*, New York, Holt, Rinehart and Winston.

WOODS, P. (1981) 'Understanding through talk' in ADELMAN, C. (Ed.)

Robert G. Burgess

   Uttering Muttering: Collecting, Using and Reporting Talk for Social and Educational Research, London, Grant McIntyre, pp. 13–26.
WOODS, P. (1983) *Sociology and the School: An Interactionist Viewpoint*, London, Routledge and Kegan Paul.

4 A Case for Case Records?: A Discussion of Some Aspects of Lawrence Stenhouse's Work in Case Study Methodology

Jean Rudduck

Some of Lawrence Stenhouse's colleagues were surprised and somewhat disappointed when, in the late 1970s, he moved out of curriculum research and development into the area of case study methodology (where, characteristically, he immediately tried to take centre stage!). But as Skilbeck (1983) points out, there was a continuity, for his interest in 'humanistic methodology in general and case study in particular' must be understood 'in the context of his overall view of education, knowledge, teaching and learning':

> ... he was interested in research method basically for its educative potential not for reasons of the disinterested pursuit of knowledge. Central to Stenhouse's view of education is the teacher — not the pupil, the school, the providing authorities or the policy makers. It is the teacher, purposive and free, informed by knowledge and understanding, with clearly articulated values and a repertoire of practical skills, he saw as the central agent in the educational enterprise and the ultimate focus of his views on research. His theory of education is essentially a theory of teacher professionalism, autonomy and development ... He summed up his concern for the teacher by saying that 'it is the task of all educationalists outside the classroom to serve the teacher'.

Stenhouse came into case study work on the attack, challenging sociologists, somewhat unfairly perhaps, for producing case studies that were elitist and idiosyncratic (1977). He proposed that more attention be paid to the rights of practitioners as partners in case study and as readers of case study reports, and to the needs of students who, as case study work burgeons at Master's and Doctoral level, are embarking on research without the support of widely agreed principles of procedure that would strengthen their practice and that would also strengthen the judgment of the assessors of their practice (1981a). And he urged that more thought be given, in case study work, to issues of verification and cumulation (1980a). The idea of the 'case record' developed partly as a response to these concerns and partly as a response to the practical problems of reporting research in multi-site case study programmes.

The 'Case Record'

The idea of the case record was first explored in a project (1975–78) designed by Stenhouse to document a programme of dissemination undertaken by a group of teacher researchers who had taken part in the project. Conferences run by them during a period of two to three years were to be the focus. The study as a whole was a variation of the 'multi-site' approach, with cases spread out over time and studied sequentially by the same field worker rather than spread out over space and studied simultaneously by a team of field workers. His advice to the field worker responsible for the study (myself) was to try to suspend judgment until the field work was over and to avoid panic during the intervening period, as the data mountain grew, by producing, for each conference, a 'case record' that would freeze the data in an orderly but untheorized form (see Rudduck and Stenhouse, 1979; Rudduck, 1984). In the event, each case record included transcripts of interviews with the teacher-researchers and transcripts of recordings of their planning and evaluation meetings; transcripts of discussions that they led and lectures that they gave; field worker observations; and documents (for example, conference handouts). The set of case records constituted the primary source for the analysis of teacher-led conferences as a medium for the dissemination of classroom research experiences.

By the end of the project (1978) Stenhouse had formalized his views and had identified two 'states' of field work data: the 'case data', which represent the totality of the material collected; and the 'case record', which is a lightly edited, ordered, indexed and public version of the case data. He also identified two ways of moving forward from the case record: to the 'case study' which is the product of the field worker's reflective engagement with an individual case record; and, in a multi-site programme, to the overview, which seeks generalizations across case records.

The prudence of our experimental use of case records in the dissemination study (1975–78) was confirmed, in our view, by the experience of Stake and Easley in their multi-site enquiry into science curricula in American schools (1978). In the US project, each field worker in the team was commissioned to produce a case study and it was from these studies that Stake wrote the executive summary or overview. Stenhouse reviewed the work (1981b) and pointed to the constraints on Stake in having to work from the restricted data base of materials that had been fashioned into an interpretative statement — a case study — by each field worker. Stenhouse suggested that the 'evidence was progressively eroded' — first by the field workers' distillation of the case data into case studies and then by the generalizations of the executive summary itself: for the reader it was the conclusions that survived while the data against which they could be checked disappeared from view. Stenhouse's major multi-site programme (funded by the British Library Research and Development Department, 1980–83) was so designed that he would not need to write his overview from a collection of case studies but instead (as in the earlier project) from the relatively untheorized and only lightly edited word-hoards (to use an Old English kenning) of the case records; if individual institutions involved in the project wanted a case study for their own use, then this was to be negotiated with their field worker. Thus, despite the threat of an end-of-field-work encounter with a mammoth data base, Stenhouse chose to work with relatively raw data rather than with the refined products of case studies.

So, the idea of the case records developed as a practical solution to a practical problem of reportage in multi-site study, but it was also explored as part of Stenhouse's search for ways of refining verification in relation to case study work (see Silver, 1983, p. 303). The line Stenhouse takes on verification reflects his commitment to the procedures of historical enquiry and, at the same time, his concern for the democratization of research and the responsibility of educational researchers to appeal to the professional judgment of practitioners (cf. Stenhouse, 1984). He proposed that 'no qualitatively based theorizing in education should be regarded as acceptable unless its argument stands or falls on the interpretation of accessible and well-cited sources, so that the interpretation offered can be critically examined' (1978; see also Nias, 1978). Conventionally the data that lie behind a case study are not made public and Stenhouse argues that in case study work case records might be regarded as parallel to the primary sources of historical enquiry — which are publicly accessible:

> the primary sources of history are essentially documents or
> artefacts in the public domain and the inference of facts from
> the sources is verified by virtue of their being accessible to a
> number of professional historians who discuss their status
> and significance ... (1979a)

Thus, the contemporary and created documentation of the educational case record is the equivalent of the 'inherited documentation' of history. But, if the case record is to be maximally useful as a primary source, then it should be as raw as possible: this means that the field worker must accept the discipline of operating in the field with a parsimony of interpretation. Now this argument holds better for the interview-based study conducted in the limited time span of condensed field work (the approach that Stenhouse used) than for the longer term, participant-observer studies within the ethnographic tradition as represented, say, by the work of Lacey (1970) and Ball (1981). In condensed field work it is more feasible to defer interpretation until the data gathering is complete, and case records that are parsimonious of theory are therefore more readily achieved. If the field worker is to produce a case study, or if the multi-site programme director is to produce an overview, then analysis and interpretation develop out of interaction with the finite body of data (i.e. an armchair, after the event task). Thus, the data and the field worker's response to the data exist as separate entities. But to ask the field worker who works within the ethnographic tradition to defer theory-making until the period of field work is over is to deny what is distinctive about the approach, for it is the process of interaction between observation and analysis and explanation that creates theory (Lacey, 1981). In this approach the field worker will start to formulate and test hypotheses during field work, and the field work data will therefore represent a narrative of the field worker's emerging pattern of speculation and explanation. In terms of verification, case records consisting of such data would offer less than the interview transcripts that are the staple ingredient of Stenhouse's case records although they would be useful as evidence of the process of conducting case studies within the ethnographic tradition — see Ball's plea in this volume (page 5) for the building of a methodological archive. Thus the idea of the case record, while it raises important issues about verification, may not provide a convincing way forward outside the particular tradition that Stenhouse was trying to develop.

Stenhouse saw the case record, then, as a way of providing access to the data on which publicly-reported interpretations are based. Another concern was with the language in which case studies are reported and it was this concern that prompted his criticism of some ethnographic studies as 'elitist'. He asks whether it is legitimate to express interpretations of the life of a school community in terms of theories not in the consciousness of the actors in the school studied (1982) but he goes further than this, proposing that authors of case studies should not disenfranchise teacher audiences by retreating from a practitioner vernacular. Again he turns to history for support: history, he claims (and the implicit comparison is with sociology)

> is the most accessible of studies. We turn to histories of art or football or country life because they further our understanding by retrospective generalizations and summaries of experience which ask for little technical language other than that of the subject — art, football or country life — with which the interested reader may be presumed to be familiar. Case study in an historical tradition would attempt to treat education in a language comprehensible to the educator (though it might aspire to build out that language). (1981a; see also Nias, 1978)

If verification through the scrutiny of case records is not a convincing possibility in relation to case studies conducted within the ethnographic tradition, then at the very least (Stenhouse's argument would seem to run) interpretations and explanations should be couched in a language that is accessible to criticism through the professional 'second record'[1] of the practitioner reader. Whether or not practitioners should be regarded as the main, or even as an important, audience is probably the nub of the contention between field workers who see themselves as contributing to sociological research and field workers who see themselves as contributing to educational research. Stenhouse's position is clear: 'The essence of educational research is the development through theorizing of the capacity to reflect about and therefore to improve practice ... Educational theory may appropriately draw on the so-called "contributory disciplines" but their contribution is piecemeal within a theory whose integrative principle is to provide understanding in support of educational action' (1978).

We should perhaps note in passing that in multi-site programmes as Stenhouse conceived them, publicly-available case studies may not be produced at all. This is a reasonable position given the economy of exposure in condensed field work: observation-based studies, conducted over a longer period of time, offer a much stronger possibility of the field worker achieving an in-depth understanding of the tight and culturally complex weave of life and work in a particular institution. What I am suggesting, therefore, is that when Stenhouse claimed that the yield of field work is a case record which is then used as an historian would use his sources (1981a), his argument fits the particular tradition that he was trying to build — a feature of which is the development of an archive of case records which would support a broad-based and cumulative understanding of aspects of schooling. The contemporary 'educational archive' would be a resource for present and future researchers. Future researchers, interested in the history of education, would find in the archive data that would provide insight into the intimacies of the process of schooling in a variety of settings. More than that: the existence of an archive would enable researchers

> ... to find extensions and implications beyond the points from which they began, discover their own ignorance, re-examine their assumptions ... and discover that even what appears most straightforward and taken-for-granted may become the focus of differing interpretations and profound controversy ... A 'case' may become the necessary starting point for other 'cases', for a process of fresh historical debate and understanding ... (Silver, 1983, p. 302)

Present researchers could use the archive in similar ways:

> For example, if I had a doctoral student undertaking a case study of a comprehensive school, he could use case records of other comprehensive schools, just as, if I had a doctoral student working on the history of an abbey, he could use work on other abbeys. (Stenhouse, 1981a)

Researchers consulting the archive would act in relation to its contents as historians would act in relation to the collection of sources relevant to a particular enquiry. And as, over time, more cases (or case records) were lodged in the archive, so continual reassessment of provisional interpretations and explanations would be possible:

> Just as generalizations about Iron Age settlements are modified as more sites are investigated, so generalization about schools or educational problems would be subject to re-

appraisal as more cases became available in the (archive). (Stenhouse, 1977)

Silver parallels the comment:

> The historian stands at the intersection of the generalized images which result from past experience, and the revised images which result from fresh 'cases' and from reflection on them, and reaction to (or against) them. (1983, p. 303)

Interestingly, Stenhouse changed his view of what the basis of the archive should be. In a paper written in 1977 he discusses the 'general survey' which a contemporary educational archive could support (giving as examples 'the role of deputy head' or 'mixed ability teaching in comprehensive schools between 1970 and 2000' and it is clear that the survey would rest on the cumulative comparison of case *studies* 'in which discrepancies and surprises' would be 'pursued back into the case records'. Thus, the archive was to include case studies with their associated records. Later, however, mainly as a result of his involvement in multi-site programmes where the main yield was the case record, his view of the archive shifted to one in which records would be the major component. The logic of his revised position seems to be this: case studies, which offer a sophisticated interpretation of evidence and which aspire to theory would not, by their very nature, provide sufficiently textured detail to allow hypotheses to be pursued across instances in the same class. In his last multi-site proposal, called *School Report* (1980b), the archive was to consist entirely of records.[2] and [3] The proposal was not funded and it is the multi-site programme supported by the British Library (the Library Access and Sixth Form Study (LASS) project) that we have to look at in order to see whether the case Stenhouse made for case records stands up in practice.

Using Case Records: The Experience of the LASS Project

The LASS project was concerned with libraries, library usage and independent thinking in academic sixth-form courses. It was conducted in twenty-four sixth-form settings by eighteen collaborating field workers (cf. Stenhouse, 1984). The selection of institutions took account of the need to have access to different environmental and social settings and different levels of library provision. There were . fourteen comprehensive schools, two sixth-form colleges, three public boarding schools, three independent day schools, one further education and one tertiary college. The main method of data gathering was the interview, and interviews were conducted with over 200 sixth-form students, approximately 200 sixth-form teachers, approximately fifty library staff and approximately sixty heads, principals and teachers with special responsibility for the sixth form.[4] Interviews lasted, on average, forty minutes and most interviewees were interviewed for only one session. Interviews were tape recorded and transcribed, and transcripts were returned to the interviewees for clearance before being placed in the archive.

The field workers were contracted to do two things: first, to prepare for the institution they were working in, something — usually a case study or an issues paper — that would serve the interests of the institution (staff rather than students were consulted as to what was wanted; some institutions asked for nothing); second, to produce for the project, by an agreed date, a case record. It was expected that the bulk of each case record would be a series of anonymized and indexed interview transcripts in the form in which interviewees had agreed they might be placed in a public archive.[5] In addition, there might be documents (historical or contemporary statements issued by the institution about itself); records of book stock; sketch maps of the library in relation to the rest of the institution; photographs of the library; field workers' descriptions of the library; field workers' reflections on the conduct of the study, and observations and notes. The responsibility for writing the overview, across the twenty-four records, was to be the project director's.

As a result of Lawrence Stenhouse's illness, however, the writing of the overview was delayed. After he died, I took over this responsibility (the original project coordinator was by then working on another research project) but there was no definitive structure: all I knew was that had he had 'but world enough and time' he would have immersed himself in the data and attempted an issues-based report. I decided to work out my own strategy for writing-up — essentially one of survival for, though a field worker responsible for one of the twenty-four case records, I was not familiar with the archive, was working under considerable stress, and was determined to meet the revised deadline for the sake of the sponsors who had responded to delay with generosity and patience.

My approach was guided by common sense and conscience. I started by quickly reading through three complete case records (an average record included about 200 pages of transcript). I then made a decision to divide the report into three sections corresponding to the three groups of interviewees: students, teachers and librarians. Thus, what I lost, from the outset, was a sense of the integrity of the individual cases. I was not too unhappy about this since Lawrence Stenhouse had already suggested that the product of a multi-site project was likely to be closer to a survey than a case study. Moreover, he had established a ground rule within the project that prohibited any field worker — or person subsequently using the archive — from attempting to write a case study from a case record unless he or she had been responsible for producing the record through field work. The next move was to invite David Hopkins (just back from Canada and temporarily out of a job) to take responsibility for one of the three sections of the report. He had not participated in the project in any way but he was familiar with the writings of Lawrence Stenhouse, on curriculum and teacher research, and the three of us had worked together in Canada in 1980. My concern was to share the work load and thereby to ensure that the task was completed in good time, but there was another pay-off: he was someone who came new to the case records and to the idea of an archive of case records and was, therefore, in a good position to examine their potential. He, in turn, was assisted by Susan Ground-water-Smith, on study leave from the University of Sydney, Australia. These two authors worked relatively independently of each other and of me and their interpretation of the overall situation in schools was to some extent a check on my interpretation. (What we did not do, however, because of the pressure of time, was to triangulate on the evidence that each of us was working on individually.) The archive served us well, although I think (see later) that we may have been somewhat superficial in our assessment of the status of the interview data.

Having carved up the data into three fairly penetrable thickets, and having farmed one out, I started to work on the student transcripts (I later moved on to the librarian transcripts). I first read enough transcripts, fairly quickly, to get a sense of the main contours of the responses. I then went back and read each transcript slowly, pencil marking key passages ('key' in terms of their contributing to the patterns of response that my initial reading had detected). I then dictated key passages and these 'thinnings' were transcribed. I read through the transcribed passages to identify sorting categories, and cut and distributed the passages. It was clear, early on, that there was little in the data that was not broadly predictable to someone familiar with the workings of academic sixth-form courses, school libraries and the 'A' level examinations; moreover, what the data allowed us to say at a broad level of analysis had been said in an earlier report (Schools Council, 1975) which had had little impact on practice. Our responsibility, it seemed, was to harness the peculiar strength of our' data — its vivid authenticity — in order to compel attention among practitioners, who were the main audience for the report. We relied therefore rather heavily on quotation to stake out the main response patterns and to illustrate variations. In a sense, we offered a 'reading' of a text, with exemplary passages (see Hull, 1984). What we gave away was the power to explain variations in responses in terms of the conventions of different institutional settings or different 'A' level groups, although it is possible to do this by returning to the archive since the evidence offered in the text is referenced to particular interviews in particular institutions. What we gained was the capacity to mirror the reality — and the commonality — of experiences in a way which preserved opportunities for readers of the overview to examine and try to explain their own experiences in a more insightful way.

In writing the overview we were aware of the presence of the archive as a sort of super-ego (there was no 'throw-it-in-the-waste-bin-if-the-evidence-doesn't-fit' escape hatch). And yet, I wonder, except for an occasional visit by groups of students interested in methodology, will anyone seriously bother to read and re-interpret the case records? Is the topic significant enough to warrant such zealous pursuit of the fairness of our selection and interpretation of the evidence? (Compare for example the furore of re-interpretation that statistically based generalizations about school effectiveness and examination results are capable of generating.) In terms of verification, therefore, we felt comfortable in knowing that the evidence in which we had grounded our interpretations was accessible, but we were sceptical as to whether the possible next step — re-examination of the data base — would actually be taken. That is not to say, however, that the case records were not invaluable as a resource in writing across cases: we were relieved to meet the data, massive though it was, without the final patina of interpretation that transformation into a set of case studies would have required.

Another aspiration for the use of the case records was not, however, realized. Lawrence Stenhouse was at pains to ensure that the field workers who took part in the study were professionally motivated and that involvement might yield more for those who wanted it than just methodological experience. Each field worker was therefore invited to propose a topic that was not at odds with the main focus, and other field workers guaranteed to bear such topics in mind in their enquiries. The idea was that the field worker who had nominated a topic should have the right to trawl the case records and prepare for publication a monograph on that topic. As it happened, most field workers rested content with the experience itself (some also had a fee). Some aspiring monograph writers did nominate a topic, but by the time the archive was ready for plundering, they were committed to other research tasks. Thus, there is more in the case records than we caught in the particular net of our concern when it came to writing the overview. For instance, the records offer good orientation data for students contemplating a study of such things as social groupings in the sixth-form or differences in opportunity at sixth-form level between maintained and non-maintained schools. Thus, the usefulness of the archive in feeding related enquiries has not been tested.

The LASS approach was essentially experimental and we can suggest ways in which similar multi-site enquiries might be improved if they are designed to produce case records that might feed the development of a national archive. First, there would need to be tighter procedures than we worked to in relation to the referencing and indexing of the records. Our field workers had, in the interests of experiment, some freedom of manoeuvre in devizing their feature lists and referencing systems but what looked like creativity at the periphery looked like confusion at the centre! A particular problem of indexing was whether field workers should adopt a strict convention and only index a term if it actually appeared on the page of transcript or whether, as some of us urged, there was a case for reasonable interpretation so that a passage would be referenced if it was clearly about independence of mind even if the actual words were not used. Another problem was with base line data. The records would have been easier to handle if there had been standard data offered in a standard format on such topics as size of school, the number of students in the sixth form, the number following different 'A' level courses, the amount of library allowances over the last x years, the qualifications and terms of appointment of library staff, opening hours of the library and so on. As it was, such data — essential for the archive — had to be laboriously hunted in likely habitats (i.e. in interviews with heads or with librarians).

A third problem was the uncertain status of the non-transcript material. Some field workers had meticulously anonymized documents that had been issued by their institution at some stage in its history and, had there been time and resources, I could have done the same for documents that were not so anonymized. More problematic were the field worker notes which offered data of a different order from the transcripts and 'found' documents. Here the richness was largely methodological: the notes provided insights into such things as the status and conduct of the field worker's 'host'; the institutional position of key informants; how interviewees had been identified; what level of institutional awareness of the enquiry there was; the setting or settings in which interviews had been conducted and the perceived effects of those settings, and so on. Again, we felt the need for a common agenda among field workers so that, given the state of our present curiosities, the experience of conducting condensed field work might be more systematically documented. And then there was the problem of knowing how to handle the observational notes that some field workers offered which were, in the main, less attempts to validate statements made by interviewees than to build an impression of the institutional climate (the notes focused on such things as morning assembly, for instance). And finally there were the fruits of evolving individual curiosities: one field worker, for instance, became intrigued by the relationship between note-making and essay writing at sixth form level and assiduously sought evidence in waste paper bins in the library so that he could see what had been discarded at draft stage! I am not bidding here for total comparability of data, for historians (who were invoked by the project team as providing some sort of model for our work) are used to dealing with data of very different kinds: all I am saying is that the problems of handling such data in the context of writing from an archive of case records deserve more attention than we were able to give, given the time constraints that we were working under. Our way out of the dilemma in writing the overview was to work from the interview data only, and we regarded this as an unsatisfactory solution. Another area that we failed to give close attention to at the time of writing the overview was the status of the interview data and the interview transcripts. In the last two years (since the LASS project ended, in fact) several papers have been written that expose the dilemmas (see Dixon, 1980; Tripp, 1982; Hull, 1984; Bartlett, 1984a and 1984b). Some of these are discussed below.

Interviews, 'Documents' and 'Texts' and the Task of Interpretation

Tripp (1982) is critical of the general level of competence and sensitivity in interviewing: 'Some researchers seem to consider the mere fact of interviewing participants face to face and avoiding multiple choice questionnaires constitutes an adequate exploration of the participant's views'. His main criticism is that the single interview (such as we used in the LASS project) affords only a limited opportunity for the interviewee, given the strangeness of the interview situation, to formulate responses that represent the meanings he or she would want to acknowledge. The one-off interview, says Tripp, suits the person whose views are already well-formulated and rehearsed: this means that within a population of respondents interviewed only once, there will be considerable differences in the stability of the views expressed, some being preliminary explorations or views not so far articulated, and therefore provisional, and some being an assured summary. Tripp argues for a strategy that might help to equalize the status of the views offered and he proposes a series of 'discussions' (in place of the one-off interview) which would allow time for the interviewee to develop and reflect on the ideas offered, would enable the interviewee to take some responsibility for establishing the agenda for the discussion, and would give space for potentially significant areas of experience (that the interviewee might remain silent about in the one-off interview) to be recognized and explored. Tripp's point is persuasive and worthwhile — but it is difficult to assess its significance for multi-site studies of the LASS kind which employ condensed fieldwork (and therefore impose a time constraint) and which see the evidence gathered across cases as contributing to a survey-type report. We were, in fact, surprised at the collective richness of the data contained in the case records and elicited through one-off interviews.

Tripp also questions the status of the interview transcript (a basic ingredient of our case records), suggesting that the conventions of talk are so different from the conventions of the written word in their 'generative and communicative powers' that the one cannot be regarded as an unproblematic substitute for the other. The transcript, he says, in fact represents 'a massive transformation of data'. At the very least, one must acknowledge that non-verbal signals and the sense of mutual presence are lost: 'Bald words alone endure translation' says Hull (1984): 'The interactive situation is pressed neatly flat, like washing from a mangle'. Tripp seeks to replace the literal text of the interview by what he calls a 'jointly authorized statement' which would represent an agreed account of the meanings that the interviewee wanted to communicate. Tripp explains:

... an accurate record of the actual words as originally

spoken is of less importance than the effective transformation by the researcher of what was actually said into what the participants are prepared to have written about what they said.

Tripp may be underestimating the temptation here for the interviewee to play safe and produce a bland paraphrase of what he or she said in the face of uncertainty about how the words might ultimately be used, thereby defeating one of his purposes in conducting the series of discussions that he advocates.

In challenging the sanctity of the original words offered in the brief encounter of the one-off interview and arguing for a reflected-on and negotiated text, Tripp is according a particular status to the interviewer or fellow discussant: the interviewer, by virtue of his or her partnership in the process of eliciting and negotiating an agreed text, derives a particular authority in relation to the exegesis of the text: the interviewer comes to have 'an exclusive authority' over the meanings of the words and hence an exclusive right to transmit those meanings to readers of the subsequent report. Tripp's conclusion, then, is to trust the interviewer, in writing the report, to use his or her personal knowledge 'to exclude all meanings which misrepresent how ... the participants viewed and interpreted the issues'. Tripp goes even further and suggests that it may be unhelpful for the researcher in writing the report to expose the evidence that lies behind the interpretation — even by offering illustrative quotations — for verbatim statements give the reader a chance to reinterpret — and misinterpret — the meaning intended by the interviewee. Tripp's paper does not refer to Stenhouse's work on case records but it would seem to represent an interesting challenge.

Hull, a colleague of Stenhouse and someone familiar with the LASS project, also questions some aspects of Stenhouse's approach — in particular the wisdom of allowing a researcher to write the overview from the records (i.e. interview transcripts) whose production he or she has not been present at or shared in. Hull suggests that the interviewer through the data carried in his or her memory of the interview and not represented in the textual record of the interview, has in a sense 'a black market of private understandings'. (The found or inherited documents of history offer no such advantage for all historians encounter them on more or less equal terms, provided that they can claim reasonable scholarship in the topic under enquiry.) According to Hull the researcher has the power therefore to 'read between the lines' of the interview record; it follows that even if interview transcripts are open to critical scrutiny by a community of professionals, their interpretations are likely to be less valid than the interpretation offered by the interviewer-researcher. Tripp and Hull appear to be leading us back to the position taken by the ethnographers and that Stenhouse set out to question! The dilemma for Hull is how to find an approach that maintains integrity to the meanings that are between the lines of the transcript and the requirement that research be a public discourse.

In writing the overview of the LASS project we could only pay attention to the surface meanings of the documents or texts (i.e. the interview transcripts); we based our interpretations on passages that our professional second records (i.e. our substantive records as educationalists and our procedural records as interviewers) helped us to identify as offering an unambiguous statement of a perspective worthy of attention. Our blithely pragmatic approach seems somewhat naive in the light of recent papers whose authors have immersed themselves in (or at least gone ankle deep into) hermeneutics (and, in particular, Ricoeur's (1976) theory of interpretation). But then, as Bartlett says, case study work has for some time been remarkable for its neglect of theories of interpretation, concentrating instead on the procedure of data gathering.

Within the historical hermeneutic tradition,[6] in which Stenhouse's work can be located, there are two sets of rules (Bartlett, 1984b): 'Rules as principles of procedure aimed at democratizing the research' and rules as 'a means for discovering "truth" '. Lawrence Stenhouse, by and large, concentrated mainly on the former (but see Bartlett's discussion of his categories of evidence offered in interview and his assessment of the quality of evidence offered within each category).[7] What Stenhouse did was to turn to the conventions of historical enquiry to examine possibilities for the democratization of case-study research; what recent papers have done is to highlight some of the fundamental dilemmas of interview-based case study work, where interview data are preserved as case record 'texts', and to look at hermeneutics for some support in establishing principles of procedure in interpretation. What we can say, without any shadow of doubt, is that Stenhouse's work in the field, though not fully thought through, has opened up a worthwhile debate — as Skilbeck recognized:

> The case study as Stenhouse left it, is a tantalisingly open element of methodology. Taken in one direction, it leads us to the perfection of ... documentation; in another, it is a key factor in the revitalization and democratization of educational practice and educational knowledge. (1983)

Notes

1 The idea of the 'second record' comes from Hexter's book, *The History Primer* (1972, chapter 4). Stenhouse introduced the idea in a paper written in 1979 (b). He begins by talking about fiction, suggesting that 'in realistic fictions verification depends upon the reader's judgments about the trustworthiness of a portrayal in terms of verisimilitude'. He goes on to suggest that the 'organized trace of the reader's experience' to which appeal is made in the verification of a realistic fiction might be called a 'general second record'. If the account offered is not confirmed by the general second record of the reader, 'either the portrayal will be dismissed or it must be upheld by a revision of the records of one's own experience'. Stenhouse then moves the argument across from fiction to history and thence to case study. In a later paper (1982) he distinguishes between the 'general second record' and the 'professional second record' (i.e. that of the educationalist). Stenhouse argues that while verification may appeal to the second record of the reader, authentication requires a first record — the documents of the case.

2 According to the proposal, *School Report* (1980b), thirty or so schools would each have a case study worker attached for a period of five years, the case study workers coming from institutions of higher education. In the first year a base-line case record would be prepared and, during the next four-and-a-half years, nine issues-based records would be prepared (the focus being, in the main, issues of contemporary concern). Thus, nine issue-based records would be produced for each school. The thirty plus records on each issue would, shortly after completion, be worked on to produce a report across institutions. In addition to the nine reports, a well-organized archive of evidence about secondary schools in the 1980s would be established.

3 New technology makes the idea of a records-based archive relatively feasible: microfiche systems of data storage would simplify the process of holding and handling the data of the case records and a computerized index system would assist the search.

4 The numbers are deliberately approximated to avoid giving the impression that there was a pre-determined number of interviews for each category of interviewee. Each field worker interviewed as many students, teachers and library staff as was feasible and as seemed relevant given the circumstances and focus of the study.

5 Interview transcripts were returned to each interviewee for clearance and for any necessary emendation. In the main, interviewees made alterations that clarified the meaning they intended, which was less clear in the written text than it may have been in the oral communication of the interview. Factual errors were also corrected. In some cases passages were deleted. A few interviews were not cleared (and were not therefore placed in the archive) — mainly because the interviewees had left the institution by the time the transcribed interview was returned and were not easily traceable.

6 Bartlett (1984b) associates Lawrence Stenhouse's work with the historical-hermeneutic tradition and lists the distinguishing features of his

approach (I have selected those items that focus on the task of interpretation):

The act of interpretation may occur distanced from the social context in which the evidence is derived.

The act of interpretation is based on evidence derived from discourse in interview and fixated in text archived as case records.

Interpretation of a single case or across cases ... involves a process of refinement of judgments based on text evidence archived in case records.

Verification of interpretation is possible through a process of critical scrutiny of texts (case records) by researchers and through intersubjectivity of judgments.

Public access to text evidence in archived case records is necessary to this process of critical intersubjectivity and refinement of researcher judgment about an instance from a class or population.

Text evidence is made public after following principled procedures (negotiation, access and confidentiality are key concepts) that preserve the ethical and political rights of participants in the research.

The act of interpretation of texts is related to a theory of action whereby participants' reflections on human experience — consciousness — inform their actions.

7 Stenhouse's categories of interview data which Bartlett (1984b) cogently criticizes are these: assumption; testimony; witness; hearsay; account; and reflection (Stenhouse, 1979b; based partly on Gottschalk's work, 1945).

References

BALL, S.J. (1981) *Beachside Comprehensive: A Case-Study of Secondary Schooling*, Cambridge, Cambridge University Press.

BARTLETT, V.L. (1984a) 'Historical narrative and event meaning in educational research', mimeo, Department of Education, University of Queensland.

BARTLETT, V.L. (1984b) 'The rules of the game: case study method and interpretation theory', mimeo, Department of Education, University of Queensland.

DIXON, K. (1980) 'The words in themselves — the appraisal of oral reports in case studies', mimeo, Vancouver, Simon Fraser University.

GOTTSCHALK, L. *et al* (1945) *The Use of Personal Documents in History, Anthropology and Sociology*, Bulletin No. 53, New York, Social Science Research Council.

HEXTER, J.H. (1972) *The History Primer*, London, Allen Lane (first published in New York by Basic Books Inc. 1971).

HULL, C. (1984) 'Between the lines: the analysis of interview data as an exact art', *Research Intelligence*, 15, pp. 8–11.

LACEY, C. (1970) *Hightown Grammar*, Manchester, Manchester University Press.

LACEY, C. (1981) 'Case studies and theory', mimeo (draft of a talk given at the British Educational Research Association annual conference), University of Sussex.

NIAS, J. (1978) 'Sociological research: some analogies with historical method', *Cambridge Journal of Education*, 8, pp. 32–44.

RICOEUR, P. (1976) *Interpretation Theory: Discourse and the Surplus of Meaning*, Texas, University of Texas Press.

RUDDUCK, J. (1984) 'A study in the dissemination of action research', in BURGESS, R.G. (Ed.) *The Research Process in Educational Settings: Ten Case Studies*, Lewes, Falmer Press.

RUDDUCK, J. and HOPKINS, D. (1984) *The Sixth Form and Libraries: Problems of Access to Knowledge*, British Library Research and Development Department.

RUDDUCK, J. and STENHOUSE, L. (1979) A Study in the Dissemination of Action Research, Report to the Social Science Research Council, No. HR 3483/1.

SCHOOLS COUNCIL (1975) *Private Study in the Sixth Form*, Occasional Bulletin.

SILVER, H. (1983) *Education as History*, London, Methuen.

SKILBECK, M. (1983) 'Lawrence Stenhouse: research methodology', *British Educational Research Journal*, 9, 1, pp. 11–20.

STAKE, R. and EASLEY, J. (1978) *Case Studies in Science Education*, Vol. XV, executive summary, Center for Instructional Research and Curriculum Evaluation, University of Illinois.

STENHOUSE, L. (1977) 'Exemplary case records: towards a descriptive educational research tradition grounded in science', a proposal to the Social Science Research Council.

STENHOUSE, L. (1978) 'Case study and case records: towards a contemporary history of education', *British Educational Research Journal*, 4, 2, pp. 21–39.

STENHOUSE, L. (1979a) 'The verification of descriptive case studies', later published in KEMMIS, S., BARTLETT, L. and GILLARD, G. (Eds.) (1982) *Perspectives on Case Study 2: The Quasi-Historical Approach*, (Vol. 3, in a series on *Case Study Methods*,) Deakin University Press.

STENHOUSE, L. (1979b) 'Gathering evidence by interview in educational research', later published in KEMMIS, S., BARTLETT, L. and GILLARD, G. (Eds.) (1982) *Perspectives on Case Study 2: The Quasi-Historical Approach*, (Vol. 3, in a series on *Case Study Methods*) Deakin University Press.

STENHOUSE, L. (1980a) 'The study of samples and the study of cases', *British Educational Research Journal*, 6, 1, pp. 1–6.

STENHOUSE, L. (1980b) 'School Report: A multi-site case study programme,' Proposal to the Social Science Research Council.

STENHOUSE, L. (1981a) 'The problem of standards in illuminative research', *Scottish Educational Review*, 11, 1, pp. 5–10.

STENHOUSE, L. (1981b) A review of 'The status of pre-college science, mathematics and social studies educational practices in the US schools', *Proceedings of the* (American) *National Academy of Education.*

STENHOUSE, L. (1982) 'Case study in educational research and evaluation', in FISCHER, D. (Ed.) *Fallstudien in der Pädagogik: Aufgaben, Methoden, Wirlungen,* Konstanz, Faude.

STENHOUSE, L. (1984) 'Library access, library use and user education in academic sixth forms: an autobiographical account', in BURGESS, R.G. (Ed.) *The Research Process in Educational Settings: Ten Case Studies,* Lewes, Falmer Press.

5   *History, Context and Qualitative Methods in the Study of Curriculum*

Ivor Goodson

This paper begins from a belief in qualitative methods and argues for a broadening of those methods to rehabilitate life stories and integrate studies of historical context. By way of exemplification the paper focuses on the work in *School Subjects and Curriculum Change*.[1] In the introductory section the reasons for concentrating on life story and curriculum history data are explored by analyzing some of the inadequacies of research methods as perceived in the mid-1970s when the study began.

It should be noted that since then studies have emerged which have also sought to address these inadequacies. Studies of teacher socialization have focused on teacher culture and careers,[2] whilst a range of 'strategies' studies have pointed to the importance of background and biography.[3] This work has considerably extended the range and theoretical aspiration of qualitative studies but in this paper I shall stay with the original intention of exploring the role of historical studies in redressing certain emergent tendencies within qualitative methods.

In retrospect several reasons would seem to have led to a prediliction for historical and biographical work when devizing a research programme. First, it grew out of my teaching experience. Certainly after Countesthorpe (recently described as an 'unemulated educational maverick') I was susceptible to Nisbet's arguments in *Social Change and History*. Here he argues that we are often deluded into thinking fundamental social change is taking place because we do not take account of a vital distinction between:

> readjustment or individual deviance within a social structure
> (whose effects, although possibly cumulative, are never suf-
> ficient to alter the structure or the basic postulates of a society
> or institution) and the more fundamental though enigmatic

> change of structure, type, pattern or paradigm. (Nisbet, 1969,
> in Webster, 1971, pp. 204–5)

To pursue this distinction demands, I think, that we undertake historical work. This holds whether we seek to understand how change is contained, as readjustment or individual deviance in particular schools like Countesthorpe or within curriculum reforms in general.

The documents and statements of the curriculum reform movement inaugurated in the 1960s reveal a widespread belief that there could be a more or less complete break with past tradition. A belief in short that history in general and curriculum history in particular could somehow be *transcended*. Writing in 1968 Professor Kerr asserted that 'at the practical and organizational levels, the new curricula promise to revolutionize English education' (Kerr, 1971, p. 1880). Retrospectively, there still seems something admirable, however misconceived, about such belief in contemporary possibility that history seemed of little relevance. At a time when traditional curriculum practice was thought to be on the point of being overthrown it was perhaps unsurprising that so many reforms paid scant attention to the evolution and establishment of traditional practice. In the event radical change did not occur. By 1975 when the research began one was in a position of needing to re-examine the emergence and survival of the 'traditional' as well as the failure to generalize, institutionalize and sustain the 'innovative'.

But if this was a view from the curriculum chalkface it later became clear that the *transcendent* view of curriculum change had infected many of those involved in researching schools and curriculum. The irony is supreme but for the best of reasons. Once again it is partly explained by an historical climate of opinion where curriculum change was thought the order of the day. Hence Parlett and Hamilton in their influential paper, though claiming general application, focused on the evaluation of innovation. They wanted 'to study the innovatory project; how it operates, how it is influenced by the various school situations in which it is applied; what those directly concerned regard as its advantages and disadvantages' (Parlett and Hamilton, 1972). Their preoccupation with 'those directly concerned', with 'what it is like to be participating' was to characterize a major school of evaluators and case study workers. Indeed, this posture characterized those researchers both most sympathetic and sensitive to the aspirations of the innovators. Above all they wanted to 'capture and portray the world as it appears to the people in it'.

Some went even further: 'in a sense for the case study worker what *seems* true is more important than what is true' (Walker 1974, p. 80).

Writing later, with a strong sense of my own delusions on curriculum reform, I saw the evaluators who had studied my school as merely confirming the participants' myopia.

> Focusing the evaluator's work on the charting of the subjective perceptions of participants is to deny much of its potential — particularly to those evaluators aspiring to 'strong action'-implications. The analysis of subjective perceptions and intentions is incomplete without analysis of the historical context in which they occur. To deprive the subject of such knowledge would be to condemn new evaluation to the level of social control — a bizarre fate for a model often aspiring to 'democratic' intuitions. (Goodson, 1977, p. 160)

Yet if many of those employing qualitative methods in evaluation and case study took a transendent view of history they were not alone. By a peculiar convergence many contemporary interactionist and ethnographic studies were similarly ahistorical.

The experimental model of sociological investigation with its emphasis on single studies to test pre-selected hypotheses, whilst for long dominant, neglected participant perspectives and interactional processes. Paradoxically, the interactionist and ethnographic models which were conceived in reaction to this model have often focused on situation and occasion with the result that biography and historical background have continued to be neglected.

Partly this may have arisen by anthropological analogy. For instance, Philip Jackson's work on *Life in Classrooms*, although full of insight, presents teachers as a particular kind of species reproducing within busy, tiring and unchanging environments:

> Not only is the classroom a relatively stable physical environment, it also provides a fairly constant social context. Behind the same old desks sit the same old students, in front of the familiar blackboard stands the familiar teacher. (Jackson, 1968, p. 72)

As a result in these accounts the teacher becomes depersonalized, neutral, above all eminently *interchangeable:* the same old familiar teacher we know so well.

A second characteristic assumption is also epitomized in Jackson, the assumption of *timelessness:* this is at one with interchangeability — whatever the time, whoever the teacher, everything is much the same. This anti-historical approach is a common feature in interactionist and ethnographic approaches.[4] Payne, for instance, asserts that:

> A fundamental assumption of the ethnomethodological approach is that the social world is essentially an ongoing achieved world. The everyday world of social events, settings and relationships is all the time created and achieved by the members of society and these events, settings and relationships are assumed to have no existence independent of the occasion of their production. (Payne, 1976, p. 33)

But while there is some truth in this the actors creating the social events which Payne describes do, nevertheless, have an existence which is independent of and previous to the social events in which they are involved. Such a neglect of historical and biographical background makes problematic the construction of general categories within which to situate those ethnographic and interactionist accounts of specific events. Hence it would be possible for a variety of social events to be portrayed and for their internal logic to be laid bare without getting at any general understanding of why events differ and why what is common to certain events, in particular school lessons, recurs over time.[5]

Recently these inadequacies have been conceded by ethnographers themselves. Woods has spoken of studies that 'tend to become a representation of a culture, a picture frozen in time', and has argued that as a result

> This immediately compromises the main aim and offends, for interactionists, the basic principle of 'process and flux'. However conscious of past and future the ethnographer may be consideration of those must always be of a different order to that of the present period of data collection. The fact is, however, that few ethnographic studies (my own included) have taken past and future into consideration to any extent.[6]

The reason for the omission of these fundamental concerns is openly expressed: 'we have looked at situations as we have found them, and have become so "immersed" that we have spent much of our time documenting and classifying. The problems of the moment consume much of time, effort and ingenuity.' The danger then is clearly that we end up with a range of idiosyncratic studies 'of the moment' or as Hargreaves puts it a 'proliferation of unique case studies' (Hargreaves, 1978, p. 9).

'A Story of Action within a Theory of Context'[7]

Apart from those studies, particularly by symbolic interactionists, which specifically denied the significance of contextual background, the reasons for ignoring historical context seem to have been twofold. Neglect arose from an essentially sympathetic and corrective concern for letting the participants speak, with charting their immediate perceptions of events. The focus was often on innovative processes which it was assumed would constitute the new educational order. But also neglect grew from procedural pragmatism: a detailed study of occasion and setting is itself a major and time-consuming enterprise.

In one sense then the study of historical context provides complementary data to the data focusing on contemporary participants and events. But I think that historical studies offer more than this. With studies confined to the view of participants at a moment in time, to the here and now of events, the essential omission was data on the *constraints beyond* the event, the school, the classroom and the participant. What above all is needed, therefore, is a method that stays with the participants, stays with the complexity of the social process but catches some understanding of the constraints beyond.

By paradox in reaction to the crude empiricism of some quantitative methods, the corrective concern with participants and immediate events often left research wholly confined within that frame of reference. The pursuit of historical data could break this stranglehold and open up the prospect of developing cognitive maps of process and of decision-making, of individuals and interest groups at work over time. Above all, history allows access to the recurrent patterns and powerful legacies on which all contemporary action must build. The footnote for much of the educational research focusing solely on participants and immediate events is therefore clear:

> Men make their own history, but they do not make it just as they please; they do not make it under circumstances chosen by themselves, but under circumstances directly encountered, given and transmitted from the past.[8]

Focusing investigation on participants' perceptions and short span interactive situations is then to 'take the problem as given'; what is needed is data on how circumstances are 'transmitted from the past'. By developing our analysis from further back we throw more light on the present and afford insights into the constraints imminent in transmitted circumstance.

The human process by which men make their own history does not take place in circumstances of their own choosing, but as both men and circumstances do vary over time so too do the potentialities for negotiating reality. Historical study seeks to understand how thought and action has evolved in past social circumstances. Following this evolution through time to the present affords insights into how those circumstances we experience as contemporary 'reality' have been negotiated, constructed and reconstructed over time.

Life Stories and Curriculum History

The argument for historical study of education is, of course, well-founded. But the concern here is not with history for the sake of history. Rigidly periodized 'history of education' poses severe problems since links with contemporary education often remain under-developed, or a kind of continuity thesis is assumed to operate. The preoccupation should ultimately be with history for the sake of understanding contemporary curriculum issues. The qualitative concern with contemporary individuals and events is maintained but historical study of context is added to ensure that the constraints beyond the individual and the event are fully illuminated.

With respect to contemporary curriculum there are three levels (though of course this is in a sense falsely dichotomous) that are amenable to historical study:

(i)   The individual life story.[9] The process of change is continuous throughout a person's life 'both in episodic encounters and in longer-lasting socialisation processes over the life history'. (Blumer quoted in Hammersley and Woods, 1976, p. 3).

(ii) The group or collective level: professions, subjects or disciplines, for instance, evolve as social movements over time.

(iii) The relational level, the various permutations of relations between individuals, between groups and between individuals and groups; and the way these relations change over time.

At the time of planning *School Subjects and Curriculum Change* (Goodson, 1982) the blending of individual history and curriculum history had been recently explored in Mary Waring's study of Nuffield science. For Waring the understanding of curriculum innovation is simply not possible without a history of context:

If we are to understand events, whether of thought or of action, knowledge of the background is essential. Knowledge of events is merely the raw material of history: to be an intelligible reconstruction of the past, events must be related to other events, and to the assumptions and practices of the milieu. Hence they must be made the subject of inquiry, their origins as products of particular social and historical circumstance ... (Waring, 1979, p. 12)

Waring's focus on individual background as well as curriculum history grew from an awareness of how the Nuffield innovations were implemented:

Organizers of individual Nuffield projects were given considerable autonomy with regard to the interpretation and carrying out of their brief, and to the selection and deployment of their teams. As a result, these aspects reflect very clearly the background and personality of the men and women chosen. (Waring, 1979, p. 12)

This belief in the importance of individual history and personality is confirmed in the study (although the role of ideological bias is conceded):

The evidence in this study supports the view that, while differences of degree no doubt existed between individuals, the sincerity, the commitment and the dedicated work over a long time on the part of the principal characters at least, and probably of many others, dwarf and transcend whatever vested interest may have been operating. (Waring, 1979, p. 15)

Whilst I am unsure about the primacy of individual will over vested interests (hardly a lesson of history!) the contention does add force to the need to explore curriculum at both the individual and collective level. Combining life stories with contextual history seems therefore a strategy for building on the wide range of case study, evaluative and interactionist work.

In this way a methodology is established which stays with the focus on participation and eventfulness but which allows examination of the constraints beyond, which in fact allows us to see how *over time* individual will and fundamental vested interests interrelate.

School Subjects and Curriculum Change

Symptomatic of the focus on participants and events has been the absence of work on school subjects. Young has of course spoken of these as 'no more than socio-cultural constructs of a particular time' (Young, 1971, p. 23) but a historical view of curriculum would attribute considerably more significance than this. In choosing to research school subjects I was cognizant that in studies of schooling the subject provides *par excellence* a context where antecedent structures collide with contemporary action; the school subject provides one obvious manifestation of historical legacies or as Waring puts it 'monumental accretions' with which contemporary actors have to work.

Williams made the case for studying the content of education over twenty years ago. He argued that:

> The cultural choices involved in the selection of content have an organic relation to the social choices involved in the practical organization. If we are to discuss education adequately, we must examine, in historical and analytic terms, this organic relation, for to be conscious of a choice made is to be conscious of further and alternative choices. (Williams, 1965, pp. 145–6)

Developing this notion of school subjects being dependent on previous choices the concern in *School Subjects and Curriculum Change* was to begin with the histories of those teachers who had played a central role in defining a school subject over the last half century. The school subject in question, rural studies, changed from being a deeply utilitarian subject based on gardening in the 1920s to a subject offering 'O' and 'A' levels in environmental studies in the 1970s. By collecting the life stories of key participant teachers spanning this generation it was hoped that insights might be provided not only of how the curriculum changes but of how structural constraints are evidenced in such a process. Understanding a curriculum innovation such as the launching of environmental studies required a detailed understanding of historical context and life stories provided a valuable access point to this context.

In talking to the key participants understandably a range of personal values and idiosyncracies emerged but on certain points their life stories substantially concurred. At this point, however, a number of doubts surfaced. The most significant was that I was clearly, in talking to the main innovators, following one of the tactics for which I had indicted earlier research. The innovators did represent a group who had been able to 'hijack' the subject association and thereby change the direction and definition of the subject. But they in no way represented the range of traditions and 'alternative visions' among the teachers of the subject. In fact the fascinating aspect of the testimonies of the key participants was their cognizance of 'other voices in other rooms', of the alternative traditions and choices, which were closed off in pursuit of the status and resources that would promote the subject.

At this point the research might have progressed in a number of directions. I was aware of three that seemed sustainable: (i) to fill out the life stories of the key participants into fully-fledged life histories which would be of sufficient depth to capture and portray the main issues within this curriculum area; (ii) to collect a wider range of life stories, to try and cover the main 'traditions' and sub-groups within the subject, and (iii) to develop a detailed documentary history of the subject of the conflicts over the innovations that were generated, during a period of over half a century.

In retrospect all three of these strategies seem to offer both problems and possibilities but in the event strategy (i) was rejected. The main reason was that the focus on the innovative in-group seemed unrepresentative and in a strong sense 'against the grain' of much of the history of the subject. To be too focused on this group opened up the problem mentioned in the introduction where historical perspective is lost by a focus on 'innovation' which might in the longer span turn out to be merely 'abberration'.

To seek a way of overcoming the problems of uniqueness and idiosyncrasy which combine with substantial methodological problems in the life history method a combination of strategies (ii) and (iii) was adopted. A number of additional life stories of non-innovators were collected, whilst the main focus of the study turned towards documentary research of the history of the subject. Combining a range of life stories with subject history resembles the methods adopted in a range of recent 'oral histories'. Certainly the combination offered a strategy to 'triangulate' the data and thereby partially assess the reliability of the findings (Denzin, 1970).

The problem in this paper is how to characterize the blend of curriculum history and life story data without involving a substantive account. The major intention in the next section is therefore to fill out the argument with some data which give a 'feel' of combining life stories with historical context.

Of course the account has all the normal problems of trying to evidence the general category with one very specific case. In addition, it should be remembered that in assembling final accounts not just one but a range of life stories would be presented in combination with studies of historical context.

The following section deals with certain critical episodes in one teacher's life. They are chosen because they represent a common viewpoint in the life story data collected: namely a conviction that the embrace of specialist examination subject identity was a watershed in the original educational visions of a generation of rural studies teachers. But above all the concern in the section is to provide an account of certain critical decision points in one teacher's life: critical in the sense that the teacher, who is now retired, regards these episodes as the main turning point in his professional life.

The work began with a long series of interviews with the subject teacher — covering a period of eight years up until his retirement and after. Again and again, in the interviews the teacher returned to the episodes when in his terms 'the dream began to fade', 'the alternative vision died'.

Critical Episodes in a Teacher's Life

1947–1954 — The Innovative Secondary Modern

The 1944 Education Act foreshadowed the tripartite system of grammar, technical and secondary modern schools. The compulsory school leaving age was raised to fifteen in 1947. The Act marks the beginning of the modern era of curriculum conflict not so much because of its details but because from this date onwards curriculum conflict becomes more visible, public and national. Glass has noted that in this respect there was no 'pre-war parallel', for there was now:

> a recognition that secondary education is a proper subject for discussion and study ... in striking contrast to the pre-war position when attempts to investigate access to the various stages of education tended to be looked at by the Government as attacks on the class structure. (Glass, 1971, p. 35)

In the emerging secondary modern schools the curriculum was initially free from the consideration of external examinations. This freedom allowed some schools, always a minority, to experiment with their curricula and to pursue vocational and child-centred objectives. Social studies and civics courses, for instance, were rapidly established in a number of the schools. Kathleen Gibberd has argued that the secondary modern school as conceived in 1944 was never intended to work to any universal syllabus to take any external examination: 'it was to be a field for experiment.' She considered that:

> Behind the official words and regulations there was a call to the teacher who believed in education for its own sake and longed for a free hand with children who were not natural learners. Many of those who responded gave an individual character to their schools. (Gibberd, 1962, p. 103)

However, the period during which certain secondary moderns were a 'field for experiment' with vocational, child-centred and integrated curricula was to prove very limited. This can be evidenced by following the changes in rural education in the secondary state sector.

Rural Education

The origins of rural studies are both conceptually and chronologically widely spread but it is possible to distinguish two paramount themes. Firstly were those advocates who stressed the utilitarian aspects of education allied to husbandry and agriculture. This theme has very early origins; for instance, in 1651 Samuel Hartlib proposed in his *Essay for Advancement of Husbandry Learning* that the science of husbandry should be taught to apprentices (Adamson, 1962, p. 103). The second group advocated the use of the rural environment as part of an educational method: they were concerned with the pedagogic potential of such work. Rousseau summarized the arguments in his book *Emile*, written in 1767.

In the inter-war years a number of circulars on 'Rural Education' were issued. In May 1925 a Board of Education Circular asserted that:

> it appears desirable at the present time to emphasize afresh the principle that the education given in rural schools should be ultimately related to rural conditions of life.

The Circular added:

> liking and aptitude for practical rural work are dependent on early experience, and an education which tends to deter children from gaining such experience has a definitely anti-

rural bias and is liable to divert them from rural occupations.
(Board of Education, 1925, p. 6)

Alongside this starkly utilitarian reason the syllabus design followed
the pedagogic guidelines laid down in a book on school gardening
and handiwork written by Gunton and Hawkes in 1922. These
teachers saw rural education as 'the hub of the curriculum wheel'. All
the subjects of the curriculum were to be taught within a rural,
practical context (Gunton and Hawkes, 1922).

In the period following the 1944 Education Act the latter theme
was enthusiastically revived by certain innovative secondary modern
schools 'stimulated by the thinking that had produced the 1944
Education Act and the secondary modern schools, teachers began to
search again in our rural heritage for whatever might be used
educationally to advantage' (Carson and Colton, 1962, p. 3). In some
secondary moderns the vision of rural studies as the 'curriculum hub'
connecting school to environment and life had a marked influence.
Their work was summarized and promoted in A.B. Allen's book
Rural Education published in 1950:

> Taking agriculture and horticulture as our foundation sub-
> jects we see the interrelationship within the curriculum.
> Agriculture leads into elementary science, general biology,
> nature study, world history and world geography. It also
> leads into mathematics with its costing problems, renumera-
> tion and balance sheets. Horticulture leads into elementary
> science (and so is linked with agriculture), and local history.
> (Allen, 1950, p. 16)

Entering the Profession — Secondary Modern Innovations

At the time the new secondary moderns, a few embracing the
integrated concept of rural education, were being launched Patrick
Johnson was completing his training at Wandsworth Emergency
College. His choice of subject was initially somewhat fortuitous:

> Well, I didn't really know what subject I wanted to do. In fact
> I really wanted to do English. But when I got home after the
> war I didn't feel I could be couped up inside. I moved into
> Kent where all my wife Jean's people were farm workers on
> the fruit farms ... I heard there was a thing called rural
> studies.

First Job: Snodland (age 27–34)

In November 1947 he got a Teachers' Certificate and then had to do a probationary year. His first year was spent teaching general subjects at a school called Snodland ...

> Gardening it was really, but I taught everything. It was a secondary modern, a very early one, illiterate kids — their standard was terrible, just after the war. It was a big elementary school at a place called Snodland, with a big cement works on the Medway estuary, Rochester direction. Terrible place, the kids were very backward. I always remember the first day I arrived. The head said, 'Good God! A teacher!' and grabbed me, shoved me inside a classroom saying 'this is your lot' and shut the door! Then I was faced by this mob who hadn't had a teacher for some years during the war. I fought a running battle with them.

IG   What had they been doing, then?

PJ   Well, they had been going into the classroom occasionally. They literally could not read or write. They were desperate kids, nice kids but they were absolutely, completely illiterate at twelve years of age. And undisciplined too.

IG   So did you just have one class?

PJ   Yes, I did everything — PE, music, everything.

IG   So you weren't a rural studies teacher in your first post.

PJ   No, there was a lesson called gardening, and I did some of that as well.

Wrotham Secondary Modern (age 34–38)

Patrick's next job for his second probationary year was at a new secondary modern at Wrotham. The head, 'one of the very exceptional headmasters', had run the village school where his wife and son had attended. The head was very enthusiastic about school gardens and invited Patrick to come and teach rural science:

> So I said 'yes', I could see the opportunities ... I'd often talked with him of things I'd like to do. When he started the new school I went along to teach rural science. The new school consisted of three Nissen huts in a field. Literally, that was all. The type made of clay bricks with cinders, half way

between Wrotham and Borough Green. That was the school. There wasn't a classroom. One of them, the largest, doubled for assembly and art room. One half was elementarily equipped as a lab. The others were ordinary classrooms. I had an ordinary classroom and I had a fourth year class, which was then the top leaving class of the school. There were three streams and the third and fourth year classes were called 4F (farming) and 4P (practical) with extra needlework and cooking, and 4A (academic) where the kids did extra English and so on. But of course there were no examinations, so in fact A wasn't the top class, but they probably did turn out a few who could read and write. They were really equivalent and we used to sit down once a year and think out who would we get into each class. Well, 4F class, which I had ... we established a school farm. We built this up from nothing. We had one and a half acres of land along the playing fields as it was too steep for football pitches. I got that fenced off, got bits of wire and so on ... as things developed I had my class for practically everything — not quite every subject, but a good deal and I developed my ideas on this farm. We built bits and pieces gradually. We built a pigsty, and the 4 Practical did the actual building of that. We built a rabbit house which we built up. Eventually we kept about two calves, about six goats, a pig and a litter; we had a poultry run and hens of course, a dairy which we fitted out, and I managed to get from Gascoynes, because my father was a friend of the chairman or something, dairy equipment.

Johnson taught 4F for about two thirds of their timetable, other teachers taught science and woodwork. He was much influenced by the idea of rural education as the 'curriculum hub' which his headmaster actively encouraged.

I taught them maths, English, history etc., all tied in completely, because, for example, maths I based as much as possible on the farm activities. In fact, I used a series of books which was popular then, called *Rural Arithmetic* — the other I can't quite remember the title of. They were all about problems of the land: for example if you were mixing things for the pigs, you didn't buy ready-made meal for the pigs. You calculated by the weight what meal they require, you broke this down, the various ingredients of the meal, you got them all out separately, weighed them up, mixed them up and it had to work out right to fourteen rations, one for every morning and evening of the week. That was a piece of arithmetic it could take two people most of the day to do.

We were fairly poorly off for books in those days, frankly, so we read a lot of literature associated with the countryside. We didn't overdo this to the extent of doing nothing else. They wrote compositions. We had an English textbook, which I at any rate kept an eye on to make sure some sort of progression of spelling was maintained. But a lot of English was straightforwardly connected with the farm. For example, they each had to write a diary every day and they had to write a summary at the end of the week. It was passed on to the next students who took on the animals. That was a good piece of English, and I had said that must be perfect — no spelling mistakes, no blots — nothing!

Johnson reckons that these were some of the happiest days of his teaching career. His own enthusiasm (and that of his wife) coupled with the interest of the children seem to have generated considerable motivation to learn:

IG   Did they respond pretty well?
PJ   They absolutely lapped it up, loved it. You'd never get absences unless the kid was really ill. You'd get kids ... often at the weekends ... We had to feed them at the weekends — there was no-one else to. I can't remember any occasion when the kids didn't turn up at the weekend. It may have happened but I can't remember.
IG   So you had to spend a lot of time at weekends?
PJ   Lived up there. But Joan helped a lot too. Frankly we hadn't any money to be doing anything else in those days. Until it reached a stage when my kids were getting a bit older and I took a job during the holidays because I needed the money — pay was poor. But I still did that as well.

Johnson attributed the main influences on his developing concept of rural education to his contacts with the Kent farm workers' family which he had married into and which he lived among:

I did a lot of walking about the orchards in Kent and talking to farm workers and I can remember lots of occasions when the attitude of these people struck me very much. I had a strong feeling that education wasn't just book-learning —

that's an old phrase — it involved in fact skills in the field and commonsense applied to a problem.

Johnson feels that he dealt with many very able pupils in 4F; partly a reflection of the social structure in Kent in the early 1950s. The pupils were, with one exception (for whom he could not find a job), boys, the most able of whom today would be in the sixth forms, who went as agricultural apprentices to farms who were glad to get them. 'Good farms, good employers!' I asked at this point if he felt any resentment that they were forced to go on to the land:

PJ No, first of all because I didn't know anything about 'A' levels at my level of teaching. Grammar schools were a separate world and while I knew my own background, I never associated these kids with it. It never occurred to me at the time that these kids could have got into the sixth form. It didn't occur to me at that time that they were bright.

IG Why didn't it occur to you that these children were bright?

PJ They were bright to me but it didn't occur to me that that meant they should have an academic education. Because I was meeting people throughout the war — meeting people then whose field of work was similar to farm workers and were every bit as bright. I don't think this is true today. One of the effects of the introduction of the 11+ was to cream the working class of its bright people who went into academic jobs. You constantly hear it's happened in places like India — all being bank clerks or professionals. There were a lot of intelligent people in the working class then, who by and large are not there today. They have all been creamed off into sixth forms and professional jobs. At that time I know there were people as simple farm workers who were highly educated — not educated — but highly cultured intelligent people. I didn't find it a problem at the time, nor did the kids, it was never raised.

Secondary Modern Examinations

From the early 1950s more and more secondary modern schools began to focus on external examinations. This posed insuperable problems for those heads and teachers in secondary moderns who were exploring new integrated modes of curricula such as rural education.

More parents began to realize that certification led to better jobs, teachers found examinations a useful source of motivation and heads began to use examinations as a means of raising their school's reputation and status. For some heads support for the GCE may have stemmed from an initial rebellious non-acceptance of the whole tripartite philosophy. But soon 'success in this examination started a national avalanche'. By 1961–63, when Partridge studied a secondary modern school, the competitive nature of the 'examination race' was clearly apparent: 'with the public demand for academic attainments, reflecting the fact that education has become the main avenue of social mobility in our society, GCE successes would immeasurably enhance the repute of such a school, and hence the standing and status of the headmaster' (Partridge, 1968, p. 68). The rapid take-up of the GCE in secondary moderns led to an exhaustive enquiry by the Ministry of Education, culminating in the Beloe Report which recommended that secondary modern schools should have their own examinations. In 1965, therefore, the CSE was inaugurated. The rapidity with which external examinations came to dominate secondary modern school curricula meant that many of the characteristics of grammar school curricula were reproduced.

Towards Rural Studies Examinations

As the tripartite system of education gradually emerged in the form of new school buildings and modified curricula, it became clear that rural studies and gardening were only developing in the secondary modern schools. In 1952 a questionnaire survey of gardening and rural studies teachers in Kent produced, with three exceptions, the reply from grammar and technical schools of 'subject not taught', whilst in sixty-three of the sixty-five secondary modern schools the subject was given an important position in the curriculum.[10]

Rural education having been decimated as a concept within the increasingly exam-conscious secondary moderns it now became clear that the successor subject of rural studies faced major problems. Writing in 1957 Mervyn Pritchard described the situation in this way:

> There appear to be two extremes of thought in secondary modern schools:
>
> (a) a concentration on external examinations;
> (b) those who won't have them at any price.
>
> In those schools where the brighter pupils are examined it is unusual to find rural science as one of the subjects taken and

as the pupils concentrate more and more narrowly on their examination subjects it is unusual to find rural science used as a social subject such as craft, art or music may be.

Even where pupils are not examined there appears to be a concentration of the teaching of the subject in streams of classes of duller children. (Pritchard, 1957, p. 4)

In 1957 the Hertfordshire Association of Teachers of Gardening and Rural Subjects, worried by the loss of status and influence of the subject, carried out a similar survey to the Kent one. This time, significantly, questionnaires were sent only to secondary modern schools. The financial treatment of rural studies showed clearly the priorities of the secondary modern headmasters: 'It is surprising to learn ... that some schools allow the Rural Science Department no money at all while others are so small that the financial pinch entails great worry to the teachers'. Of the thirty-nine schools that returned questionnaires, fifteen had no classroom allotted for rural studies.

Generally the standard of provision for rural subjects appears to be below that of other practical subjects. Few schools are equipped satisfactorily with the items required for a good horticultural or agricultural course at secondary school level.

Why have ten schools, for example, inadequate garden-ing tools? The large number of inadequate or unsatisfactory items listed is striking. In particular, fifteen tool rooms and seventeen potting rooms are thought to be inadequate.

Of the fifty-three teachers involved, twenty-six were unqualified in gardening or rural studies and the general 'image' of rural studies teachers was of a low status, low morale group. Not only was the status of the rural studies teacher questionable but his isolation on the staff was often confirmed by placing the rural studies facilities in a distant corner of the school grounds.[11]

The concern of rural studies teachers at the deteriorating status and position of their subject led to a variety of responses in the latter part of the 1950s. Mervyn Pritchard exhorted:

as often as possible the rural studies teacher should mix with his colleagues, even if he has to kick off muddy gum boots to drink his cup of tea. Much useful interchange of knowledge and information is carried out among the staffroom gossip. Informal discussion of school policy can be helped along judiciously by the rural science teacher. Frequent contact can convince our colleagues of one's normality and value. (Pritchard, 1957, p. 5)

Apart from such exhortations some teachers were concerned to develop a 'philosophy of rural studies'. In 1954 Carson and Colton produced a paper which appeared in the Kent Association Journal, and later in 1957, in the Lincolnshire 'Rural Science News'. It was a systematic attempt to think through a subject philosophy, a first, embryonic attempt to define a subject, and one equipped with a contemporary rationale. They argued:

> For this study to justify its inclusion in the school curriculum it must be shown to play a vital part in developing a fully educated citizen who is aware in his heart of his kinship with the rest of life and yet realizes the unique qualities of the human spirit. (Rural Science News, 1957)

Carson and Colton were editors of the Kent Association of Teachers of Gardening and Rural Science Journal. The 'Rural Science' appendage was added at Carson's insistence when the Association was formed in 1949. The Association was predated by an ephemeral association of rural science teachers in 1925, and by a small association in Nottingham founded in 1940, and the Manchester Teachers' Gardening Circle founded in 1941.

By 1954 the Kent Journal was beginning to define a philosophy for rural studies and soon after claimed, 'this Association has constantly sought parity of esteem with the rest of the curriculum for all rural studies' (Kent Journal, 1954).

At the same time new rural studies associations were forming in other counties, normally to pursue the aims expressed in the Kent Journal. By now rural studies was a specialized subject of very low status, literally fighting for its existence in the exam-conscious secondary modern schools. In 1960 the County Subject Association banded together to form a National Rural Studies Association with its own journal. The 1961 journal stated in 'The Constitution':

> The aim of this association shall be 'to develop and coordinate rural studies'. Rural studies includes nature study, natural history pursuits of all kinds, the study of farming and the activities of the countryside, as taught in primary and secondary schools. Rural studies should be regarded as an art, a science and a craft; a subject as well as a method of teaching. (National Rural Studies Association Journal, 1961, p. 5)

The Association soon became involved in promoting examinations in rural studies. They initiated a pilot CSE project and although many practising teachers complained at the inappropriateness of written examinations a range of new CSEs in rural studies were duly promoted.

1954–1958 Secondary Modern Certification (age 34–38)

In 1953 the headmaster at Wrotham who had so strongly promoted rural education left; his successor was more examination conscious. Johnson began to look out for a new job and in the spring term of 1954 noticed a post at Royston in Hertfordshire where a teacher was required to start an ambitious rural studies programme. On the interviewing panel was a rural studies adviser, Geoff Whitby (he was, in fact, the first rural studies adviser and was steeped in the concept of rural education in which Hertfordshire had long been a pioneer).

> Whitby asked me about rural education and I described what I'd been doing in Kent, and I could see at once that I'd got the job. I should guess he'd never met anyone else who had done this sort of thing. The Head saw it differently. This was very interesting. He didn't see it as rural education in that sense because he was already thinking ahead to raising the standards of this school to what could eventually be CSE. None of this existed but he was thinking in terms of this. Although I understood when I got there I could have the same set up as in Kent, with three top classes and I could have anyone who wanted to volunteer for the subject, it never in fact worked out. The classes were streamed; I only ever got the lower of the three streams. While at first I could do what I liked with that bottom stream, and I did the same sort of things as in Kent, over the next few years this was whittled away from me, and more specialism invaded the curriculum and these kids eventually spent practically no time in running the farm. Whereas in Kent they did the whole operation of running the farm in lesson time, in Herts they had to do it before school. So it never really got going.

The problems were in fact both internal and external to the school. Inside the school there was streaming and a belief that it was vocational training for agriculture. Outside the school the community remained hostile to the whole concept, partly a result of the very different social structure of Hertfordshire compared with Kent. In Kent farm workers were better paid and treated and respected because their job was skilled.

> In Hertfordshire there was a long history of poverty on the land going back to Arthur Young's travels. If you meet any of the farm workers in this area there are tales of great poverty even in this day. So there was a feeling that going on the land here was nothing but condemnation ... nothing but ploughing and sowing, no other skills, very little mixed farming, no orchards.

But beyond the different social structure of the new locality Johnson had moved towards an awareness that 'society was changing'.

> The concern was that selection was important, children were getting into grammar schools and other people were beginning to see what was happening to them. Therefore they wanted their children to do as well academically as possible in order to get better jobs ... certainly the atmosphere was different.

Johnson's disillusionment with his new school grew as he realized he would only ever be given the problem children and those stigmatized as less able. In 1956, his third year, he had a series of interviews with the head:

> I had arguments with Young. I made my case and he was adamant that this was not what was required today. They gave a school leaving certificate, and they required qualifications in other things. In my opinion he never really saw what I was up to.

At the time he felt a deep sense of professional betrayal. After all in Kent he had seen a working model of rural education as an integrated 'eminently satisfactory situation of mixed ability type'. Again and again in his retirement interviews he returns to this critical point when as he puts it 'my dream faded', 'my vision of educating children faltered'. However, at the time, although disappointed, there were other goals:

> My ambition was to be a head, and I had long talks with Young about how I could get to be a head. It became increasingly obvious to me that as a rural studies man I wasn't going to get a look in.

1958–1979 Rural Studies and Environmental Studies Adviser
(age 38–59)

In 1958 Johnson was asked by the Rural Studies Adviser who had
brought him to Hertfordshire if he would like to take over his job.

> I didn't think twice when Whitby asked. I thought an
> opening like this, I'll do something good in this. I started off
> in 1958 with part-time, half my time, and he worked the other
> half for a year and then he retired, and I got his job. By this
> time I'd really given up hope of getting rural studies seen in
> the way I'd taught it in Kent. Then I saw it as a specialist
> subject which had certain weak links. For the first two to
> three years I did two things; I read all about the rural
> education tradition in the papers Whitby gave me on his
> background, etc. At the same time I was visiting the secon-
> dary school teachers and stimulated them to get themselves
> organized to try and get any kids other than the least able, to
> get them better facilities in their schools. I spent the first three
> to four years with this aim.

At this stage in his life Johnson was enthused by the prospect of
using his influence as an adviser to change things. Initially this
enthusiasm carried him over the loss of 'hope of getting real rural
education' for by now it was clear that whatever his preference the
specialist subject was taking over.

IG   What kind of people were they, as you travelled round in
      1958–60?

PJ   They were pre-war teachers of gardening who'd come back, and
      there were people of my own generation living through the war
      who came into teaching. Gradually then we began to get the
      post-war younger teacher coming in and the colleges who
      specialized in rural studies from the 1960s onwards. Before that
      they were the older chaps generally.

IG   So what did you decide would be your strategy? By then you
      were involved in the National Association?

PJ   No, we started the National Association in 1960. I called the
      first meeting in the name of the Herts Association. We knew
      there were various other groups around the country. I have no
      idea how we found that out.

IG   What was the thinking behind calling this meeting?

PJ   It was quite definitely to raise the standard of rural studies as a subject and the status of it because we decided that until it was raised nationally we wouldn't be able to do much in Herts. 'If you're not given a proper classroom refuse to teach this subject in any old place, and as adviser call me in', was what I told my teachers, and I will say 'this chap is entitled to a classroom just the same as anyone else'. To some heads this was a bit of a shock. They'd never been faced with this problem. If it rained they all just sat in the bicycle shed. We had Broad who was sympathetic to ideas ... we produced that report, and as a result every school from 1960 onwards where I was adviser, we got minimal provisions called the Rural Studies Unit in Herts.

From this point on Johnson became a leading campaigner for rural studies as a subject — self-promotion and subject promotion became finally and inextricably linked. This pursuit of subject promotion over time was reflected upon in an article he wrote in 1963 for the Rural Studies Association Journal. It begins with the polarity that teachers actually have two duties 'one to their classes and one the educational climate in which they worked'. It was argued that the subject had to respond to these 'changing climates' to ensure influence and resources.

During the next few years considerable changes are likely both in the framework of our school system and in the curricula within school and if rural studies is to retain its influence, then those teachers who believe in the subject must be clear about their aims and ready to adapt their methods to new conditions.

He concluded:

Thus the climate is changing continually, now perhaps more rapidly than ever before. But rural studies teachers are used to British weather. Have we not all got a lesson up our sleeves for the sudden downpour or the unexpected fine day? Within the educational climate too, we are ready with new ideas to meet whatever the weather has in store! (National Rural Studies Association Journal, 1963, pp. 14–15)

In fact what the weather had in store at this time was the new Beloe examinations for secondary moderns. Rural studies became one of the pilot studies for the new examination and despite a range of evidence that it was ill-suited to written examination, subject opportunism demanded a positive response to the changing climate. As a result CSEs in rural studies were promoted wherever possible. This embracing of examinations was pursued obsessively when the comprehensive system was launched. Rural studies then, Johnson thought, had to 'adapt or perish'. Again the response was opportunistic. Rural studies was changed into environmental studies, and a new 'A' level in the subject was launched for as Johnson says 'this way, you got more money, better kids, better careers'. (See Goodson, 1982)

The Alternative Vision: A Retrospect

Although during the period when he was building his career Johnson embraced the notion of his subject as an examinable specialism, in later years doubts surfaced. On his retirement he stated quite clearly that it was the embrace of the specialist subject examination that killed his educational vision. 'This was when my dream began to fade, I was not aware of it at the time.' For him now his alternative vision, his dream, is all powerful:

> My alternative vision was that in more general terms, and I'm still convinced this is true, a lot of kids don't learn through paper and pencil and that we do far too much of this. A lot of kids could achieve success and use all the mental skills that we talk about in the classroom such as analyzing and comparing through physical activities. Through such things as building the school farm, looking after animals. I used to talk about the fact that the real reason for keeping the farm wasn't to teach farm work. With the farm it was a completely renewing set of problems and the fact it was a farm was incidental. You were thinking in educational terms of process with these kids. That's the sort of dream I was well aware of giving up, and talked about it a number of times. I always felt dissatisfied since and I've met many teachers who have come across the same realization, not in quite such explicit terms as they'd never had the chance of doing it, whereas I had. I meet them now in schools ... a teacher whom I met today knew that the teaching she was doing with these less able girls was not the right way to educate these girls, but what was the right way she couldn't think. Well, I know what is the right way. The right way is the sort of thing we were doing in 1947 whether it's using the farm or whatever. The attitude is that you use your hands. You don't always sit at a desk necessarily. You

are facing problems of a three-dimensional kind at an adult level. You use terms like 'man's problems'; and this is no longer feasible in a school situation. I couldn't tell that girl today to do that sort of thing; she wouldn't succeed at all.

To my mind one of the tragedies of education in my life, and I would call this the secondary modern ethos, maybe it's one of many, but I don't know, was that the best thing that secondary moderns did was to promote this idea that it's just as good to be a skilled craftsman as, say, a white collar worker, and that you get as much satisfaction and challenge from it, at your own level. This was what was really behind what we were doing in Kent. The fact that this is no longer recognized in schools at all is I think responsible for the problems we have in school today, both academically with the less able and with the anti-school group and the apathetic group.

Conclusion

I have included this episode in a subject teacher's life mainly just to give a 'feel' for the data, the way that life story and historical context combine. Above all the strength of beginning curriculum research from life story data is that *from the outset* the work is firmly focused on the working lives of practitioners. Other researchers have commented in similar manner on the peculiar force of this kind of data as the initial strategy in a research programme:

> When one conducts a life history interview the findings become alive in terms of historical processes and structural constraints. People do not wander round the world in a timeless, structureless limbo. They themselves acknowledge the importance of historical factors and structural constraints (although, of course, they would not use such pompous language). The analysis of life histories actually pushes one first of all to the problems of constraints bearing down upon the construction of any one life ... (Faraday and Plummer, 1979, p. 780)

In articulating their response to historical factors and structural constraints life story tellers provide us with sensitizing devices for the analysis of these constraints and the manner in which they are experienced. We are alerted to historical legacies and structural constraints and can pursue understanding of aspects such as, in the instance given, strategies for self and subject promotion and career construction.

Certainly in the life of Patrick Johnson we gain insights into him wrestling with imperatives in the social structure. From his early professional life he develops a vision of how schools might be, this vision is challenged and defeated as subject specialism and examinations invade the early secondary modern schools; we see how self-promotion and subject promotion interrelate; and we see how one educational ideology is initially replaced by another as the teacher's career is constructed; the ideological renunciation only follows his retirement at the end of his career. Our attention is therefore left on the link between the structuring of material interests, strategies for career aggrandisement and the acceptance of particular educational ideologies.

I believe the instance gives some grounds for seeing how Bogdan's exhortation might work. He argued that the fully-researched life history should allow us to:

> See an individual in relation to the history of his time, and how he is influenced by the various religious, social, psychological and economic currents present in his world. It permits us to view the intersection of the life history of men with the history of society, thereby enabling us to understand better the choices, contingencies and options open to the individual. (Bogdan, 1974, p. 4)

A combination of life stories and curriculum histories should then offer an antidote to the depersonalized, ahistorical accounts of schooling to which we are only too accustomed. Above all we gain insights into individuals coming to terms with imperatives in the social structure. From the collection of a range of life stories located in historical context we can discern what is general within a range of individual studies. We can thereby develop our understanding from a base that is clearly grounded within personal biography and perception.

Critical Questions

In this paper I have taken the view that a combination of life story and curriculum history data can both broaden and deepen our accounts of schooling and curriculum. But a range of critical questions remain. Certain problems are specific to life story data, others specific to curriculum history and a further set of questions arise from the relationship between the two.

Firstly, life stories provide us with only partial accounts collected at certain stages in a life. If we seek a full retrospective life story then we come at the stage Vonnegut has described so well in his most recent novel. He argues that sociologists have ignored the fact that

> We all see our lives as stories ... If a person survives an ordinary span of sixty years or more, there is every chance that his or her life as a shapely story has ended; and all that is to be experienced is epilogue. Life is not over, but the story is. (Glendenning, 1983, p. 47)

But John Mortimer has summarized the problems of writing an autobiography at this stage. In the last paragraph he says:

> That is how it was, a part of life seen from a point of view. Much more happened that I cannot tell or remember. To others it would be, I am quite sure, a different story. (Mortimer, 1983, p. 256)

At root the problem is to retain and defend the authenticity of the participant's account. But to do this such problems of lapsed memory or partial or selective recall must be faced. We only get a part of the picture, to be sure a vital part, but we need to push for more of the picture, more bits of the jigsaw.

In part the problem is addressed by triangulation through collecting a range of life stories, and by developing a documentary history of the context. Certainly in *School Subjects and Curriculum Change* a wealth of subject journals, committee minutes, personal letters and memoirs were used to 'interrogate the evidence'.

The development of research which moves from a range of life stories to curriculum history concentrates on the focus of the work; arguably in a way which challenges the authenticity of the accounts and certainly in ways which affect the relationship between the life story teller and the researcher. By moving from life story to curriculum history control is passing irrevocably to the researcher. In addition the life story data are being concentrated onto particular issues and themes. In this case the linkage with the history of a subject could well have led, in spite of the range of life stories gathered, to an over-concentration on the career conscious, upwardly-mobile teachers. Once again there is the danger of an over-emphasis on the unrepresentative.

I have explored elsewhere the relationship to theory of the work.[12] But in this respect it must be noted that as with life stories, so with curriculum histories, the specificity of their focus can act against their capacity for generalization. *School Subjects and Curriculum Change* concentrates on one specialist subject history. But what about pastoral systems? Do the findings apply to subjects like classics, economics or even sociology? What about subjects where industrial and external forces are more clearly involved? What about conditions where the autonomy of the educational system (and 'rules of the game' for self and subject promotion) is challenged?

A central question is the nature of the interpretation, the role of the commentary. As Bertaux has reminded us moving from the personal life story to wider histories involves considerable questions of methodological reliability:

> What is really at stake is the relationship between the sociologist and the people who make his work possible by accepting to be interviewed on their life experiences. (Bertaux, 1981, p. 9)

This question is deeply significant both at the ethical and procedural level.

The ethical and procedural questions relate closely to the relationship between life story teller and researcher and the potential for mutuality. This is further related to the question of 'audience'. If the earlier contention that life story data placed in a historical context offer the opportunity for research which 'engages' teachers is correct then the prospects for mutuality are enhanced. In developing life stories teachers could be involved in work which would illuminate and feed back into the conditions and understandings of their working lives.

Acknowledgements

To my University of Sussex colleagues Stephen Ball and Michael Eraut, and in particular to Barry Cooper.

Notes

1 GOODSON (1982).
2 For instance LACEY (1977).

3 For instance Peter Woods' work on POLLARD (1982).
4 The criticism of ethnography's lack of history is well featured in BURGESS (1982). See also DELAMONT (1981).
5 The comments on assumptions derive from my paper (GOODSON, 1983a).
6 See WOODS (1985, p. 54). For further comment see also WOODS (1983).
7 A phrase often used by Lawrence Stenhouse.
8 See MARX, The Eighteenth Brumaire, in MARX/ENGELS, as for instance *Selected Works*, Vol. 1, London, Lawrence and Wishart, 1951.
9 Bertaux has drawn our attention to the significance of the distinction between life stories and life histories. In this paper the work would be defined as life stories rather than life histories. See BERTAUX (1981).
10 Survey by Kent Rural Studies Association, 1952.
11 Survey by Hertfordshire Association of Teachers of Gardening and Rural Subjects, 1957.
12 See GOODSON (1983b).

References

ADAMSON, J.W. (1951) *Pioneers of Modern Education 1600–1700*, Cambridge, Cambridge University Press.
ALLEN, A.B. (1950) *Rural Education*, London, Allman and Son.
BERTAUX, D. (Ed.) (1981) *Biography and Society* London, Sage.
BLUMER, M. (1976) quoted in HAMMERSLEY, M. and WOODS, P. (Eds.) *The Process of Schooling*, London, Routledge and Kegan Paul.
BOARD OF EDUATION (1925) *Circular 1365*, 28 May, London, HMSO.
BOGDAN, R. (1974) *Being Different: the Autobiography of Jane Fry*, London, Wiley.
BURGESS, R.G. (Ed.) (1982) *Field Research: A Sourcebook and Field Manual*, London, Allen and Unwin.
CARSON, S. and COLTON, R. (1962) *The Teaching of Rural Studies*, London, Edward Arnold.
DELAMONT, S. (1981) 'All too familiar?: A decade of classroom research', *Educational Analysis*, 3, 1, pp. 69–83.
DENZIN, N.K. (1970) *The Research Act*, Chicago, Aldine.
FARADAY, A. and PLUMMER, K. (1979) 'Doing life histories', *Sociological Review*, 27, 4.
GIBBERD, K. (1962) *No Place Like School*, London, Michael Joseph.
GLASS, D.V. (1971) 'Education and social change in modern England' in HOOPER, R. (Ed.) *The Curriculum: Context, Design and Development*, Edinburgh, Oliver and Boyd.
GLENDENNING, V. (1983) 'The slaughterhouse epilogue', *Sunday Times*, 20 February.
GOODSON, I. (1977) 'Evaluation and evolution' in NORRIS, N. (Ed.) *Theory in Practice*, SAFARI Project, Norwich, Centre for Applied Research in Education, University of East Anglia.
GOODSON, I. (1982) *School Subjects and Curriculum Change*, London, Croom Helm.

GOODSON, I. (1983a) 'Life histories and the study of teaching' in HAMMERS-LEY, M. (Ed.) *The Ethnography of Schooling*, Driffield, Nafferton.

GOODSON, I. (1983b) 'Subjects for study: aspects of a social history of curriculum', *Journal of Curriculum Studies*, Autumn.

GUNTON, M.W. and HAWKES, C.W. (1922) *School Gardening and Handiwork*, London, Pitman.

HARGREAVES, D. (1978) 'Whatever happened to symbolic interactionism?' in BARTON, L. and MEIGHAN, R. (Eds.) *Sociological Interpretation of Schooling and Classrooms: A Reappraisal*, Driffield, Nafferton.

JACKSON, P.W. (1968) *Life in Classrooms*, New York, Holt, Rinehart and Winston.

KENT JOURNAL, (1954) No. 4.

KERR, J. (1971) 'The problem of curriculum reform' in HOOPER, R. (Ed.) *The Curriculum: Context, Design and Development*, Edinburgh, Oliver and Boyd.

LACEY, C. (1977) *The Socialization of Teachers*, London, Methuen.

MORTIMER, J. (1983) *Clinging to the Wreckage*, Harmondsworth, Penguin.

National Rural Studies Association Journal, (1961).

National Rural Studies Association Journal (1963) 'The changing climate'

NISBET, R.A. (1969) *Social Change and History*, quoted in WEBSTER, J.R. (1971) 'Curriculum change and crisis', *British Journal of Educational Studies*, 3.

PARLETT, M. and HAMILTON, D. (1972) *Evaluation as Illumination: A New Approach to the Study of Innovatory Programs*, Occasional Paper 9, Edinburgh, Centre for Research in Educational Sciences, 1972.

PARTRIDGE, J. (1968) *Life in a Secondary Modern School*, Harmondsworth, Penguin.

PAYNE, G. (1976) 'Making a lesson happen' in HAMMERSLEY, M. and WOODS, P. (Eds.) *The Process of Schooling*, London, Routledge and Kegan Paul.

PLUMMER, K. (1983) *Documents of Life*, London, Allen and Unwin.

POLLARD, A. (1982) 'A model of coping strategies', *British Journal of Sociology of Education*, 3, 1.

PRITCHARD, M. (1957) 'The rural science teacher in the school society', *Journal of the Hertfordshire Association of Gardening and Rural Subjects*, 2, September.

Rural Science News (1957) 10, 1, January.

WALKER, R. (1974) 'The conduct of educational case study' in *Innovation, Evaluation, Research and the Problem of Control: Some Interim Papers*, SAFARI Project, Norwich, Centre for Applied Research in Education, University of East Anglia.

WARING, M. (1975) *Aspects of the Dynamics of Curriculum Reform in Secondary School Science*, unpublished PhD thesis, University of London.

WARING, M. (1979) *Social Pressures and Curriculum Innovation: A Study of the Nuffield Foundation Science Teaching Project*, London, Methuen.

WILLIAMS, R. (1965) *The Long Revolution*, Harmondsworth, Penguin.

WOODS, P. (1983) *Sociology and the School: An Interactionist Viewpoint*, London, Routledge and Kegan Paul.

WOODS, P. (1985) 'Ethnography and theory construction', in BURGESS, R.G. (Ed.) *Field Methods in the Study of Education*, Lewes, Falmer Press.

YOUNG, M.F.D., (1971) 'Curriculum as socially organised knowledge' in YOUNG, M.F.D. (Ed.) *Knowledge and Control: New Directions for the Sociology of Education*, London, Collier-MacMillan.

6   In Pursuit of the Past: Some Problems in the Collection, Analysis and Use of Historical Documentary Evidence

Alison Andrew

Introduction

The collection, analysis and use of historical documentary evidence raises methodological issues and problems for all researchers, whilst the sociologist involved in historical research faces further difficulties and dilemmas brought about by the often uncomfortable straddling of two separate academic disciplines. The aim of this paper is to examine some of these issues drawing on personal experience of research into working-class experiences of education in a Northern industrial town, Preston, in the nineteenth century. Areas of discussion include: history and sociology and the relationship between them; the use of historical documentary sources; the availability and representativeness of 'historical data'; the relationship between theory and 'facts'; and problems of historical and sociological interpretation. The discussion will focus particularly on methodological approaches and strategies and their influence on the final outcome of the research.

The Sociologist as Historian

It is possible, and I believe desirable, to argue against the treatment of sociology and history as distinct intellectual enterprises, to argue not simply for a rather limited collaboration but for the inherent interconnectedness of the two. Certainly a strong case can be made for the relative poverty of sociology without a historical perspective. This is argued persuasively by Mills (1959) in his classic account of the 'sociological imagination' and is also taken up by Goodson in this volume (page 121). Nevertheless, the current situation is that the majority of sociologists embarking upon historical research will become acutely aware of the inadequacy of their preparation for the task. This said, it is obviously the case that sociological approaches to history will vary. Historical data may be used to illustrate or support theoretical propositions or to provide context for a particular empirical study. In these instances it may be sufficient to 'borrow' material from the historians and concentrate one's time and effort on the matter more immediately in hand. However, for the sociologist whose central questions concern the past rather than the present, this clearly will not do.

The would-be historical sociologist with an initial training in sociology faces the task of self-education as a historian before the research project can proceed. This involves some important methodological considerations but is also to some extent a question of simple methods: acquainting oneself with the mysteries of the local record office, the Public Record Office, the British Museum and the tortuous organization of official publications. It is necessary to become familiar with the kinds of primary sources which contain information about the past, and how and where these are available. Secondary sources present another potential minefield. It is less easy outside one's own subject area to recognize what may be useful and what may be entirely marginal. Is it really necessary to read yet another tract on the economic advantages of the 'spinning jenny' or the extra production enabled by the development of the larger 'mule', in order to gain some understanding of working-class life in the nineteenth-century cotton towns? Where are new books and articles reviewed and summarized? Which are the most useful journals? How much work has already been done on a particular topic? This list of questions faced by the researcher in a relatively unfamiliar discipline could be greatly extended, and each one represents hours of labour and uncertainty. A plea can be made for more guidance, for expertise and experience to be brought together to spare at least the worst of these traumatic struggles; but for the time being researchers must take comfort in the fact that few, if any, of us manage to avoid them entirely (see, for example, Purvis in this volume, page 179).

In addition to this confusion over methods, sociologists engaged in historical research face the problem of the extent of their acquaintance with a particular historical period and with academic debates of relevance to the research topic. My own research may provide some examples here. It is largely concerned with the growth in the nineteenth century of both formal and informal networks of educational activity which embraced the working class, and the course of their future development, focusing not on administrative structures but on the beliefs and practices of working-class participants. A broad definition of the word 'education' has both formed a starting point for the research, and emerged from it. The sources studied revealed a large number of activities which in nineteenth-century Preston were regarded by working people as important educationally and which formed an integral part of working-class life. These activities included involvement in the Chartist movement, participation in religious organizations, trade union membership and leisure pursuits, as well as attendance at more conventional schools and classes. Education in its more informal guise was highly valued, and whilst it often coexisted with more conventional provided schooling there is evidence to show that it was frequently also in opposition to it. Throughout the earlier part of the century a 'tradition' can be traced which emphasized the importance of indigenous forms of working-class educational activity and resisted the notion of outside interference. There is some indication on a national level that by the last third of the century those members of the working class who placed a high value on education had moved from a defence of their own forms to a demand for state aid and a welcoming of the 1870 Education Act as a step in the right direction (see, for example, Simon, 1974; McCann, 1970). Either way, resistance or welcome, the passing of this Act might have been expected to elicit a response. The present research, however, has failed to find any such response in Preston itself; the 'trail' of working-class educational endeavour in the town goes cold at this point.

In order to understand fully all these developments it may well be necessary to engage in various debates within nineteenth-century historiography: the significance and extent of Chartism in Britain; the question of whether Methodism can be understood as either a radical or a conservative influence in nineteenth-century politics and class relationships; the existence or otherwise of a 'labour aristocracy' which led to the increasing conservatism of the British working class in the later nineteenth century, and so on. Academic debts are of course legion; all researchers rely to a great extent on the work and inspiration of others in the field. Yet some engagement in the substantive concerns of the historian as they impinge on the research topic cannot and should not be avoided. It is crucial both to enable sound theoretical insight and to facilitate a proper understanding of the source material. This requirement may make historical sociology a difficult and time-consuming task, but unless people and institutions are to be ripped out of their context it is undoubtedly essential.

Working with Historical Sources

It may also be necessary for sociologists working with historical documentary evidence to question some of their fundamental methodological assumptions. Methodology texts frequently warn of the dangers of allowing methods to determine problems: we are exhorted to begin with our 'problems', hypotheses or areas of interest and to select the methods most appropriate to them. Obviously historical 'problems' or questions require historical research but the availability or otherwise of documentary evidence will itself exert a crucial influence on the research and even the choice of research problem. The historican makes no bones about this; it is not unusual for a particular town to be selected for study because excellent records relating to it survive. This approach is less clumsy than it might seem. It is difficult to pursue even the most urgent investigations and fervent interests if the evidence needed does not exist.

Documents have differential survival rates and those which do survive do not always provide all the information required. The fundamental difference between historical research and other forms of social enquiry is the impossibility of 'going back' to ask for further explanation and elaboration. This leads to all kinds of problems (see Purvis in this volume, page 179). The answers to a great many questions are simply not available, since the necessary records either never existed or failed to survive. There is the frustration of events reported without follow-up, individuals not clearly identified, ambiguous accounts or those which provide a wealth of detail except that which is desperately sought. Characters in the plot are 'lost'; do they die, move away, cease to be seen as of interest, or, in the case of women, marry and change their names? Diaries tell enough about people or events to underline their importance but no trace of them can be found elsewhere. Even more prosaically, the material which is so central to the research suddenly changes in character or runs out; the newspaper for a particular (crucial) week has been destroyed; the discovery in the record office catalogue of some immensely exciting document leads only to the information that it disappeared mysteriously five years ago, or is damaged beyond restoration. Material which might enable a wealth of insight can be tantalizingly elusive. The 1845 Report of the Commissioners Inquiry into the State of

Large Towns includes a report from Preston which records that documents giving an account of the state of school rooms for the poor accompany it. Other references to this enquiry suggest that it was detailed and wide-ranging, but the documents have so far proved impossible to locate and do not appear to have survived along with the main body of the report. There are many similar instances, often reflecting accidental wastage and loss.

There is also, however, the problem of what Williams (1965) calls a 'selective tradition' in the transmission of culture. Even those who live within a particular period have only partial knowledge of all its character and aspects, and since only some of them will leave behind documentary evidence, what is passed on to future generations is a very fragmented picture. In addition to this, as Williams points out, within any period, some things are given value and emphasis whilst others are not, Beethoven rather than The Beatles for example. There is, too, the problem of more conscious distortion. 'Historical data' may be created, suppressed or destroyed for specific purposes: think of the wartime propaganda machine or the recent alleged epidemic of 'shredding' of official papers. This represents a crucial gap between 'fact' and evidence.

Much of what we know about the past has been selected for us by others on the basis of their judgments of what is important, a process which, as Williams claims, is compounded by continual re-selection and interpretation, and which is influenced by the relationships of different interests in society including class interests. This latter consideration is particularly important in the case of research which focuses on any subordinate group in society (like the working class). Attempts to reconstruct the history of such groups will be influenced by the interpretations and judgments both of the dominant contemporary values and of those which succeed them.

There are dilemmas here for the sociologist. Is the focus of a historical research project constrained and modified by availability of evidence to such an extent that the questions we ask and conclusions we arrive at must be narrower than we would wish? Or is this perhaps an unduly pessimistic view? Certainly it is possible to overstate the case here. There is an alternative strategy illustrated particularly in recent years by developments in labour history and in feminist history, which involves the reading of 'gaps' of silences, the interpretation of the absence of evidence as well as its presence. It may be argued that if we are ever to 'rescue' the nineteenth century of the cotton factory worker, or to understand the significance of sexual divisions in society, this kind of interpolation is essential. It is, nevertheless, not an easy task. How can the silences be read without at least some 'clues' as to their meaning? Can we take these clues from our own knowledge and insights alone or does this impose the present on the past in a way which simply negates the historical enterprise? These are questions to which I shall return elsewhere in this chapter.

A less obvious problem, perhaps, is that those who work with historical documentary evidence have both too little and too much available to them. Your never find exactly what you need; on the other hand where, in the huge amount of nineteenth-century material in particular, do you start? The classification systems of the libraries and record offices may be of little use, although the catalogues are of course indispensable. Many sociologists embark on historical research in order to question current definitions, to uncover the real reasons for the growth and development in particular ways of particular institutions. Research which asks how current definitions of education and knowledge came about, what kinds of competing definitions may have existed and why one set of ideas came to dominate will not find all the answers in files or on shelves marked 'Education', 'Schools', 'DES' or 'Teacher Training'. As I hope to show, there is good reason to believe that for groups of people in the nineteenth century 'education' may not necessarily have been associated with classrooms or schools. There may have been greater emphasis on learning through 'doing', for instance, as when acquiring skills by working alongside those with greater experience; or there may have been a feeling that political involvement, learning about society and how to change it, was more valuable than a formal schooling in 'the three Rs' or their more sophisticated variations. These are just two examples of possible alternative approaches to education. But the categorization of historical documents follows to a large extent the dominant definitions of a particular period and if we are to read silences we need also to look at material which gives little hint that evidence we need may be lurking inside it. The research which forms the basis of this paper led to newspapers, trade union records, Bishop's visitations, factory inspectors' reports, riot depositions and a wide range of other documentation not directly concerned with 'education'.

There are several consequences of this approach. Firstly, one is for much of the time working in the dark. Decisions about what to look at and what to ignore may largely be a hit and miss affair, and the staff of the various institutions may not, through no fault of their own, be able to offer much help. Tell them you are looking at school boards and their operation and they can lead you to the appropriate file. But how can you convey to them possible alternative definitions of education which are themselves dependent on the research for clearer formulation?

This leads to the second consequence, which is that this kind of research is time-consuming, frustrating, often unrewarding, and frequently leads to a feeling of wasted time and effort. It is possible to work for weeks without finding any useful material at all. This may lead to the suggestion that there is, after all, nothing to discover, that the putative events or situations simply did not exist. The temptation to give in to this suggestion should, I believe, be resisted, unless the sources are so completely barren that they yield nothing whatsoever to support the tentative hypotheses of the research. More usually there will be flashes of discovery, fragments of clues, and enough supporting material from secondary sources to convince the researcher that it is indeed necessary to dig deep in order to acquire an understanding of those matters which are 'hidden from history'.

Thirdly, the wide range of material which historical researchers often have to handle means that some kind of sampling, whether deliberate or otherwise, is inevitable. It is obviously impossible to study every document which may include references relevant to the research. Choices have to be made, but on what basis? Secondary works are useful, pointing us in the direction of material which may be relevant, but there are dangers here too. It could be that previous researchers have not always tapped the most useful sources even when their concerns overlap with our own. Yet there may be an unconscious feeling that more unlikely sources will prove disappointing; how otherwise could they have been ignored for so long? We should beware of absorbing a kind of received wisdom about which avenues of investigation are likely to prove worthwhile.

It may be the case that a thorough review of the literature and potential sources can only be followed by a 'dive in at the deep end', an immersion in primary documentary data at an early stage of the research plan. No rigid overall scheme of action is likely to be either possible or adequate in this early phase. The data will itself suggest alternative sources and possible further lines of investigation. Saran (in this volume, page 228) refers to a process of 'abduction' by which total immersion in the data enables us to make 'imaginative leaps' which lead to new avenues of thought. This process is likely to be stifled by any insistence on the need for a fully worked out research plan to be drawn up in advance. Increasing knowledgeability gained from the research process gives insight into the distribution and selection of information and allows more informed choices to be made.

Yet having gained some idea of the kinds of sources which are likely to be most useful, it may still be the case that the documents within a particular class are far too numerous to be covered in their entirety. Newspapers, for example, are an obvious source of information on many aspects of nineteenth-century life, but there have been many of them, they usually appeared weekly, and a large number survive. This means that some kind of selective reading is essential, but how is this to proceed? One method of selection is to focus on 'significant' events or periods, guided by information from secondary sources. We know for example which were the years when Chartism was an important force in the Northern textile areas, and we might therefore expect these same periods to be ones in which trade union and political educational activities were taking place. This approach poses a number of difficulties however. It presupposes that other times and other activities were less significant in relation to the central concerns of the research; it runs the possible risk of interpreting a set of extraordinary circumstances as more generally applicable; and it does not enable us to explain why changes occurred over time, to understand continuities *and* apparent breaks in activity.

An alternative method of sampling may be the adoption of a more random approach, the selection of one newspaper a month, every tenth newspaper, or every newspaper from each alternate year, for example. This method presents difficulties in following up particular stories, in concentrating on periods which we suspect may be exceptionally fertile, and in relating this data to evidence obtained from other sources. This latter point provides us with what may be the best solution to the problem: the use of a variety of sources simultaneously so that an overall pattern begins to emerge which suggests directions for further research. An approach such as this has the advantage of allowing the primary sources to exert most influence on the research, so that its conclusions are less predetermined; but it does inevitably involve a great deal of fishing around almost blindly, which can cause crises of confidence and requires constant awareness of the selective nature of the sources which are actually available.

There can be no 'formula' for decisions of this kind which have to be made in the course of any historical research project. A 'feel' for the period, the relevant questions and the sources is ultimately what guides the methodology of any particular piece of research and this can only properly be gained as part of the research process itself. It should inform all the important decisions, including the issue of where and when the research should stop, itself a form of sampling. Ideally it may be that the research should be considered finished when all the classes of documents relevant to it have been exhausted, but for the nineteenth century at least, with its proliferation of material, this is really not a practical proposition. There is a sense, inevitably, in which the research is over whenever it is time to stop; it has a habit of expanding to fill the space available and contracting accordingly. Whilst not entirely 'scientific' this is probably the case with research of all kinds in most academic disciplines. There is however also a sense in which a kind of law of diminishing returns sets in, a time when the sources, while still fascinating, provide supporting evidence rather than turning up new lines of thought and investigation. This is rarely as final as it sounds; more usually there remain many unanswered questions, but since these threaten to lead into whole new areas and, on a practical level, whole new boxes and rooms full of documents, the decision is taken to call a halt.

It is clearly the case then that the sources themselves do, and must, exert a crucial influence on the research process, but the sources on which we rely in historical research are rarely above suspicion. Their validity and reliability must always be held up for scrutiny. Problems include the operation of the 'selective tradition'; the issue of authenticity; who a document was written for and by; whether it constitutes a first-hand, second-hand or even more remote account; whether confidential or not, public or private, forced or voluntary and so on. These and other considerations are addressed at length elsewhere by other writers and I do not therefore propose to rehearse them all here (see, for example, Gottschalk, *et al,* 1945; Platt, 1981; Johnson, n.d.; and Burgess, 1982, for a longer list of suggested reading).

Theories, 'Facts' and the Role of Interpretation

Many of the problems raised in this paper emphasize the role of the historical researcher as *interpreter.* It is, therefore, the contention here that in spite of the obvious centrality of historical documents to historical research, there is no straightforward sense in which history simply 'speaks for itself'. The collection and presentation of historical material is inevitably selective, and to some extent at least this selection and interpretation relies on the questions asked of the material, or in other words the theoretical perspective which is brought to bear on any particular piece of research. If history is to have any meaning at all, this is clearly unavoidable. There may, for example, be a correct answer to the question of how many working-class children failed to attend elementary school regularly, but how significant is that bare statistic alone? Is it not rather how we arrive at it and what we do with it that renders it important? It has been suggested that scarcity and lack of control of data in historical research may be most successfully overcome by a 'grounded' or inductive strategy — deriving categories and problems from the data itself (for example, the discussion in Platt, 1981). But as one historian comments:

> Those who tried to create theory out of facts never under-stood that it was only theory that could constitute them as facts in the first place. Similarly those who focused history upon the event failed to realize that events are only meaningful in terms of a structure which will establish them as such. (Jones, 1972)

Perhaps the tendency to polarize such approaches into a kind of 'chicken and egg' debate is ultimately unhelpful. Theoretical suppositions and ways of looking at the world will mediate 'facts' and 'historical truths' whilst the raw material of a study will almost inevitably modify questions asked, avenues to be explored, and the framing of theory itself (see Carr, 1964). An insistence on historical 'truth' and historical 'facts' as problematical does not in any case have to imply that historians simply write the past according to their own personal and theoretical preferences. History may only answer the questions that we put to it but we do not necessarily get the answers we expect. Historical documentary evidence has an inconvenient tendency not to fit neatly into a carefully prepared scheme of things. This raises the issue of how such contradictory material is to be handled. Should it lead to a corresponding modification of problems and theories or is it simply to be ignored? Much may depend on the integrity of the researcher, which means that in historical research as in other forms of social enquiry a certain amount has to be taken on trust. There are however, checks available too, such as a reworking of the primary sources, comparison with other research and information from other sources, and perhaps a healthy suspicion of the precise model, the too neat theories, the pat conclusions. The past, like the present, does not fit too easily into little boxes. And although the past does not in any automatic way 'speak for itself' historical documentary evidence might provide its own answers to issues of validity and reliability in sometimes unexpected ways, as the following example shows.

When Chartism was an active force in the Northern textile districts the local press carried regular reports of Chartist meetings and events, as did organs of the radical press such as *The Northern Star*. These reports often conflicted in their accounts of numbers attending and the fervour and quality of the support. A certain amount of exaggeration must be allowed for on both sides and a number of other factors must be taken into consideration when attempting to account for the discrepancy. One interesting point here though is that the traditional, 'establishment' press always stressed the large numbers of 'mere youths' present at such gatherings, with the sometimes overt, sometimes implied suggestion that theirs was not a serious contribution. But other evidence which emerges from the research shows clearly that these 'mere youths' were neither like the teenagers of today nor like the middle-class youth of the nineteenth century. There was no prolonged adolescence through full-time education, and often work commenced at an early age. Young people had similar experiences to older people of labour/capital relations and these were important in their lives. They even to some extent had families to support since *all* contributions to the family economy were essential. Working-class autobiographies show that even very young people felt this responsibility keenly (Vincent, 1981). They did belong to trade unions and their role within them did not go unnoticed. It was reported during the 1853/54 strike and lock-out in Preston that one of the Sunday School Superintendents had kept the girls behind after class and asked them to sign their names that they would have no more to do with the union.[1]

This raises once again a crucial issue for those involved in the study of historical documents. Can the past be understood from the perspectives of the present? Is it possible to recreate the texture of the past, to understand the experiences and relationships of different groups of people in their historical context? More specifically, can insight be gained into the lives and beliefs, hopes and opinions of those groups who have been subordinate in society? Can one uncover the relationship of the working class to education in nineteenth-century Preston and what difficulties does such an endeavour present?

In the same way that theory is important for 'facts' so our twentieth-century perceptions can be useful for understanding other lives and other times. There are dangers in interpreting nineteenth-century material in terms of twentieth-century concepts, but our own insights and experience can sharpen perceptions and raise important sociological questions. Recent attempts to recover women's history probably provide illustrations of both the advantages and the disadvantages of distance (see Purvis, in this volume, page 179 for further discussion of this issue). Whatever the value of hindsight, one cardinal rule must surely be that

> ... whatever questions are brought to historical materials, *historical procedures must be followed* and the material will only answer those questions which are *historically relevant.* (Thompson, 1976)

In other words, questions that we might pose in relation to education in the twentieth century might not be relevant to a study of working-class educational activity over a century ago. As has been pointed out elsewhere (Macfarlane, 1977), one result of studying a society merely through documentary evidence is that the impact of that society is less immediate and less devastating than say the 'culture-shock' of the anthropologist. Many historians and sociologists enquiring into the past are investigating changes and developments in their own societies and may therefore fall into the trap of failing to question whether or not their most basic assumptions about those societies apply to the period under study. In order really to understand the past, acts of imagination are required, but more than this, historical research demands responsiveness to the sources and a willingness to see even the most fundamental concepts overturned.

In recent years historians of education have illustrated the benefits of this kind of approach and have shown the inadequacy of adopting narrow definitions and parameters. 'Education' need not mean schools and classrooms as we now know them and much evidence has been produced which indicates that working-class educational activity in the nineteenth century often explicitly challenged the dominant model (see, for example, Simon, 1974; Johnson, 1979; Harrison, 1961; Thompson, 1968). There may be a danger, however, of a new orthodoxy influencing researchers beginning to work in the field. The research project described in this paper began as a proposal to look at independent working-class educational activity in the nineteenth century and the extent to which this involved a different approach to education from that of the philanthropical provision of the period. The underlying assumption in this case was that the research would focus on a radical section of the working class whose own educational philosophies involved a theoretical rejection of other educational provision. Months of panic when this independent radical working-class educational activity failed to materialize led only slowly to the realization that although it did exist, its form and content was not that which was being sought. There is no 'pure' form of independent working-class educational activity untouched by contact with the middle-classes and untainted by conservative or conventional attitudes, beliefs and aspirations. The equally central hypothesis that working-class engagement in educational activity did not necessarily occur most importantly in 'schools' or 'classrooms' but had a closer connection with areas of everyday life such as work and the family is, however, borne out by the research, which shows that a large number of activities were regarded as important from a working-class point of view. Radical working-class approaches to education do emerge strongly from the source material which, nevertheless, indicates that distinctions between, for example, religion and secularity, formality and informality, class independence and class co-operation, may be overstated.

This is of crucial importance. Revisionist historians (for example, Simon, 1974; Johnson, 1979) have, on the whole, not underestimated the complexities of the working-class relationship to education; nevertheless, their deliberate opposing of conventional accounts with evidence of an alternative, radical tradition in education (in itself an act of recovery of immense significance) means in one sense that they continue to see working-class cultural forms from the viewpoint of the middle classes. This is due to the fact that even when the relationship between working-class educational activity and provided schooling is seen as one of opposition, it is the latter which sets the terms of the debate.

Data obtained from historical documentary evidence relating to nineteenth-century Preston and other towns in the Northern textile area suggests that rather than asking why working-class people rejected provided education it may be more fruitful to begin with some questions which can be summarized briefly as follows:

What kinds of activities were members of the working class involved in during this period as part of their daily lives?

What kinds of knowledge and skills did they feel that they required in order both to participate in these activities and to become involved in others?

Where would they go or what means would they adopt in order to acquire such knowledge and skills?

This 'model' for the research seems to avoid the danger of imposing taken-for-granted twentieth-century definitions in another historical context; at least so far as the major focus of investigation is concerned. But it is important to note that the model itself is inseparable from the actual process of research and has, in fact, emerged from it, as the following section shows.

Whose Account Counts?

It is not too difficult to construct some kind of picture of the social structure and life of a nineteenth-century cotton town with the aid of secondary sources, contemporary histories, trade directories, business records, government reports, maps, census material, newspapers, autobiographies and so on. There may be gaps in the account and unfortunate absences of detail, but the real problem in this research centred on how to answer those questions dealing with working-class attitudes, habits, values, beliefs and aspirations. The 'selective tradition' which operates in the recording, preservation and survival of the past is of central significance here. Working-class people in the nineteenth century were less likely than their middle-class contemporaries to set down written records of their activities and such documents as they did produce had less chance of preservation and survival. Ordinary workers in this period had little power and little control over many aspects of their own lives. Self-conscious recording of their activities was, therefore, not often seen by them as being of immense significance. Nor did they enjoy freedom of expression. Almost every week for many years the letters column of the *Preston Chronicle* included a statement of its reasons for refusing to print letters which had been submitted for publication. This in effect took the form of a blackout on anything which was considered 'subversive' or 'undesirable' in its influence.

Trade union reports and records, along with those of radical associations rarely survive in their entirety, particularly those from around the 1830s and 1840s when membership of such organizations entailed no small degree of risk. It is recorded with regard to the Preston Spinners and Minders Institute that the local authorities were very suspicious of their gatherings and that they were always closely watched by the police, particularly during the 1841 proceedings.

> ... At the meetings of the society, in that year, policemen put in an appearance regularly, to note the way in which matters were going — whether they were in the direction of con-

spiracy and revolt, of Chartism, machinery-breaking etc. or were simply on the side of friendly aid and pacific association.[2]

A constant complaint of working people was the lack of venues in which to carry out their collective activities, and the fact that they were rarely granted access to the 'public' buildings of the town. Between 1823 and 1859 named meeting places of the Spinners and Minders Institute include the 'Green Man', 'Hen and Chickens', 'Grey Horse' or 'Seven Stars', 'Black Bull', 'Black-a-Moors Head', 'Farmers Arms' and the 'Albion' singing rooms.[3] In these circumstances it is not surprising that only fragmentary evidence of their activities remains.

An added difficulty for the researcher investigating aspects of working-class life in the nineteenth century is the importance in this period of an oral tradition which by its very nature goes largely unrecorded. At a time when many workers were not literate, cultural traditions were passed on through families, the church, friendly societies, trade unions and other forms of close association. Books and journals were read aloud in public houses and workplaces. Public addresses, sermons and radical oratory played an important part in the dissemination of information and opinion: Chartist 'lecturers', for example, undertook 'missionary' tours throughout the country. Handbills and pamphlets were usually written in a style conducive to reading aloud, designed to make an impact orally. Ballad singers and theatre groups entertained, informed and provoked debate. There are many illustrations of the importance of folklore and music, as when the aims and attitudes of the Preston workers involved in the 1853/54 strike and lockout were summarized in the songs which formed a part of their response.[4]

Documents which enable a view of the world through the eyes of working-class people do exist, but they are relatively scarce and elusive. In the interest of breadth of information as well as an appreciation of the relationships between different groups in society, it is therefore necessary also to devote considerable attention to the commentary and actions of interested middle-class observers. This frequently results in conflicting evidence which provides on the one hand insights into differences in perception and interests, and on the other, ample illustration of the extent to which historical research demands both interpretation and some kind of theoretical framework on which to hang 'the facts' obtained from historical documentary material.

The 1830s saw a burgeoning of all kinds of educational institutions and activities instigated by the bourgeoisie and aimed at the 'lower orders' in society. These included church and other philanthropic elementary schools for children, evening classes and Sunday schools and the increasingly common Mechanics' Institutes. The working class, however, 'failed' to respond as anticipated to these endeavours. Throughout the years of the existence of the Preston Institution for the Diffusion of Useful Knowledge (the Mechanics' Institute) constant reference was made to this fact. The report of the Seventh Annual Meeting of the Institution regretted:

> that those individuals for whose particular benefit such efforts were originally made do not in greater numbers avail themselves of the proffered advantages ...[5]

At the Thirteenth Annual General Meeting the list of members was said to be as follows:

6 ladies	17 mechanics
14 gentlemen	34 joiners and other operatives
3 bankers	6 youths at school
40 manufacturers	6 factory hands
76 tradesmen	29 miscellaneous
85 clerks and shopmen	

As the report states:

> From this classification it appears that the great bulk of our population who are employed in factories, derive no direct advantage from this valuable institution ...[6]

One speaker, regretting this fact, claimed that 'the working classes seemed to have turned their backs upon learning'. The surviving statements of working people themselves do not suggest that this can have been the case.

In October 1860 the Spinners and Minders Institute sent to the *Preston Chronicle* an appeal for funds and resources to support their newly-established Institute for mutual improvement. The Spinners and Minders had been involved in 'improving' activities on many occasions in the past, but this latest endeavour was on an altogether grander scale, as the following extract shows:

> We have taken a large room, capable of accommodating 1000 persons at least. Already we have expended a large sum of money in re-fittings, and given the room that attractive

appearance calculated to engage the attention of those who attend. We propose, during the winter evenings, to open our rooms as a school, for the especial benefit of our members, and for that purpose we have to purchase a large quantity of school books, copy books, arithmetic, slates, etc; but still a higher class of books are necessary for the study of more elevated and better cultivated minds. Our object is to give factory operatives an opportunity to avail themselves of the time now afforded by the present Factory Act ... To aid us in carrying out the above object, we humbly solicit a donation or a few books, such books to be divested of all religious opinions ...[7]

A second letter to the newspaper claimed that the movement had been 'signally successful', between 1000 and 1100 operatives having joined the Institute. Alongside this letter were printed the contents of a circular sent by the Committee of the Institute to the operative spinners and minders, giving details of donations and books, and including thanks to donors. It goes on to say:

Two of those who have denied us, and one of our supporters, believe that the Mechanics' Institution is sufficient to meet all the requirements of the working classes; granting that it is so — why was it not erected in a situation more convenient for working men, for whose especial benefit, some parties contend, it was established? or why not long since opened branches in various parts of the town, at a cheaper rate than what is charged at the present time, 10s. per year? It is a well-known fact which requires no explanation, that there is a natural shyness amongst the working classes in mixing with the middle and higher classes. We can accommodate comfortably 1000 persons in our Institute. We propose to establish a very fair library for the edification of our own classes ...[8]

The educational activities of the Operative Spinners and Minders Institute were obviously not a flash in the pan. In May 1863 the *Chronicle* reported that the Secretary, Mr. Banks, had written to the guardians requesting that they would grant them a sum of money in order to employ teachers at the Institute. The application was considered by the Labour Committee of the guardians, when it was resolved 'that the matter could not be entertained by them'.[9]

Clearly the lack of response to the Mechanics' Institute was not simply, or even largely, due to lack of interest in education on the part of working people and indeed references to their activities throughout the nineteenth century support this claim. The early cotton unions, the Preston Operative Radical Association and the Chartist Association all had reading rooms, classes and lectures and all emphasized the importance of education to the workers.[10]

Frequent references occur in speeches made at workers' gatherings to the lack of resources and time for education for themselves and their children, and this seemed to be an important issue for those who supported moves to reduce working hours. Following the Ten Hours Act many reports of increased numbers at evening schools and classes appear in the press and in business records, like the one reproduced below:

> On Wednesday evening a meeting of factory operatives was held at Mr. Hool's Temperance Hotel, to devise plans for improving the time obtained by the passing of the Ten Hours' Bill. It was finally agreed to open a school for mutual instruction, in reading, writing, arithmetic, and the English grammar, and, if possible, to have a newsroom and lectures . . .[11]

Self-help activities flourished, as shown in this entry from the journal of the chaplain to the Preston House of Correction:

> H.H. was sentenced to 2 months' imprisonment at the last sessions. In my conversations with him I had been struck with a most uncouth appearance, dialect, and manner, combined with information quite unusual in one of his station. Today he gave me the following account —
>
>> I am forty-four years old. I worked at the print works at A — for 11s. a week. I have a wife and seven children. I went first to a Baptist and then to a Swedenborgian Sunday School until I was sixteen. I learned to read and write. I married when I was twenty-one. I was always fond of reading. I read all Swedenborg's works before I was married. Afterwards I read Goldsmith, Hume and Smollett. For thirteen or fourteen years I earned from 20s. to 30s. a week; and I spent all I could spare in books, although I drank a little occasionally. My books altogether cost me between £50 and £60. In botany alone I spent more than £10. After I read Hume and Smollett I tried to master Guthrie's Geography; then I read Goldsmith's Greece and Rome; then Rollin's Ancient His-

tory; then I bought Goldsmith's Natural History, edited by Brown. I joined a chemical society at A —, and bought Murray's Elementary Chemistry and Ure's Chemical Dictionaries. I took 20s. worth of Dr. Adam Clarke's New Testament. When I took to botany the Swedenborgian minister said a little Greek would assist me and he made me a present of a Greek Testament; after that I got one of Bagster's editions, Greek and English; and I also bought two Greek 'lexicons'. The Swedenborgian minister lent me Frey's Hebrew lexicon, and I made some way in it so that when reading theology I could make out any Hebrew words. I made most labour at botany, and got so far as to understand the cryptogamous plants. I only studied the system of Linnaeus; though Smith's Grammar contained both his system and Jussieu's ...[12]

According to the conventional, most readily available sources, the educational condition of Preston's working class can be summarized in Clay's words as:

ignorance ... (which) has its great dark masses sometimes contrasted, not relieved, with strange and useless glimmerings of light.[13]

Yet a more flexible approach to the sources, an emphasis on alternative kinds of documentary evidence, yields quite another impression. The evidence, in short, is conflicting, and why should this surprise us? If different groups in society have different interests, different cultures and different ways of looking at the world, then surely their accounts will also vary. It is important to realize that not only educational development but the very definition of education itself has been constructed in specific social and historical contexts, through struggle and conflict. The operation of the 'selective tradition' in the transmission of culture provides its own illustration of the process. Definitions which ultimately do not prevail are 'hidden' from us and present special problems of recovery.

This argument does not necessarily imply that working-class educational aims and activities were deliberately suppressed by more powerful forces; what I am suggesting is that they were not understood as 'education', that they simply failed to fit the definitional requirements of the word. There were a variety of reasons why this should have been the case.

'Education' as seen by those who constructed philanthropic and, later, state provision was a formal process which took place in institutions approved for the purpose. It was age-specific and often sex-specific and involved the transmission of narrowly defined knowledge supposedly devoid of all political or 'prejudiced' taint. It could only be guided and organized by those of a higher culture and intellect. On all these points, activities which were seen as educational by the working class often fell short (see, for example, Simon, 1974; Johnson, 1979; Harrison, 1961). A description of educational facilities in the city of Manchester in 1842 contained this paragraph:

> A social hall has been recently erected by some of the followers of Mr. Robert Owen, but as it is much used for political meetings and the propagation of peculiar opinions, it cannot be described as an ordinary educational institution.[14]

This is an exceptionally explicit expression of what was more usually a taken-for-granted assumption and has obvious implications for researchers looking for evidence of educational activity.

The conflict of interests and definitions is well illustrated by many of the remarks of those workers who were involved in radical political activity. In 1837 a cotton operatives' union urged members to remain with them and announced that if they did they would be sent to school 'in order to learn what were their rights'.[15] Later in the same year a quarterly meeting of the Preston Operative Radical Association reported the establishment of a Reading Room, delivery of a series of lectures and dissemination of other information to 'obtain those rights and liberties which have so long and so unjustly been kept from us'.[16] The local Chartist Association distributed tracts containing political knowledge throughout the 1830s and 1840s, which they saw as 'a grand auxiliary to the cause'.[17] At times the conflict over what constituted 'ignorance' and 'knowledge' was more explicitly expressed, as in the following extract from a speech made by one of the leaders of the 1844 strike and lock-out:

> They tell us the working classes are ignorant, that we don't understand the laws by which capital and labour are regulated. What is there about the matter we don't understand? ... when the working classes begin to want more money they are taunted about their ignorance. These political economists, however, will fail to convince you that 18s. a week is preferable to 20s. We all have brains enough to know what would be best for us in that respect, whatever Mr. Turner or

Sir James Kay-Shuttleworth may say ... Political economy. What is it? the doctrine of buying cheap and selling dear ... The sooner we can rout out political economy from the world, the better it will be for the working classes of this country.[18]

James Waddington, also involved in the strike, was even more explicit as the following report of his speech shows. It began:

We were told that the only remedy for our difficulties was the education of the people — especially an education in political economy. Now he contended that in the present condition of society, without an alteration of the relationship between capital and labour, the education of the people would only make strikes more frequent than they were, because as you educate the people you make them less capable of bearing tyranny and of submitting to oppression and degradation (Hear, Hear). Then he said that education was not preventative of strikes unless that education should teach the people of this country how to make labour and capital identical. It was of no use saying — for this was a favourite teaching of the manufacturers — that their interests were identical. When they told them that, they told them what ought to be, but not what is. (Hear, Hear) The interests of labour and capital were *not* identical with each other. The interest of capital was to buy labour as cheap as possible ... The interest of the labourer was to sell his labour as high as he could.[19]

As early as 1836 a speaker at a meeting of the Cotton Spinners' Union had expatiated upon the benefits of education

... as opening the eyes of those who had the opportunity of acquiring it, to a proper consciousness of their own importance in society, and of the comparative insignificance of their adversaries who now lorded and tyrannised over them.[20]

The middle classes on the other hand stressed the power of 'education' to counter such views. Speaking of self-educated radicals Clay claimed that:

The mysteries of spelling and grammar are impenetrable to them, but they will undertake to unloose the knottiest points of policy. Surely it is by the spread of education that the power and importance of these 'blind leaders of the blind' is to be counteracted.[21]

There is, therefore, evidence of working-class approaches to education in the nineteenth century which differ from those of the middle-class providers. It is in this context that the question 'whose account counts?' becomes particularly relevant and has methodological implications. One possible research strategy is to attempt to reconcile different accounts, to resolve the problem of conflicting definitions, to arrive at the 'correct' answer, the 'truth'. A more appropriate response is to accept that no general consensual version of history is possible, and that monolithic accounts are unlikely to be either adequate or satisfactory. Different groups do have different interests, experiences and cultural forms, and do provide alternative definitions and accounts of these. The research project described in this chapter therefore involved a clear guiding principle: it set out quite explicitly to recover working-class experiences of education and as a result has given priority to working-class accounts.

How far the kinds of activities engaged in by those members of the working class whose statements survive are typical of the class as a whole is another question. Does the very nature of the documents which give us this insight mean that they constitute the testimony only of exceptional people? To what extent do leaders represent movements as a whole? There are several ways of dealing with these problems. Firstly, by asking what is meant by 'representative'. In statistical terms we are unlikely to be able to make a statement one way or the other; the evidence is too fragmentary and inconclusive. But even minority movements can have enormous social significance and are often tacitly supported by many people who have neither the time nor the resources to be among the most vocal. The documents quoted above are 'representative' in the sense that they provide an articulation of viewpoints or movements which clearly were important, judging by their persistence both in Preston and nationally (as other research has shown) and by middle-class reaction and concern. Secondly, directly autobiographical material like diaries and memoirs should be used with caution and in conjunction with other sources. Thirdly, we can regretfully accept the difficulty of gaining insight into the everyday lives, experiences, beliefs and motivations of the great mass of 'ordinary people'. We are at best interpreting half-clues, relying on information not directly commissioned by us. This inevitably leads to some superficiality. For in-depth analyses and statements we are to a large extent dependent on those who, for whatever reason, are prepared to speak on behalf of others. This, it must be acknowledged, is also the case with contemporary research. Fourthly, we should abandon the tendency to polarize arguments and

oppose activities without at the same time recognizing the relationships between them. The truly 'extreme' position is a rare one. It
all comes back to the necessity to avoid imposing our own concepts
on the source material in a way that the sources themselves will not
bear. Neither the lifestyle and cultural modes of the middle classes
nor those of the working class existed in isolation. Each was
influenced, modified and transformed by those of the other. If we
accept, as the evidence suggests we must, that even radical working
class leaders with 'alternative' views on education had often attended
church elementary schools, were sometimes fervent Methodists,
frequently had aspirations to 'respectability' and were in many cases
loyal to the company for which they worked as well as trying to
change what they saw as an unacceptable, exploitative, social structure, then we begin to realize the futility of seeking to establish
whether or not they were representatives of an alternative culture
which can in some way be measured for ideological correctness.
Finally, referencing and indication of the sources of the claims we
make is crucial. The evidence is presented; readers can decide how
convincing it is and, if appropriate, supply evidence of their own to
either support or refute it. This is after all how our knowledge of the
past progresses.

Conclusion

All research contains gaps; some due to theoretical oversight, others
to lack of material and inadequacy of sources, still others to constraints of time, energy and expertise. There is one important sense in
which the work discussed here is not representative of working-class
life and activity in the nineteenth century: women play less of a role
in it than men. This research, by historical accident, did not begin as a
specifically feminist endeavour; the scarcity of evidence relating
directly to women's lives and experiences therefore meant that
bringing their concerns to the forefront would have entailed the
abandonment of the project as it stood and the adoption of a radically
different approach. Since this fact itself did not emerge clearly until an
advanced stage of the research had been reached, a complete reworking of it was never really a serious proposition. There *are* important
questions to be answered about female involvement in working class
educational activity in the nineteenth century whose neglect hopefully does not entirely invalidate the current research enterprise.

It should be clear from this review of some of the problems

involved in the collection, analysis and use of historical documentary evidence that this activity, no less than other forms of social research, involves a process of interaction. The interaction in this instance takes place not directly between the researcher and the researched, but between the researcher and the sources, which are both acted on and exert their own influence on the research process and outcome. Interpretation and meaning are as central here as ever.

There is another sense too in which the personal cannot be ruled out in historical research. It is unfortunately the case that dreadful handwriting, the later numbers of two thousand newspapers, and the new box of sources discovered when that part of the research was approaching completion, may not always receive the same diligent perusal granted to other material. The intention is not to defend such lapses; any researcher whose intentions are 'honourable' will attempt to minimize their effect, but in order to do just this we must be prepared to acknowledge that the human element intrudes even into our relationships with dusty documents, and other relics of the past.

Any attempt to outline the problems caused by a particular approach to research may seem to lead to the conclusion that the whole enterprise is impossible and should immediately be abandoned. This would surely be unduly pessimistic. All social research is by its very nature problematical; historical investigation need not produce results of any less validity than those of any other form of social enquiry. Furthermore, to neglect a line of enquiry simply because of the methodological problems posed by it is to let methods determine problems in a most undesirable way. There is much we need to know about the past; the collection and analysis of historical documentary evidence may guide us towards at least some of the answers.

Acknowledgements

I should like to thank participants at the July 1983 Whitelands College Workshop on Qualitative Methodology and the Study of Education for their assistance in clarifying some of the issues raised in this chapter. I should also like to thank Bob Burgess for inviting me to contribute, and Tim O'Shea for his support and helpful comments.

Notes

1 *Preston Chronicle*, 29 October 1853.
2 HEWITSON, A. (1883) *History of Preston.*

3 *Ibid.*
4 See for example, Various Writers (1887) *Fortunes Made in Business,* London; Ashworth Cuttings in the Lancashire Record Office, DDPr 138/87a. *Household Words,* 10 December, 1853; THOMPSON (1968) and VINCENT (1981) give other examples.
5 *Preston Chronicle,* 10 October, 1835.
6 *Ibid.,* 9 October, 1841.
7 *Ibid.,* 20 October, 1860.
8 *Ibid.,* 22 December, 1860.
9 *Ibid.,* 23 May, 1863.
10 See for example, *Preston Chronicle,* 26 November, 1836; *Ibid,* 11 November, 1837; BANKS, T. (1894) *A Short Sketch of the Cotton Trade of Preston for the Last Sixty-Seven Years,* Preston; *Northern Star,* 24 June, 1848.
11 *Preston Chronicle,* 10 July, 1847.
12 1844 Report of the Chaplain of the Preston House of Correction, Lancashire Record Office, QGR/2/39.
13 *Ibid.*
14 *Illustrated Itinerary of Lancashire,* 1842, Lancashire Record Office.
15 *Preston Chronicle,* 28 January 1837.
16 *Ibid.,* 11 November, 1837.
17 *Northern Star,* 31 October, 1840.
18 *Preston Guardian,* 28 January, 1854.
19 *Ibid.,* 15 March, 1854.
20 *Preston Chronicle,* 26 November, 1836.
21 1840 Report of the Chaplain of the Preston House of Correction, Lancashire Record Office, QGR/2/31.

References

BURGESS, R.G. (Ed.) (1982) *Field Research: a Sourcebook and Field Manual,* London, George Allen and Unwin.
CARR, E.H. (1964) *What is History?* Harmondsworth, Penguin.
GOTTSCHALK, L. et al. (1945) *The Use of Personal Documents in History, Anthropology and Sociology,* Bulletin No. 53, New York, Social Science Research Council, pp. 79–175.
HARRISON, J.F.C. (1961) *Learning and Living 1790–1960,* London, Routledge and Kegan Paul.
JOHNSON, R. (1979) 'Really useful knowledge: radical education and working-class culture 1790–1848' in CLARKE, J. et al (Eds.) *Working Class Culture,* London, Hutchinson, pp. 75–102.
JOHNSON, R. (n.d.) *The Blue Books and Education, 1816–1896: The Critical Reading of Official Sources,* Birmingham, Centre for Contemporary Cultural Studies, Occasional Papers.
JONES, G.S. (1972) 'History: the poverty of empiricism' in BLACKBURN, R. (Ed.) *Ideology in Social Science,* London, Fontana, pp. 97–115.
McCANN, W.P. (1970) 'Trade unionists, artisans and the 1870 Education Act', *British Journal of Educational Studies,* 18, 2, pp. 134–50.

MacFarlane, A. (1977) 'History, anthropology and the study of communities', *Social History*, 5, pp. 631–52.

Mills, C.W. (1959) *The Sociological Imagination*, New York, Oxford University Press.

Platt, J. (1981) 'Reading data: evidence and proof in documentary research', parts 1 and 2, *Sociological Review*, 29, 1, pp. 31–66.

Simon, B. (1974) *The Two Nations and the Educational Structure 1780–1870*, London, Lawrence and Wishart.

Thompson, E.P. (1968) *The Making of the English Working Class*, Harmondsworth, Penguin.

Thompson, E.P. (1976) 'On history, sociology and historical relevance', *British Journal of Sociology*, 27, 3, pp. 387–402.

Vincent, D. (1981) *Bread, Knowledge and Freedom: A Study of Nineteenth-Century Working Class Autobiography*, London, Europa.

Williams, R. (1965) *The Long Revolution*, Harmondsworth, Penguin.

7   Reflections Upon Doing Historical Documentary Research From a Feminist Perspective

June Purvis

Introduction

For the last five years or so, I have been engaged in documentary research into the education of working-class women in nineteenth-century England.[1] My education, training and teaching experience has, however, been as a sociologist, not a historian. Yet I wanted to undertake historical research and specifically to focus upon women. My interest in researching women in the past meant that it was impossible for me to avoid contemporary interest in feminism. Thus I also became involved in discussing some of the issues in present-day feminist debates, attending feminist conferences and reading contemporary feminist literature. What I had to confront, therefore, was not just the vast outpourings of feminist scholarship during the last decade but also the impact of feminism upon my own views and my own experience. This impact has been very significant for me as a person and for the shaping of my research. Of equal, or greater, importance for shaping my research has been the encouragement and help given to me by my supervisor, who is herself a feminist. I could discuss ideas with her and write papers in an atmosphere that was exploratory and supportive rather than closed and conflictual. My good fortune in this has frequently been illustrated for me when I compare my experiences with those of other feminist researchers I know who have told me about 'battles' with supervisors who were unsympathetic to a feminist perspective. Perhaps first of all I should attempt to define what I mean by 'feminism' and 'feminist research'.

Feminist Research

A number of definitions of feminism have been offered. Janet Radcliffe-Richards (1980, p. 1), for example, argues that the essence of feminism is the belief that women suffer from systematic social injustices because of their sex. Ann Oakley (1981a, p. 335) suggests that feminism is about putting women first — about judging their interests to be important and insufficiently represented and accommodated within mainstream politics and the academic world. Dale Spender (1982, p. 7) claims that a feminist is a woman who does not accept man's socially-sanctioned view of himself and that feminism refers to the alternative meanings put forward by feminists. Feminism involves all of the things that are offered in these definitions, but it is also important to emphasize that feminism is not just a set of beliefs or a particular perspective — it is a political movement. And as a political movement it seeks certain changes, in particular the eradication of the injustices that women experience because of their sex.

Just how one defines feminism is obviously related to how one defines feminist research. It is important to note, however, that research about women is not *necessarily* feminist research. One may write about women without adopting a feminist perspective. Neither is feminist research something that is confined to the academic world (Reuben, 1978, p. 228). Many feminist researchers do not hold academic posts. It may be, as Kelly (1978, p. 225) has suggested, that it is much easier to say what feminist research is not, than what it is. However, for me, feminist research involves, above all else, a questioning of the form and content of knowledge in our society since it is claimed that this knowledge is primarily made by men and created through the eyes of men. And within the academic world, feminist research claims that 'mainstream' research operates within a male-centred paradigm where man and man's experiences are taken as the norm. Consequently within 'mainstream' research women tend to be hidden or marginalized or, if present at all, to be represented through the perspective of men. As Dorothy Smith (1979, p. 138) has argued, the forms of thought, the concepts and vocabulary of academic discourse are a landscape in which 'women are strangers' since women had no part in its making. In particular she criticizes sociology for excluding the concerns and perspectives of women. Similarly, Margaret Stacey (1981 and 1983) suggests that sociology is a male-dominated discipline in which the boundaries and conceptual tools are devized by men and about the concerns of men. Consequently 'mainstream' academic research is often called 'malestream' research by many feminists.

Feminist research involves then a questioning of many of the sexist assumptions of 'man-made' knowledge. In particular, it differs from 'mainstream' or 'malestream' knowledge in regard to (a) the questions that are regarded as of primary interest and (b) the methodological framework that is used. Let us explore this issue a little further.

Feminist research seeks to bring 'women's issues' (Daniels, 1975, p. 369) into the academic disciplines, to make women visible. Oakley (1974), for example, argues:

> A feminist perspective consists of keeping in the forefront of one's mind the lifestyles, activities and interests of more than half of humanity — women. Many different arguments or blueprints for a sexually egalitarian society can be, and have been, constructed on this basis ... their common focus is on making visible the invisible: bringing women 'out from under' into the twin spheres of social reality and cultural belief-systems. (p. 3)

But much more than simply making women visible is involved since feminists may also study men. In particular, I would like to suggest that in feminist research, the primary questions focus around the power relations between the sexes, the sexual division of labour and the way these affect the lives of men and women. A common assumption within feminism generally is that women are oppressed, in a variety of ways, by men, and the feminist researcher will obviously be sensitive to this issue. Thus 'patriarchy', that process by which men dominate and exercise control over women, is a common concept in feminist research.[2] However, the feminist researcher will also be aware that patriarchy is often a 'catch-all' phrase, and that one will expect to find 'spaces' where patriarchy does not apply and 'resistance' from women at some forms of patriarchal control. Rowbotham (1979) encapsulates some of these problems when she notes that:

> 'Patriarchy' implies a structure which is fixed, rather than the kaleidoscope of forms within which women and men have encountered one another. It does not carry any notion of how women might act to transform their situation as a sex. Nor does it even convey a sense of how women have resolutely manoeuvred for a better position within the general context

of subordination — by shifting for themselves, turning the tables, ruling the roost, wearing the trousers, hen-pecking, gossiping, bustling, or (in the words of a woman I once overheard) just 'going drip, drip at him'. (p. 970)

In addition to all these issues, feminist researchers often try to make recommendations or draw out the complexities of their work in a way that will help other women to analyze their situation.

The methodological framework within which feminist research is conducted differs from malestream research in a number of ways. First of all, an important premise is that *women must not only be made visible but also heard.* Thus it is frequently stressed that an attempt must be made to capture the personal experience of women and to let women's voices be recorded since this will challenge the male paradigms that have governed research so far. Duelli Klein (1983), for example, notes:

> 'Feminist' for me implies assuming a perspective in which women's experiences, ideas and needs (different and differing as they may be) are valid in their own right, and androcentric-ity — man-as-the-norm — stops being the only recognized frame of reference for human beings. (p. 89)

The emphasis upon letting women's voices be heard has led to a tendency to adopt certain research techniques such as participant observation and interviewing rather than quantitative analysis.[3] For the historian, however, especially the historian researching the distant past, letting women's voices be heard can be a problem. And this is a point I will come back to later.

A second important methodological premise of feminist research is that *the primary audience is women.* This does not mean, of course, that men are not part of the audience — many feminist researchers hope they will be. But men are not the primary audience, and neither are academics. Since the main audience is women, the hope is often expressed that the research will help women to understand their situation and perhaps change it. Westkott (1983) and Leonard (1983), for example, argue that women's studies is linked to the wider political movement of feminism and that it essentially involves a strategy for change in the lives of the female students. And other writers make recommendations for change that they think will help improve the situation of women. Downing (1981, p. 100), for example, ends her article on an analysis of secretarial work by suggesting that if women wish to preserve their hard-won rights to financial independence through paid employment, then the only solution is collective organization with other women: trade unions, she continues, will only cease to be male-dominated when women join and change them from within to defend their interests as working women.

A third important aspect of the methodological framework of feminist research is *a questioning of many of the assumptions embodied in 'malestream' academic research.* Some of the most common assumptions that have been questioned by feminists include the following — though this is by no means an exhaustive list:

(a)   The distinction between 'objective' and 'subjective' knowledge is frequently criticized as being an arbitrary distinction that is based on male standards. In traditional mainstream research, 'objective' knowledge is seen as the only form of 'scholarly' and 'rational' enquiry, and 'subjective' knowledge and personal experience are considered as outside the boundaries of academic research. A number of writers have questioned this basic assumption. Rich (1980, p. 241), for example, points out that even science (which we might regard as the epitome of 'objective' knowledge) is not 'objective' but value-laden with biases that are white and male, racist and sexist. Others (for example, Stanley and Wise, 1979 and 1983, and Du Bois 1983) argue that subjective knowledge and personal experience are an integral part of the research process and that the polarization into 'objective' and 'subjective' knowledge only falsifies the experience and reality of life. And Morgan (1981, p. 97) raises the issue of how far academic discourse is in fact a male discourse which shelters behind labels such as 'rationality', 'scientific' or 'scholarly'.

(b)   The hierarchies of knowledge within most academic work are frequently questioned too as being hierarchies that are based on knowledge that relates to only one half of the human race, i.e., men. Dorothy Smith (1978, p. 287), for example, speaks about women's exclusion from man's culture and notes that at the university level it is men who occupy positions of dominance in regard to such things as setting standards, producing social knowledge, acting as 'gatekeepers' over what is admitted into the system of distribution, innovating in thought or knowledge or values: as a result, the perspectives and interests of one sex and one class, i.e., middle-class men, are overwhelmingly represented in mainstream writings.

(c) The classifications of knowledge within mainstream thought are no longer accepted by many feminists. Dale Spender, for example, in *Women of Ideas and What Men Have Done to Them* (1982) argues that since men have ordered and controlled knowledge in their own interests and women's ways of classifying and analyzing the world have been repeatedly erased, it would be inappropriate for her to continue with conventional male practices when constructing an index for the subject matter of her book. So she attempts to make up categories as they relate to women, even though this necessitates making up some new terms. Some of the new categories for the index include the following:— 'burial of women's contributions' (p. 575), 'completion complex (i.e., the incompleteness of a woman without a man)' (p. 575), and 'theft of women's resources' (p. 580).

(d) The language in which mainstream academic research is conducted is increasingly being questioned by feminists. It is not just the use of words such as 'he' and 'mankind' to refer to men and women, and the substitution of non-sexist words such as 's/he', 'they' and 'humanity' that has been raised. Some writers such as Dale Spender (1980), assert that language has been created within a patriarchal order and that it is a source of oppression for women. Thus words associated with women, she continues, carry a lower status than those associated with men, and, in addition, words associated with women often carry a sexual stigma which transmits and reinforces the unequal relations between the sexes. Words such as 'bachelor' and 'spinster', for example, denote unmarried adults: but while the former presents a positive image for males, the latter is negative for females (p. 17). While Spender's claim that language itself is oppressive for women has been challenged by some writers (see, for example, Black and Coward, 1981), feminist researchers have undoubtedly sensitized the academic community to the sexist nature of much academic discourse. The use of the word 'he' to refer to men and women perpetuates the idea of man-as-the-norm in our language, and serves only to hide and marginalize the presence of women.

(e) The concepts used in most academic discourse are questioned too. 'Social class', for example, has often been criticized as a concept that has been defined in relation to the occupation, income and lifestyle held by men. Married women are given no independent social class ranking but are usually subsumed 'within' the social ranking of their husbands.[4] The idea of a 'career' within an occupation or profession is another concept that has been defined in relation to the lifestyles of men. Acker (1983, p. 129), for example, in a review of the sociological work on women and teaching, notes that women teachers are 'almost inevitably' discussed in terms of their marital status: whenever reasons are advanced for 'lack of ambition' in a teaching career, marriage is always cited as a reason, even when not accompanied by any empirical evidence comparing single and married women. Yet she found no published sources which discussed any conflicts that married men might experience in regard to career and marital commitments:

> Nor do researchers remark on the assistance men's families might provide towards fulfilling career ambitions. The literature on academic and certain other professional workers (and countless book prefaces) suggests that men are often enabled to immerse themselves fully in their careers because they have a 70-hour-a-week housewife backing them up. (p. 129)

A fourth important aspect of the methodological framework of feminist research is that the *research itself should be written up in an 'accessible' style* that can be read by the primary audience of women rather than an 'academic' style that will be read mainly by an elite of experts. Roberts (1981, p. 26), for example, notes that there is little point in feminist sociologists writing up their research in a type of academic discourse that can only be understood by a 'coterie of sociologists'.

A Challenge to 'Men's Studies'

Overall then, my introduction to organized feminism as a political movement and my reading of the writings of feminists sensitized me to certain issues during the time that I was collecting my research data and attempting to write it up. I became increasingly aware that if one used a feminist perspective when undertaking historical documentary research then this was a part of a wider process of challenging male definitions of knowledge. In the immortal words of the title of one of Dale Spender's edited collections of readings, a feminist perspective in any of the academic disciplines, whether it was history, sociology, education, philosophy, psychology, political science, anthropology, law, medicine, biology or science meant 'Men's Studies Modified' (1981).

I began to read feminist history, which is a booming area of study in this country,[5] as well as feminist sociology. In particular, I became aware of the need for women to know their own history and to use that history to make a point about the position of women in our society today. Today it is frequently assumed that women are entering the labour force in large numbers for the first time. Yet when I began collecting my research material, I became aware of the fact that working-class women had never left paid work. The jobs that women do today are frequently characterized as 'women's work' yet in nineteenth century England, women were engaged in jobs that today are seen as 'men's work', such as coal-mining (see John, 1980). Examples like this revealed only too well that when I was researching the education of working-class women in the nineteenth century, I must continually question what 'mainstream' male-defined history had to say.

My reading of mainstream academic texts in the history of education revealed that little attention had been given to women, especially working-class women.[6] And my curiosity was aroused. Initially, I began an exploratory search with this question in my mind — were working-class women to be found in various forms of nineteenth-century adult education or not? As my research developed and I found evidence of their presence, and as I read feminist literature, the question I was asking began to change. In particular, I became interested in the relationships between the middle-class providers of education and the working-class adults who were the recipients of such provision, and the relationships between working-class men and women. As I became more involved in my research and in further reading, the question was narrowed down even further — what are the specific types of relations between the sexes constructed by the middle class for the working class in various forms of adult education provision? This is a question to which I will return later.

What I shall do in the rest of this paper is explore some of the problems I encountered when undertaking my research, and when organizing and interpreting my material. Let us look at the former issue first of all.

Problems of Undertaking Research

I can well remember the bewilderment, and yet excitement, of that first term when I began my reading of documents of various kinds in the British Library. I had not undertaken any historical research before, and I had to learn, as Alison Andrew notes (in this volume, page 153), simple techniques such as acquainting myself with the organization of publications in not only the British Library but also in the other institutions I visited. Overall, I think the problems of undertaking my research may be grouped into two major areas — deciding the scope of my research and the consultation of sources.

Deciding the Scope of my Research

When I first began my research, I intended to cover the whole of nineteenth-century England and to look at all forms of adult education provision for working-class women. Such a scheme was far too grandiose! As my research proceeded I found that I had to make choices about what I should study in depth.

Some of the choices I made involved the following. First of all, I had to decide whether to focus upon forms of adult education provided by the middle class for working-class women or forms of education organized by working-class women themselves. Within the latter, one might include such things as mutual improvement societies, self-help groups or classes offered by the Women's Co-operative Guild, established in 1883, and usually regarded as the first separatist working-class women's organization (Gaffin, 1977, p. 14). Now it was difficult to focus upon forms of education provided by working-class women themselves since, though many written records exist about the activities of the Women's Co-operative Guild, I could find hardly any written records about mutual improvement or self-help groups. This does not mean, of course, that the latter did not exist. They very probably did. But any record of the meetings of such groups may have been oral rather than written. And any written records that did exist may have been destroyed as 'worthless' documents, of no interest to posterity. I decided, therefore, to focus upon those forms of adult education for working-class women for which I could find plenty of written texts, i.e., that provision offered by the middle class.

A second choice I had to make was whether to cover all forms of adult education offered by the middle class to working-class women or whether to concentrate upon a few. Initially, I decided on the former course, and collected much information about a range of formal and informal educational forms — such as adult Sunday schools, evening classes, Bible classes, mechanics' institutes and working men's colleges. I also came across references to classes for women in some of the political, rather than educational, movements such as co-operation and socialism. The Owenite movement, for example, one of the most popular socialist movements during the first half of the nineteenth century, offered a variety of educational programmes, including classes for women. While spanning a wide range of educational forms gave me a 'feel' for the nineteenth century and greatly aided my understanding of what was going on at that time, I found I had to narrow my focus. Thus I decided to concentrate upon the major adult education movements of the nineteenth century in which the middle class were active providers — the Mechanics' Institute Movement and the Working Men's College Movement.

A third choice I confronted was whether a comparison between the education of working-class women in these adult education movements with the education of middle-class women, especially in higher education, would be fruitful. I did undertake some research into the struggle of middle-class women to enter the masculine stronghold of the universities (Purvis, 1981a, pp. 57–61). I found that as early as 1828, women had been allowed to attend the lectures for male undergraduates at King's College and University College, London, but that the struggle to enter the ancient Universities of Oxford and Cambridge became particularly mobilized in the late 1860s and 1870s. The fact that women students at these two universities were not awarded degrees on the same terms as men until 1919 and 1947 respectively indicated that here was a rich field for feminist research. However, the theme of middle-class women in higher education had already received a great deal of attention from other writers, and so I decided not to cover the topic. The theme of the education of working-class women had, however, been neglected at all levels, and so I decided to concentrate upon this.

A fourth choice was whether to focus upon mechanics' institutes and working men's and working women's colleges (a few single sex colleges for women were established within the Working Men's College Movement) in urban or rural areas, and whether to investigate regional differences. To some extent my choice was dictated by where the institutes and colleges were established and whether any written records existed. By 1841, for example, it has been estimated that 261 mechanics' institutes were in existence with the largest concentration — about 22 per cent — being in the West Riding and in Lancashire (Kelly, 1957, p. 230). In 1849, in the Yorkshire and Lancashire institutes alone, some 1200 and 600 women are recorded respectively (Tylecote, 1957, p. 265). Fortunately, the records of many of the Yorkshire institutes, as well as some of the larger

Lancashire institutes, such as the one at Manchester, have been well preserved. And I therefore studied these documents in detail. However, I was diligent about trying to find out about mechanics, institutes in other urban centres, such as London, as well as institutes in rural areas. When I found that a mechanics' institute had existed in addition to those institutes that I had already read about, I usually wrote to the local records office to enquire whether any documents, written or visual, had survived. Sometimes, some documents were found, sometimes not.

As my research proceeded, I found I could not examine the education of working-class women without also looking at their schooling as girls. The state of the latter helped, in many ways, to set the conditions of entry into adult education and to influence the kinds of curricula that might be offered. I also found that it was impossible to write about the education of working-class women without reference to the various ideologies about women's social and economic position in society.

In particular, I have suggested (Purvis, 1981a, pp. 45–51) that a 'domestic ideology' about women, held by the bourgeoisie, was the dominant ideology about women's position in the nineteenth century. A number of assumptions were embedded in this domestic ideology. First of all, it was assumed that women should ideally be located within the private sphere of the home as full-time wives and mothers while men would be located within the public sphere of waged work, earning sufficient to support an economically dependent wife and any children. Secondly, it was assumed that women were 'relative' beings, defined in relation to men and children rather than as autonomous individuals in their own right. Thirdly, it was assumed that women were 'inferior' to men and that they should be 'subordinate' to men. Perhaps the epitome of these beliefs regarding women's position may be found in some sentences uttered by Dr. Withers Moore in 1886 when he addressed the British Medical Association on the inappropriateness of higher education for women:

> That one truism says it all — women are made and meant to be, not men, but mothers of men. A noble mother, a noble wife — are not these the designations in which we find the highest ideal of noble womanhood? Woman was formed to be man's helpmeet, not his rival; heart, not head, sustainer, not leader. (p. 315)

Bourgeois domestic ideology formed part of the context within which educational classes for working-class women were established and formulated. And within this domestic ideology we find that the bourgeoisie upheld a class-specific ideal for working-class women — that of the 'good woman', the practical, efficient 'housewife' who was a competent wife and mother. This ideal is in contrast to the ideal bourgeoisie upheld for their own womenfolk, that of the 'perfect wife and mother', a ladylike manager of a household who employed servants to do the routine domestic chores.

All these factors then, that is, the choices I had to make, the necessity of investigating the schooling of working-class girls and various ideologies about women's position in society, helped to shape the scope of my research. For two-and-a-half years I read a host of nineteenth-century texts and also tried to keep up-to-date with many of the debates in present-day feminist literature. And during this time I was gradually narrowing the boundaries of my research and deepening my concerns. At all levels, I was interested in the relationships between working-class boys and girls and working-class men and women, not just in the females alone. The power relations between the sexes, a primary question in feminist research, was one of my main questions too. Yet I was also very much aware of, and in sympathy with, the main questions in social history which, in this country, have been influenced by a Marxist concern with the power relations between social classes and class conflict. Thus class relations, as well as the relationships between working-class men and women, became a central foci of my analysis too.

Consultation of Sources

Sociological research methods texts have devoted little attention to the use of documentary sources. Platt (1981, p. 31), for example, found in a survey of eighteen such general textbooks on research methods that only seven devoted a significant amount of space to anything to do with the use of documents, and that these texts often either conflated the point with other points or concentrated on only one type of use. What I learnt, I learnt through trial and error and through thinking about the issues involved. Initially, when I first began my research, I undertook an intensive reading of what are usually called 'secondary' sources, and then delved into 'primary' sources.

A primary source is usually regarded as a source which came into being during the period of the past that the researcher is studying. As Marwick (1970, p. 4) has noted, primary sources are the basic raw material out of which history is made. A secondary source, on the other hand, is usually regarded as an interpretation of the past, an interpretation that is written much later by a person who is looking back upon a period in the past (*ibid*). A reading of the secondary sources that have been written by twentieth-century historians on the two major adult education movements on which I was concentrating — the Mechanics' Institute Movement and the Working Men's College Movement — revealed that these texts were mainly focused around the activities of men. Harrison's account (1954) of the London Working Men's College, for example, which is regarded as a 'classic' account, does include a few references to the admission of women, classes for women and various separatist working women's colleges: but the number of pages devoted to discussing these matters number no more than four, even at a most generous estimate. Tylecote's (1957) analysis of the Mechanics' Institute Movement in Lancashire and Yorkshire before 1851 did contain many more references to the education of women but once again this was a small part of the total work.

Other secondary sources I read included books on the social condition of nineteenth-century England, more specialized texts on education and biographies of influential nineteenth-century figures. The Reverend Frederick Denison Maurice, for example, was a leading figure in the Working Men's College Movement and a number of biographies have been written about him.[7] I also read biographies of well known nineteenth-century women such as Emily Davies, Elizabeth Garrett-Anderson, Mary Carpenter and Octavia Hill.[8] Biographies of less well-known figures, and especially of working-class women, were harder to find. When I was reading these texts I was particularly looking for any references to the daily life of working-class women, especially their education. And I was also looking for any information that might tell me something about the power relationships between the sexes and the sexual division of labour.

My reading of the secondary sources gave me not only a 'feel' for the nineteenth century but also many primary sources that I could follow up. I 're-read' these primary sources in order to find out whether the relative neglect amongst present-day historians to the theme of the education of working-class women was due to selective bias on the part of the historian or to the absence of the necessary information within the documents themselves. Fortunately, I found plenty of references to the education of women within the records kept by the mechanics' institutes and working men's and working women's colleges — though often the information was less complete than I would have liked and sometimes it was ambiguous.

Elsewhere (Purvis, 1984), I have classified the kinds of texts that may be involved in qualitative research into three broad categories — official texts, published commentary and reporting, and personal texts. Official texts includes such documents as government reports, official letters and reports of organizations; published commentary and reporting includes newspapers, journals and writings of 'key' political and social figures; personal texts includes personal letters, diaries and autobiographies. Each of these broad categories of texts may present its own problems for the researcher. In the rest of the discussion in this section, I will look at each of these categories in turn in regard to the primary sources I consulted.

Contemporary feminist criticisms of official texts, and especially government reports and statistics, will alert the feminist who is studying the past about problems when interpreting such historical documents. The categories of analysis used in official documents may, for example, obscure certain aspects of the life of the nineteenth-century woman. In the 1851 Census, for example, 57 per cent of all women over the age of 20 who were living in London were recorded as without an occupation. Yet, as Alexander (1976, p. 64) has noted, this is an unrealistic assumption since the vast majority of these women were working-class women who were expected to contribute to the family income. In particular, Alexander suggests that the waged work of a married woman might be 'hidden' behind that of her husband. Thus a married woman might help to run a shop or help in a trade, such as shoe-making. In addition, since the male 'head' of the household filled in the census form, he probably thought (especially if he was a skilled artisan or an aspiring tradesman) that his wife was a 'housewife and mother' and not a paid worker (*ibid.*, p. 64).

Other problems arise too for the researcher trying to find out about working-class women in the nineteenth century through studying the official documents of the time. Government reports on education and paid work, for example, contain a mass of information and, in particular, a mass of oral evidence. We are given, however, no information about the views and assumptions of those who submitted the evidence, nor of the way in which they acquired their information. Did they acquire the information through first-hand experience, through observation, through listening to what someone else said? In particular, 'official' personnel such as government inspectors of schools that received state aid (from 1833) are a rich source of information about the life and conditions of working-class people and the education of working-class children and adults. But these inspectors were men and, in particular, middle-class men of a conservative, rather than radical, persuasion. The evidence they submit is therefore couched within a particular ideological framework. In particular, I have found that these inspectors upheld, in varying degrees, a 'deficit' model of the working-class woman, i.e., she is seen as an incompetent wife and mother, unable to cook a nourishing meal, unable to make clothes for her family, and unable to make the home comfortable. Consequently she drives her husband to the 'alehouse' when (the assumption is) he should be at home. Kay-Shuttleworth (1862, p. 130), Secretary to the Committee of Council on Education from 1839–1849 and responsible for overseeing the school inspectorate, epitomizes this view when he asserts that the employment of married working-class women in the mills in Manchester has not only a 'fatal influence' on the health and life of the infants in the family but also 'deranges the comfort of the workman's household. He escapes from a slatternly home and ill-cooked meal to the tavern.' Consequently, when the inspectors do describe and/or advocate education for working-class girls and women it is often in terms of its potential usefulness for an 'improvement' in a domestic role. The feminist researcher reading statements such as that quoted above will be aware then, that such statements are made from the viewpoint of men and not from the viewpoint of women, especially the working-class women who are being criticized. 'Official' personnel giving evidence in nineteenth-century reports rarely gave consideration to the double workload of the working-class wife as paid worker and unpaid housewife, nor to the fact that her earned income was necessary for family survival, nor to the need for adequate substitute child care provision.

In a number of government reports we also find oral evidence given not by 'official' personnel, but by 'ordinary' men and women. Forty-one year old Mrs. Britton, for example, the wife of a farm labourer, was 'examined' by the Poor Law Commissioners in 1843 and told them:

> I went to school till I was eight years old ... At ten years old I went to work at a factory in Calne, where I was till I was 26. I have been married 15 years. My husband is an agricultural labourer. I have seven children, all boys ... I have worked in the fields ... When at work in the spring I have received 10d. a day, but that is higher than the wages of women in general ... When working I never had any beer, and I never felt the

want of it. I never felt that my health was hurt by the work.
(Reports, 1843, p. 66)

Being 'examined' by official personnel may have been an intimidating
experience for working-class men and women, and witnesses may
have coloured their evidence to suit the occasion. The researcher
using oral evidence that has been collected in this way is constantly
aware of this problem.

Another readily available source for documentary research in the
nineteenth century is that category of texts I have called published
commentary and reporting — which includes newspapers, journals,
the writings of 'key' social and political figures as well as a mass of
other published material. During the course of my research I
consulted a range of newspapers, especially those that were part of a
radical political movement amongst the working class — such as the
Northern Star (a Chartist newspaper), *The New Moral World* (official
newspaper of Owenism) and *The Poor Man's Guardian* (which
crusaded particularly for the vote for working-class men). Journals I
consulted included those associated with the Mechanics' Institute
Movement and the Working Men's College Movement — such as, for
example, *The Working Men's College Journal* — as well as some of
the women's journals, such as *The Englishwoman's Journal* and *The
Englishwoman's Review*. The issue of 'bias' in reporting is a particularly acute one for the researcher using such sources. If we take old
newspapers, for example, it is often difficult to sort out the degree of
bias in any of the articles. As Thompson (1978, pp. 92–3) has noted,
an eye-witness account of an event or an interview reported by a
journalist may not only suffer from 'inaccuracy' but also be 'selected,
shaped and filtered' through a particular, but to the historian, uncertain, bias.

The issue of 'bias' is pertinent to the writings of 'key' social and
political figures. Such figures in the nineteenth century were usually
men, especially middle-class men, and their accounts of education for
working-class women are usually written from a particular perspective. Since the middle class in the nineteenth century had a higher
level of literacy than the working class, more time to write and more
opportunity to have published what was written, they are over-
represented in the mass of other published material. And 'bias', once
again, will be found in such publications. In particular, middle-class
women often wrote about 'woman's role in society' or 'woman's true
mission'. Mrs. Ellis, for example, wrote some highly successful books
on *The Women of England* (1839), *The Daughters of England* (1842),

The Mother of England (1843a) and *The Wives of England* (1843b). Any accounts of working-class women and their education that we may find are couched however (like the accounts written by middle-class men) within a particular perspective.

The third category of texts that I consulted was personal texts such as personal letters, diaries and autobiographies. I have already noted that an important premise of the methodological framework within which feminist research is conducted is that women's voices must be heard. Finding the voice of working-class women in the nineteenth century was highly problematic for me since I had no access to oral research. I had therefore to rely upon those personal texts that I could find.

While I found a number of personal texts that had been written by working-class men, especially autobiographies, I could find few personal documents that had been written by working-class women, especially those women who participated in the forms of adult education in which I was interested. Occasionally, in my frequent visits to the British Library or to the secondhand and antiquarian bookshops, I did stumble across an autobiographical extract or a letter. My excitement on these occasions always reminded me of the sentence in Thompson's epic book *The Making of the English Working Class* (1963, reprinted 1972, p. 13) — 'I am seeking to rescue the poor stockinger, the Luddite cropper, the "obsolete" hand-loom weaver, the "utopian" artisan, and even the deluded follower of Joanna Southcott, from the enormous condescension of posterity'.

Using personal documents in historical documentary research presents its own particular problems (see Burgess, 1982; Plummer, 1983; and Purvis, 1984 for further discussion of this issue). When, for example, one finds a well-written, articulate letter signed 'By a working woman', or 'A female factory worker' or 'One of the female oppressed', does one infer, both from the signature and the context of the letter, that the woman is a working-class woman? One must always question whether such a document is authentic and whether it is a first-hand account. In particular, the researcher does not know under what conditions the document was produced and whether it was edited before it was published. In addition, to ask how representative any one personal document written by working-class women might be of working-class women as a whole is a question that cannot be answered. As Rock (1976, p. 367) has commented, there are great regions of experience and happenings in the past that can never be recovered.

Using autobiographical evidence can be problematic too. Autobiographies are usually written late in life and may contain 'the oft-repeated recollections of others' (Clifford, 1978, p. 188), especially of childhood, as well as inaccurate reporting of events in adult life. And autobiographies about the nineteenth century vastly over-represent the middle class and vastly under-represent the working class, especially working-class women.

Despite these problems, personal texts are invaluable when one is undertaking historical documentary research from a feminist perspective. Such documents may provide, as in the case of letters, diaries and autobiographies written by working-class men and women, information about the power relationships between the sexes on a 'personal level'. In particular, the accounts written by working-class women themselves enable their voice to be heard amongst that mass of historical documents that reflects the views of those 'from above' rather than those 'from below'.

Now that I have discussed some of the problems I encountered when undertaking my research, I will explore the problems I met when organizing and interpreting my material.

Problems of Organizing and Interpreting Material

A basic problem that any researcher using documentary sources faces is — how do I know when I have collected enough data? As Platt (1981, p. 39) observes, how many defunct journals' review sections, secondhand book catalogues or publishers' advertisements in the back of old books must one read before being entitled to conclude that a further search is not likely to turn up anything new? In my own case, I felt I had reached a point where, within the limits of time, I had consulted as many primary sources as I could. I felt I had developed a 'picture' of the issues I was investigating and that certain patterns were beginning to emerge from the huge amount of data I had collected. When attempting to write up and interpret my material, I did, however, encounter a number of problems and I will discuss some of these now.

First of all, when trying to organize my material I found the category of 'woman' a problematic one. In particular, I had to confront the issue of what is a 'girl' and what is a 'woman' in nineteenth-century terms. Sometimes it appeared that when a 'girl' left school or home she acquired adult status while at other times it related much more to an actual age, such as fourteen years old. I had also expected that there would be marked differences in the experience of life between 'single' and 'married' working-class women. Yet I found that the single/married dichotomy hid a range of different categories of women — such as single parents, widows with children, widows without children, wives with husbands who were 'absent' in the navy or in prison. Overall, I decided that the category of 'woman' was a blurred category, and that in terms of life styles and educational recruitment, whether a working-class woman was 'single', that is, unmarried or, for example, a childless widow, or whether she was a 'wife' and/or 'mother' was significant.

Secondly, I found that it was impossible to write some account of adult education for working-class women without taking into account the economic and social conditions of their lives. And it was feminist research on the lives of women that helped me to shape my approach to this issue. Thus feminists have frequently argued that the division between 'the family' and 'paid work' that is common in mainstream academic research in disciplines such as sociology and history is a division that relates to the lives of men but not of women. And I found when writing up my research that I could not divide up my material into a chapter on 'the family' and another on 'paid work' since for working-class women in the nineteenth century, one sets the conditions for the other. Thus I wrote one chapter which attempts to integrate, rather than separate, these two aspects of daily life.

Some contemporary feminists would claim that to focus upon the daily experience of life for women is the essence of feminist research. Other contemporary feminists would dispute this and assert that one must first of all analyze the structural aspects of women's position. I tried to take some kind of middle road and to argue in my chapter on the family and paid work that the experience of life for working-class women in the nineteenth century was structured[9] — both by their location within a particular social class grouping and by their situation *vis-à-vis* men. Thus the relationship with men within the family and within employment is critical for working-class women and this is something that anyone writing from a feminist perspective must consider. In particular, men in the role of husbands could determine the conditions under which working-class women were able or not able to participate in adult education. As late as 1907, for example, a husband within the co-operative movement is reported as being against his wife attending the Women's Co-operative Guild — 'My wife? What does she want with meetings? Let her stay at home and wash my moleskin trousers!' (cited in Nash, 1907, p. 76). Thus, working-class women were not necessarily independent actors since they were often seen as the property of men, both materially and psychologically.

Thirdly, I also found that it was impossible to write an account of adult education for working-class women without examining the various ideologies about 'woman's place' in the nineteenth century. And I wrote about these ideologies separately from the conditions of family life and employment for working-class women. This is, of course, highly problematic since the sets of beliefs about woman's place in society are integral to the conditions of living for women and not separate from them. However, for me as a researcher, it was interesting to investigate these ideologies about women in their own right. Thus I looked at the writings of a wide range of people to see where the beliefs about women might be located.[10] Overall, as I have indicated earlier, the dominant ideology about women was that held by the bourgeoisie who believed that the ideal location for women was in the private sphere of the home as full-time wives and mothers. I then sought to explore the extent to which the various ideologies about women, and in particular the 'domestic ideology' held by the bourgeoisie, were reaffirmed or challenged in educational classes for working-class women.

Fourthly, the main focus of my research was to examine how the ideologies about women were played out in specific educational institutions, i.e., the mechanics' institutes and the colleges within the Working Men's College Movement. A major problem here was that one could not assume that statements made about women by people who were influential in these two major adult education movements described what actually happened in practice. And unfortunately, I found hardly any records written by working-class women themselves describing their education as they experienced it. I had to rely upon 'official' records of the various institutes and colleges which, however, did reveal marked divisions between the sexes in regard to terms of admission, categories of membership, curricula and use of various educational facilities. Thus rarely did working-class women enjoy equality of access with men to adult education classes and rarely were they offered the same curricula choices. The patriarchal structure of nineteenth-century society, whereby women were expected to be subordinate to men within a variety of power structures, pervaded the institutes and colleges. In particular, the idea of 'separate spheres' between the sexes, a prominent feature of the dominant bourgeois domestic ideology, influenced educational provision so that women were usually offered separate and different curricula that reinforced their subordinate status. For example, at the

Mechanics' Institute in Lockwood, Yorkshire, where 212 male and forty-five female members are recorded in 1856, men are offered classes in reading, writing, arithmetic, algebra, mensuration, history, geography, grammar, music, freehand and ornamental drawing while women were offered reading, writing, arithmetic, knitting, sewing and marking (quoted in Purvis, 1980, p. 201). Even within the Working Men's College Movement, where separate colleges for women were established, the range of topics for women never matched that range offered to men — especially in mathematics. Within the colleges, women might be offered a wider range of curricula than the 3Rs, sewing and cookery that might be offered in the institutes. But in the colleges too, the education of women was usually conceived as education for the development of others, especially men and children, than education for the development of self (Purvis, 1981b, p. 243).

Fifthly, I became more and more aware as I was writing up and interpreting my material of just how problematic it was for the present-day researcher to know the meaning of education for those working-class women who did attend adult classes. At one level, it appears that the mechanics' institutes and the various colleges offered working-class women a highly conservative kind of education that was simply a form of social control. Yet for those working-class women who actually made the effort to attend an adult education class, on a voluntary basis, after long hours of waged work as factory hands, milliners, domestic servants, dressmakers or home workers of various kinds, such an educational experience may have been liberating. It may have been a form of 'fighting back' against the daily grind of life, against the views of society about women's subordinate place, against the prejudices of husbands, lovers, brothers, fathers and sons.

Conclusion

In conclusion, I would like to raise some general issues that I have thought about in regard to undertaking historical documentary research from a feminist perspective.

Within mainstream academic circles, I have occasionally encountered the argument that a 'commitment' to a feminist perspective is a hindrance to 'genuine scholarship'. Indeed, when I first presented this paper at a conference in the summer of 1983 both myself and Sue Scott (who had also presented a paper from a feminist perspective) were attacked by one conference participant for being 'biased' and 'value laden' and not engaging in 'proper' research.

In my view, both historical and sociological research will always be selective in the use of data and the construction of theory. In particular, historical facts do not just 'emerge': they are 'chosen', and which facts are selected depends, to some extent, upon the questions that the researcher is asking. The historian E.H. Carr (1961 and 1978) emphasizes this point when he says:

> The facts speak only when the historian calls on them: it is he who decides to which facts to give the floor, and in what order or context ... The historian is necessarily selective. The belief in a hard core of historical facts existing objectively and independently of the interpretation of the historian is a preposterous fallacy, but one which it is very hard to eradicate. (pp. 11–12)

This does not necessarily mean, however, that the research is biased in the sense of being prejudiced. What is important is that the person researching the past, from whatever perspective, keeps a relatively open mind and expects to find 'spaces' which refute what was thought to be the case, and 'contradictions' which upset the patterns that were expected.

In my experience, a feminist perspective is a major help and not a hindrance to research. The feminist undertaking documentary research into the past has to go back to the primary sources and be a 'better' detective than many other researchers have been before because an analysis of the situation of women and of the power relationships between the sexes has been 'hidden' and 'obscured'. The balance between the forces of history and actors in history is continually present in feminist research, and the stereotyped view of women as voiceless, passive, determined beings who are made by history, but do not make history, is questioned. The questioning relates, however, not only to the stereotypical assumptions about women but also to the methodological framework, the boundaries and concepts that are a part of mainstream, male-oriented research. A questioning mind is an advantage, not a disadvantage, in the world of scholarship. And the questions that feminist research poses about the in-built sexist assumptions within malestream academic disciplines is an existing challenge that must be welcomed, not bypassed.

If one is a woman and a feminist, the process of undertaking research from a feminist perspective is also a means by which one may attain a better understanding of one's own life and of the lives of the women one may be researching. Feminist research is essentially a reflexive process whereby one's own consciousness may provide insights into the experience of women in the past and vice versa. Researching the education of working-class women in nineteenth-century England has meant for me personally an increasing awareness of the change and continuity between past and present, of the gains and struggles of women living a century ago and of women living today. And it is this awareness that has made my research a personal involvement. One becomes conscious of what has been achieved and what is yet to be struggled for.

The struggle to include feminist scholarship as valid scholarship within the academic world continues. And some strides have been made in this respect during the last decade. Feminist books are now included on reading lists for students in adult and higher education, and feminist books are regularly reviewed in the press. For example, Barbara Taylor's (1983) superb analysis of socialism and feminism in the nineteenth century received highly acclaimed reviews. Raymond Williams referred to it as 'an admirable piece of research, clearly and thoroughly presented ... absolutely necessary reading' (*The Guardian*, 17 March 1983). Judith Chernaik (*New Society*, 24 March 1983) called the book an 'admirable historical study' and Marina Warner (*Sunday Times*, 20 March 1983) spoke of it as 'eloquent history'. The feminist challenge to 'men's studies' continues. And it is a challenge that owes the greatest debt of all to those women past and present who have been, and who are, part of that force in history which demands that women's voices and women's perspectives be heard and acknowledged as half of the human race.

Acknowledgement

I would like to express my great debt to Madeleine Arnot, Lecturer in Educational Studies at the Open University, for her constant support, criticism of my work and invaluable suggestions. Any inadequacies in this paper are, however, my own.

Notes

1 I would like to offer my grateful thanks to the Social Science Research Council and the Open University for funding the research.

2 Patriarchy is a problematic concept. For discussion of some of the various definitions and uses see BEECHEY (1979), EISENSTEIN (1979) and McDONOUGH and HARRISON (1978).

3 For a discussion of the problems a feminist might face when undertaking what might be considered a 'proper' interview with women see OAKLEY (1981b).

4 For an attempt to include the paid employment of wives and husbands in a 'family' social classification see BRITTEN and HEATH (1983).

5 In this country, feminist history began to 'take off' after the publication of Sheila Rowbotham's *Hidden from History: 300 Years of Women's Oppression and the Fight Against It* (1973).

6 See, for example, LAWSON and SILVER (1973) and SIMON (1974).

7 See, for example, HIGHAM (1947) and MASTERMAN (1907).

8 See, for example, STEPHEN (1927), MANTON (1965), MANTON (1976) and BELL (1942).

9 ACKER, BARRY and ESSEVELD (1983) make a similar point — 'Although we view people as active agents in their own lives and as such constructors of their social worlds, we do not see that activity as isolated and subjective. Rather, we locate individual experience in society and history, embedded within a set of social relations which produce both the possibilities and limitations of that experience' (pp. 424–5). They go on to point out in a footnote that the term 'social relation' gives centrality to the organization of social life without positing either 'the individual' or 'the social structure' as separate and oppositional.

10 In particular, I looked at the writings of influential people within religious circles, political circles, medical circles and educational circles and also literature that was highly popular, such as the writings of Mrs. Ellis.

References

ACKER, J., BARRY, K. and ESSEVELD, J. (1983) 'Objectivity and truth: problems in doing feminist research', *Women's Studies International Forum*, 6, 4, pp. 423–35.

ACKER, S. (1983) 'Women and teaching: a semi-detached sociology of a semi-profession', in WALKER, S. and BARTON, L. (Eds.) *Gender, Class and Education*, Lewes, Falmer Press.

ALEXANDER, S. (1976) 'Women's work in nineteenth-century London: a study of the years 1820–50', in MITCHELL, J. and OAKLEY, A. (Eds.) *The Rights and Wrongs of Women*, Harmondsworth, Penguin.

BEECHEY, V. (1979) 'On patriarchy', *Feminist Review*, 3.

BELL, E. (1942) *Octavia Hill*, London, Constable.

BLACK, M. and COWARD, R. (1981) 'Linguistic, social and sexual relations: a review of Dale Spender's "Man Made Language" ', *Screen Education*, 39.

BRITTEN, N. and HEATH, A. (1983) 'Women, men and social class', in GAMARNIKOW, E., MORGAN, D.H.J., PURVIS, J. and TAYLORSON, D.E. (Eds.) *Gender, Class and Work*, London, Heinemann.

BURGESS, R.G. (1982) 'Personal documents, oral sources and life histories' in BURGESS, R.G. (Ed.) *Field Research: a Sourcebook and Field Manual,* London, Allen and Unwin.

CARR, E.H. (1978) *What is History?* Harmondsworth, Penguin Books first published by Macmillan in 1961.

CLIFFORD, G.J. (1978) 'History as experience: the uses of personal-history documents in the history of education', *History of Ecucation, 7,* 3, pp. 183–96.

DANIELS, A. (1975) 'Feminist perspectives in sociological research', in MILLMAN, M. and KANTER, M. (Eds.) *Another Voice,* New York, Anchor Books.

DOWNING, H. (1981), 'They call me a life-size Meccano set: super-secretary or super-slave?', in McROBBIE, A. and McCABE, T. (Eds.) *Feminism for Girls,* London, Routledge and Kegan Paul.

DU BOIS, B. (1983) 'Passionate scholarship: notes on values, knowing and method in feminist social science', in BOWLES, G. and DUELLI KLEIN, R. (Eds.) *Theories of Women's Studies,* London, Routledge and Kegan Paul.

DUELLI KLEIN, R. (1983) 'How to do what we want to do: thoughts about feminist methodology' in BOWLES, G. and DUELLI KLEIN, R. (Eds.) *Theories of Women's Studies,* London, Routledge and Kegan Paul.

EISENSTEIN, Z.R. (Ed.) (1979) *Capitalist Patriarchy and the Case for Socialist Feminism,* New York, Monthly Review Press.

ELLIS, MRS. (1839) *The Women of England, their Social Duties and Domestic Habits,* London, Fisher, Son and Co.

ELLIS, MRS. (1842) *The Daughters of England, their Position in Society, Character and Responsibilities,* London, Fisher, Son and Co.

ELLIS, MRS. (1843a) *The Mothers of England, their Influence and Responsibility,* London, Fisher, Son and Co.

ELLIS, MRS. (1843b) *The Wives of England, their Relative Duties, Domestic Influence and Social Obligations,* London, Fisher, Son and Co.

GAFFIN, J. (1977) 'Women and co-operation', in MIDDLETON, L. (Ed.) *Women in the Labour Movement,* London, Croom Helm.

HARRISON, J.F.C. (1954) *A History of the Working Men's College,* London, Routledge and Kegan Paul.

HIGHAM, F. (1947) *Frederick Denison Maurice,* London, SCM Press Ltd.

JOHN, A.V. (1980) *By the Sweat of Their Brow: Women Workers at Victorian Coal Mines,* London, Croom Helm.

KAY-SHUTTLEWORTH, SIR J. (1862) *Four Periods of Public Education as Reviewed in 1832–1839–1846–1862,* London, Longman, Green, Longman, and Roberts.

KELLY, A. (1978) 'Feminism and research', *Women's Studies International Quarterly,* 1, 3, pp. 225–32.

KELLY, T. (1957) *George Birkbeck: Pioneer of Adult Education,* Liverpool, University of Liverpool Press.

LAWSON, J. and SILVER, H. (1973) *A Social History of Education in England,* London, Methuen.

LEONARD, D. (1983) 'Moving Forward', in Open University Course, *The Changing Experience of Women,* Course U221 (Unit 16), Milton

Keynes, Open University Press.

MANTON, J. (1965) *Elizabeth Garrett Anderson*, London, Methuen.

MANTON, J. (1976) *Mary Carpenter and the Children of the Streets*, London, Heinemann.

MARWICK, A. (1970) 'Primary Sources', in Open University, *Humanities Foundation Course*, Course A100 (Unit 6), Milton Keynes, Open University Press.

MASTERMAN, C.F.G. (1907) *Frederick Denison Maurice*, London, A.R. Mowbray and Co.

MCDONOUGH, R. and HARRISON, R. (1978) 'Patriarchy and relations of production', in KUHN, A. and WOLPE, A.M. (Eds.) *Feminism and Materialism*, London, Routledge and Kegan Paul.

MOORE, DR. W. (1866) Presidential address to the British Medical Association, reported in *The Lancet*, 14 August.

MORGAN, D. (1981) 'Men, masculinity and the process of sociological enquiry', in ROBERTS, H. (Ed.) *Doing Feminist Research*, London, Routledge and Kegan Paul.

NASH, R. (1907) 'Co-operator and citizen', in VILLIERS, B. (Ed.) *The Case for Women's Suffrage*, London, T. Fisher Unwin.

OAKLEY, A. (1974) *The Sociology of Housework*, London, Martin Robertson.

OAKLEY, A. (1981a) *Subject Women*, Oxford, Martin Robertson.

OAKLEY, A. (1981b) 'Interviewing women: a contradiction in terms', in ROBERTS, H. (Ed.) *Doing Feminist Research*, London, Routledge and Kegan Paul.

PLATT, J. (1981) 'Evidence and proof in documentary research: 1: some specific problems of documentary research', *Sociological Review*, 29, 1, pp. 31–52.

PLUMMER, K. (1983) *Documents of Life*, London, Allen and Unwin.

PURVIS, J. (1980) 'Working-class women and adult education in nineteenth-century Britain', *History of Education*, 9, 3, pp. 193–212.

PURVIS, J. (1981a) 'Towards a history of women's education in nineteenth-century Britain: a sociological analysis', *Westminster Studies in Education*, 4, pp. 45–79.

PURVIS, J. (1981b) '"Women's sphere is essentially domestic, private life being confined to men" (Comte): separate spheres and inequality in the education of working-class women, 1854–1900', *History of Education*, 10, 4, pp. 227–43.

PURVIS, J. (1984) 'Understanding Texts', in Open University, *Conflict and Change in Education: a Sociological Introduction*, Course E205 (Unit 15) Milton Keynes, Open University Press.

REPORTS ON SPECIAL ASSISTANT POOR LAW COMMISSIONERS (1843) *On the Employment of Women and Children in Agriculture*, London, W. Clowes and Sons.

REUBEN, E. (1978) 'In defiance of the evidence: notes on feminist scholarship', *Women's Studies International Quarterly*, 1, 3, pp. 215–8.

RICH, A. (1980) *On Lies, Secrets and Silence*, London, Virago.

RICHARDS, J.R. (1980) *The Sceptical Feminist*, London, Routledge and Kegan Paul.

ROBERTS, H. (1981) 'Women and their doctors: power and powerlessness in the research process', in ROBERTS, H. (Ed.) *Doing Feminist Research*, London, Routledge and Kegan Paul.

ROCK, P. (1976) 'Some problems of interpretative historiography', *British Journal of Sociology*, September, pp. 353–69.

ROWBOTHAM, S. (1973) *Hidden from History: 300 Years of Women's Oppression and the Fight Against It*, London, Pluto Press.

ROWBOTHAM, S. (1979) 'The trouble with "patriarchy" ', *New Statesman*, 21–28 December, pp. 970–1.

SCOTT, S. forthcoming 'Feminist methods and qualitative research: A discussion of some of the issues', in BURGESS, R.G. (Ed.) *Issues in Educational Research*, Lewes, Falmer Press.

SIMON, B. (1974) *The Two Nations and the Educational Structure 1780-1870*, London, Lawrence and Wishart.

SMITH, D.E. (1978) 'A peculiar eclipsing: women's exclusion from man's culture', *Women's Studies International Quarterly*, 1, 4, pp. 281–95.

SMITH, D.E. (1979) 'A sociology for women', in SHERMAN, J.A. and BECK, E.T. (Eds.) *The Prism of Sex: Essays in the Sociology of Knowledge*, Wisconsin, University of Wisconsin Press.

SPENDER, D. (1980) *Man Made Language*, London, Routledge and Kegan Paul.

SPENDER, D. (Ed.) (1981) *Men's Studies Modified*, Oxford, Pergamon Press.

SPENDER, D. (1982) *Women of Ideas and What Men Have Done to Them*, London, Routledge and Kegan Paul.

STACEY, M. (1981) 'The division of labour revisited, or overcoming the two Adams', in ABRAMS, P., DEEM, R., FINCH, J. and ROCK, P. (Eds.) *Practice and Progress: British Sociology 1950–1980*, London, Allen and Unwin.

STACEY, M. (1983) 'Social sciences and the state: fighting like a woman' in GAMARNIKOW, E., MORGAN, D., PURVIS, J. and TAYLORSON, D.E. (Eds.) *The Public and Private*, London, Heinemann.

STANLEY, L. and WISE, S. (1979) 'Feminist research, feminist consciousness and experiences of sexism', *Women's Studies International Quarterly*, 2, 3, pp. 359–74.

STANLEY, L. and WISE, S. (1983) *Breaking Out: Feminist Consciousness and Feminist Research*, London, Routledge and Kegan Paul.

STEPHEN, B. (1927) *Emily Davies and Girton College*, London, Constable and Co.

TAYLOR, B. (1983) *Eve and the New Jerusalem*, London, Virago.

THOMPSON, E.P. (1972) *The Making of the English Working Class*, Harmondsworth, Penguin Books, first published by Victor Gollancz in 1963.

THOMPSON, P. (1978) *The Voice of the Past*, Oxford, Oxford University Press.

TYLECOTE, M. (1957) *The Mechanics' Institutes of Lancashire and Yorkshire*, Manchester, Manchester University Press.

WESTKOTT, M. (1983) 'Women's studies as a strategy for change: between criticism and vision' in BOWLES, G. and DUELLI KLEIN, R. (Eds.) *Theories of Women's Studies*, London, Routledge and Kegan Paul.

8 The Use of Archives and Interviews in Research on Educational Policy

Rene Saran

Introduction

Methodological Pluralism

Qualitative methodology in the social sciences has enjoyed a revival in the last decade or two. Filstead (1970) even argued that the trend towards quantification — associated with the attempt to make sociology respectable — actually lessened our understanding of the empirical social world. In place of the deductive method borrowed from the more respected natural sciences, Filstead commended the use of inductive 'grounded theory' as developed by Glaser and Strauss (1967) in the late 1960s.

As a researcher of policy-making in education, deeply steeped in seeking and analyzing empirical evidence, I have often been aware of the gap between theory and empirical evidence, especially as I felt some lack of theory in my own work. The idea that appropriate theory might somehow spring from empirical evidence rather than *vice versa* had considerable appeal. Even after reading Glaser and Strauss, however, bridge-building between evidence and theory remained remarkably difficult. How was it to be done? Some researchers, who, like myself, have gathered data from archives and interviews, have reported that prior theories with which their re-search began did not always stand up in the light of the empirical evidence. For example, Foster and Sheppard (1980) concluded their chapter on the use of archives with excellent advice:

> Perhaps the most important point for all those wishing to use primary source material ... is that the reader should approach the material with an open mind in order to get the most from it ... Having read around the subject, the next

step is to see what the documents tell you rather than look for individual theories to be proved. You may be surprised by your own conclusions. (Foster and Sheppard, 1980, p. 210)

The major aim of this paper is to describe and explain the methods I believe I used to see what archival and interview data told me and how from these 'messages' I made a creative leap to hypotheses and mini-theory building. Post-hoc introspection of what I had actually done led me to the conclusion that our understanding of social life is more likely to be advanced by methodological pluralism than by reliance on any one approach alone.

Spiral-Like Process

To help readers understand the research process in my project I am deliberately presenting it in an ordered form, rather than describing what is often the confused state of mind of the researcher whilst at work. But I am fully aware that the actual research process is usually a messy business, with periods of excitement, panic, disillusionment and dull slog experienced in no given order. Even when one reaches the end of a tunnel, one could usually start all over again, time permitting. Whilst involved in the process, one is often only dimly aware of the methods employed.

Thus I have found this critical post-hoc appraisal of my own research methods immensely valuable. It has involved a search for clarity about what I actually do. The writing of this paper, initially for workshop discussion, was itself an exciting and challenging experience. Its analysis of my methods reflects an inter-disciplinary input, for it was preceded by several hours of discussion with two friends, one a philosopher, the other an experimental psychologist.

Discussion with people of various backgrounds has always had an important role in my search for meaning and explanation. Regular participation over many years in discussions, often on ethical topics, using the socratic method developed a capacity for empathy. The facility to enter into other people's feelings, to understand their purposes, aims and value assumptions has profoundly influenced my approach to archives and the way I interview policy-makers.

Through writing the initial draft of this chapter I came to see the research process as an ongoing spiral-like activity with no specific start and no specific end. Every question has its antecedents, every statement made or 'answer' found in turn could lead to further questions. The search is for truth in the form of increasing clarity of meaning, explanation, generality and — eventually — a general theory about social phenomena being investigated. It proved helpful to me to identify more clearly the methods I had actually used, even though not necessarily in a given sequence. These were three: abduction, deduction and induction. Often they are used at one and the same time, but each will be briefly described.

For the purpose of illustration I shall draw extensively on my study of teachers' salaries negotiations, with special reference to data gathered from historical archives and interviews with policy-makers. The following section, therefore, provides a brief outline of the aims and scope of my study before discussing qualitative methodology on page 228.

The Burnham Project

Origins

Between 1979 and 1981, the Social Science Research Council (SSRC) financed a study on 'Burnham since 1945: analysis and critical examination of the need for reform'. The first application for a grant had been made (and failed) five years earlier. The refusal of a grant in 1974 was based on my inadequate knowledge of the proposed research topic: I had not talked to enough people, and not been promised access to sufficient sources. This experience illustrates a vicious circle: to do the research one often needs a grant; to get the grant one has to do pilot work and secure access. As regards the Burnham project, this problem was solved by my keeping the topic ticking over alongside my teaching duties, by the City of London Polytechnic allocating an Inner London Education Authority (ILEA) financed research assistant to the project for three years, and by a small grant from elsewhere, to allow progress to be made between 1976 and 1979. Together these factors culminated in a revised and strengthened application and the SSRC grant in 1979.

But how does one actually get a research idea and then pursue it? Reform and change never occur in a vacuum. Awareness by researchers of contemporary problems, or their current theoretical perspectives, can lead to questions about the past which may illuminate the present. June Purvis argues that the conjuncture between past and present is less sharp than many people might suggest, that insights from the past do enable us to ask questions about the present, just as awareness of the present may lead to interesting questions about the past (see page 179).

Sociologists are often the first to admit that sociological research is weak on history. But the scene is changing. In the field of health policy this is illustrated by *Rewriting Nursing History* (Davies, 1980), a work which seeks to replace conventional history — often a mere narrative and chronology of events — by a more analytical approach offering insights through comparison, criticism and the historian's reflections. Here there is less concern with narrative, more with explanation of patterns of events.

Four of the chapters in this book on qualitative methods arise from historical research. June Purvis and Alison Andrew write about their research on nineteenth-century documents; they share the difficulty that they cannot interrogate their characters, other than by an imaginary 'dialogue with the dead' (Silver, 1983), while Ivor Goodson (see page 121) and I both applied an historical approach to more recent events since 1945. We were thus able to engage in a dialogue with the living as part of our data gathering activity.

In my case, interest in the Burnham research arose from participation in policy-making at local level, an involvement which in turn had arisen out of an earlier major research project on secondary schools policy and administration (Saran, 1973). Whereas Alison Andrew approached her nineteenth-century study from a prior theoretical perspective, the tendency in my case is to select twentieth-century research topics from the identification of contemporary policy problems. I am, of course, fully aware that my perception of 'problems' is influenced by my own value position, which possibly brings Alison Andrew's approach and mine closer to each other than appears at first sight. I am convinced that my value stance led to the particular interest I developed in the Burnham unit total system. I saw this mechanism as reflecting the elitist attributes of the selective secondary system. So there is a circular relationship at work in our minds. It can be argued that theoretical insights should arise from the data that are collected but this presents two problems. First, no-one starts with a value-free position; further, if one 'waits' for theoretical insights to arise from data, sometimes none may arise! I am very conscious of the difficulty, yet I have experienced the insight coming to me from immersion in data. How this occurred I will explain later, where I write about 'imaginative leaps'.

In contrast to some colleagues who engage in action research my own predisposition is to participate in the policy-making debate, before and after, rather than during, the research process. But the two activities are not in water-tight compartments. In the early 1970s I was active in the Association for the Advancement of State Education in Camden, a pressure group concerned with improving the maintained sector of educational provision. Another executive member in our group argued that certain desirable policy options for the 16 to 19 year olds were non-starters due to the Burnham salaries structure. This discovery led me to search the literature, where I found very little to help me understand anything about the Burnham structure as a constraint on educational policy options. This pointed to a good research topic, hence the 1974 SSRC application. Ten years later, through writing and speaking activities, an informed contribution to current policy analysis has become possible, based on historical insights gained through intensive sifting of documentary data. Once such historical insights had evolved, the necessary up-dating of one's knowledge for ongoing policy debates can be achieved through journals, newspapers and interviews of current policy-makers.

A spin-off for the researcher from involvement in public policy and dialogue with policy-makers is that new research questions often spring to mind. One's awareness of possibilities as well as constraints is heightened. No researcher commences the process with a *tabula rasa* or content and value-free mind. Initial questions reflect judgments about what is worthwhile investigating.

Scope

The aims I set myself for the Burnham research were very broad, and I intended to cover a period of some thirty years: 1944–1974. In the end, recognition of the value of relevant policy inputs led to an extension into the 1980s. The required SSRC end-of-grant report, written in November 1981, summarized the project as follows:[1]

> Overall the aims of this investigation have remained unchanged. They were, firstly, to analyze political power relationships within and between the organizations of employers and teacher unions represented on the Burnham (Main) Committee; secondly, to gain insights into the objectives and values underlying the Burnham salaries system. Reform of Burnham attracted greater public attention as the research progressed, and emphasis was therefore placed on keeping abreast of current developments.
>
> The first aim involved examination of Burnham machin-

ery as itself reflecting power relationships with ensuing conflicts over its reform. The second aim was pursued by reconstruction of teacher union demands and management offers during salary negotiations in order to establish how far the salaries structure over time reflected the changing pattern of school organization.

In-depth analysis of selected committee decisions drew on archive data from the Burnham Committee (including verbatim minutes) and some constituent organizations, and on extended open-ended interviews with leading negotiators and some others. Evidence covered the stages by which salary settlements were reached, the politics of negotiating tactics and alliances, and the effects of settlements on career and promotion structures.

The negotiating environment changed as government policies on incomes, cash limits and statutory controls over local government expenditure evolved. In the light of these changes, the Secretary of State's more interventionist role had to be assessed, and new pressure to end separation of salary negotiations from those of conditions understood.

The study aims to open up new possibilities for policy-makers by clarifying beyond doubt and in detail the implications of the present system. Precise alternatives will emerge only when negotiators themselves initiate change and test out the acceptability of new policies. However, in the light of its post-war evolution, tentative recommendations for reform of the Burnham system in the 1980s are made. (Saran, 1981c)

So far, a number of articles have emerged from the project (Saran and Verber, 1979/80; Saran, 1981a and 1981b; Saran, 1982a, 1982b and 1982c), and a book is partly written. The end of grant report set out under certain headings the main findings which were summarized under the headings: Burnham negotiating machinery; Burnham negotiations and the salaries structure; Recommendations.

Research Sources and Data Gathering

(a) *Archives.* In discussing the use of archives for nursing history Foster and Sheppard state:

The strict definition of an archive is a document which is produced by an individual or institution in the normal course of life or work and which provides a record or part of the history of that individual or institution. Archives are mainly written documents — that is, manuscripts or typescripts — but photographs and sound recordings can also be classified as archives, as can some printed material. (Foster and Sheppard, 1980, p. 200)

Foster and Sheppard refer to sets of documents that were equally relevant to the Burnham investigation. Thus, annual reports of teacher unions, as well as specialized journals or newspapers, belong to the relevant printed material (for example National Union of Teachers (NUT) *Annual Reports,* and the NUT's weekly paper *The Teacher;* the journal *Education,* and newspapers like the *Times Educational Supplement*). The researcher has to seek out such printed material in libraries. The NUT Library at Hamilton House (open as a reference library to the public), the London Institute of Education Library, and the Department of Education and Science (DES) Library are excellent specialized libraries in London where such material can often be found or guidance given as to where else it might be found. For archival documents, like minutes of formal public bodies (for example the Burnham Committee or the Education Committee of a local education authority), or of relevant teacher organizations, societies or educational charities, or of employer organizations, access has to be obtained from the particular organizations. Many of them keep their own archives, some hand over older records for safe keeping to university libraries. Thus, the Association of Education Committees (AEC) records have been lodged at the University of Leeds (except for the Burnham Management Panel archives lodged at the City of London Polytechnic). Records belonging to the NUT, the National Association of Schoolmasters/Union of Women Teachers (NAS/UWT) and to the Association of County Councils (ACC), were used at the headquarters of those organizations, where I was kindly given facilities to peruse documents once access was granted. There is also the Public Record Office at Kew, where the public has, generally speaking, the right of access to administrative records after thirty years have elapsed under the Public Records Act of 1958. For the Burnham project, for example, I could have used Ministry of Education records lodged at the Public Records Office concerning the 1944/45 negotiations between Butler and the representatives of unions and employers to reconstitute the Burnham Committee following the 1944 Education Act. In the end it was the pressure of time that prevented my using these records.

Securing access to archives is often difficult for the social scientist. The researcher's work may suffer from inadequate data as well as too much. Initially, I had great difficulty in getting access to unpublished material, yet the SSRC grant application required me to show I had such access. I had had more success by the time the second application was made, and once the grant was secured, I was soon flooded with possible data. Pressure of time necessitated selecting what I could use.

My first round of letters asking for access was written in May 1974 to the secretaries of organizations represented on the Teachers' and Management panels respectively. The following is an example:

I am writing to enquire whether you might give sympathetic consideration to cooperating over an investigation into the Burnham negotiations and agreements since the 1944 Education Act. In the light of recent discussions on the reform of the Burnham machinery, I intend to undertake a pilot academic study of Burnham since the war.

My Polytechnic is supporting an application to the SSRC for a research grant to cover such a pilot study. We have already taken up informal contact with the SSRC, but when submitting the formal application it would be desirable to be able to indicate to which source material access is being granted.

As the (name of organization) occupies the leading position/is represented on the (name of) Panel of Burnham, I assume that many of the records concerning the work of the (name of) Panel for Primary and Secondary Schools will be in your possession. I hope therefore you may see your way to granting me permission to peruse relevant records and documents covering your involvement in negotiations since the war.

For your interest I attach a brief curriculum vitae, from which you will see that I have wide experience in industry and education, and that my research interest and published work is in the field of educational administration.

The breakthrough came when Lord Alexander in the mid-1970s agreed to deposit at the City of London Polytechnic the Burnham Management Panel archives. Alexander had been Secretary of the AEC, which was until 1974 one of the organizations represented on the Management Panel of Burnham, and for nearly thirty years he had also been Secretary to the employers' side. Within two years of

Table 1: Major Sources for the Burnham Project

1 Teachers' organizations

NUT Archives	Teachers' Panel Minutes 1944–74. NUT Executive Minutes 1969–70. NUT Annual Reports 1944–81. Selected issues of Union journal, Union rules, pamphlets, etc, 1944 onwards
NAS/UWT Archives	Selected documents, reports, etc., from 1962 onwards Selected issues of Union journal 1962–81 Union rules
Assistant Masters Association Archives (at the Institute of Education, University of London)	Minutes of Executive 1944–60s Selected Issues of Union journal, especially reports of Council meetings 1944–77 Selected documents 1944–60s Salaries circulars 1969–73 (supplied by Head Office)

2 Management organizations

Burnham Management Panel Archives (at the City of London Polytechnic)	1940s to early 1970s, including verbatim minutes of Burnham Committee (Primary and Secondary) 1951 to early 1970s Large collection of Management Panel working documents on Burnham machinery and on salary offers and salaries structure
Association of County Councils	Education Committee reports to Executive Council 1961–77 Burnham files relating especially to early 1960s through to early 1970s. Letters and working documents
LACSAB	Burnham Management Panel circulars 1974–81.

3 Government reports, theses, etc.

Barnes, S.E. (1959) 'Individual, Local and National Bargaining for Teachers'
Salaries in England and Wales: a study of the period 1858–1944', PhD
thesis, University of London

Burnham Reports: Primary and Secondary 1945–1980, London, HMSO

Clegg Report (1980) Report No. 7 *Teachers,* Standing Commission on Pay
Comparability, Cmnd. 7880, London, HMSO

Green Book (1941) *Education After the War,* Board of Education

Hansard, particularly 1960–65, London, HMSO

Houghton Report (1974) *Report of the Committee of Inquiry into the Pay of
Non-University Teachers,* Cmnd, 5848, London, HMSO

Macfarlane Report (1981) *Education for 16 to 19 Year Olds,* London, DES

McNair Report (1944) *Teachers and Youth Leaders,* London, HMSO

AEC ceasing to be represented on the Burnham Committee, it was disbanded. The death of an organization can thus be an opportune moment for the researcher to seek access to records (cf. Saran, 1973).

Permission to use the Teachers' Panel papers proved more difficult to obtain; the minutes were made available only some time after commencement of the SSRC grant. Archival records at the ACC were consulted at a later stage of the research, for a particular sub-topic, by which time access problems had been eased because policy-makers in the constituent organizations of the Burnham Committee were more *au fait* with my investigation. By then I had conducted interviews with at least some of them, and the SSRC grant had given prestige to the research.

Table 1 gives a list of primary sources used for the Burnham project. Sections 1 and 2 comprise archives of the two negotiating sides, section 3 mainly published government documents. I relied heavily on 'official documents' — time pressure and the long period covered by the project being two reasons. But it should be borne in mind that the combination of official documents used in no way conveyed only one view of the negotiations, because comparisons of data were made from documents of a range of organizations repre- sented on the Burnham Committee whose views did not necessarily coincide. In addition, on selected topics which became prominent in the research, I consulted journals, newspapers and other contempor- ary accounts for comparative purposes. For example, when engaged in detailed analysis of the 1969/70 negotiations, in which eventually the Secretary of State intervened personally, I used *Teachers in Turmoil* (Burke, 1971), an account of the events written shortly afterwards by a well-informed observer. This focused my attention on aspects of the teachers' strike which had not been emphasized as much by the official sources. The matching of such evidence from a varied range of documents is an essential part of the historian's craft.

From Table 1 it may be noted that negotiations in the full Burnham Committee are recorded verbatim. I had an uninterrupted run of these from 1951 to the early 1970s. Many hours were spent perusing this record. It became exasperatingly boring. Yet this introduction to the negotiating process and settlements gave me an immense amount of raw data, providing an outline map of the research field. From the verbatim record it could be noted that the Burnham Committee is made up of two panels, each comprising representatives from several union and employer organizations. One learned that there was a single spokesman (and it always was a *man*) for each side; that the full Committee often adjourned for panel

Table 2: *Formal Network of Burnham Committee (Primary & Secondary) 1981*

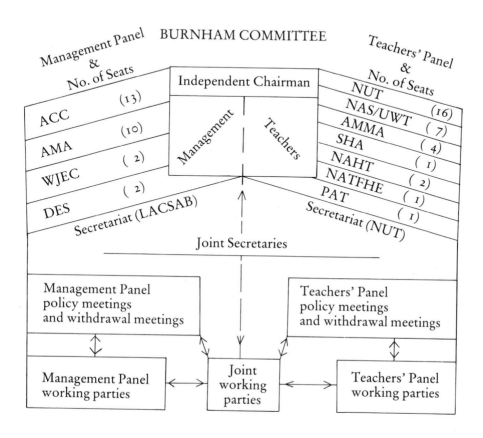

Acronyms

ACC	Association of County Councils
AMA	Association of Metropolitan Authorities
AMMA	Assistant Masters and Mistresses Association
DES	Department of Education and Science (the two DES members have a veto vote on global sums and a weighted vote on questions of distribution at Management Panel Meetings)
LACSAB	Local Authorities Conditions of Service Advisory Board
NAHT	National Association of Head Teachers
NAS/UWT	National Association of Schoolmasters/Union of Women Teachers
NATFHE	National Association of Teachers in Further and Higher Education
NUT	National Union of Teachers
PAT	Professional Association of Teachers
SHA	Secondary Heads Association
WJEC	Welsh Joint Education Committee

Rene Saran

Table 3:   Decision Process in Burnham Negotiations 1970–71

Management Panel — MP
Teachers' Panel — TP

Background
1   Termination date previous two-year agreement 31 March 1971. This
    was amended by 1970 interim award of £120, commencing 1 April 1970,
    on account. A new agreement, to be negotiated, was to commence
    partially 1 January 1971, fully 1 April 1971.
2   Negotiations commenced   3 July 1970   )
    Sent to arbitration   5 March 1971   )   13 months
    Arbitrators' report   22 July 1971   )
    Draft order based on arbitral award 9 August 1971   )
    Number of full Burnham Committee meetings — 9 (one stretched over 4
    days)
    Number of times Working Party met — 2
3   Arbitration Award: 10 per cent all teachers from 1 April 1971;
    Assimilation of all teachers to 5 new scales and Head and Deputy Head
    Teacher Scales.

Below are given recorded details for two of the nine meetings, the remainder
having been omitted from this table.

First meeting
TP claim: Basic scale £1,250–£2,200 (10 equal increments)
            Graduate addition: £175.   Consolidation grad. addition at
                                         maximum, by extension non-grad.
                                         scale to reach grad. maximum
                                         (£2,375).

            Good Honours: £175.
            Unit Totals: Same value for all children to 15.

withdrawal meetings on a given day, and for periods of days or weeks
to consult their constituent organizations. The mechanics of the
negotiating process thus became much clearer to me. Unlike someone
familiar with the details of industrial relations and wage negotiations,
I did not have this sort of knowledge.

   In addition, from Management and Teachers' Panel documents it
became apparent that these panels have two types of meetings:
ordinary ones at which, in the main, major policy decisions are made
prior to commencement of negotiations; and withdrawal meetings
(already mentioned) during negotiations to decide on immediate
negotiating tactics and on refusal, amendment or acceptance of
proposals made by the other Panel.

   Whereas at the early stages of the project I was very ignorant
about the Burnham Committee set-up, by the later stages I had

Posts of Special Responsibility Rationalization
needed   —   suggest 6 grades of post at £150, by £150 to £900
maximum.

MP: Suggest Working Party on structure, as agreed last round of
negotiations.

TP: Prefers MP thinking to be presented full Committee first. TP dislikes
negotiations in sub-committee: difficult to discuss structure unless
clothed with figures; once figures considered, is negotiation.

Adjournment to enable MP to prepare response to claim.

Fourth meeting

MP: *Basic + Allowances or Scales:*   Salary must relate to total activities,
including teaching, organization etc. Means scales. Can't divide salary
between teaching (basic scale element) and other tasks (allowances);
for H.T., large school, basic would be almost nil. MP incremental
structure related to salary and job, whereas on basic scale increments
same for all.
Unit Totals.   MP rejects TP proposals.
Promotion Anomalies.   TP criticism valid — alternative proposals
put forward. Renewed appeal for Working
Party.

TP: No case made out for Scales. MP keeps saying: These are our
proposals, let's have a Working Party. TP does not like Working
Parties; can result in commitments. Dislike refers specially to
discussion of hypothetical cases.
But TP unanimously agreed to join Working Party 'provided MP
does not rule out the possibility of a settlement which includes the
concept of a basic scale'.

(Working Party met twice)

gained enough insights mainly from archival data to compile a
diagram of the formal network, as shown in Table 2. To my
knowledge no records of withdrawal meetings are kept by either side,
although I found occasional references or records relating to such
meetings. For the Teachers' Panel, I had a complete run of ordinary
Panel meetings from 1944–74. By contrast, the Management Panel
kept no regular minutes of its ordinary meetings during the era of
Alexander's secretaryship (1947–73), though the archives contained
occasional typed minutes, as well as a book of easily decipherable
shorthand notes of Management Panel meetings covering several
years in the 1950s. The latter document recorded the views of
individual Management Panel members on the unit total system, of
which I made a special study.

Minutes of meetings (official documents) enable the researcher to peep behind the curtain, but they reveal only part of the drama. One respondent in an interview said such evidence was no more than the 'tip of an iceberg'. I had shown him one type of decision-process chart prepared from data contained in the verbatim Burnham Committee minutes, of which Table 3 is an example. Despite the 'tip of an iceberg' comment, the researcher has to jump in somewhere, to acquire a map of the research topic. For me, the extensive Management Panel papers proved invaluable, because a chronological record could be compiled therefrom of the decision-making process and content on certain issues, drawing on dated background discussion documents and even on correspondence. My earlier research on secondary policy had taught me that where committee records were underpinned by access to working documents and even correspondence, the insights gained into the policy-making process were of an altogether different complexity. The difficulties and excitement of such reconstructions of past events will be discussed later.

(b) *Interviews.* Interviews were sought mainly with leading policy-makers or other people well informed about the Burnham scene, to supplement data gathered from archives. A total of thirty-three persons were interviewed mainly in 1980 and 1981. Each interview lasted for anything between one to three hours. A few interviews were secured at an early stage of the research for purposes of general orientation: some as long ago as 1974–75. Thereafter interviews were left for a later stage for two reasons. I could hardly expect very busy people to give me a second chance to see them, although some were good enough to answer my questions during two, or even three, separate sessions. Thus, I had to be prepared to ask all major questions at one session, which meant I had first to identify these questions myself. The second reason was that successful use of the unstructured interview requires very careful preparation, based on prior analysis of raw data drawn from archives and secondary sources. The researcher must do the hard spade-work first. Good interviews are the bonus which follows. Just how I actually conducted my interviews is described below, to convey something of their chemistry.

First I want to explain why I favour, in the research I undertake, the informality and open-endedness of the unstructured interview. Drawing on modern textbooks, one may conclude that interviews, which can take many forms, can be 'placed on a continuum with structured interviews at one end and unstructured interviews at the other' (Burgess, 1982, p. 107). Unstructured interviews can, and should, in fact, be firmly controlled by the researcher. If also described as 'conversation', then the unstructured interview is 'conversation with a purpose', a 'unique instrument of the social investigator' (Webb and Webb, 1932, p. 130) or a 'controlled conversation' guided by the researcher 'to the service of his research interest' (Palmer, 1928, p. 171). Thus, what initially sounds totally unstructured (like the session of patient with therapist) is, in fact, conducted within a framework established by the researcher, so that 'the unstructured interview is flexible, but it is also controlled' (Burgess, 1982, p. 107).

The unstructured interview can take various forms (Burgess, 1982, p. 108–9). Mine may be described as both 'non-directive' and 'conversational', though they are almost always at least partly directed on my initiative. Occasionally, a respondent simply takes over, do what I will. The 'non-directive' aspect facilitates flexibility, a freer response, and allows for the modification of questions or even pursuit of new and unexpected topics, provided they are relevant. An interview that takes the form of 'conversation' may also be described as a dialogue between researcher and informant, so that a real exchange of views may take place.

How then do I prepare for interviews? For all stages of preparation it is vital to draw on one's existing knowledge of the research topic. Indeed, it is that knowledge which determines the list of likely and useful informants. First, then, advance approaches have to be made, usually by letter. These have to be carefully drafted to inform the respondent about the researcher's background and the nature of the investigation, as well as to indicate broadly the areas on which questions would concentrate, tapping the person's special knowledge. Such letters were written on Polytechnic letter-headed paper and were always typed. Here are some examples of initial approaches to leading policy-makers, including Teachers' Panel and Management Panel members, ministers and civil servants:

Examples of the opening paragraph of the letter were as follows:

(i) I am taking the liberty of writing to you about my current SSRC financed research project, which covers the Burnham salary negotiations since 1945. I am now half-way through the two-year grant period and have done a considerable amount of archival and other research, some interviews, some preliminary analysis and draft writing.

(ii) I gather that you are now retired, having served for many years on the Teachers' Panel in connection with the Burnham (P and S) Salary Negotiations. May I introduce myself? I have been interested in educational policy-making for many years, and teach — among other things — decision-making in British Government at the Polytechnic. But at the moment I am on sabbatical leave on a Social Science Research Grant, working on a study on the Burnham Salary Negotiations since 1945, with a cut-off point probably in 1974–75, with the Houghton award. I have had cooperation from both sides, and have already read the Teachers' Panel minutes from 1944 to the early 1970s at the NUT Library.

In turn I prepared specially tailored paragraphs for particular respondents as follows:

(i) As you are a recognized authority on the work of ..., I wondered whether you might be willing and able to spare the time to grant me an interview. You would, I am sure, be particularly knowledgeable about the events leading up to the 1965 Remuneration of Teachers' Act, and your views on that piece of legislation would interest me very much. But there may well be other aspects of my study on which you could be helpful, given your long experience in ...

(ii) I would very much like to have an opportunity of talking to a few 'backbench' members of the Teachers' Panel who had a reasonably long period as Panel members, and wondered whether you might be willing to see me sometime. Naturally what I would be most interested in is to hear your views about cooperation (or lack of it) between the various unions on the Teachers' Panel. I believe you played a prominent role during the negotiations for an interim flat-rate claim in the winter of 1969–70, and that is a round of negotiations in respect of which I discovered some unusual and interesting features — at least looked at through the eyes of an 'outside' researcher.

(iii) Your secretary suggested that I should indicate briefly in writing the questions I would wish to raise. I am of course interested in the Burnham negotiating machinery but know that the Remuneration of Teachers' Act is at present a highly sensitive issue. Possibly you would prefer not to discuss it at this particular time. My other major interest is the structure of teachers' salaries. Regardless of the precise form of the machinery through which negotiations are conducted, the parties always have to start their discussions from the status quo. In what respect does the structure fall short of the school system's present needs? The most recent criticism of the salaries structure is contained in paragraph 70 of the Clegg Report. How do you assess this? What, if any, possibilities exist to simplify the structure and what are the major difficulties in effecting changes? For example, how important is (a) the cost factor — especially in respect of safeguarding? (b) resistance to change — on one, or on both sides? (c) lack of agreement within or between the two panels over proposals for reform?

Finally I stated:

> I would greatly appreciate your granting me an interview, and would be happy either to travel to ... or to meet you in town, whichever is more convenient to you.

Before going to an interview, I always prepare a set of specially tailored questions. I do not necessarily ask them in a particular order, as that would make for a rigid, rather than a flexible, flow of answers. Whyte (1982, p. 112) refers to two types of responses in unstructured interviews:

> the objective and the subjective. Objective responses would be descriptive answers to questions like 'who did that?' whereas subjective ones would be evaluative answers to questions like 'how did you feel about that?'

Being well prepared helps the researcher to judge the accuracy with which a respondent is able to reconstruct past events from memory, that is, descriptive answers. It may also give the researcher a 'feel' about the degree of frankness with which evaluative answers are given. The kinds of questions that I posed are shown in the following examples:

Example 1:   Questions related to proposed changes in the Salaries Structure in 1971, when a system of five scales replaced a basic scale plus responsibility allowances

How did ideas for a new structure emerge in the 1960s?

What was Lord Alexander's response to proposals for change?

What was the LCC/ILEA's attitude to the unit total system?

By what mechanisms did the LCC/ILEA arrive at its policy views on Burnham?

Why was the Management Panel relatively unresponsive to teacher pressure on the age weighting of the unit total system?

Do older children require lower pupil-teacher ratios?

What prevented the Teachers' Panel, and the NUT in particular, from accepting the new salaries structure?

Falling school rolls are a source of difficulty for Burnham now. Did the emergence of middle and comprehensive schools at an earlier date affect your Panel's thinking about changes in the salaries structure?

Example 2: Questions on the 1965 Remuneration of Teachers' Act, which gave the DES direct representation on the Burnham Management Panel

What were the views of various teacher associations on the Teachers' Panel?

What in your view were the real motives of the DES? How soon were these apparent? Was the DES concerned primarily about the global sum of the salaries bill, the distribution of that bill, or controlling the local authorities' willingness to pay?

How did the Act affect subsequent negotiations?

All round, very few people refused to see me. One did so due to illness, and has died since. Another pleaded old age and faulty memory of events experienced some twenty years previously. Two crucial policy-makers — who were still involved in Burnham affairs — did not respond to my letters; I interpreted this as reluctance to face questions from a well-informed researcher at a time when rather sensitive negotiations were still in progress.

Many researchers record the actual interview on tape. I do not. Knowledge of shorthand enables me to dispense with this instrument. Experience suggests that tape-recording of interviews may be counter-productive when interviewing policy-makers about sensitive issues, but this objection might not apply to non-sensitive research. True, respondents may well forget the machine is switched on. Equally well they may not, and this will influence the free flow of comments. I vividly remember one interview where during the first two minutes I sensed that it was my notebook which froze my respondent. I quietly put it away and the atmosphere instantly became relaxed. Even when extensive notes have been taken during an interview, the researcher needs to write up the interview fully as soon as possible to ensure as near accurate reconstruction as possible of the main 'facts' and nuances of judgment conveyed during the dialogue. In my write-up I may undertake some ordering, for example, if the same topic was dealt with twice during the interview, it makes sense to place these responses together. Interview notes are one form of raw data. When asking particular questions later, or working on a topic, such notes are used to extract relevant bits of information. The following is an example of my write-up of part of an interview conducted in 1980 with a Teachers' Panel representative about the 1971 changes in the salaries structure. It articulates the informant's perceptions of the employers' as well as the NUT's views:

> Local authorities wanted to introduce scales because they felt they could not staff schools on basic scale and allowances given for qualifications and extra responsibilities. What they wanted to be able to do was to attract teachers to specific posts in schools which did not prove possible on basis of allowances. Shortage subjects could not be solved by such allowances. Another problem was if a new subject was to be developed. So one reason was shortage subjects; another was that the responsibility scheme did not enable authorities to give someone a considerable increase in salary at a particular point in time. Say a head of department of a large English department — he could have the allowance for that — but if the particular teacher was still relatively young, that allowance would not mean offering a good salary because he would still be low on the basic scale. The Management Panel wanted to be able to prevent a person from going to other jobs — for example in further education or even outside teaching. Further education had scales.
>
> The NUT was afraid that the scale system would be used to make certain posts attractive, and thereby salary of run of

the mill teacher would be depressed. May be this is, to some extent, true. It is easier to depress Scale 1 teachers, if the difficult posts can be filled by having Scales 3 and 4 to offer. The NUT represents all teachers and wants a good salary for everybody. It feared salary scales would be manipulated in such a way that Scale 1 would be kept low.

Writing-up interviews is time-consuming, but crucial if the data is to be useful for later reference and analyses in conjunction with other data on the same topic.

I want finally to paint a picture of my techniques and the 'feel' of the interview situation. In this connection I found Silver (1983) interesting. He views history as imaginative reconstruction, involving a dialogue with the dead. However unsatisfactory, the conversation has to take place 'within the controlling imagination of the historian', 'in order to treat evidence as elusive and unreliable and the opposite of the inert'. The researcher needs to understand, enter into, what Vickers (1965) has called the appreciative judgments of the policy-maker, his reality as well as his value judgments. People's appreciative perspective affects policy options at a particular time. Klein (1980) has argued that interviewing of policy-makers is an unreliable method for establishing what happened. But interviews could be crucial for testing the researcher's hunches and hypotheses, for entering into the atmosphere of the policy-maker. Without this one could get the bare facts wildly wrong. Policy studies, he argued, are an artistic rather than a scientific activity, and a novel has to be recognizable to the people who are in it.

Perhaps the sensitive researcher can enter into situations even more fully than the participant. Having read some of my earlier published work, one participant expressed amazement that I, an outsider, had understood more than he had ever done. Possibly the involved person is prevented from seeing the situation as dispassionately as an outsider may through reliving the events. Collingwood (1939) has argued that the historian has greater need of the head than the heart, for it is with the intellect that the historian re-enacts past events. I wonder, however, whether historical imagination does not in fact act as a bridge between the researcher's intellect and feelings. The unstructured interview is well suited to feel oneself into the situation of the policy-maker.

Experience has taught me that busy policy-makers are prepared to discuss in some depth an area of work which has been (sometimes still is) an important part of their life's experience with someone who asks searching questions, which stem from serious study and a prior grasp of the issue. Indeed, respondents are at times fascinated by the developing open-ended dialogue. Not infrequently it is the interested respondent who starts questioning the researcher.

The skill of interviewing can be learned. There are certain basic rules, for example never to tell one respondent what another has said. The researcher is in a similar situation to the Lobby correspondent. The moment the respondent senses that confidentialities may not be respected, free-flowing responses dry up. During the first few minutes of an interview the experienced policy-maker sizes up the researcher, who has to be finely sensitive in order to secure the respondent's cooperation. Whilst maturity is not simply a function of age, it probably helps if the researcher's age, experience and sensitivity facilitates quick rapport and the establishment of a relationship of trust. Throughout the interview the researcher has to make judgments about how the interview feels to the other person. There may be questions which the respondent does not wish to answer, because the issue was, or continues to be, politically or personally very sensitive. It might be wise to omit such a question. One has to feel that in one's bones. One wants, after all, to avoid 'more or less courteous dismissal' (Webb and Webb, 1932, p. 136).

Policy-makers work through a wide network involving many relationships of trust with other people. That alone means that an insensitive researcher could threaten the future effectiveness of the policy-maker. Some questions which can be successfully asked at the later stages of an interview could kill it if asked at the outset. Whyte (1982, pp. 113–7) counsels the researcher to discuss descriptive rather than evaluative topics at the beginning in order to establish rapport and confidence. Touchy topics should be left to a later interview. In my case there often is no later interview, so some questions may have to be omitted. I agree with much of Whyte's advice and the care needed in interpreting answers received. For example, recollections by informants of past feelings are often selected to fit into their current points of view. The well-informed researcher can test answers for implausibility, unreliability, and by grasp of what Whyte calls the 'informant's mental set' and how this influences any interpretation of events. But ultimately the researcher arrives only at approximations of reality in terms of what happened, and only at insightful awareness of the ambivalence of human motive and behaviour.

Even in reading archive material, let alone when questioning the living participant, I endeavour to assume the actor's sincerity of purpose and motive. One needs empathy to enter into other people's feelings to understand their purposes, aims and value assumptions. The 'principle of charity' is a good guide, until and unless one's evidence convinces one to the contrary.

Qualitative Methodology

The Three Methods

In the introduction reference was made to three methods which I use repeatedly in a spiral-like research process — abduction, deduction and induction. The traditional dichotomy between induction and deduction was first challenged by C.S. Peirce (1934), who replaced it with a trichotomy. He argued that traditional logic confused two meanings under the term 'induction'. He introduced the additional term of 'abduction' to distinguish the process of hypothesis *formation* from the process of hypothesis *testing*, for which he reserved the term induction. Glaser and Strauss in their 'grounded theory' approach fail to make this distinction.

In this section each method is briefly described. The reader is warned yet again, however, that the spiral-like research process is messy, that the methods described are not employed each separately in a given sequence, that indeed the researcher is often unaware what method is being used at a given moment.

Abduction. The name 'abduction' originated from C.S. Peirce (1934). The method may be described as a 'meta-method', requiring the researcher to be creatively inventive. No hypothesis emerges from the facts themselves. The human mind has to 'invent' it. Thus abduction is an inner mental process, resulting — when one is successful — in an *imaginative leap*. The inner recognition of a hypothesis involves the use of intuition, it is spontaneous, it brings into play one's emotions — intellectual creation can be enormously exciting. All scientists experience it, as Archimedes did in the bath! So our hypotheses result from reflection; Germans refer to the moment of imaginitive insight as an Aha-Erlebnis — the Aha experience (Bühler, 1908). Prior to the invention of appropriate hypotheses, raw data has no meaning. The researcher may possess 'all the facts' (what is all?), yet understand nothing. Thus mere fact gathering could proceed without method, resulting in a random collection of data.

However, the type of research I do requires immersion in empirical facts, for it is from such total immersion that my hypotheses are born (akin to 'grounded theory' building). As random, unordered facts do not in themselves produce hypotheses, a mental process of abduction is essential. Abstract, speculative, imaginative thought is at work, but it springs or bursts forth from a sea of facts crammed into the human mind. It is, of course, the case that the spiral-like activity has involved the researcher in a process distinguishable from the purely random collection of data. The searching for empirical evidence is itself a selective activity, since the researcher has certain questions or criteria in mind and is not a mere sponge absorbing everything. In the early stages of one's work, however, questions or criteria are often so vague or so broad that the mind is closer to Popper's bucket than to his searchlight (Popper, 1972). Gradually, as knowledge and understanding is built up, questions become more specific, the search more selective, the process more refined.

Deduction. The invention of a hypothesis (a general principle or statement) enables the researcher to put order into the previously unordered, or poorly ordered, facts. The process of deduction involves returning to detailed data, but *with new eyes,* to deduce or order the facts in a new way. The individual cases are viewed as (or deduced to be) particular examples of the general principle contained in the hypothesis. The researcher at this stage has to beware of an enchanting love affair with the hypothesis — that is, not to 'squeeze' the facts to fit the principle or generality contained in the provisional hypothesis.

Induction. Having deduced or inferred the individual facts from the hypothesis, the researcher's work may be checked by the process of induction. This involves making comparisons between the deduced (ordered with new eyes) facts and the previously unordered given facts. Thus the hypothesis is tested by ascertaining whether the deduced facts agree with all the particular examples the researcher has to hand (or which come to hand with further work) in the collected data. Induction is thus a method for testing an hypothesis not for inventing it.

Finally, the following diagram may be helpful as a summary of the three methods, or of Peirce's trichotomy:

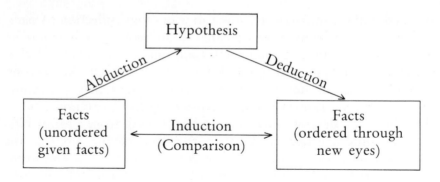

Application of Methods

Archives and interviews offer researchers two data sources. My task here is to describe and analyze, with examples from the Burnham project, how I actually applied the methods of abduction, deduction and induction in collecting and interpreting the data. Using these methods involves particular mental processes, which — unlike the trichotomy summarized above — do not operate in separate boxes. Briefly, then, abduction involves invention, deduction a new ordering of data, induction a testing by means of comparison.

Where interviews are used to test out the researcher's hunches or provisional hypotheses, then the mental process of invention or abduction is at work before conversing with a respondent. This influences the questions asked. An interview may produce new data, which in turn is then processed by the researcher's mind, using the other two methods of ordering as well as testing the new data to see whether the provisional hypothesis can accommodate it. This activity may lead to yet further inventive 'leaps', to refine one's hypothesis, if testing showed up its inadequacies. With careful prior preparation one can gain some chinks of light to help solve puzzles and fill gaps that have arisen from pondering data from previous interviews and/or written sources. But this is only possible if one already knows and has ordered into significant categories a great many facts, which has involved using all the three methods.

The success with which all three methods are applied is enhanced by the use of graphic representation to display data to myself. Table 2 is an example. The technique of drawing diagrams, charts, or even briefly summarizing particular data on a few sheets, can be an invaluable instrument for the researcher in the process of refining questions, aiding the spiral-like development towards greater clarity, meaning, explanation and generality. It thus assists making imaginative leaps (abduction) because one suddenly 'sees' something which massive detailed written notes failed to reveal; it facilitates new ordering of raw data, for example into a chart (deduction); finally, and almost simultaneously, one checks by comparison whether all one's known data ('facts') are accommodated in the chart under the invented categories of the hypothesis (induction). Graphic representations may also assist the researcher's writing up of results. The charts are used for purposes of clarification and simplification; when one then writes, one can do so with better structure, even though one often reintroduces (but in a more ordered way) the complexities of social reality.

Example 1: The Salaries Structure
Initially the search for empirical data seeks to answer very broad questions. My research assistant's first task was to identify the major characteristics of the salaries structure for schoolteachers for the period 1945–74 from the printed Burnham reports and other sources. We needed an *overview* of the structure, before we could ask more refined questions. Early work enabled us to select *criteria* which became headings for a chronological chart. These criteria could also be called provisional mini-hypotheses, for they reflected our judgment — arrived at by abduction — that the selected headings expressed a generality under which we could order — or deduce with new eyes — data drawn from many Burnham reports. Building up the chart involved the process of induction as well, because we checked that our invented headings were adequate, that we could order into the chosen categories all the raw data about the salaries structure which we had and continued to discover. Where certain data did not 'fit' into existing categories, new headings had to be invented and added to the chart.

We were able to invent headings for ordering our 'facts' partly as a result of immersion in our data, partly because we had prior wider knowledge and understanding, as well as experience, of trade union-employer relations — that is, the mind is never *tabula rasa*. By grouping our data under headings like responsibility, allowances, graduate additions, unit totals/school group, promotion differentials, we compiled a chart which gave us an ordered overview of the evolution of the salaries structure. At a glance this highlighted changes as well as continuities in the structure. Our new understanding, gained through use of the three methods and the technique of drawing a chart, enabled us to start asking new, more refined, questions about the revealed continuities and discontinuities. This well illustrates the spiral-like process in the use of one's methods: we were now searching for answers at a more informed level because raw data had been turned into ordered data. We asked why certain observed changes had occurred, as well as what explained observed non-changes.

Example 2: Innovation and Resistance to Change
Once an overview led to more refined questions, it was possible to seek and test one's own tentative explanations through interviews. Asking questions means one has inadequate evidence, or one has an unsolved puzzle. During unstructured interviews roles are sometimes reversed. One relatively new member of the Burnham Committee asked whether my historical knowledge of the Burnham negotiations threw light on the way actual changes of structure had been accomplished. I immediately responded with vivid descriptions of the negotiating difficulties in securing the 1956 and the 1971 settlements, the two which, since 1945, had introduced important changes in structure. However, this did not satisfy the Burnham member. Why had proposals for change been put forward, and who had taken the initiative, with what results? I decided to analyze part of my accumulated data in a new way. This experience illustrates how the search for explanations by participants who were interviewed influenced decisions about further work.

It was not possible to discover the reasons for change or non-change in the salaries structure from the chart documenting particular changes. But other charts had been compiled to document stages of the negotiating process during which salary settlements are hammered out between the bargaining sides. Chronological decision charts proved a useful method for reconstructing the decision process. Thus a comparison of the decision process in 1956 and 1971 could be undertaken by use of the charts for those two years (the one for 1971 is reproduced as Table 3). In particular, I was making the comparison from the point of view of the politics of innovation and resistance to change, so that pointers or partial answers might spring to mind to the new questions. One respondent had told me that the decision charts were only the 'tip of an iceberg'. Nevertheless, the comparative pondering of this ordered existing data helped me to open up the unseen part. Analysis of the decision process, in contrast to the end product of a salaries settlement, threw light on the changing negotiating positions of the two sides. Data from Management and Teachers' Panel archives illuminated the role played by individual participants or by particular groups in innovation or resistance to change. Whilst working on this sub-topic I sought access to the archives of one individual organization not previously used, as other data pointed to important initiatives for change originating from that quarter. Marshalling the available evidence brought certain insights which came to me by the process of abduction, which formed the conclusions of an article (Saran, 1982a). These threw light on why and how initiatives for change were taken and their fate during negotiations.

Example 3: Changes in Burnham Machinery

In giving this example I want to describe in detail the process of abduction. In working on this topic I experienced an actual very specific and memorable moment when I made an imaginative leap, alighted on a hypothesis, perhaps a mini-theory, which in turn in-fluenced further work on the project in most fruitful ways.

In my data collection, I initially concentrated on documenting the changes in the Burnham negotiating machinery since 1944. I needed to know the detail of the organizational framework within which salary negotiations were conducted. My efforts (using archives, *Hansard* and other published sources) led to the construc-tion of a dreary chronological record (ordered by dates, thus not entirely random) of the evolution of formal structures.

Boredom resulted in a shift of research interest to another aspect of the project, at least for a while. Such a break can actually be helpful to the researcher, because on returning to the topic one often is struck by previously unnoticed points. When on this occasion I returned to contemplating my data on the Burnham machinery, I became aware that participants had often seemed more excited about changes in machinery than in the substance of negotiated settlements. This puzzled me. Why had there been disputes over machinery — a mere means for arriving at agreements? This question was a considerable refinement of my original much broader one of simply asking what the Burnham machinery looked like and how it had changed. Until I could answer the more refined question I was unable to give meaning to my data beyond a dreary chronological sequence.

Some days later whilst preparing a meal, a sudden imaginative insight seemed to provide the clue: the participants' keen interest in changes of machinery was explicable because such changes were seen as a means to strengthen (or weaken) the bargaining power of participants. I dropped the knife and ran out into the sun, exclaiming to my husband, 'I think I have found the explanation!' A provisional hypothesis began to take shape:

Table 4: Negotiating Machinery as An Expression of Power Relationships: Burnham 1944–1980

Changes in Burnham Committee Machinery	Effect on Power Relationships		
	Within a Panel		Between the Panels
	Management Panel	Teachers' Panel	
1944 Education Act: Sect. 89 (i) Organizations/ number of Representatives on Burnham Committee decided by Secretary of State.	AEC > LAAs (AEC dominant despite numerical minority on Panel; AEC provides secretariat)	NUT > JOINT 4 (NUT had absolute numerical majority; NUT provides secretariat)	Balanced: MP = NUT
		MP protect minority Joint 4 interests (eg. over differentials).	(a) Benefitted teachers, as LEAs could no longer refuse to pay Burnham rates, as some had done pre-war.
(ii) Secretary of State's powers over negotiated settlements (a) Acceptance made settlements statutorily binding on LEAs (b) Settlement could be rejected	(b) LAAs/AEC > DES (DES as non-member has reserve power only at end of negotiating process)		
(iii) No provision for retrospection or arbitration			MP > TP (Management offers had to be accepted within time limit — no established method for backdating or resolving deadlock)
Rules of procedure not written — thus conventions — for example confidentiality, one spokesman per side			Assumption of trust and flexibility between the sides

Event				
1962 Membership: NAS and NAHT recognized by Secretary of State		NUT > NAS + the rest (but NAS challenges NUT dominance thus threatens unity of TP)	NAS challenge of Burnham procedural conventions causes standstill in negotiations; thus NAS weakens power of Burnham Committee. Secretary of State intervenes, resulting in written procedural rules — a less flexible but more open system — by 1965	Not known, but TP divisions believed to benefit MP
1964 Burnham Secretariat: Alexander of AEC ceases to be sole MP Secretary; LACSAB provides joint MP Secretary	LAAs > AEC (first organizational attempt to curb AEC's dominance)			Not known but over time likely to increase influence of local government spokesmen who are not committed educationalists, which may be detrimental to teachers' power
1965 Renumeration of Teachers' Act: (i) DES membership of MP DES powers under Concordat	DES >> LAAs/AEC (Veto vote over global sum; weighted vote over distribution of salaries; as a member, DES gained access to information on MP proceedings, but lost power of rejection of agreements)	Following 1965 Act, NUT absolute numerical majority preserved by decision of Secretary of State		MP >> TP (Central Government able to limit global sum available, thus curbing previous flexibility in negotiations)
(ii) Retrospection				TP > MP (Time pressure for concluding settlements reduced. TP power enhanced by greater effectiveness of delaying tactics, strike weapon)

Table 4 (continued): Negotiating Machinery as An Expression of Power Relationships: Burnham 1944–1980

Changes in Burnham Committee Machinery	Effect on Power Relationships		
	Within a Panel		Between the Panels
	Management Panel	Teachers' Panel	
(iii) Provision for Arbitration (Arbitration arrangements by Secretary of State provide for 'compulsory' arbitration — on ruling of independent chairman unilateral request for arbitration may be granted)	TP minority interests may benefit from fact that NUT dominance could be curbed by MP requesting compulsory arbitration (for example over differentials)		1965–75 MP > TP (TP fear that arbitration not independent of government incomes policy; MP seeking 'deadlock proof' machinery, but independent chairman's ruling preserves some balance of power between sides) 1975–80 TP > MP (MP fear loss of bargaining power at time of cash limits if TP secures cost of living and comparability claims via arbitration without having to 'trade off' concessions MP seeks)
(iv) Two resolutions Procedure in Parliament to set aside Arbitration Award (Government power of last resort, if national economic circumstances warrant)	Government > LAAs (although DES as a MP member normally has to accept arbitration award, Government has reserve power to reject via Parliament)		TP < MP (Because independence of arbitrators can be overridden — but so far reserve power not used)

1974 Membership: Secretary of State disaffiliates AEC.	LAAs inherited AEC's power (1976 AEC disbanded)	Not known, but influence of LA Treasurers — rather than committed educationalists — over negotiations believed to be greater, thus TP <
1980 Consultations over amendment/repeal (?) of Remuneration of Teachers' Act, to date limited to MP members. There are 3 major issues: (i) Proposed changes in arbitration arrangements		Not known. But LAAs are seeking to enhance their bargaining power by making access to arbitration more difficult for teachers, hoping thereby to secure concessions from TP during negotiations in return for salary settlements.
(ii) Linking negotiations for Salaries with those for Conditions	Not known. DES has no direct voice over conditions of service negotiated through CLEA. DES may seek to enhance its power — LAAs are likely to resist this. (But see also below: DES/LAAs may make a deal giving DES some voice over conditions in return for reduced power over salaries)	Not known, but LAAs seek specific concessions on conditions of service which TP will resist as undermining their power of sanctions (eg. withdrawal of cooperation over meals supervision is not in breach of contract since under the 1968 Agreement these duties are voluntary. Teachers are therefore able to resort to disruptive sanctions at cost of LAs, whereas use of strike weapon is expensive for teacher unions)
(iii) DES powers over Salaries under Concordat	LAAs < DES at present. (LAAs argue that cash limits and Heseltine's new Land Bill No. 2. make the veto vote over global sum obsolete, and seek to reduce DES powers)	LAAs and probably TP as well (certainly the NUT) expect that curbing the power of DES would restore the earlier balance of power between the two sides, from which both parties assume future negotiations would benefit

> Changes in negotiating machinery strengthen or weaken (enhance or curb) the relative powers of bargaining partners. (Saran, 1981b)

This was a general statement. It was usable for further work. Its creation had undoubtedly been helped by reading some secondary literature on industrial relations (Clegg, 1979; Kahn-Freund, 1979; Thomson and Beaumont, 1978). Feverish writing of draft chapters ensued; following the imaginative leap by abduction to a hypothesis, all previously gathered data could now be ordered in a new manner (the process of deduction) and could then be checked against the original facts (the process of induction). The activity of reordering and checking provided a range of themes around which meaningful interpretative chapters could be written. About a year later, in preparation for a conference paper, I returned to the topic yet again and compiled the chart reproduced in Table 4 which sets out the effects on power relationships of given changes in machinery. By way of visual display, under appropriately selected headings, the chart tested the 'truth' of my hypothesis in the light of all the given facts I had accumulated. I pondered with respect to each change the relative shifts of power between the bargaining partners. A further refinement was to establish relative shifts of power within each side, also included in the chart. This was an idea I had come across in reading about industrial relations. In a complex negotiating set-up where a number of organizations are represented on each side, clearly relative power shifts may occur not only between, but also within, each side.

There followed at a later stage another idea as to how the 'power relationships' hypothesis might be tested. I had meanwhile done a lot of work on the Burnham Committee verbatim minutes in order to document the stages of the negotiating process during which salary settlements are worked out. I had been interested in both the decision process and in decision content, as example 2 above illustrates. Perhaps one could now correlate the shifts of relative power associated with a particular change in machinery with known changes in negotiating outcome. One could ask the question whether particular salary settlements were favourable to the side which had enhanced its bargaining power, unfavourable to the side whose power had been curbed. Looking at data on machinery with new eyes had opened up new possibilities for interpreting the salaries structure. By this means the hypothesis about power relationships might serve to link the two major areas of the research: the changing formal organizational structure viewed as a system of power relations; the salaries settlements viewed as negotiating outcome reflecting those power relationships. The mental structure for a book began to take shape; chapter headings within that structure came to mind.

The task of integrating my written-up data into a coherent book still remains. It will be a challenge to see whether I succeed in knitting together two major areas of the research on the lines indicated above. It seems that the researcher's task never ends!

Conclusion

Various scholars have described the process by which new ideas are generated (for example, Wallas, 1926; Hadamard, 1945). It involves the constant interaction of intense preoccupation or immersion, periods of gestation or incubation, and moments of illumination.

To use appropriate research methods successfully, one needs to stand back from time to time to reflect on one's methods and to improve them. It is probably true that thinking about them very deliberately at the time of working on a particular project might make one very self-conscious about the skill, and this could be counter-productive. But this paper has been written as a post-hoc analysis of the methods actually used in handling archive and interview data. I anticipate that it will also assist me in future research.

Acknowledgements

I wish to thank the editor, Robert Burgess, for his helpful comments on my workshop paper before revision for this chapter. Two friends gave me stimulus, encouragement and ideas for writing the original paper: I am most grateful to Paul Branton, Department of Occupational Psychology, Birkbeck College, University of London, and to Fernando Leal, University of Guadalajara, Mexico.

Note

1 The Burnham (Main) Committee, referred to in this summary, negotiates the salaries of schoolteachers, not of lecturers in the public sector of further and higher education, for which there is a separate Burnham Committee.

References

BÜHLER, K. (1908), 'Tatsachen und Probleme zu einer Psychologie der Denkvorgänge II. über Gedankenzusammenhänge', *Archiv für die Gesamte Psychologie*, 12, pp. 1–23 (specially pp. 17 ff.)

BURGESS, R.G. (1982), 'The unstructured interview as conversation', in BURGESS, R.G. (Ed.) *Field Research: A Sourcebook and Field Manual*, London, Allen and Unwin.

BURKE, V. (1971) *Teachers in Turmoil*, Harmondsworth, Penguin.

CLEGG, H.A. (1979) *The Changing System of Industrial Relations in Great Britain*, Oxford, Basil Blackwell.

COLLINGWOOD, R.G. (1939) *An Autobiography*, Oxford University Press, see especially Chapter IX; cf. also his posthumous (1946) *The Idea of History*, Oxford, Oxford University Press.

DAVIES, C. (Ed.) (1980) *Rewriting Nursing History*, London, Croom Helm.

FILSTEAD, W.J. (1970) *Qualitative Methodology*, Chicago, Markham Publishing Co.

FOSTER, J. and SHEPPARD, J. (1980) 'Archives and the history of nursing', in DAVIES, C. (Ed.) *Rewriting Nursing History*, London, Croom Helm.

GLASER, B.G. and STRAUSS, A.L. (1967) *The Discovery of Grounded Theory: Strategies for Qualitative Research*, Chicago, Aldine Publishing Co.

HADAMARD, J. (1945) *The Psychology of Invention in the Mathematical Field*, Princeton, University Press.

KAHN-FREUND, O. (1979) *Labour Relations — Heritage and Adjustment*, Oxford, University Press (for the British Academy).

KLEIN, R. (1980) 'Policy options at a time of stringency', lecture at the City of London Polytechnic, 19 November.

PALMER, V.M. (1928) *Field Studies in Sociology: A Students Manual*, Chicago, University of Chicago Press, cited by BURGESS, R.G. (1982) 'The unstructured interview as a conversation'.

PIERCE, C.S. (1934) in HARTSHORNE, C. and WEISS, P. (Eds.) ([1]1934, [2]1965) *Collected Papers of Charles Sanders Pierce*, Cambridge, Mass., The Belknap Press, Vol. 5, pp. 99 ff.

POPPER, K.R. (1972) 'The bucket and the searchlight: two theories of knowledge', in *Objective Knowledge*, Oxford, Clarendon Press.

SARAN, R. (1973) *Policy-Making in Secondary Education*, Oxford, Clarendon Press.

SARAN, R. (1981a) 'Debate: do you feel undervalued', *Junior Education*, February, p. 11.

SARAN, R. (1981b) 'Negotiating machinery as an expression of power relationships: the case of Burnham 1944–1980', in RIBBINS, P. and THOMAS, H. (Eds.) *Research in Educational Management and Administration*, Proceedings of the Second British Educational Management and Administration Society/Social Science Research Council Research Seminar, Occasional Publication of the British Educational Management and Administration Society, pp. 35–46.

SARAN, R. (1981c) Social Science Research Council end-of-grant report, reference HR/6170/2.

SARAN, R. (1982a) 'The politics of bargaining relationships during Burnham negotiations', *Educational Management and Administration*, 10, 2, pp. 39–43.

SARAN, R. (1982b) *Reform of Teachers' Salary Structure*, University of Liverpool, School of Education Occasional Papers, pp. 1–30.

SARAN, R. (1982c) 'Why quality must pay in the classroom', *Times Educational Supplement*, 22 October, Platform Page 4.

SARAN, R. and VERBER, L. (1979/80) 'The Burnham unit total system: career structure and resource allocation 1948–1974', *Educational Administration*, 8, 1, pp. 113–38.

SILVER, H. (1983) 'Case study and historical research', in *Education as History*, London, Methuen.

THOMSON, A.J.W. and BEAUMONT, P.B. (1978) *Public Sector Bargaining: A Study of Relative Gain*, Farnborough, Saxon House.

VICKERS, SIR G. (1965) *The Art of Judgment — A Study of Policy Making*, London, Chapman and Hall.

WALLAS, G. (1926) *The Art of Thought*, New York, Harcourt Brace.

WEBB, S and WEBB, B. (1932) *Methods of Social Study*, London, Longmans, Green, cited by BURGESS, R.G. (1982) 'The unstructured interview as a conversation'.

WHYTE, W.F. (1982) 'Interviewing in field research', in BURGESS, R.G. (Ed.) *Field Research: A Sourcebook and Field Manual*, London, Allen and Unwin.

9 Ethnomethodology and the Study of Deviance in Schools

Stephen Hester

From an ethnomethodological perspective the facts of social life — social realities — are inseparable from the methods of their constitution in social interaction. Indeed, in a strong sense, social reality *is* its methodic constitution. In this paper I shall discuss some methodological issues pertaining to the use of such a perspective in investigating the phenomenon of 'deviance' in schools.[1]

Developing an Ethnomethodological Stance

The research which is the subject of this paper emerged out of an earlier study of deviance of classrooms (Hargreaves, Hester and Mellor, 1975). The central focus of that work had been the 'labelling' of deviant acts and persons within the context of classroom interaction. This focus had yielded analyses of the nature of rules in classrooms, teachers' methods for bringing rules into play, the knowledge drawn upon by pupils (and assumed by teachers) in interpreting teachers' talk as rule invocations and deviance imputations, and the ways in which teachers achieved a sense of pupil conduct as deviant. In addition, a 'theory of typing' had been presented. This attempted to summarize how teachers arrived at typifications of pupils, both in general and with particular reference to deviant pupils. Finally, teachers' decision-making in relation to the problem of how to react to deviant conduct when it occurred was explored in detail. Throughout, the focal point of analysis was on the use of 'commonsense knowledge' in making sense of deviance in classrooms. In the research to be discussed here the initial aim was to develop this earlier work through an examination of the social processes whereby some deviant pupils are referred to and subsequently assessed by agencies outside the school setting, particularly those associated with the provision of special education. The intention was to identify a collection of conditions or contingencies relating to the subjection of these children to this referral process. In doing this it was anticipated that 'what happens next', a question which had not been addressed in *Deviance in Classrooms,* could be explained.

This research was not only continuous at a substantive level with that in *Deviance in Classrooms;* it also adhered at the outset to the 'phenomenological' approach which had been employed there. This meant that the aim of the research was to produce, firstly, a description of the 'meanings' of deviance from the 'standpoint' of the actors (teachers, social workers, educational psychologists, psychiatrists, etc.) who were involved in the referral and assessment process and, secondly, an analysis of how such meanings were constituted or arrived at. In terms of the subject matter of the research these two 'methodological imperatives' required a focus on the commonsense knowledge (the criteria, assumptions, rules of thumb, models, typifications, and other 'interpretive phenomena') which was employed in the organizational processing of deviant pupils. It was thought that interviews with, and observations of the social interaction between, the various educational personnel who were participants in this processing would help in the discovery of such knowledge. Through its inference and documentation it was anticipated that the ultimate goal of the construction of a phenomenological theory of referral would be reached.[2]

The initial list of questions for research was as follows:

(i) Under what conditions do teachers seek the assistance of agencies outside the school setting with respect to 'deviant' children?

(ii) What kinds of typifications of children do teachers use in describing children when they refer them?

(iii) How do the staff of special education agencies translate teachers' descriptions into their own operational frameworks of meaning?

(iv) How do agency staff assess children referred to them?

(v) How do agency staff devize remedial strategies for referred children?

The method for gathering data to provide a basis for eventual answers to these questions, and to learn more about the social interactions between teachers and agency staff, consisted initially of establishing contact with an agency to which teachers referred children. It was thought that this would enable (a) the selection of a sample of previous referrals and its retrospective examination through interviews with teachers and agency staff; and (b) the interception of a sample of 'new' referrals with a view to monitoring their organizational processing. Interviews and observation were to be the methods to accomplish this monitoring. Access to such a research setting presented few difficulties: a colleague knew someone who worked as a Principal Educational Psychologist at a local Child and Family Guidance Clinic. After a series of discussions with him and his colleagues, and also negotiations with the teachers in the schools within the catchment area of the Clinic, fieldwork began. Visits were made several times a week to the Clinic and the social workers and educational psychologists who had agreed to be interviewed provided detailed information about their work.[3] The central focus at this stage was the different types of referral which the Clinic handled and the reasons underlying their referral. At the same time, the staff were also accompanied on their visits to schools where they discussed both old and new referrals with teachers. These visits were openly observed and in many cases tape-recorded. As soon as possible after each visit interviews about what had happened were held with staff.

As the fieldwork progressed and the data began to accumulate, a number of developments occurred which resulted in the abandonment of the original commitment to 'phenomenological sociology' and to the methods of 'observation' and 'interviews' as methods for generating data to be used in the construction of a phenomenological theory of referral. In retrospect, and in inevitably oversimplified terms, the complex series of events and experiences which occasioned this can be summed up as revolving around the following methodological issues: the partiality of data, the production of sociological accounts, and the observability of interpretive processes. Coming to terms with these issues meant a reorientation of perspective towards ethnomethodology and conversation analysis.

The Partiality of Relevant Data

It was not long after the research began that the realization occurred that it was not going to be possible to observe the 'full' course of events relating to the organizational processing of each referral, from its initial recognition as a 'problem about which something ought to be done' to 'case closure', in any selected sample of cases. In the first place there was the sheer physical problem of being present at all of the relevant meetings and encounters connected with each of the cases selected for study. Secondly, and perhaps more importantly, it became clear that the processing of cases and the involvement of staff with referred pupils extended typically over considerable periods of time, sometimes years. Such a time-span clearly precluded anything approaching a comprehensive observational coverage of staff's work on cases let alone the complex series of events leading to the referral in the first place. These events often extended way back into the child's biography and his or her relationships with others, and they were obviously beyond the scope of observation. If the natural history of referral began long before researchers appeared on the scene and was likely to continue after they had left it then much of the 'process' would be hidden from view. Even if the time or resources had been available for 'constant monitoring' the limited period of fieldwork could only provide a fragment of the material which seemed relevant to an understanding of the referral process.

The realization that only isolated and dissociated glimpses and images of the phenomena which were of interest could be obtained led to reflections on how these could be related to the original project of producing a phenomenological theory of referral. How could such fragmentary data serve as a reliable resource for a valid theory? The conventional ethnographic response to this problem seemed reassuring: this was to recognize that such fragmentary data is an inevitable condition of doing research and that it was a positivist dream or delusion to suppose otherwise. Further, anthropologists and sociologists typically manage to make something out of their research materials however 'thin', 'partial' or 'fragmented' they may be. Such achievements could have served to assuage any anxieties about the data because it could be observed that other researchers — both predecessors and contemporaries — had been able to 'piece together' their data and produce acceptable findings. Even if 'complete' description was in principle impossible (cf. Sacks, 1963) there remained, however, a sense in which sociologists just scratch the surface when they conduct research, qualitative no less than quantitative. Their data, in other words, is always partial in the sense that it consists of only glimpsed fragments of the social life being investigated.

The Production of Sociological Accounts

Even if the partiality of data could be construed as a 'problem' with which the sociologist has to live because it is an endemic feature of sociological work, further reflection on this matter led to more serious doubts about the methodological path being followed. What soon became thrown into sharp relief was the methodic and accomplished character of sociological accounts and the problematic nature of the process whereby sociologists produce generalizations from the relative and particular data at their disposal. The doubts expressed themselves in several ways. Firstly, doubts surfaced about the relationship between the sociologist's use of descriptive terms like 'process' (for example, 'the referral process') — as devices for making sense of events in the life of those people being studied — and the ways in which those people themselves made sense of such events, assuming that they did so. The notion of 'process' indexed a systematicity, an interconnectedness, which perhaps was not a feature of how the people being studied experienced their lives in society. When sociologists begin their research with notions like 'process', which they deem in advance as relevant for capturing the nature of social life, and then treat observed events as indicators of such notions, they risk imposing an analytical structure on those events which is alien to those who experience them from within. This doubt, then, pointed to the need for a greater sensitivity to the members' ways of experiencing events and to enhanced scepticism about sociological versions of those experiences.[4]

The second way in which doubt was expressed about the methodological path which had been laid out for the construction of a phenomenological theory of referral concerned the question of how the sociologist demonstrates the relationship or relevance of an account to those of the people being studied. Even if the sociologist does not impose some a priori conceptual scheme — like 'social process' — and instead attempts to develop some 'grounded' and 'adequate' account from the bits and pieces of talk and action collected in the course of research there remains the problem that the sociologist has to interpret the meanings of that talk and action in order to arrive at inferences about what is going on 'out there'. Thus, for the construction of a phenomenological theory of referral interpretive work would have to be done on members' talk and action in order to infer the knowledge (criteria, assumptions, models, rules, etc.) which underpinned the referral process. In this, of course, the sociologist shares the same 'predicament' as the members themselves — they too are constantly engaged in similar processes of practical reasoning in order to decide the 'facts of the case', the 'kind of problem we face here', 'what are we going to do about this', and so on. Both members and sociologists, in other words, make use of certain 'resources' in producing a sense for their experiences. However, such interpretive work is seldom revealed or even addressed in phenomenological versions of social life. The knowledge used by analysts is typically treated as an unexplicated resource, rather than as a topic in its own right (cf. Zimmerman and Pollner, 1971). It is through the use of such resources that depictions of 'what is going on out there' are produced; sociological accounts are constitutive of that which they describe, rather than being simple or neutral reflections of independent realities. The implication of this is that these resources which are drawn upon in constructing sociological accounts need to be revealed rather than taken for granted.

A third problem which surfaced at this stage of the research was this: if the original intention of examining staff talk and action, whether in interviews or in 'natural' settings, in order to abstract some general theory of referral was to be followed through, then meanings would have to be dissociated from their original contexts of expression. The problems here are two-fold. First, there is no guarantee that such 'decontextualized' meanings are generalizable to contexts other than those in which they were originally produced. Second, the assumption would have to be made that meanings are settled in a once-and-for-all fashion through some shared agreement on usage. However, if the view is taken that all usage is necessarily situated usage then the assumption that knowledge exists independently of social context is untenable. In other words, therefore, if meanings are more appropriately seen as being continually elaborated, with members of a culture arriving at 'correct meanings' only for practical purposes through an examination of the particular settings in which they find themselves, then a radically different kind of approach from that originally conceived was implied. The requirement was for an approach which took into consideration the contextually embedded character of the social constitution of social meanings on the part of both members (in the work of teaching and child and family guidance) and researcher (in the work of observation and sociological analysis).

The Observability of Interpretive Processes

Earlier ethnographic and phenomenological sociological work appeared to have ignored this emerging critique. More than this, it typically entailed a commitment to a mentalistic or cognitive model of interpretive processes. This model is exemplified in the work of

Schutz (1964 and 1967) and Cicourel (1964, 1968 and 1972). The processes of interpretation are here largely covert mental activities which can only be investigated retrospectively and indirectly. By way of contrast, ethnomethodologists and, in particular, conversation analysts, had set about the task of studying such matters as 'understanding', 'sense making', 'using knowledge', 'typifying', etc., without recourse to such a decontextualized model. The view here is that interpretation is not simply a covert mental process which 'surface' categorizations presuppose. Rather, these surface categorizations are themselves acts of interpretation. Furthermore, for the researcher who wishes to conduct empirical work on interpretive processes then there is no other place to go but to the study of such surface phenomena. Other interpretive 'activities' are, in the final analysis, analytic constructions imposed upon them. It was thus that in the context of this research 'interpretation' came to be seen as synonymous with the activity of description, with a focus on description at the level of members' talk demanding first consideration. Following this route enables the sociologist to avoid providing an account of social processes through the invocation of 'procedures', 'rules', 'assumptions', 'knowledge', etc., and other dubious entities 'under the skull'.

As a result of these reflections, then, the goal of constructing a phenomenological theory of referral from interview and observational material was eventually viewed as an inappropriate way in which to proceed. The conclusion was reached that the most appropriate direction for further research was the close examination of talk about pupil deviance in particular settings, with a focus on the locally managed, situated construction of the meanings of deviance. The problem was to find a way of proceeding which showed (a) how the members (teachers, educational psychologists, and social workers) described deviance; (b) how the researcher produced an understanding of what the members were doing; and (c) complied with the constraints of the critique which had been generated. As had been argued by others (cf. Atkinson and Drew, 1979) ethnomethodological ethnography did not look promising since it, like its symbolic interactionist counterpart, typically entails a failure to explicate adequately its own production and, most importantly, fails to come to terms with the situated character of interpretive processes. If the sociologist wishes to examine how members use their practical reasoning in processing referrals on particular occasions, to do so in a way which avoids the pitfalls of the cognitive approach and which also reveals the constitutive character of sociological analysis, then it becomes necessary at least to provide the reader with the materials which are used in the production of that analysis. This not only 'situates' the analysis, it also allows the 'findings', 'conclusions', and 'practical reasoning' used in generating them to be displayed, inspected, challenged, checked or modified with reference to the same data as that used by the analyst. It seemed that conversation analysis, in its provision of transcripts of naturally occurring talk, had most fully come to terms with the issues involved here. Accordingly, this became the methodological strategy for further research.

Audio-tape recordings were made and subsequently transcribed of a large number of meetings in a variety of contexts in which children were discussed by teachers, educational psychologists and social workers. These included routine visits to schools by educational psychologists, case conferences within schools involving teachers, psychologists, social workers and others, staff meetings within the Clinic, work allocation meetings, intelligence tests and interviews, etc. The aim was to analyze the organization of the naturally occurring talk in these settings wherein deviance was described, and where decisions were taken about managing it.

Conversation Analysis and the Social Constitution of Deviance in Educational Settings

The path of conversation analysis seems to have become the dominant form of enquiry within ethnomethodology, particularly in Britain. Its central focus is the sequential organization of talk itself. With respect to the research being discussed here it has resulted in studies of the opening and closing of meetings, the organization of reporting (story-telling) within case conferences, the topical organization of talk about children, the selection of descriptions and the use of membership categorization devices, and the use of contrastive and other devices in the production of reports and stories. However, such work is not without methodological problems of its own, at least insofar as the investigation of substantive issues like 'deviance' is concerned. Hence, rather than focus on the detail of the products of these analyses the following remarks will be confined to the methodological issues which were encountered in making use of this approach.[5] The central problem is this: in searching through the transcripts and listening to the tape recordings for sequential regularities and uniformities there is a sense in which the researcher tends to lose sight of what the talk is about — its subject matter (for example, 'deviance') — as opposed to the organization of the talk itself. Whilst it may be justifiably claimed that the pay-off from conversation analysis is considerable — its capacity to comply with ethnomethodological principles of enquiry, and its illumination of the social organization of talk in particular settings — there is, nevertheless, a sense in which its concern with the 'formal' features of talk tends to divert attention away from the 'substance' of that talk.[6] There is, in other words, something of a 'tension' between the formal and substantive concerns of enquiry within conversation analysis, with any illumination of the latter being more a by-product of analysis of the former than a central focus of research.[7] When studying 'making reports', 'describing people', 'turn-taking', 'doing agreements', 'opening and closing topics', and the rest, it is difficult to resist the conclusion that 'any setting will do'. Against this, the notion of 'speech exchange system', as a device for referring to the different ways in which turn-taking is organized in relation to different projects, can be said to imply a concern with talk in substantive contexts (for example, courtrooms, classrooms, case conferences) but once again, even here, the focus is more on the form than on the content of the discourse in question. Even if the researcher argues that talk accomplishes the description and ascription of deviance and that therefore a focus on the talk itself will illuminate deviance, this seems insufficient to refute the charge that the subject matter of the talk — the children and their supposed problems — tends to be rather left out of the picture.

These misgivings about conversation analysis resulted in the use of a closely-related perspective from within the family of ethnomethodological approaches, specifically the work of Pollner (1974a, 1974b, 1975 and 1978). Here it seemed that the focus had been not so much on how talk itself is organized but on what may be accomplished in and through the talk, and yet at the same time Pollner had conducted his analyses with reference to transcripts of naturally occurring talk. In general, what Pollner appears to be saying is that talk about the social world embodies presuppositions which reflexively constitute the character of the world being talked about. More specifically, the presupposed facticity of a social phenomenon is reflexively confirmed in talk which takes such a phenomenon as a pre-given ground for talk in relation to it. Pollner (1974a) has suggested that talk about the world rests upon and displays an 'idiom of mundane reason', consisting of a set of assumptions and operations of practical reasoning based upon them. In his early work, he examined how the assumption of an objective and intersubjective social world was used in the solution of 'reality disjunctures', in particular in solving the puzzle posed by conflicting versions of events in witnesses' testimony in traffic courts. Thus, the judge's presumption that people cannot be in two places at one time, that they cannot be going at two speeds in their cars at the same time, etc., enables conclusions such as one of the witnesses is mistaken, or is telling lies, to be reached and the 'reality disjuncture' solved. Without an assumption of this kind the spectre of a world of multiple ontological possibilities and realities is raised; with the 'common-sense' view of the world shattered there would be no authoritative way of choosing between competing versions of reality. But with the assumption of an objective and intersubjective social world, of course, the facticity of our world and the objects within it is continually sustained and the chaos of multiple realities avoided. In a later study (1978) Pollner builds upon this earlier work in making a distinction between 'mundane' and 'constitutive' versions or models of deviance. Where the former conceives of deviance as a pre-given feature of an act or person and as the independent cause of social reaction to it, the constitutive version conceives of the mundane or commonsense version, with its assumption of the pre-given facticity of deviance, as being constitutive of the reality of deviance in the first place. Deviance is created by members as they mask their creativity from themselves through their assumption that deviance is independent of their creative work.

Pollner's approach appeared to be one offering great potential in clarifying how teachers and staff from the Child and Family Guidance Clinic constituted the reality of the problems of deviance in schools with which they had to deal. It was thus that the research began to pay close attention to the 'reification' of deviance: those human practices whereby human accomplishments are conceived of as having an existence which is independent of those practices. But what were these practices? Pollner had indicated that the use of the mundane version of deviance was one such practice. He had also spoken of 'talking practices' as constitutive of objective and inter-subjective realities, but he had very little to say, it seemed, about the precise character of such practices. The search for 'practices' in the talk about deviant pupils thus became the research task.

Initial analysis of the materials suggested that it was indeed possible to locate within the talk of teachers and educational psychologists the presupposition of a pre-given object called deviance, which is the cause of their social reactions towards it. This can be heard in the talk of such persons in at least two senses. Firstly, it can be heard when children are described or typified. In these descriptions or typifications the speakers can be heard to display an orientation to some pre-given features of the child as grounds for the description. Consider the following extract from a case conference about a primary school pupil:

SA/273

```
 1  EP:   or perhaps it wasn't that__perhaps it was just that__you
 2        know he wasn't listening to what was going on__he was
 3        more interested in his cowboys and indians__but er he
 4        comes out on testing as er ESN__but=
 5  T1:              [hmm]
 6  EP:  =whether that's a true picture__of Simon I don't know but
 7        as I said we want to find out whether individual home
 8        tuition working one to one is gunna boost his attainments
 9        to such a point where we can do testing again to see
10        whether or not he is ESN or whatever its ermm his
11        behaviour you know that's interfering with his learning__
12        but from the er report and from ( ........ ) errmm
13        people have been saying this afternoon my impression is
14        that he is a slow learner and he is ESN and that his
15        behaviour is probably__a result of his inability to__er
16        cope with ( ...... ) independent study__you know
17        frustration's been talked about
18  T1:   mm
```

A possible reading of this transcript is that the educational psychologist (EP) can be heard to maintain a distinction (lines 6 to 10) between the 'picture' of Simon which is yielded by the test results and the 'true picture' of Simon. This extract can thus be heard to display a conception of 'testing' as a passive activity, one conducted under the auspices of the presupposition of some pre-given degree of educational subnormality as an objective feature of the child in question. Indeed, the educational psychologist (lines 9 to 10) states that he wishes to do testing again to discover 'whether or not he is ESN or whatever'. Such a view of testing to decide whether a child is 'really' ESN or not is achieved on the basis of the assumption that the child's normality/subnormality is inherent: it has an existence which is independent of its recognition and it is the pre-existing cause of the description provided by the activity of testing.

A second way in which reification of deviance can be said to occur is when members speak of social reactions to deviance. In particular, it can be heard in talk which uses prior typifications as taken for granted grounds for devizing ways of intervening in the case of deviance. This can be heard in the following extract where an educational psychologist is discussing an intervention strategy with a teacher (this time in an infant school).

WIS/30

```
 1  EP:  on the other hand I-I could perhaps give you errm a sort
 2        of err an observation sheet [which] umm you know you
               might be able =
 3  T1:                              [umm]
 4  EP:  =to they're fairly easy to use [they] wouldn't take up much
           [time] =
 5  T1:   [yeah]                          [yeah]
 6  EP:  =in fact (0.5) umm (0.9) you could almost sit in the bath an
 7        do it you know [thinking] about what happened
 8  T1:                  [yes a ha]                      yeah
 9  EP:  errmm but once we'd got (0.7) a description in those (0.5)
10        pretty hard terms
11  T1:  mhmm
12  EP:  we'd be able to look at something and err look at what we
13        can change in the classr [oom]
14  T2:                            [mm]
15  T1:  yeah
16  EP:  err or how we can treat him differently
17  T1:  mmhmm
18  EP:  errmm (1.2) yeah I mean I think I'm talking along some
19        behavioural lines y'know [errgh even] some kind of modi-
           fication =
20: T1:                           [mmhmm]
21  EP:  =[of behaviour]
22  T1:   [yeah mhmm]
```

In this extract, then, the educational psychologist (EP) can be heard to propose the use of certain measures with a view to modifying the behaviour of the child in the classroom. As a starting point in this programme of intervention he suggests that the teacher completes a behavioural observation sheet on the 'actual behaviour' of the pupil as it occurs in the classroom. On the basis of these 'hard' descriptions, then, it is suggested that steps can be taken to modify the pupil's behaviour.

Such a way of proceeding can be seen to reify the (deviant) behaviour of the pupil concerned because, firstly, it treats as non-problematic the recognition of 'actual behaviours'. That is to say, the completion of the behavioural observation sheet and hence the typification of behaviours is conceived of as an essentially passive and neutral activity where the typifier produces descriptions which are occasioned by the factual features of the behaviours which are being observed. Secondly, in devizing programmes of behaviour modification the behaviours are further reified in so far as they are then oriented to as the pre-given and unquestioned grounds for such programmes. By conceiving of their task as identifying and modifying pre-given and non-problematic behaviours, users of such a procedure for managing deviance in schools can be seen to 'manage' to reify precisely those troublesome behaviours which they wish to modify.

So far it has been suggested that it is possible to locate within the talk of teachers and psychologists an orientation to deviance as something which is independent and objective, as the source of description and social reaction. There is, however, another aspect to the reification of deviance in schools besides the use of the assumption of the objective character of deviance. Thus, it is not just that educationists are constructing an objective world of pupil deviance through their reliance upon such a world in their talk. Rather, they are at the same time producing for each other a sense of that world as 'there' for each of them. In other words, deviance is not just an objective phenomenon for these speakers, it is an intersubjective one too. The question then arises — how is this intersubjectivity achieved? Previous discussions of intersubjectivity (for example, Cicourel, 1972; and Schutz, 1964, and 1967) had conceived of it as a kind of pre-given condition of social interaction. By way of contrast, the critique of the cognitive approach outlined earlier leads to the analysis of intersubjectivity as a practical and situated accomplishment of social interaction itself. Members do not simply assume a reciprocity of perspectives or an intersubjectivity for their social relations, they also have to demonstrate that intersubjectivity to one another in the course of their social interaction. The question for research thus became: in what ways is the intersubjectivity of deviance accomplished in the social interaction of teachers, educational psychologists and others? Pollner had pointed to an answer to this question when he had spoken of 'talking practices' as constitutive or objective and intersubjective realities, but he had revealed little about their nature. For a fuller answer it was necessary to look elsewhere — to the details of the talk itself. Ironically, in so doing the research returned full circle to conversation analysis.

The investigations into intersubjectivity which followed suggest that it is interactionally achieved through such everyday talking practices as agreements and corroborations,[8] through sequences in which speakers monitor each other's understanding of their talk, through the production of topically continuous utterances, and probably through a host of as yet unanalyzed other talking practices. By way of illustration, consider the following examples of corroboration sequences:

MP/1160
```
      1   T1: In the dining hall today__he was messing around (0.6)
      2       doing ridiculous things (0.7) throwing some potato at
              somebody
→     3   T2: yeah that's him
→     4   T1: right
```

MP/82
```
      1   T1: right an you can imagine you know who the hell's
      2       pinched my bloody expensive stuff right an he just sits
→     3   T2: he forces con⌈fron he⌈forces confronta⌈tion ⌉
→     4   T1:              ⌊stands⌋    (0.5)      ⌊that's⌋right

→     5   T2: yeah
```

PS/902
```
      1   EP: r-really I think (0.4) Peter is a totally amoral
→     2   T1: mhmm⌈    ⌉
      3   EP:     ⌊child⌋ ⌉
→     4   T2:     ⌊yes⌋  ⌉
→     5   T1:         ⌊mhmm (0.5) totally
→     6   T2:  yes this is what I said
```

Each of the arrowed utterances can be heard as an agreement with or corroboration of prior utterances or descriptions. In the first extract (MP/1160, line 3) T2 appears to be saying that the example of the pupil's behaviour which is described as 'ridiculous' (throwing some potato at somebody) is an appropriate one, it is typical, it is correct. This is then followed by an agreement with the prior corroborative utterance (line 4). In the second extract (MP/82, line 3) T2's remark that the pupil 'forces confrontation' can be heard both to formulate and confirm the description made in the preceding utterance ('he just sits'), this formulation itself being then corroborated in line 4 ('stands', 'that's right'). Finally, in the third extract there is a series of corroborations following close on one another. The first appears at line 2 ('mhmm'). This utterance can be heard as an agreement with or at least an acknowledgement of the description begun in line 1. The completed description (line 3) is then followed with an overlapped agreement and re-emphasis at line 5, and finally a restatement of the agreement at line 6. In each extract speakers can be heard to demonstrate to the other speakers that they 'see things the same way', even if strictly speaking, they have experienced these things from their own unique individual positions. They announce their common orientation towards the object in question (the child) and thereby remind each other that they share a common world. It is almost as if they are 'celebrating' their common attitudes towards the children through such talk.

The kinds of 'second assessments' considered above seem a fairly 'obvious' way in which to appreciate the means whereby talking practices accomplish an intersubjectivity of objects in the social world. Other examples include those sequences where speakers appear to deliberately check on or monitor each other's understanding of the talk. One particular variant of this can be seen where a first speaker invites a second speaker to confirm that they share a body of knowledge, a co-orientation, a shared perspective on the world. The following extract can be viewed as containing such a sequence:

WJS/22

    1 EP: mother has had a black eye recently (1.0) and umm (1.0)
    2   she has a part-time job in an office (1.5) tch Alex is fairly
    3   happy in school but he's not at all well motivated (0.8) err
→   4   rather a difficult sort of boy (s,v) y'know y'know__
            $\begin{bmatrix} \text{umm} \\ \end{bmatrix}$ (0.6)
→   5 T1: $\begin{bmatrix} \text{mhmm} \end{bmatrix}$

    6 EP: but they'd like to err__improve him but she sees the
    7   primary problem (0.9) in (0.5) the home

Thus, at line 4 the EP checks with the teacher (T1) that he 'knows' what he means. Furthermore, note how the teacher (line 5) then confirms that he understands the EP's remarks at precisely the less than half-second gap (___) between the end of the EP's second 'y'know' and the beginning of the EP's next utterance — 'umm', suggesting a finely coordinated sequence of turns within the overall extended turn which comprises the EP's report/story about the child and its family. With this sequence the speakers can be said to have demonstrated their intersubjective participation in a common world. In particular, they have shown to each other that they know what the other means when they make use of such descriptions as 'rather a difficult sort of boy'. Thereby, it can be argued the intersubjective aspect of the reification of deviance is socially accomplished.

The irony of this move from conversation analysis to the study of the relationship between talking practices and the reification of deviance is that it led full circle back to conversation analysis. Thus, it was soon found that in order to locate these talking practices and then to order and classify them in some way a method of working essentially similar to conversation analysis was required. The analytic search was for regularities, repetitions, uniformities, — that is, reportable and orderly conversational structures in terms of which speakers constituted their talk about deviance. It seemed insufficient to say that the speakers achieved the reification of deviance through talking practices and to then proceed to list the various kinds. It seemed a natural next step to produce a more thorough-going understanding of these structures, specifically the sequential organization of the talking practices which had been located.

This inclination to examine further the nature of the talk itself was reinforced by the suspicion that the analysis of the relation between talking practices and the reification of deviance was based upon a contravention of a central tenet of ethnomethodology, namely that of examining what it is that the members themselves were oriented to in their speech. It seemed that the research was in danger of substituting or confusing a sociological problem (how is deviance reified) with the members' own problems to which they were oriented in their talk. It was possible to bring off a reading that members' talking practices served (had the function of?) to reify deviance, to demonstrate intersubjectivity, etc., but was it the case that the members conceived of their speech in these analytical terms? A negative reply to this question seemed the most convincing. To be sure, the members were very likely to have been oriented to agreeing with each other, to checking that they understood each other, but to say that these practices amounted to 'demonstrating intersubjectivity' or 'treating deviance as a pre-given object' was to place an analyst's gloss on what they were doing. It was to use members' practices as resources in the solution of analytical problems. In the interest of taking seriously the methodological constraint to illuminate that which the members themselves were oriented to conversation analysis looked the surer path. The gain was in its methodological rigour; the loss was in its insensitivity to the substantive issue of deviance in schools. How far the researcher is prepared to compromise, and sacrifice rigour for substantive analysis, depends upon how far the researcher is prepared to refrain from ethnomethodological enquiry and avoid the methodological constraints it implies.

Transcript Notation

The transcript notation utilized here follows that contained in Schenkein (1978).

1. *Overlapping Utterances*

   Overlapping utterances are indicated by square brackets. The point at which overlap begins is represented by a single left-hand bracket; where overlap ceases this is marked by a single right-hand bracket.

   ```
   MT: he's ⌈not__in your group y'know⌉ umm
   FT:      ⌊   yeh no yes he is umm   ⌋
   ```

2. *Contiguous Utterances*

   When there is no interval between adjacent utterances, the second being latched immediately to the first (without overlapping it), the utterances are linked together with an equal sign:

   ```
   FT: that's the blonde haired one=
   MT: =that's right yes a ha
   ```

   The equal sign is also used to link different parts of a single speaker's utterance when those parts have been separated by transcript design even though they comprise a continuous flow of speech. This is usually occasioned by the need to transcribe an intervening interruption or overlapped utterance.

   ```
   MT: Please Sir Stephen White ⌈heh he⌉ h .thh well let Stephen=
   FT:                          ⌊ yeah ⌋
   ```

MT: =come an ask an this sort of .hh

3 Intervals Within and Between Utterances

When intervals in the stream of talk occur, they are timed in tenths of a second and inserted within parentheses, either within an utterance:

MT: I mean I haven't got a quiet voice (0.8) it tends to be ...

or between utterances

MT: and he paid not the slightest scrap of attention he might well have been deaf
(1.4)
FT: mhmm

A short (less that 0.5 seconds) pause which is untimed is indicated by a dash:

MT: now at present__erm__I don't seem to have that problem

4 Transcriptionist Doubt

Other than the timings of intervals, items enclosed within single parentheses are in doubt, as in:

MT: and umm I suppose (I must have) s-since I haven't marked them

When single parentheses are empty, but for dots, then this indicates that no hearing could be achieved for the talk in question:

EP: well [that seems something you're happy] about dealing
    with
FT: [(that's all ....)]

Notes

1 For those unfamiliar with ethnomethodology, there are some good introductions available. See, for example, LEITER (1980) and MEHAN and WOOD (1978). However, as introductions and summaries they do lack something of the originals on which they are based. Cf. ATKINSON and DREW (1979), GARFINKEL (1967), GARFINKEL and SACKS (1970), PSATHAS (1979), SCHENKEIN (1978), SUDNOW (1969 and 1972) and TURNER (1974).
2 For further discussion of the methodological issues involved in construct-

ing phenomenological theories see especially SCHUTZ (1964 and 1967).

3 It was something of a disappointment that the child psychiatrists to whom children were sometimes referred by the Clinic staff refused to cooperate in any way in the research.

4 Phenomenological sociologists have attempted to address the problem of ensuring the consistency of sociological accounts with those of the subjects of study in terms of the 'postulate of adequacy' (cf. HARGREAVES, HESTER and MELLOR, 1975; and SCHUTZ, 1967). It is beyond the scope of the present discussion to examine in detail the problems involved in ensuring the production of 'adequate' accounts. Briefly, however, even though the postulate is represented as a device to be used in the production of sociological accounts which are qualitatively distinct from the kind produced by positivist approaches within sociology, a major presupposition of the postulate — that there is some independent 'subjective reality' to which sociological accounts are supposed to correspond — in fact reproduces the dualism which underpins positivist sociology. A fuller discussion of this and other methodological issues raised by the postulate is contained in HESTER (1981b).

5 The detail of these analyses is contained in HESTER and NEWTON (in preparation).

6 ATKINSON and DREW (1979, p. 22) describe the methodological constraints of ethnomethodology in the following way:

> In pursuing such studies ... researchers were to operate under a number of analytic constraints or injunctions ... thus, the general exhortation to view what seemed to be obvious, mundane and commonplace as 'anthropologically strange' was to be a constant reminder to analysts that obviousness was itself an orderly and methodic product of their *members'* interpretive competences ... a closely related ... constraint was entailed by the way in which ... social actors were viewed as practical rule-using 'analysts', rather than as pre-programmed rule-governed 'cultural dopes' ... the ... analyst's task was not to stipulate what rules members *really* were 'following' or 'governed by', but to locate rules to which they might be 'orienting to' and using in producing a recognizable orderliness in some setting ... (this) demanded ... that traditional sociological recommendations about the importance of looking at actors' orientations to actions, and of avoiding the imposition of observers' constructions were to be taken more seriously than in the past. That is, any solution which involved paying lip service to such matters as a prelude to stipulating observers' versions, would be regarded as unacceptable.

7 The 'tensions' within ethnomethodology and conversation analysis are discussed more fully in HESTER (1981a).

8 Agreements and corroborations are part of a class of utterances referred to by POMERANTZ (1975) as 'second assessments'.

References

ATKINSON, J.M. and DREW, P. (1979) *Order in Court: The Organization of Verbal Interaction in Judicial Settings*, London, Macmillan.

CICOUREL, A. (1964) *Method and Measurement in Sociology*, New York, Free Press.

CICOUREL, A. (1968) *The Social Organization of Juvenile Justice*, New York, Wiley.

CICOUREL, A. (1972) *Cognitive Sociology*, Harmondsworth, Penguin.

GARFINKEL, H. (1967) *Studies in Ethnomethodology*, Englewood Cliffs, N.J., Prentice Hall.

GARFINKEL, H. and SACKS, H. (1970) 'The formal properties of practical actions', in MCKINNEY, J.C. and TIRYAKIAN, A. (Eds.) *Theoretical Sociology*, New York, Appleton-Century-Crofts.

HARGREAVES, D., HESTER, S. and MELLOR, F. (1975) *Deviance in Classrooms*, London, Routledge and Kegan Paul.

HESTER, S. (1981a) 'Two tensions in ethnomethodology and conversation analysis', *Sociology*, May, pp. 108–16.

HESTER, S. (1981b) 'Ethnography and the postulate of adequacy', unpublished seminar paper, Ontario Institute for Studies in Education.

HESTER, S. and NEWTON, J. (n.d.) *The Language of Deviance in Schools: Ethnomethodological Aspects of the Work of the Child and Family Guidance Service*, (in preparation).

LEITER, K. (1980) *A Primer on Ethnomethodology*, Oxford, Oxford University Press.

MCKINNEY, J.C. and TIRYAKIAN, A. (Eds.) (1970) *Theoretical Sociology*, New York, Appleton-Century-Crofts.

MEHAN, H. and WOOD, H. (1975) *The Reality of Ethnomethodology*, New York, Wiley.

POLLNER, M. (1974a) 'Mundane reasoning', *Philosophy of Social Science*, 4, pp. 35–54.

POLLNER, M. (1974b) 'Sociological and commonsense versions of the labelling process', in TURNER, R. (Ed.) *Ethnomethodology*, Harmondsworth, Penguin.

POLLNER, M. (1975) 'The very coinage of your brain: the anatomy of reality disjunctures', *Philosophy of Social Science*, 5, pp. 411–30.

POLLNER, M. (1978) 'Constitutive and mundane versions of labelling theory', *Human Studies*, 1, pp. 269–285.

POMERANTZ, A. (1975) 'Second Assessments: A Study of Some Features of Agreements/Disagreements' unpublished PhD dissertation, University of California at Irvine.

PSATHAS, G. (1979) *Everyday Language: Studies in Ethnomethodology*, Irvington Publishers, Inc.

SACKS, H. (1963) 'Sociological description', *Berkeley Journal of Sociology*, 8, pp. 1–17.

SCHENKEIN, J. (1978) *Studies in the Organization of Conversational Interaction*, New York, Academic Press.

SCHUTZ, A. (1964) *Collected Papers I: Studies in Social Theory*, The Hague, Martinus Nijhoff.

SCHUTZ, A. (1967) *Collected Papers II: The Problem of Social Reality*, The Hague, Martinus Nijhoff.

SUDNOW, D. (1969) *Passing On: The Social Organization of Dying*, Englewood Cliffs, N.J., Prentice Hall.

SUDNOW, D. (Ed.) (1972) *Studies in Social Interaction*, New York, Free Press.

TURNER, R. (Ed.) (1974) *Ethnomethodology*, Harmondsworth, Penguin.

ZIMMERMAN, D. and POLLNER, M. (1971) 'The everyday world as phenomena', in DOUGLAS, J.D. (Ed.) *Understanding Everyday Life*, London, Routledge and Kegan Paul.

10 Ethnographic Conversation Analysis: An Approach to Classroom Talk

David Hustler and George Payne

Introduction

In this paper we address three interrelated themes. First, the central concern is to explicate some aspects of a particular methodological approach: 'ethnographic conversational analysis' for want of a better phrase; second, this is developed through a focus on attributions of and displays of competence in educational settings; third, we display both these methodological and substantive themes through the presentation of empirical studies. Inevitably, at times, these three themes will seem to be pulling in differing directions: the alternative, however, is to present papers reinforcing notions about theoretical and methodological issues as being separate domains. Another way into this paper, and into what we mean by ethnographic conversational analysis, is to start with the section entitled Wendy's Story. In this introductory section we sketch in some of the background to this approach.

Since, as the latest American import, ethnomethodology captured the imagination of some of us in the early 1970s, it has become a somewhat diverse enterprise. We will not survey this diversity in any detail, but need to touch on some of the differing strands so as to locate our own concerns and ambitions as regards the study of, and study for, education.

Those who might be characterized as ethnographic ethnomethodologists have utilized the conventional data-gathering techniques associated with ethnography — participant observation, informal interviews, etc — in studies of the practical reasoning displayed by participants in their accomplishment of social order in particular settings. As Atkinson and Drew have noted, such studies might be seen as not so different from symbolic interactionist ethnographies.

In the first chapter of their book *Order in Court: The Organization of Verbal Interaction in Judicial Settings*, Atkinson and Drew draw some interesting distinctions between ethnography and conversational analysis and point to several relevant ethnomethodological writings in order to do this (Atkinson and Drew, 1979). We would also note that many of these researchers seemed to have as their focus, not so much what others might take as the substance of the setting, but rather how that substance documents and further explores the properties of invariant interpretive rules. The latter focus was on occasion also used to point to the supposed inadequacies of, for example, participant observation which was uninformed by ethnomethodological principles. Then again, the analysis could at times be less on this, and more on the further refinement of our understanding of these self-same invariant properties of practical reasoning: this time as rendered through an analysis of the ethnographic ethnomethodologist's production of a research account. What some took to be the seeds sown by Garfinkel, ironicizing sociology wholesale, flowered in a few studies, as did a confusion as to what precisely an empirical study in this tradition was designed to relate to. Whilst some sociologists such as Blum and McHugh flirted with Socrates as a solution, the confusion as to the targets and concerns is clear in some of the better-known studies such as Cicourel's *The Social Organisation of Juvenile Justice* (1976) which maintained the ambivalent ambitions originally apparent in his *Method and Measurement* (1964).

For many sociologists attracted to ethnomethodology by, amongst other things, the promise of an empirically rigorous approach to the study of social life, another developing strand within ethnomethodology beckoned. This lay in the work of Harvey Sacks and his colleagues, the approach known as conversational analysis and the approach which has fundamentally informed our own work within the sociology of education.[1] An early paper by Sacks, 'Sociological description' (Sacks, 1963) provides in our view the most concise argument for this development. He makes the simple point that human beings, in interaction with one another, use their capacity to describe the world and through this descriptive work render that world sensible. Social scientists, however, far from attempting to describe and analyze how that is achieved, have rather pointed to its inadequacies, its incompleteness, and so on, or, we would add, have taken such descriptive work solely as tokens of underlying meanings. Perhaps it is this last point which displays one critical distinction between a conversation analyst and a symbolic interactionist as regards their approach to talk. For symbolic interactionists the talk is used to give researchers access to their subjects' meanings and interactional patterns, is related to developing models of these meanings drawing very often on other sources of data apart from talk, and is presented to illustrate and document these meanings and interactional patterns. One of the clearest accounts of this approach, along symbolic interactionist lines, is provided by Peter Woods in his 'Understanding through talk' (Woods, 1981). The work of conversational analysis takes as its central core of research materials, transcriptions of tape-recordings of naturally occurring talk. These are our basic materials although we should point out that we have more in common with aspects of Sacks' original position than with more recent developments in conversational analysis. In particular we have not found ourselves comfortable with what some take to be the excessively formal analyses of sequencing and turn-taking, where, as Button puts it, the goal is that of 'describing and documenting the operation and organization of stretches of conversation as activity in its own right ... and making no claims to be capturing wider sociological concerns' (Button, 1977).

Such an approach is not for us sufficiently attuned to the ways in which conversational materials can be used in the analysis of how interactional encounters are accomplished in particular contexts: contexts such as the classroom and the school. Such contexts are of central concern to us and our belief, and our finding, is that conversational analysis can speak to such settings in fruitful ways. We then, unlike some sociologists, would not go along with the suggestion that Garfinkel's notion of 'ethnomethodological indifference' must necessarily be translated into irrelevance as well, a point which Stephen Hester develops, although along slightly different lines, in his paper (page 243). Perhaps this depends on the sort of ethnomethodology one does. What do we mean then by ethnographic conversational analysis? We mean a form of conversational analysis which remains sensitive to the orientations people are working with in particular settings: settings such as story-time in an infant classroom for example. Participants in the classroom use and display their knowledge about schools and classrooms to talk in the way they do. What sort of knowledge that might be is one of the concerns of the analysis. In that analysis, researchers too are inevitably making use of their own commonsense knowledge about such settings, and it is part and parcel of this approach to attempt to give the reader at least some access to this knowledge too. We develop this briefly in later sections.

David Hustler and George Payne

What we present in the main body of this paper are some selected aspects of two empirical analyses. First and foremost, we wish to use these analyses to point to some issues associated with this variant within qualitative methodology, and to consider some of the analytical machinery available. Our more general concern is to document some ways in which this approach can be principled, rigorous, yet practical. The analysis will of necessity have to be brief, but it has always been our preference to tie discussions or exhortations about theoretical and/or methodological issues to empirical analyses. Furthermore, there is across our selection a common substantive theme, the notion of 'competence'. Before moving to the empirical analyses, we need to comment on this notion.

Competence

Competence is a concept which has general currency in the study of education. It is, however, a concept which suffers from a certain looseness of definition routinely being associated with notions of ability and achievement. Many years ago Parsons identified two dimensions of achievement, the cognitive and the moral or social, and suggested that the latter is often used in making inferences and judgments about the former. In many respects the argument still holds today. From a very different starting point we believe we can illustrate some concerns of ethnomethodology as outlined above, and extend our understanding of the notion of competence as it is naturally used in educational situations, especially classrooms.

Classrooms are conducted largely through talk. Talk is the medium through which classroom life, teaching, learning, being a teacher or a pupil are accomplished. At the most mundane level, talk is the very bedrock of the social achievement of routine classroom interaction. On arrival at school, young children are already competent conversationalists[2]; that is to say they can talk themselves through their day-to-day lives without difficulty. It is true, of course, that a child may find himself or herself short on vocabulary at times but that does not deny his or her observable interactional ability to engage in talk.

Even the youngest of pupils enter school with a measure of cultural competence which they can variably display and which we argue can be influential in that it provides teachers with materials, for making a wider range of judgments about them.

The cultural competence we refer to is, however, a complex

phenomenon. This complexity can be broadly placed within the framework of Sacks *et al*'s conceptualisation of context free and context sensitive methodic practices. The methodic practices are the cultural apparatus members use in displaying their social competence.

It is Sacks *et al*'s argument that these methodic practices have generalizable features which will be observable whatever the context of their use, but that in their use in any situation they will also display context sensitive features. Thus, for example, general context free features of turn-taking practices will be observable together with the particularized context sensitive features called for in such situations as natural multi-party conversations, large or small meetings, debates, discussion groups, telephone conversations, etc.

Similarly, at the time when children come to school, they are able to participate in conversations and talk in a host of situations displaying context sensitive uses of generalized context free methodic practices. But school will be a new situation for them; social organization of school life is different in some ways from that of other social situations. Classroom lessons are occasions which have distinguishable organizations of talk. Books have been written on the subject of 'Classroom Language' for example which describe and analyze the characteristic of the talk produced by teachers and pupils.[3] This observation, however, is obviously not meant to imply that we see the organization of classroom talk as something entirely separate or separable from other contexts.

There are several aspects of the organization of classroom talk which are evident in other social occasions. Additionally, of course, classroom talk is by no means identical in its organization from one lesson to another, from one activity to another.

The recognition of a child as a socially competent pupil presumably hinges on the displayed capacity to cope with these subtleties. We will demonstrate what we mean by this statement by reference to our first empirical study.

Elsewhere (Payne and Hustler, 1980) we have described some of the methods and procedures used by a teacher as he handles a fairly large number of pupils as a single collectivity or whole. In that analysis it was suggested that the handling of the pupils as a class was being accomplished by a combination of such methodical practices or cultural procedures as providing for the identification of those present as one (the teacher) and the rest (the pupils); the presentation and preservation of a single topic of talk to be attended to simultaneously by everyone; organizing the talk of the occasion as over-

whelmingly two-party talk although there were between twenty-five
to thirty people present there; and providing for the collective movement of the pupils from one task to another through such practices as
using repetitions, making use of the pupils' orientation to the lessons
as an agenda of various tasks and producing a running commentary
on the progress of the collective changeover.

Throughout the analysis the emphasis was upon the teacher's
accomplishment, the teacher's interactional competence, almost totally ignoring the work of the pupils in the interaction. But it is
clearly the case that pupils are, in collaboration with the teacher,
jointly responsible for the orderly organization of the lesson. From
the perspective of the pupil, utterances have to be produced at the
right moment in the right sequence in an appropriate form of
organization and to display appropriate topical coherence. Those
pupils who can manage these aspects of the talk production com-
petently are likely to be seen in a favourable light by the teacher;
those who cannot handle this complex interactional organization are
likely to be viewed differently — possibly as a 'nuisance' and perhaps
even as 'dim' or 'not with it'. The example of 'Wendy's story' relates
to these possibilities, although it is the methodological issues raised
which are more central to this chapter.

Wendy's Story

The following analysis is based on a brief extract from a transcript of
a story-time session in an infant classroom.

A start will be made with one small extract: utterances 92–104,
which can be termed 'Wendy's Story'. Starting here provides a
resource for displaying, firstly some relevant issues in terms of one
particular analytical approach to these materials, secondly some
substantive points regarding attributions of competence at talk production. 'Wendy's Story' is not where the analysis started: it is being
used here as a device for relating to these issues. Here is Wendy's
Story extracted from the transcript[4]:

92	T	What about you Wendy
93	Wendy	Well uh- I got lost // (one day)
94	C	KATHY
95	T	Yes
96	Wendy	and uh -- and -- I can't remember (the rest)
97	T	You got lost did w- were you going shopping

98	Wendy	Uhm - yes I (was with) Mummy ( ) a- a- no I wasn't going shopping with ( )
99	C	hahhhh
100		Wendy and I went and looked in the shop and she wasn't there ( ) and she (caught) up ( )
101	C	hahhhh
102	T	and did you think for a moment you'd been left on your own
103	Wendy	Y(hhh)es
104	T	and you felt lonely - - Yes Melanie

These utterances can be heard in their more extended sequential context, as involving the eventual telling of a story, *and* the telling of that story at a certain 'stage' during story-time in an infant classroom. Also certain utterances, for example, 93 and 96, seem to be taken by the teacher as insufficient, or as displaying some sort of incompetence on the part of Wendy. The intention here is to bring these three points together: to see how this hearing of incompetence hinges on at least (i) the immediate sequential organization of the talk; and (ii) commonsense knowledge of aspects of the infant school and story-time in particular. Separating these two out is merely an analytical convenience, since they interrelate to provide for the participants and the researcher orientations allowing for both the hearing of particular utterances as inappropriate or appropriate, and for the participants' own sensible talk productions. What should already be clear about this approach, is that the transcript is not to be taken as 'the data'; the data, more fundamentally, consists of the commonsense knowledge and practical reasoning which participants can be said to be using and displaying through their talk.

(i)   *The Sequential Organization of the Talk*

Harvey Sacks, in particular, built up a considerable number of analyses of story-telling in natural conversation (Sacks, 1970) as involving, amongst other things, interactional collaboration between participants, and as having interactional structures to which participants orient. Problems facing participants include: for the person wishing to tell a story, getting the floor for that story; making apparent what a completion to that story will look like (without having to say 'That's the end' 'now laugh' or 'cry'!), so that embarrassing silences will be avoided and so that orderly transition of speaking turns can take place. Hearers, generally, need to monitor a story so as to be able to display a recognition of its completion at the appropriate time, as well as displaying an adequate understanding. Often this display of understanding is done through the telling of a second story which can be seen to 'fit' the first. Sacks has suggested an oriented-to-interactional structure as follows:

(a)	STORY-PREFACE (REQUEST)	for example A	Something terrible happened on the way here
(b)	ACCEPTANCE	for example B	Oh dear, what?
(c)	STORY	for example A	((A tells what happened))
(d)	HEARING/SECOND STORY	for example B	Oh, that's terrible. ((and B may go on to tell a 'similar' story))

Wendy's story however seems to have an interactional structure which differs from the above pattern in some respects and which is closer to another class of stories found in natural conversation: stories which can be termed 'invited story' (Cuff and Francis, 1978). The pattern here consists of:

Speaker:

A	(a)	Story Invitation/Request
B	(b)	Story/Acceptance
A	(c)	Story Closing/Hearing
A	(d)	Story Invitation (to C).

What should be made clear is that these structures are not to be viewed as rules *governing* the production of talk, but rather as *oriented* to rules which allow participants to produce and hear certain utterances in certain ways, and as doing certain activities: for example, 'being rude' or 'being interactionally incompetent', or as 'monopolizing the floor'. The last might be illustrated in the first pattern should a speaker, in the 'acceptance' slot produce 'Did it really — well, let me tell you something really terrible...'.

In a variety of respects it can be suggested that in utterances 92–104, the teacher at least is expecting a story from Wendy. In fact, in utterance 97 she goes on to provide some resources which Wendy might use (and does!) to construct a sequence of events leading to her state of being lost; a state which the teacher then incorporates into the relevant theme of 'feeling lonely'. This last incorporation documents a more general feature of invited stories, since in such stories it commonly rests with the inviter to judge the appropriateness or otherwise of a story, in the context of the invitation. Respondents will, in a sense, always be offering only possible completions — what might be thought of as 'is this what you were after'. In utterances 102 and 104, the teacher continues the story himself, in such a way as to display its relevance to the initial invitation. Invited stories generally, and certainly Wendy's Story, can then be termed *joint productions* in a very real sense.

More generally again, in terms of the sequential organization of the talk, to make sense of all or any part of Wendy's Story, it is necessary to locate these utterances in a broader sequential context. It is important to note that earlier utterances establish a pool of potential story-tellers on the theme of having felt lonely; also that what is being developed is a *round* of invited stories, all of which can be viewed as joint productions, and two of which precede Wendy's Story. *Now*, that Wendy's Story is a joint production can be seen to be in part a consequential feature of the invited story format; however, by contrast with some of the surrounding stories it might be argued that in Wendy's case the teacher not only makes her eventual story explicitly relevant, but also has to provide the resources for a story — as a recognizable sequence of events — to begin with. This is however a marginal point: more fundamental is the suggestion that the participants are not only orienting to story-telling, and to telling these stories in an invited story format, but also orienting to a continuing round of such stories. These orientations provide resources for considering the work that certain utterances are doing; they also provide us and the participants with resources for a situated hearing of certain utterances as for example particularly skilful in solving certain problems, or as in some sense inappropriate, as requiring further work.

(ii)   *Common-sense Knowledge of the Infant School and Story-time in particular*

So far, when considering competence at talk production, at least the principle of looking to the orientations concerning the sequential organization of the talk has been discussed and perhaps partly established.

Hearings, however are also made in terms of more general orientations to the setting: what is at issue here is the *occasioned* nature of the talk, and how participants' background knowledge of what is involved in an infant school story-time can provide central resources for making sense of particular utterances and activities.

Without documenting these points now, it can be strongly argued on the basis of the complete set of materials that: teacher and children know that what they are doing is story-time, and that it is a scheduled occasion in the school day; they also know that the teacher is to be oriented to for the overall internal scheduling and control of the occasion; they also know that story-time is routinely more than the telling of a story by the teacher. More specifically, they know that story-time is an occasion with an 'agenda' (Anderson, 1979). This does not mean that story-times are pre-planned or predictable over their entire course; it means that there are recurrent formal features of story-times which make up an 'agenda' to which participants orient in terms of what might routinely, typically, be expected to take place. These and other aspects of the participants' background knowledge are displayed through their talk and serve to provide resources for producing what they produce and hearing what they hear — as for example, sensible, appropriate, being cheeky, and so forth.

Wendy's story is embedded in a round of invited stories, which it can be argued is oriented to as a routine, to be largely expected, part of the story-time: the post-story work. This work (i) routinely commences with the teacher initiating some story-related activity for the children; (ii) routinely the teacher asks questions with a strong thematic relationship to her story; (iii) routinely, too, post-story time is a place for the telling of the children's own stories.

Wendy's 'Well ah ... I got lost // (one day)' would appear to be precisely on target in terms of thematic relevance, since being lost is presumably a good basis for the state of feeling lonely. It seems, however, that the utterance is insufficient and perhaps this lies in its not being recognizable as a story. Both the sequential organization of the talk *and* the way in which the story-time agenda is being concretely realized, make the production of a story as interactionally occasioned. In fact the sequential organization of the talk as a round of invited stories is what seems to constitute the occasion in a routine way as an unexceptional display of a post-story stage in story-time. This brings together the two sets of resources, which were earlier separated for analytical convenience, as mutually interdependent. It must be at least on the basis of such resources that hearings of insufficiency, inappropriateness, and so forth must be being made. The argument is that these general points hold, as apart from the substantive hearings which the reader might disagree with which have been used as a vehicle in considering this transcript.

There is one further interesting issue which these materials and their analysis raises. This involves a contrast between Wendy's story and another child's story (Paul). In its internal content, Paul's story appears to have very little relationship to the theme of having felt lonely whereas as has been noted, Wendy's first utterance has strong topical coherence. Yet Paul appears to display a recognition that a story is called for and he is also able to maintain the floor by constructing it in terms of an extended sequence of events which can be heard to culminate in a preferred candidate for conclusion and completion. He is able to embed within this sequence of events a story funny enough to evoke a response from his peers and this funny story seems to have been touched off by the talk of a previous child about ice-cream. In addition, it is possible to speculate about Paul's interest in maintaining the conversational floor, about his role of 'joker' and also about the dual directionality of his talk in that he appears to be addressing *two* audiences, his peers and the teacher. The central feature of Paul's talk is that he can construct stories, and story-time has as one of its routinely possible occurrences a time within it for the production of such stories by the children. The post-story work for story-time is in part constituted as such by the ways in which children are able to construct coherent stories in the sense that such stories are made up of a recognizable sequence of events. That certain of these stories seem to hearers to have minimal bearing on the themes nominated by the teacher may not be a central issue if competence is viewed in terms of acquiring methods of telling stories rather than the ability to produce an appropriate utterance or story in terms of topic. It would also appear that it is less important for Wendy to tune into the topic as defined by the teacher than to produce something that can be heard as a recognizable story during this stage of story-time.

Our account generates for discussion some wider substantive issues. First, a question emerges regarding the sorts of knowledge which young children are working with concerning the everyday routines of infant school life, and whether professionals can benefit from a more detailed consideration of that knowledge as displayed in teacher-child talk. A second question is the need to ask how different children come to terms in differing ways with settings such as story-time. In particular, even if we accept their skills as conversationalists, we can go on to ask the reasons why some children still find particular problems in this somewhat distinctive context involving talk between the teacher and the children as members of a class. This last question is significant in at least two senses, given the increasingly important role that the teacher-class relationship comes to play as children continue their education. On the one hand, children's early experience of participation in such settings presumably provides some basis for the nature of their participation at a later stage; on the other hand, through their participation, children are providing teachers with materials upon which attributions of competence can be based, and which can lay the foundation for children's future educational identities.

The discussion of commonsense knowledge leads us into making an important methodological point which is germane to any scrutiny of our materials in terms of the imputed competence of the parties to the talk. It will have been noted that we have avoided referring to transcription as 'the data', preferring to refer to them as the 'materials'. The reason for this apparent circumlocution is simply that a transcription does not 'speak for itself'. In order to make sense of any particular utterance, not only do we have to utilize sequencing considerations, but also we have to trade off our commonsense, background knowledge of how the social world is organized — for example, the ways of infant schools, the nature of infant-adult relationships, the fact that parents collect their children from school at the end of the school day, etc. Similarly, the parties to the talk in our materials have to use such knowledge to bring off their social world through their talk. In short, 'the data' for analysis consists of commonsense knowledge, and members' methods of organizing and deploying such knowledge, which are made available for description and analysis by means of a transcription of a bit of the everyday social world. Here the bit of the social world in which we are interested is the naturally occurring activity of story-time in an infant classroom.

We have used 'Wendy's Story' to address: (i) some substantive matters relating to attribution of, and displays of, competence; (ii) our argument that any substantive focus such as this can usefully draw on analysis in terms of both the immediate sequential organization of the talk *and* commonsense knowledge related to particular contexts. It is, in particular, this combination which leads us to feel that the term 'ethnographic conversational analysis' is appropriate. Participants and researchers trade off the latter to do what they do; as researchers, primarily committed to some sort of rigour, we should attempt to explicate the resources we are using; and (iii) some aspects of the more specific analytical machinery within conversational analysis.

Beginning Lessons

Our second brief empirical example is less developed than Wendy's Story and we use it to point to some issues which might be worthy of attention. The substantive focus is still the notion of competence, albeit in a different sort of context. Clearly our view is that an ethnomethodological approach presents a great deal of promise for exploring this notion further. With its emphasis on catching the talk of classrooms as it naturally occurs and its use of conversational analysis to study the organization of that talk in detail it can provide us with ways into exploring the issue rigorously.

It will not be necessary to be highly selective in the collection of taped materials because of the fact that displays of interactional competence should be available in the most mundane of classroom activities: starting lessons, organizing the beginning of the day in an infant school, bringing lessons to an end, as well as the multitude of question and answer sessions which permeate a school day. The point we have made earlier is that through studying these mundane aspects which form the very basis of any teacher's day these 'more important' issues such as pupil competence can emerge.

Clearly the relevance and promise of an ethnomethodological approach to the study of competence need not be confined to pupil competence. We have, for example, in our studies of teacher practices, such as cohorting, starting lessons, displaying power and control implied a consideration of teacher competence. The issue becomes interesting when considering the activities of teachers in training. Through the process of training, teachers, like pupils, are learning how to handle and produce the language of the classroom. Although student teachers will clearly have a wealth of interactional language competence they find they have to modify the organization of their talk to manage classes with an acceptable measure of competence. It is a question to some extent of learning new context sensitizing practices.

We can illustrate our point through some materials which present contrasting competence or ability in getting a lesson started. Starting off occasions or events such as meetings, parties or conversations are not activities unfamiliar to us as ordinary members of society. The accomplishment of any such beginnings will of course be situationally specific to that beginning but at the same time will draw upon those practices which can accomplish beginnings.

Beginnings of lessons display the characteristics of *beginnings* but importantly they will also be characterizable as the beginnings of *lessons*, but that is not to say every lesson beginning is identical. Rather it is to suggest that while any lesson beginning displays the contingency of that lesson beginning alone it may also be observable as a recognizable lesson beginning.

Whereas experienced teachers may not particularly notice how they get lessons started unless asked pointedly to reflect upon it, student teachers may be acutely aware of the fact that they are not very good at it.

We can refer to an analysis of a lesson beginning carried out some years ago (Payne, 1976) and which has been more recently reworked and redeveloped. In the original piece of work, the following materials were considered.

8	T:	E:r — come o:n settle down — no one's sitting down till we're all ready. (pause circa 7.00 seconds) (General background noises)
9	T:	Stand up straight — bags down. (pause circa 8.00 seconds) (General background noises getting quieter)
10	T:	Down I sai. (pause circa 5.00 seconds) (General background noises getting quieter still)
11	T:	Right quietly sit down. (pause circa 9.00 seconds) (General background noise)
12	P:	( )
13	T:	( ) *Right* now then what were we talkin about last time -- yes.
14	P:	(Sir) the Vikins how the -- were going to raid -- Wessex.
15	T:	How they were going to raid *Wessex yes* -- and what had they raided *before* Wessex.

The analysis of these materials suggested that accomplishing the beginning of this lesson involved identification and relational work by the teacher and the pupils through the use of such cultural practices as orienting to the use of standardized relationship pairs and category bound activities. The formulation of the teacher's utterances provides his learners with resources for recognizing him as now being the teacher, getting the lesson started. Those learners present who know themselves to be pupils thereby have resources for knowing that the lesson is being started for them and that they are now becoming engaged in a teacher-pupil relationship. They also know that the organization of his talk provides for their learning the activity he is engaged in is that of getting the lesson started. He is observably calling them, as a class, to order and cueing them into the beginning of a collaborative project. Then he initiates that project through providing for them contributing to the talk.[5]

A more recent and extended version of an analysis of these same materials has pointed to some aspects of their production which have some relevance for our current discussion. For example, it is suggested that the manner of the accomplishment of beginnings can have implications for whatever may follow. Beginnings of occasions are good places for laying down guidelines, setting out expectations and establishing precedents.

Now student teachers may well have had experience of starting off occasions or events and thereby know how to 'begin things' but beginning lessons requires an orientation to the features of lessons. In lessons teachers are expected to have control over what happens there. There is always the possibility in lessons that pupils are likely to contest that control in systematic ways at 'any time' in the lesson. Thus, beginnings can have a special importance in that they are times when issues can be settled at the outset.

In this lesson beginning for example the teacher can be heard to be setting up for the pupils, through his early 'showdown' around the activity of sitting down, clear indications that it is he who is going to be in charge. He is letting the pupils know that it is he who will be in charge of this occasion, he who will be controlling what can happen and they may as well get that clear from the beginning.

One aspect of the extended analysis involved a comparison between the accomplishment of this lesson beginning and another lesson beginning which appears to be less efficiently effected.

These additional are:

		((General background noises) (Teacher walking round) (Children talking))
1	T:	Right (will) everyone look this way now please. ((pause circa 3.00 seconds) (General background noises))
2	P:	( ) ((These are pupil to pupil utterances))
3	P:	( )
4	T:	Come on — turn this way please. ((pause circa 2.00 seconds) (General background noises))
5	T:	Ready — (you) ready.

		((pause circa 6.oo seconds) (General background noises))
6	P:	( ) ((These are pupil to pupil utterances))
7	P:	( )
8	T:	Come on David — now.
9	T:	Steven — turn round.
		((pause circa 15.oo seconds) (Background noises) (Children chattering))
10	P:	( ) ((Pupil to pupil utterances))
11	P:	( )
12	T:	Umm — now couple of weeks ago — David (stop) being silly.
		((pause circa 2.oo seconds))
13	T:	Couple of weeks ago — I —
		((pause circa 4.oo seconds))
14	T:	Finished Karen — couple of weeks ago — I er — mentioned I'd like you to bring in newspaper articles — for a collage — about law and order now one person's already brought some in — and I'd like to remind the rest of you — to bring some in — e:r — because I want to get this on the way (by) starting on Wednesday and carrying on next Wednesday — so tonight — as part of your homework — ((a pupil sneezes))

I want you to look through newspapers — for articles — to do with law and order — I want you to find *anything* about cases in courts — about — um — things like vandalism er hooliganism at football matches and things like this — I want you to find out any articles pictures headlines (that) you can (that) relate to this ((a pupil coughs)) together as a collage I think David you'd better come and sit down here you're a bit distracted over there.

((pause circa 15.oo seconds))

15	P:	See y' Gary.
		((pause circa 7.oo seconds))
16	T:	Now the other thing is that um — the on Wednesday ( ) started doing something some writing on age limits (were) didn't you is anybody here who wasn't here on Wednesday well — the other people -- started doing a bit of writing on age limits er and what age limits they

agreed or disagreed er strongly about — so I want you to finish this now because what I want you to do with it — I want you — to — hand them in to me at the end of this lesson — and I'm going to give out a few of the best ones — and er — put them on a banda sheet put them on a sheet — you listening Valerie — put them on a sheet — and — give them back to you so that you (all can) see what these people have written and discuss it -- as a class — so — er I want you to get on with that now for the next ten minutes or so.
((pause circa 7.00 seconds) (Background noises))

17   T: Does anybody want one of those graphs that you had last time — do you want one.
((pause circa 50.00 seconds) (Background noises))

18   T: Er settle down now I know it's Monday morning and you've not seen everybody for — weekend but settle down please.
((Lesson continues))

In these materials it would appear to be the case that the teacher has some difficulty getting his lesson started. His difficulties are made available to us through his repeated attempts to get all the pupils to look at him, his repeated attempts to introduce the topic of the lesson and his attempts to stop the pupil to pupil talk. They in turn are taken to be indications that he has problems getting the pupils organized as a class rather than as several pupils and the interrelated problem of not being able to get their collective attention. In contrast to the other teacher this one would appear to be attempting to get the lesson under way without having the pupils appropriately ordered and organized for a lesson beginning.

In general this teacher's difficulties throw into stronger relief the achieved nature of beginning a lesson; they demonstrate more obviously that beginning a lesson is *every time* a contingent 'first time' accomplishment. They also indicate that beginning a lesson may well call for particularized usage of any general cultural ability for beginning occasions or events. Those particularized usages may call for particular organizations of practices and procedures which require attending to the features of classroom lessons as occasioned social events.

The above provides only the seeds of an analysis and readers may wish to take it further. We would, however, wish to raise the following issues:

(i) The first is a substantive issue relating to competence, and the competence of student teachers in particular. Those who observe student teachers, and are called upon to make judgments on them, seem to have a remarkable capacity to recognize 'good teaching' or 'bad teaching', a 'good start' or a 'bad start'. This appears to be no particular problem, yet how that recognition is done, and what it might rest on, is somewhat more elusive. In attempting to explicate, with reference to transcribed materials, how we and others arrive at such recognitions, we might begin to address a matter of concern for more than a few!

(ii) Second, we have briefly pointed to some further analytical machinery which might help address such a concern as well as others. We are referring to the fact that Sacks and others, in a variety of empirical studies, have been involved in attempting to document content features of the commonsense knowledge with which members seem to be working in particular settings. In his early work Sacks attempted to construct analytical frameworks which would be sensitive to the commonsense knowledge displayed in particular settings. The central devices made use of were the notions of 'category-bound activities' and 'membership categorization devices'. Subsequent studies have involved researchers in making claims as to the membership categorization devices to which members are orienting in various settings.[6] In short, there is some basis, in terms of analytical equipment, for a rigorous analysis of the nature of the commonsense knowledge that members may be said to be using and displaying in particular contexts. Of necessity this has been discussed here somewhat abstractly, but it may be useful to note that this machinery is somewhat different from the frameworks developed to handle structural aspects of conversation, such as sequencing and turn-taking. Perhaps we should point out that Schegloff has provided a particularly interesting example of an attempt to interrelate the two frameworks (Schegloff, 1972).

(iii) Third, the attempt to move into 'a matter for concern' such as that in (i) above, can in our view only benefit from accepting that our observations as researchers are informed through and through by our own membership within society and within particular professional communities. Any commitment to a rigorous analysis should involve providing readers with as much access as possible to the sense-assembly procedures we are depending on to produce our analysis. This final point leads us into our concluding comments.

Implications for Teacher Research

As we briefly noted, one possibility for the reader is to take the materials presented in the previous section and attempt an analysis. In the process of doing this, a wider sense of the general methodological issues we have addressed might emerge, as well as those we have neglected. In this conclusion we will not summarize what we take to be these issues, but will note one simple point before touching on the practical relevance of such an approach for teachers. The point is this: readers and researchers have access to the same materials, the transcriptions. The reader does not depend, as in most qualitative studies (let alone quantitative), on the researcher's descriptions of events, or on an account by the researcher of the principled bases for selecting certain illustrative examples (if there is such an account). The materials are available for scrutiny, as are what the researcher makes of them. The reader can arrive at alternative 'hearings' from a transcript and/or can propose an alternative analytical apparatus. Readers have their own cultural competence, their own common-sense knowledge, and can challenge again and again with reference to the materials, the ways in which researchers have used theirs. This simple point is for us quite central to what we mean when we talk of the 'rigorous' nature of such research.

The same point is one of the features of the approach which seems to have been especially attractive to many of the teachers with whom we have worked. Equally attractive has been the ease with which such materials can be gathered, without being disruptive, in the very situation which teachers may wish to research into.

Perhaps the most useful article documenting the practical possibilities of the approach is by Digby Anderson (Anderson, 1982). One issue which he does not take up, and which we certainly did not anticipate, is how the approach can contribute to a collaborative relationship between teacher and teacher and between teachers and lecturers.[7] Over the last few years more materials are beginning to surface which point not only to the problems involved in such relationships, but also to some of the fruitful outcomes. Books such as Jon Nixon's *A Teachers' Guide to Action Research* (1981) are building on the work of contributors such as John Elliott and Clem Adelman, whose involvement with teachers in the Ford Teaching

Project was one of the major early influences (Elliott and Adelman, 1974; Adelman, 1981). An important resource are many of the projects and working papers associated with 'Teacher Pupil Interaction and the Quality of Learning', an aspect of the Schools Council Programme Two: Helping Individual Teachers to Become More Effective. There is of course a major problem which we, and others, have found in attempting to work with teachers in ways which might speak to their problems. The problem is that of imposing our own 'relevancies'[8] — whether these be relevancies in terms of familiar theoretical constructs, disciplinary problems, or 'relevancies' born of the practical contexts in which we operate. There is, in our view, no prospect of disposing of these differing relevancies — and probably a lot to be lost from attempting to mask them. What can be useful, however, is trying to make them explicit, with reference to shared materials. Ethnographic conversational analysis seems to demand a move towards that end, at least in so far as the commonsense knowledge we use becomes to some extent, not only a 'resource' but also a 'topic'. That process becomes one device, amongst others, whereby teachers' own professional knowledge can be made more available for tackling teachers' own problems. In this sense we return to our opening paragraph and our belief that the approach outlined in this paper can further both the study of and the study *for* education.

Notes

1 The groundwork for conversational analysis was done in large part by HARVEY SACKS (unpublished lectures, 1964–72). For a more accessible source, see TURNER (1974). It has informed our approach to the sociology of education in a variety of ways best indicated perhaps in PAYNE (1976), CUFF and HUSTLER (1981) and HUSTLER and PAYNE (1983).
2 See, for example, KEENAN (1975), MACKAY (1974), FRENCH and MACLURE (1981). Also see the book edited by GORDON WELLS (1981), especially the contributions of P. FRENCH.
3 There are, of course, a massive number of publications in this area now. We would particularly recommend EDWARDS and FURLONG (1978) as well as several of HAMMERSLEY's articles (1974 and 1976).
4 The transcripts in this paper draw on a set of conventions largely developed by GAIL JEFFERSON, for many years a co-worker with HARVEY SACKS. The transcription symbols are as follows:

//	talk overlapped at this point by next utterance
wh-	word started but not completed
yes-I-know	words run together quickly
-	untimed pause

(1.0)	timed pause (of one second)
( )	something said but not transcribable
(yes I know)	transcriber thinks 'yes I know' was said
((laughter))	description not transcription
YES	capitals indicates loud volume
:	indicates prolongation of syllable
(hh)	indicates aspiration — usually laughing sound in a word
T	teacher
C or P	unidentified child or pupil
CC or PP	unidentified children or pupils speaking together

5 There has been some interesting work done on initial encounters between teacher and pupils and much of it is ethnographic in character. See, for example, BALL (1980), EDWARDS and FURLONG (1978) and GANNAWAY (1976). Clearly the focus of these studies is not on beginnings of lessons as such, but it is our view that such studies could benefit from a more detailed focus on the talk in such encounters: on the formulations being used by teacher and pupils, on the sequential structuring and on the turn-taking system. At times, it seems to us, importing notions such as 'negotiation' and 'working consensus', as well as a reliance on data concerning pupils' views of teachers gathered outside the classroom, can conceal precisely *how* such initial encounters are being accomplished. What might also be neglected is a more powerful understanding of the sorts of knowledge which teachers and pupils are displaying and using to talk to each other as they do.

6 See, for example, ATKINSON and DREW (1979), WATSON (1978), SCHEGLOFF (1972) and HUSTLER and PAYNE (1983). The last publication attempts to show how the notion of membership categorization devices may provide a partial basis for linking 'micro' and 'macro' levels of analysis within sociology. The argument and analysis is developed with reference to the claim that ethnomethodologists are unable and unwilling to handle concepts such as 'power' — we dispute the claim.

7 See, for example, the report from Manchester Polytechnic's outer network group of teachers and tutors (PAYNE, CUFF, *et al*, 1983). This was linked to the Schools Council Programme Two: Teacher Pupil Interaction and the Quality of Learning. Also bearing on this is PAYNE and CUFF (1982).

8 The term 'relevancies' draws on the work of SCHUTZ (1974). We find his work in this area extremely fruitful for conceptualizing and coming to terms with the problems of collaboration involving people working in differing sectors of education. For applications of this framework see, in the context of college course construction, HUSTLER (1981), in the context of evaluation, PAYNE, HUSTLER and CUFF (1984) and, in the context of Action Research, HUSTLER and CUMMINGS (1983).

References

ADELMAN, C. (1981) 'On first hearing' in ADELMAN, C. (Ed.) *Uttering, Muttering: Collecting, Using and Reporting Talk for Social and Educational Research*, London, Grant McIntyre.

ANDERSON, D. (1979) 'The formal basis for a contextually sensitive classroom agenda', *Instructional Science*, Vol.

ANDERSON, D. (1982) 'The teacher as classroom researcher: a modest method for a new opportunity', in PAYNE, G. and CUFF, E. (Eds.) *Doing Teaching*, London, Batsford.

ATKINSON, J.M. and DREW, P. (1979) *Order in Court: the Organization of Verbal Interaction in Judicial Settings*, London, Macmillan.

BALL, S. (1980) 'Initial encounters in the classroom and the process of establishment' in WOODS, P. (Ed.) *Teacher Strategies*, London, Croom Helm.

BUTTON, G. (1977) 'Comments on conversational analysis', *Analytical Sociology*, 1.

CICOUREL, A. (1964) *Method and Measurement in Sociology*, New York, Free Press.

CICOUREL, A. (1976) *The Social Organisation of Juvenile Justice*, London, Heinemann.

CUFF, E. and FRANCIS, D. (1978) 'Some features of "invited stories" about marriage breakdown', *International Journal of the Sociology of Language*, 18.

CUFF, E. and HUSTLER, D. (1981) 'Stories and story time in an infant classroom', in FRENCH, P. and MCLURE, M. (Eds.) *Adult-Child Conversation*, London, Croom Helm.

EDWARDS, A. and FURLONG, J. (1978) *The Language of Teaching*, London, Heinemann.

ELLIOTT, J. and ADELMAN, C. (1974) 'Stranger in the classroom' *Ford T Project*, Norwich, Centre for Applied Research in Education, University of East Anglia.

FRENCH, P. and MACLURE, M. (Eds.) (1981) *Adult-Child Conversation*, London, Croom Helm.

GANNAWAY, H. (1976) 'Making sense of school', in STUBBS, M. and DELAMONT, S. (Eds.) *Explorations in Classroom Observation*, Chichester, Wiley.

GARFINKEL, H. (1967) *Studies in Ethnomethodology*, Englewood Cliffs, NJ, Prentice Hall.

HAMMERSLEY, M (1974) 'The organization of pupil participation', *Sociological Review*, 22, 3, pp. 355–68.

HAMMERSLEY, M. (1976) 'The mobilization of pupil attention' in HAMMERSLEY, M. and WOODS, P. (Eds.) *The Process of Schooling*, London, Routledge and Kegan Paul.

HUSTLER, D. (1981) 'Making a start: story time in an M.Ed. course', *Tactyc Journal*, Derby Lonsdale College.

HUSTLER, D. and CUMMINGS, C. (1983) 'Action research in an infant classroom', *Primary Contact Journal*, 1, 2, Manchester Polytechnic.

HUSTLER, D. and PAYNE, G. (1983) 'Power in the classroom', *Research in Education*, 28, pp. 49–64.

KEENAN, E. (1975) 'Coherency of children's discourse', *Journal of Psycholinguistic Research*, 4, 4.

MACKAY, R. (1974) 'Conceptions of children and models of socialization', in TURNER, R. (Ed.) *Ethnomethodology*, Harmondsworth, Penguin.

NIXON, J. (Ed.) (1981) *A Teachers' Guide to Action Research*, London, Grant McIntyre.

PAYNE, G. (1976) 'Making a lesson happen: an ethnomethodological analysis', in HAMMERSLEY, M. and WOODS, P. (Eds.) *The Process of Schooling*, London, Routledge and Kegan Paul.

PAYNE, G. and CUFF, E. (Eds.) (1982) *Doing Teaching*, London, Batsford.

PAYNE, G., CUFF, E. *et al.* (1983) *Talk and More Talk*, Schools Council Report, Manchester, Manchester Polytechnic.

PAYNE, G. and HUSTLER, D. (1980) 'Teaching the class: the practical management of a cohort', *British Journal of Sociology of Education*, 1, 1, pp. 49–66.

PAYNE, G., HUSTLER, D. and CUFF, E. (1984) *Gist or Pist: Teacher Perception of the Project 'Girls into Science and Technology'*, Evaluation Report, Manchester, Manchester Polytechnic.

SACKS, H. (1963) 'Sociological description', *Berkeley Journal of Sociology*, 8.

SACKS, H. (1964–72) 'Unpublished lectures', mimeo, University of California.

SACKS, H. (1970) 'Aspects of the sequential organization of conversation', unpublished manuscript, University of California.

SCHEGLOFF, E. (1972) 'Notes on a conversational practice: formulating place', in SUDNOW, D. (Ed.) *Studies in Social Interaction*, New York, Free Press.

SCHUTZ, A. (1974) *The Structures of the Life World*, London, Heinemann.

TURNER, R. (Ed.) (1974) *Ethnomethodology*, Harmondsworth, Penguin.

WATSON, R. (1978) 'Categorization, authorization and blame — negotiation in conversation', *Sociology*, 12, pp. 105–13.

WELLS, G. (Ed.) (1981) *Learning through Interaction*, Cambridge, Cambridge University Press.

WOODS, P. (1981) 'Understanding through talk', in ADELMAN, C. (Ed.) *Uttering, Muttering: Collecting, Using and Reporting Talk For Social and Educational Research*, London, Grant McIntyre.

11 Integrating Methodologies: If the Intellectual Relations Don't Get You, then the Social Will

Brian Davies, Peter Corbishley, John Evans and Catherine Kenrick

Only Relate

The defence of the apparently only commonsensical (a bit of this and a bit of that) in a domain, like social research, given over to specialism and even mystery, requires a special act of standing outside of the skin. When trade traffic is concentrating on either brand dominance or best buys (here are a whole bunch of people committed to the superiority of 'qualitative methods'), arguing that 'it ain't necessarily so' is bound to raise specialist hackles, to sound rather folksy or even unprincipled. Our case is that mono-methodic cases in social studies are only contingently justifiable, for example, because they are easier to handle or because they provide purity, or afford non-dissonant identification for people, and so on. It might be rejoined immediately that 'contingency' here, far from being slight, threatens all the characteristics of the Keynesian long term. Short of a belief in research after death, therefore, it might be held perfectly reasonable to accept that most people will set up house in single-style and period epistemological edifices. There they will find the fruitfulness of familiarity as ethnographers, surveyors, textual analysts, and so on. What it is not reasonable to accept, however, is that anyone will be the better either for their crying plague on other houses or confusing a habitational mode with a housing policy that solves all problems of warmth and dryness, let alone gracious living. To argue this is not to commit ourselves to either theoretical or methodological pluralism that claims the possibility of superior, synthetic *melange* (remember the dullness of the 'ultimate' taste of mixed jellies or the colour of scrambled paints). Indeed, we hold that the metaphors, models and key concepts of the major sociological approach paradigms (marx-isms, interactionisms, structural functionalisms, etc.) are, to a degree, incommensurate and do not meaningfully 'translate' from one to another. Moreover, methods *qua* techniques do not 'belong' mono-politistically to anyone. At root, what researchers do is extraordinarily simple: we look, ask and read. The organized form of these activities which we encounter in 'methods' books and research practice should not cause us to forget that observation, interviews, questionnaires, documentary analysis, and so on, are neither inherently qualitative nor quantitative. All quantification involves judgment as to qualities and all qualitative statements invoke hierarchy, number and amount to give shape to meaning.

Our 'arguments' in these areas should not be about 'all or nothing' issues (for example, to measure or not, to observe or not) but rather about how much, when. The 'why' questions seem to us, for present purposes, not worth disputing. On the grand scale, we argue that social phenomena are inherently dualistic (I mean, structure is) and multi-levelled (my moment alone, ours next together, the system or epoch's existence). At the mundane level of our research life, we ought surely to recognize that there are times and places where we do not know the issues or even inhabit the language and only the patient search for naturalistic markers makes sense. But '(S)ociological studies have *two* broad purposes. One is to chart the impact of societies upon their members; a second is to study the societies themselves in terms of the impact of their institutions upon each other and how they relate to the impact on individuals' (Brown and Harris, 1978, p. 270, our emphasis). Accepting this does not deal with problems of meaning. People's perspectives differ irremediably. Whose we take 'will depend on what we are trying to do but it is difficult to contemplate any way of dealing with such multiple perspectives without the investigator at some stage imposing his *own* viewpoint of the world. He must use his judgment not only for methodological reasons ... but because the world is capable of having an impact irrespective of the meanings a person brings to it' (*ibid*, p. 273). If we want to talk causes, methodology is not some optional irritant. 'Methodological considerations start from the fact that it will usually be possible to reach alternative conclusions about the same set of results: methodology concerns anything that enables the researcher to rule out explanations that compete with the one favoured' (*ibid*, p. 63). Fundamental to its quality are hoary issues of reliability and validity at the heart of which needs to be the avoidance of the circular and 'self defeating nature of [Social Science] definitions and the confusion of "dependent" and "independent" variables' by distinguishing 'a *unit* of study from its *qualities*' (*ibid*, p. 74). These problems, we would underline, are not resolved by a retreat from 'positivism' (how often simply used as a boo-word for activities poorly understood?) to more 'naturalistic' methods (often no more than inferior positivism on a very small scale). Avoiding positivism means avoiding the empirical, which is clearly not what ethnographers and their ilk are about. It is part of the aftermath of our own cultural revolutions that we have a generation ignorant of hard-won standards, painfully reinventing necessity, finding that poetry is not enough and that poor poetry is worse than nothing.

In our research, we have no pretence to the developed quality of Brown and Harris' grounding in model and theory. But we do share their passion for the importance (and difficulty) of naming parts and describing/measuring qualities. Our activity was only preliminary and delineative, a pair of first stages tending pragmatically toward open and descriptive techniques, hypothesis-seeking rather than testing but at the same time hopelessly overcrowded with intention.

Hopefully it will be clear at once that the title of this paper is a fraud (which we undertook at the editor's request who had Sieber's work (1973) in mind): in principle, we do not believe in 'integrating methodologies' insofar as this would involve 'integrating' theoretical perspectives. We have no new metaprinciples to offer. But we think it wilfully damaging not to juxtapose methods and their datafruits within perspectives and then to ask the more difficult question of how far it is possible, short of risking deafness by dissonance, to listen with profit to the stories yielded by differing perspectival tongues, forbidding anyone, for the moment, to drown out the others. The orientation toward research we will call eclectic.

Getting Started

As a basis for extending our discussion of these matters, we offer this comment on a piece of funded research that has failed in part as a result of over-ambition and under-management largely related to insufficiently bridled (inherent in every principled case of) eclecticism as well as the exigencies of public funding. What we need to do in the course of it is to draw your attention, with great difficulty as above, to the defence of the eclectic *per se*, as opposed to the contingent sources of semi-failure of the projects.[1] We would immediately point out the need to be wary of our account. We began with diversity in our bones but we could not have written a decade ago about these general issues in the way we now do. We knew less *and* different then. And no more or less than any other social actors do we do other than call guiding values those rules we evolve in the course of interacting with events. Having this view of the *ex post facto* as well as the initiating function of purposes, we would do well to invite you to watch our storyline waver, even though we are committed to getting it as straight as we can. We also recognize, with Bell and Newby (1977), that we cannot tell all, even if we wanted to. Perhaps even more important, even if we were not constrained by thoughts of libel or good taste *vis-à-vis* our kin, friends and enemies to edit out or generalize to the watery edge of acceptability/meaninglessness a good number of 'personal' facts and judgments, we would argue that knowing all there is to know about a research venture would be no substitute for judgment concerning its truth claims, its utility or significance. Prurience aside, reading this, reading the accounts in Bell and Newby or reading Cathy Marsh's self portrait (Marsh, 1983, p. 1–3) which merges into a locating of the survey tradition in general in Britain, one is undergoing two possible relevant experiences: one is being persuaded as to the reasonableness of a certain pattern of research events/positions, while one is learning a bit of the trade ostensively. In a trade that is all too hard and private (with all the dangers of life in entrenched positions), practice badly needs sharing, an appreciative audience cultivating.

Our trip up unstreaming goes back at least a decade to 1974. Picture the London Institute of Education Sociology Department, the creation of Mannheim, developed by Floud and greatly expanded under Bernstein to contain the largest concentration of specialist staff (six) and students (nearly eighty full-time equivalent) studying the sociology of education (not to mention the initial teacher training of sociologists just splitting off) and pursuing funded research in the area in any department in Britain, in one of its perennial miffs. Far from being gift-shop to a suffering world of schooling, thanks to the power of 'New Directions' with which the whole department was persistently identified (see Flew, 1976; Bernbaum, 1977; Demaine, 1981) to the great fury of most of its incumbents who were thus falsely labelled, we were a group of people representing in unusually strong personal form the divergencies at large in sociology. Students on our courses would certainly have found endless scope for experiencing the rigours and confusions of intellectual dissent. If they were not rapidly proselytized then they tended to spend a good deal of effort on working out a (non-existent) party-line. The moral balance was being currently held about equally among tenured staff between the centrality to sociology of traditional means of 'bringing in the news' and the reckless rectitude that marked neo-New Directions and absolved its possessors from the needless chore of poking about for mere empirical confirmation of the *a priori* reality of a rotten system. If one were trying to catch the intellectual mood of the moment, then it might, for example, be characterized by the simultaneous existence of beliefs in *Classification and Frame*[2] as marvellous insight, messy typology needing empirical treatment, *a priori* truth and bourgeois junk. There was a good deal more bellyaching and backbiting than honest and open debate about differences. Non-engagement is always potentially the upshot of either unwillingness (the need to stay different, imputations of bad faith) or inability (not knowing enough to abandon the safety of dogmatism), easily exacerbated in this context by the fact that among the putative terms of the debate was the issue of 'openness' itself. While all this was the case of the 'teaching' department, there was also the highly visible, though largely unintegrated, presence of the Sociological Research Unit (SRU). It had at its peak in terms of contract researchers employed quite dwarfed the Department. It stood, amongst other things, for the historical reality of a dominant departmental model for funded research actually being accomplished. Methodologically, the SRU stood for hard numbers applied to small samples in the highly theorized universe of sociolinguistics after a decade of Brandis, Young (D), Robinson, the Geoghans, Hawkins, Turner, Hassan etc. (not to mention Bernstein himself) and before the coming of Adlam, Holland, etc.[3] The only other valid currency was the small change of student ethnography, breathless world views balanced on vestigial fieldwork, even before the world learned to call it 'Marxist'.[4] Central to the atmosphere (from both sides, for differing reasons) was the irritation generated by the presupposition that came to be appropriated via Young (M)[5] that Seeley has said it all; make, don't take, problems, especially in respect of the double-deceptive school system. For some of us, the liberation was less than total, given grasp of the fact that rendering problematic presupposes the existence of one so that the fun of deconstruction is likely to give way to distaste with the new foundations. It was doubly regressive — and could only really be met by equal and opposite dismissal — for those with highly developed research expertise to have to face continual attempted massacre by the innocents.

Enter specific local politics: says Bernstein, it's time to diversify away from the sociolinguistic and begin to develop an empirical database for large numbers of schools involving more teaching staff in public research. He had a specific urge to understand pupil truancy and disruption in his capacity as school governor along with the 'deeper' consideration of logging the school trails of the new middle class across the system's boundaries. This seemed to require data from primary, secondary and even tertiary levels, (in the latter especially in respect of some of the more obvious new makers and repairers as in architectural education). Researchable foci of interest were the sorts of things that *Pedagogies visible and invisible*[6] seemed to point toward as moments of weakening classification and frame and their location — 'progressivism' in pedagogy, mixed ability in the grouping, subject 'integration' and learner behaviour oriented in the direction of 'free expression', for example, in art education. All the muck of our varied system plus the whole problem of little in large and *vice versa* (grandly referred to as micro/macro problems), stared back rather balefully from the prospect. All sorts of things worked to uncouple the wagon train, to make sure that there was no new research venture that would include within it a significant slice of the teaching department and research unit. In retrospect, in a context where we could only agree on course content by apportioning terms to names and the roughest of sequencing principles (academic freedom take the highly distinctive hindmost), we were hardly likely to carry off the more difficult task of a common focus for our research. Planning did take place for a project which would involve Bernstein and Davies along with Brandis (SRU) of long standing and Corbishley (much more recently arrived as a Bernstein PhD student) on the big database. Basil Bernstein, while anxious that the empire would begin to be parcelled out differently, was not completely taken by the prospect of messing around with a theoretically unsexy, ordinary secondary school 'problem', such as the focus on 'unstreaming' which was emerging in planning meetings. He stayed with developing aspects of the class cultural and social transmission thesis. Brian Davies, interested in 'explaining' relatively obvious states of affairs and in the big database as a promise for the future, but having nothing but an abandoned, failed-and-unruly organization/classroom case study under his researcher-belt, took up with Corbishley who was coming from study of professional socialization of the invisible pedagogues.[7] Both of us wanted a varied 'research experience' and BB was no doubt exercising sound and proper judgment in letting us go play data on our own, while leaving the door to advice and colleagueship wide open.

From the earliest planning/discussion stages, there was a determination to mix metaphors *qua* quantitive/qualitative, positivist/ idealist (the dialogue was naive then and is often still as bad).[8] We feared empirical work that 'took meaning seriously' but which some-how allowed absolution from the necessity to index and measure concepts, where you did not state hypotheses, but hugged them duly justified as radical *angst* until they slipped out from bosom to text, merely annoted by the field note, justified by invoking a superior macro-reality.[9] But we also recoiled from superbly measured cloudi-ness/vacuity. The problem, above all, to be dealt with was the relation of micro to macro in a way that neither sold out to isomorphism or the *a priori*, that is to say, we believed in the Big Picture but did not believe that it made all the Little Ones in its image just like that. Our ways of avoiding the metaphysics and enabling us to get on with the eclectomania was to take a view of the world as multilevel and determinate but where articulations between people and institutions were always such as to generate choice and change in life largely lived out in organization contexts. Davies had an extended interest in the organization literature, occasioned both by an early obsession with the meaning of grouping and in particular the nature of the 'iron law of streaming' and the chance of leaving knowledge/curriculum to Young (M).[10] Davies was much persuaded that the business of effective change in British education was either an issue of turning the system administratively whether by central government legislation and regulation, as for example the modern grammar school had been created between the Welsh whisky money and the regulations of 1907 largely by the principled opportunism of Morant, or by local government provision such as the change engineered by Mason, the Leicestershire chief, so as to produce junior and senior high schools of types so varied by the sixties that they allowed Wyggeston and Countesthorpe to flourish or of individual school/department/ teacher finding the right conjunction of organization/curricular inter-stice and career. The latter sort of change could usually be largely characterized as five-day wonder stuff — it died or exported with key enthusiasts, hardly ever managing to fix itself as organization habit.[11] There appeared to be a two-way problem to be tackled, of showing how the daily face of relative autonomy/structural looseness might allow change, while the harsh reality of inertia and the requirements of cultural/social reproduction ensured limit and death to novelty in organizational form. If teachers were trained incapacitants, then part of their socialization was into simultaneous belief in their indispensi-bility and powerlessness.[12] No couple could be counted more satisfactory guarantors of social assenting.

Brian Davies, Peter Corbishley, John Evans and Catherine Kenrick

In this context, the reverting and falling-flat world of secondary reorganization, with its capacity to be marched swiftly back a step more than it advanced forward by the persistent class colonists of its commanding heights, presented a fascinating and messy arena (and still does — the process has been markedly accelerated by legislation and administrative action by Tories since 1978). Within it, conjunction of substantive focus that would provide valid, non-trivial database material (solidly factual, theoretically of some interest) with a problem with a high chance of legitimating system and institutional access, selected 'unstreaming' for us. Commonsensically, there was lots of it about, whereas the system twitches toward subject integration or pedagogic new initiative were more talk than practice. The school system, particularly in our natural constituency of Greater London, was coming to a rising-rolls, high-teacher turnover boil. Schools were 'in a state' perhaps hardly imaginable to those who have come to them in recent years. Inner-city staff turnover rates were often enormously high and LEAs experienced great problems of ensuring sufficient provision, all in a context where 'going comprehensive' was recent or imminent. Indeed the range of states of reorganization within its LEAs presented a complete spectrum of stages. Purple patches of grant application drafts even talked of 'natural experiments' on our doorstep. Finding out about grouping with special reference to 'mixed ability' was sexy enough to get us in, varied enough to generate the dossier (knowing about grouping required data on intake, curriculum pattern, organizational form). It required puzzling out both as an educational social movement within the larger 'common school' impulse, and as a determined individual-organizational event that itself required explication and would be in turn more or less determining of key within-organizational processes, such as curriculum, pedagogy, social relations. It was certainly clear that schools first unstreamed and then picked up the consequences. Peter Corbishley was particularly interested in the knowledge elements, especially the subject-as-held in teacher's head. We felt justified in the commonsense 'is it worth the effort?' direction by being convinced that the whole 'mixed ability' field was currently mainly in the hands of the normative sharks, bigots and denizens of the shallow end.

There must come a time in all research planning when the enthusiasm for getting going on discovery (ever driven by accompanying motives like the gappy CV, incipient unemployment) balances out against the negativities. On the positive side for those who do the planning and proposing, there can be no mistaking that period of ferment and excitement when ideas are knocked into 'doable' shape, the tension of knowing that the activities proposed bear only a fractured and inadequate relation to the hoped-for outcomes at conceptual theoretic or policy levels. There is the reality of knocking the enthusiastic chat into grant-appliers prose, of entitling and costing, of planning to go into business. For prospective research workers already in a job who intend to add project involvement to teaching, supervision etc. there is the prospecting of where it will fit. Frequently, proposals name or proposers either have in mind or thrust upon them by colleagues or circumstances, people 'already around' on soft money. Knowing that someone with funded (in both senses) research experience is going to be available can be a very positive support at this stage. But at the same time, there can be no doubt that our excessively short time-scales in public funding, with the built-in assumptions that full-time contract researchers are young, cheap, disposable, easily trained workers having their life's creative moment, just nicely to time, is a spurious legacy of models drawn from natural science laboratory (often factory-like) contexts, insufficiently rethought for the less expert, differently time-scaled work of the social sciences and education. Rolling programmes improve matters slightly but, in our view, the question of research tenure is more fundamental and would only be solved when something as revolutionary as explicitly recognized posts and part-posts available for entry and exit by rotation of staff are available in higher education departments, to provide the platform for the established business of research bidding for soft money to run at longer time-scales than are conventional. These are matters of hindsight. At the point of preparing the ground for this (or any) application, what are important and can support or detract are the attitudes and responses of colleagues. Ours were pretty mixed. There were the pitying smiles and petty abandonments as well as the supportive pushes. They matter a great deal when one actually faces the very considerable lead-times on planning and the intractability (and for the first time buyer, unfamiliarity) of the mechanics. Maybe even more, honest comment is required from peers for the motivation to get something going pushes inexorably toward planning/offering to do too much and self-delusion as to what is temporally and technically within the prospective competence of individual or group.

Though there was pressure upon us in the 'thinking ahead' time to consider the continuing employment of existing researchers (who will write the account of the effect of this as a spur to funded research?), we were never lumbered with anyone along for the wage-ride rather than the intellectual trip. Indeed there were times to come when people stayed on wageless (or joined at very poor rates) in order to sustain or finish activity. That 'thinking ahead' time, the exploratory research project's combination of feasibility and pilot study went on in part-time vein, initially largely in Davies' hands (and then with Corbishley), over two terms in the middle of which the first proposal for funding was submitted.

Utilizing personal contacts with education officers and inspectorate staff in LEAs (in exchange for in-service favours rendered, the job one had come second in, shaking down a branch of the Taffia, that once dominant, now declining, Welsh educational organ for controlling the education of the Greater London masses), a dominant noise to be discovered was the acuteness of intake growth, staff shortage and 'reorganizational' pressures on schools and the potential difficulty to be encountered of data collection 'on site'. In carefully recorded visits to selected LEAs and schools two questions were being put: what is it that we need to know about mixed ability? (subscript, bet there's a mess in classrooms we ought to be solving, answer yeah, yeah) and what do we need to know about individual schools as a preface to knowing which ones/how many we should select for case study observation? (subscript, what is it that can be found out about schools from LEA files, without bothering them direct? answer, a lot but there are problems about giving it to you). The pitch (as in sales) mixed with supplicancy (as in product testing) outlined a project in prospect over two stages, with emphasis on the necessity of the first to the relevance of the second which would be case studies of mixed ability schools chosen for their critical interest, focusing on classroom practices. But first it was argued we needed *not* a survey but a *map* which would give complete patterns in respect of the information available, our Greater London database where each secondary school would be known for curriculum, grouping, intake, staffing, etc. . . . The two LEAs who allowed initial extended 'pilot conversations' proved misleading, i.e. more open and generous in their (duly-delivered) promises, in the upshot, in comparison with London LEAs at large, where we later found refusals were few, but species of internal inefficiency in data availability were manifold and the time taken to collect information, though highly variable, proved to be seriously underestimated because we had based plans (how else?) on our pilots. Our LEA pilots saw rather differing ways and means to provide mapping information but both were interested and supportive and the question of legitimacy of the research role was taken for granted.

Indeed, the wider issue of what these pilot, issue-forming conversations are a case of, is a fascinating one. They were one-to-one (Davies and another), not recorded, but recollected accounts were written and sent to the LEA officers concerned immediately afterwards for comment and reference. We know them as odd mixtures of sales talk, insider plotting and practical speculation. They provide a number of practical limits which underwrite what can be 'promised' in research proposals for funding. They stand on the cusp of wheeling and dealing and data collection. They become routine basis for confident claims (normally exaggerations) as to what the data-market will bear and what 'needs to be done': they serve as a check on the more unreal researcher expectations as to what is possible, and reorient them toward the necessary. What they also did practically in this instance was to indicate that visits to senior ranking LEA officials required building-in to the first stage of the research design, not only to test for the presence of 'policies' about grouping and curriculum, but to legitimate and explore the terms of entry to 'the office' for the collection of 'what?' per school data, as well as checking out on desirable terms for case studies.

An original proposal to the Social Science Research Council (SSRC) for three-year funding of a two-stage, one and two 'halves' person team in addition to the 'Director' Davies, a full-time research officer (Corbishley), a half-time project secretary (unnamed) and a statistical consultant (W. Brandis), where a first year mapping would give way to a second year case study phase and third year write up, followed a fairly standard 'some qualitative, some quantitative' style of bidding, but justified methodological variety only in descriptive terms: we wished to know the whys and how much there was of varying patterns of grouping for teaching purposes in a system (commonsensically understood to be) destreaming, that is to say, moving from more to less homogenous forms in terms of ability/ attainment measures. We would need a variety of baseline data mainly from local authority files and partly from schools of a descriptive, numerical kind, as well as conducting the more or less orthodox form of semi-structured interviews with officials in all LEAs and a 'sample' of schools (to stand for the variety of provision and experience in each) in order to describe and account for the variety of unstreaming phenomena. We emphasized a taxonomic thrust that would hopefully point beyond the present project and enable us to pick up case study sites systematically rather than on the basis of convenience and access only.[13] The second stage would concentrate on a small number (up to six) schools chosen as being of theoretical (sociological, educational) interest and would focus largely on the observation of classroom practices across the non-workshop-and-gym curriculum. The plan was referred to the Educational Research Board (ERB) of the SSRC (whereas we had hoped for Sociology) from whence it duly emerged with a no, qualified by the opportunity to discuss the matter with a member designated to gloss the disappointment and help with potential resubmission. The news he bore when Davies met him was a genuine surprise, its gist being to forget mapping part one, and to proceed direct to a case study go, on the rationale that the information which we wanted to collect was intelligence available routinely to LEAs (i.e. was not a 'problem', did not need collecting) and (subscript) didn't seem to transcend commonsense anyway. Maybe it was indicative that it was broken by a Scot, maybe uninitiated into the scant glories of Form 7, the DES return which constituted the only directly educational common informational ground among the Wenglish authorities. It was certainly an invitation to prefer purity, that is to say, to specify the problem in theoretical rather than chalkfacers' terms in a way which would have warmed quick readers of Seeley's hearts and an indication that grouping was a 'go' area but were we not a bit vague about effects, should we not be comparing something, for example, streaming with mixed-ability for pupil outcomes? Summer went, and a reapplication pressing the grounds of stage one as an essential informational base for choosing case study sites was granted from January 1975 initially on a four term basis, extended subsequently by one. One had learned a very direct lesson on how far the rumour was true that it was the case that the ERB loved to pay for the hypothesis tested. The financeable model entailed the mode where you state in advance what it is you expect to find. *Non comprendez* the claim where what one wants to state is only a puzzle without the conviction that one actually knows the relevant names of the parts, let alone being gripped by more than a light agnosticism about the limits of methodologic virtue. But they *did* pay and one never knows for sure who talked up and booted down (if at all) and what continues to be a guessing game (we went through it another three times, its heart is deciphering the ultimate restricted code of a committee secretary who has 'collected the voices' from a no doubt internally discrepant brief discussion, charged to take the really rude and naughty bits out but disabled (because nobody provided any, because the system is predicated on demand response to suspect coves called 'researchers') from giving leads capable of being built upon toward approbation).

The limits of this project's world (and it is only now, almost a decade later in a position to report) were set from the start by the personnel and the task. There were too few of the former (one research officer, one part-time secretary) with insufficiently differentiated skills and interests but with a terrible appetite for the serendipity which sprouted monthly and could not be harvested fast enough. In retrospect, where we should have cut and written, we chased and luxuriated, always in the prospect of extension and expansion. Wanting not just a person Friday from our £900 per annum half-time secretary, but a fieldworker Thursday and Tuesday too, we employed a post-post graduate sociologist whose typing came but slowly and at too much time cost, and everybody minded the shop. We lacked sufficient statistical expertise and enough data-slave power to plan and feed the data manipulation and coding sheets. In the light of the shocking response (in terms of the highly qualified, underemployed, overwhelmingly female, very large number of applicants willing to work for peanuts if it was a *real* job with real autonomy/involvement) to our initial secretarial advertisement, the temptation to have done otherwise is only retrospective. When we reappointed after three terms, we got not only more secretarial skills but research experienced psychology graduate who also shared in data-collection and analysis. The arguments on most projects in favour of the typewriter-bound full-timer must be very limited, but the risks of role sharing becoming confusion, displacement and even refusal are also real, when egalitarian exhilaration in no longer the most functional thing in the room.

There cannot be any simple prescriptions for what constitutes an effective research team. Matching amounts of appropriate expertise to task is an obvious *nostrum*. As neophytes, we were fatally caught up in offering 'value for money' and then, rather recklessly over the top (when you have offered to deliver too much, what price a bit more?) compounding it by overwork on overmany objects. We were almost certainly too indulgently egalitarian. There is surely inherent in teamwork a strain toward 'organic' organizational type, *pace* Burns and Stalker (1961), particularly when the research object is both unclear/changing/exploratory and where the means are being evolved as part of the process. 'Every person a researcher/manager', extended in degree from 'Director' to 'secretary'. Execution preponderated over the executive and the fact that the experience was a 'good one' masked the need for clear enough division of labour and limit-setting to a greater hierarchy of activities conducive to effective, limited report. While this is clear enough in retrospect, we cannot easily name the points where these splittings should have occurred.

Brian Davies, Peter Corbishley, John Evans and Catherine Kenrick

Mapping London

The first two terms set the tone, and letters to London LEA chief officers (twenty of them, the approach to ILEA was always different and an early decision had to be taken, given its quite disproportionate size, so that if it cooperated the data which it generated would need to be presented on a neo-borough basis in terms of its own ten operating divisions, which would be treated on par with the twenty other boroughs in the interests of report anonymity) requesting interview with the chief officer/inspector/adviser responsible for (secondary) schools, brought the first reply in a week and the final (chased up) one five months later. The politics of contact involved emphasizing public financing, being part of the Institute SRU and the 'mapping' nature of the exercise leading to future direct pedagogic benefit — 'how to do mixed ability better'. Against the exigency of our LEA visit being one-off contact, we prepared per school booklets into which information could be written either as delivered verbally or left for in-office completion. From the very first interview we stressed the need for access to whatever measures of school ability intake were available as an essential basis for evaluating the 'meaning' of grouping regimes. Our *de facto* pilots in two boroughs the previous summer had taken place in an atmosphere of compliant discussion. We now met responses which ranged from open welcome to counter-insurgent interrogation and hostility. It put us through a rapid course in managing very different atmospheres at initial encounter with seasoned and senior educational workhorses. The necessity to present ourselves as expert and insider were acute and trading anonymized system knowledge as it accumulated became a regular feature of project legitimation. Little gifts as to how difficult issues were handled elsewhere, the spice of new gossip about other people's problems, were more than tokens to establish goodwill. Who says old fashioned rapport is what counts knows only the sunkissed foothills of interviewing the inexpert. One's scepticism for the indulgent Gross (not to mention Mason, McEachern and Ward, 1966) melted to sympathy in prospect of the three-hour (we only made nine hours once, later, with a headteacher) interview (Philips N220, C90 cassettes, multi-directional horror in some noisy inner-city town halls), a good deal of which was directed to the state of reorganizational/institutional change in the LEA's secondary (or middle and upper) schools, usually unobtainable in completely current or unfudged form from public written sources. The natural concomitant of this was to ask about secondary transfer *qua* criteria and procedures. Two LEAs refused permission for further contact after this initial encounter — in one with additional signs being shown that we were read as impercipient dilettantes not up to grasping school realities — essentially in relation to this matter. No guarantee of confidentiality would have been enough to cover their disquiet about access to ability/transfer data, we intuited, but we know little more about the process of refusal save that in one we 'got across' a chief inspector who disliked having his borough brochure interrogated and in the other that the enthusiastic engagement of a team of advisers (in a group interview) was swiftly revanched upon when the news got upstairs that we had been seen and approved by minions. Two other boroughs never met us, both claiming a moratorium on non-pledged projects during secondary reorganization (in one of them we certainly got embroiled in a power-tinged etiquette struggle over who allowed what, as between local inspectorate and officers). Both could have been entered later but only at a point where we were already struggling with stage two. We dwell on these initial encounters because they contain within them a good illustration of how innocence is lost in open-ended research exploration, effective decisions are taken jointly with one's 'subjects' and the minutiae of 'methods' decisions emerge from the circumstances, even when one is far from the ethnographic confession.

The initial unstructured interviews (which transcripted at between five and ten thousand words in excerpted form) included laying plans, in the light of our early 'decision' to abandon our per school booklet to be filled in on the spot or left in most authorities, as to how we might return to collect the data from office files concerning staffing, pupil and a variety of other resource dimensions of schools and clarification of the best tactics subsequently for obtaining per school grouping and curricular data. Some LEAs volunteered their advisory teams to do collection on our grid[14] ('it will be good for them/for us . . .'). Others put our instrument into their schools for us, with explicit confirmation of the project's independence. Our own preference was to have the school-completed grouping data mailed direct to us but we took local advice on whether a through-the-office procedure would enhance our returns or not. An early bit of project learning concerned the extent to which centre-periphery/office-school relations within LEAs varied widely between them in substance and tone. Some LEAs clearly knew a great deal about and 'dominated' their schools from the centre, the office and local inspectorate/advisory service. Others knew little and exuded a real timidity in the face of schools' rights and reactions. Allowing some

LEAs to collect for us, or act as posting box for, school grouping returns involved sheer opportunism and pragmatism about the schools' definition of the meaning of the destiny of their returns, the effect of which upon reliability we could only hope to check upon during visits. But the choices were stark. Best guess as to percentage returns from a direct approach were bleak and only in a very few authorities was the quality of in-office intelligence so good as to enable us to feel confident with descriptions from this source only. One assented to a wish on the part of most LEAs to share the information which we wanted and they lacked. In our eventual visits to 14 per cent of the nearly 600 schools from which we had returns (and in all cooperating authorities our map has less than 10 per cent gaps), the discrepancy between them and actual arrangements was very small and in the main related to clarity of information about remedial provision and sub-details of what happened within them when grouping was by bands.

We got our first turnround on grouping returns about individual schools within weeks of our visits to interview senior officers and the work of setting up LEA in-office data collection from files began almost immediately. The interviews had nearly all been conducted two-handed by the Director and research officer. The data-collection visits were conducted by the research officer, accompanied as often as possible by the part-time research secretary. What we had anticipated from our pilot experience would take a few hours of writing in answers on our per school pre-prepared booklets for each authority, rapidly escalated to days (even weeks) in most of them. The whole unexplored world of LEA routine intelligence assembly and associated office practice opened up in all its unexpected variation. There were plenty and enough of willing informants for whom the research incursion was both novel and unthreatening. The case is that just as psychologists have done little to scale the child cognitive mountain as opposed to the psyche of the white mouse, so even greater are the gaps in our knowledge of the shape and daily working of local authority intelligence and operating systems. We had to learn absolutely *de novo* who was who in this world where, beneath the surface crust of the front office and adviser's room where schools were described in a full-gospel rhetoric of autonomy and independence, (certainly in relation to grouping and curricular decisions), unvarnished opinions of the clerical kind frequently guided administrative fiat and relation. For example, in relation to the intake of schools we know to be variously determined by the interaction of geography, ability criteria and, increasingly, parental choice, resource management considerations created the frequently non-public world of the catchment area or zone with its pragmatically shifted and more or less breachable boundaries manned by a witting clerk. Catchment-areas were regularly trimmed and augmented according to the paramount obligation firstly to create sufficient 'seats' and then secondly on grounds of efficiency to ensure that there were 'bums' enough to fill them. These marginal adjustments were almost invariably kept secret from any public gaze and a fruitful source of parental unrest. In some authorities the whole business of creating catchment areas was publicly denied for all schools. The range and strength of criteria used to allow parental choice varied considerably. 'Who parents were' and how they might pursue a thwarted cause were differentially taken into account as were the 'standing' and likely behaviour of schools. Routine decision-taking was quite likely to be invested in a specific non-senior person, whose anonymity from public gaze was strictly functional for more senior 'front' people who could use it to invoke 'themness' in the situation almost as legitimately as the disappointed family. The public and in-office 'standing' of schools became an important, if elusive, issue and we attempted to index the status of schools by improving upon sheer counts of parental preference. The paucity of available markers for the social class distribution of schools led us to think through not only things like the utility of the free-meal count but to try applying district census data to school catchments. After very considerable endeavour of our own we discovered a governmental agency with an appropriate technique just as fund-shortage was closing it down. The standing and reputation of schools after reorganization led us to seek organizational biographic data on their previous histories by official type and intake characteristics sometimes back before 1944. LEA office administrations were highly variable in their capacity for providing statistical information and the lengthening of data collection timescales completed the 'all hands on deck' i.e., all project members flat out 'collecting' syndrome. In retrospect, here was a prime case of funded work where the linked scholar (as indeed was the case in stage two) could be utilized to effect.

From this point on, we felt affirmed in the messy and expensive decision to think levels and multiform data: imagining that LEAs 'were' what LEA senior officials said they were might not under any circumstances seem more than *jejeune*, but digging in at other personnel levels, comparing words with documentary practice, observing daily routine events and their corresponding vital level of organizational intelligence did not simply give us more information, it gave us better, cross-checked insights. The sum of triangulation is (given luck) a transformation of one's view of the separate angles and extensions. If the sociological task be that of 'looking behind' describing the view the other side of the first areas we come to is hardly likely to prove penetrating enough.

As grouping returns from schools in an LEA became available and were placed alongside a preliminary description of school by type defined by size, sex, ability intake (very variously available), official-nomenclature, LEA office gossip, and previous history crude inspection of grouping patterns on the borough basis was the platform for choosing a bunch of schools in each authority to visit. The incidence of grouping types certainly varied by borough as well as very obviously by pupil age group and school subject. Other 'differentia' in data patterns emerged while we, of necessity, had to 'get on with' choosing schools for visits on a very *ad hoc* basis of 'representing' the LEA's school types, plus following interesting hunches and deviations (for example, that girls' schools did unstreaming more, the irresistible urge to see a mixed school which sex segregated for about half the curriculum). Had we the 'final patterns' before choosing our school visits samples, then we would surely have chosen differently and in some ways better. But on the other hand, the visits changed and deepened our foci of interest as the process went on so that *a priori* choosing without visits might, in turn, have missed numerous tricks. The request to schools for interviews was delivered after they would have had the experience of making a grouping return, to its head-teacher, for access to her/himself or, ideally, the substitute most fully acquainted with the exigencies of timetabling. We most frequently got heads/*and* another(s). On the basis of a pre-delivered agenda, which contained the key prompts for an otherwise open-ended interview (again cassette recorded, increasingly selectively transcribed at longer intervals from recording, though visits were immediately 'diaried' for surrounding noise and overall impressions, intuitive leads, etc.) school visits went on from March 1975 to January 1976. As early as the second school visited it was highly apparent that a look at the timetable and a sceptical orientation toward the verbally delivered 'facts' of the headmaster's account of school were essential. Above all what emerged in this interview was the extent to which, in a large school, the head's confidently delivered exposition of grouping and curricular practice simply did not accord with what happened on the ground — he simply did not know what went on when the science department met three first-year mixed ability forms with four teachers. He thought they re-sorted the children into smaller mixed ability groups following a common, identically paced worksheme, whereas in fact they set and covered different arrays of topics. The basic on-site tactic was to ask for the 'recent history of the school', which merged with the recent biography of many new(ish) heads. The emphasis on 'why this grouping?' was never forced away from 'how?' because it became abundantly clear that the changes and states being discussed were not some deep and clearly theorized purpose, but rather a set of practices pursued for conflicting and uncertain ends, whose reality ran hardly beyond the doing. Not far below the social surface *qua* individual perception may lurk spurious nonsense, rationalization masquerading as 'cause'. We complied with requests for comparative information on the solution to problems (for example, how do I get round modern language choices?) as freely as we could, in a conversational mode. The school-eye view of local authority behaviour was interestingly different, the school and individual decision-maker linked contingency of grouping and curricular decisions, grew from (often striking) anecdote to complex picture. Notwithstanding the protestation of LEAs, the incidence of mixed-ability and other grouping modes was a borough phenomenon, largely linked to reorganization type and timing. Recent or ongoing reorganization, particularly accompanied by augmented advisory teams and transition-aimed INSET, were most highly indicative of its likelihood, as were non-11–18 school types. Among other school characteristics, those with ability-compressed intakes were most likely to mix such abilities as they had (whether 'high' or 'low') and among more normally ability-spread schools, ex-grammar, girls' and catholic (though in this last case the distribution tended to be bimodal) tended to unstreaming. On visits, any available documentation on grouping or curriculum was sought and the question was raised as to what would be the right questions to ask in what locations at the subsequent case study stage. We would emphasize that these school interviews with heads and/or their nominees were essentially interviewee paced unstructured conversations around an agenda which put the emphasis on curriculum and grouping practices as school-wide events produced by people who run them. Given that we wanted to discern motives for modes in contexts we deliberately oriented the conversation start to 'tell us how things have happened' and, given opportunity to intervene in the flow, pushed for description of mechanics before declarations of purpose or hopes for outcomes. Faced with contradiction, we rarely asked for comment. Clearly we did not believe that we were getting other than authorized version, in more or less publicly edited retrospect, of school events. We were not seeking some Selznickian grasp of leadership as curator of organizational group-mind but only texts which would enable us to evaluate and locate 'top persons' ' self-reported intentions for organizational events.

'What is mixed ability?' and 'how does it come to pass'? converged as questions properly to be asked of system as well as school. The fragmentary and half- (or mis-) perceived at any one of the LEA, school 'front-office' and departmental levels took more secure shape when annotated/triangulated with data from others. This constitutes the heart of the case for methodological electicism. One's confidence in the strength of a determination is greater if it is located in more than one meaning/interactive universe. Our accumulating data was pushed toward a typology of school level 'reasons' for going mixed ability to one extent or another in specified areas. Our peak long list showed twelve main 'motives' of an analytically distinguishable kind.[15] The interview data suggested they existed in complex and often contradictory admixtures in the minds of heads and other senior school people, when squeezed for a story. It showed in awesome form how very easy the change to mixed ability *grouping* could be for a school management, without effective thought for classroom consequences, and how far these decisions were linked to specific supra-school, LEA exigencies revealed by our mapping.

Two basic motifs lay behind 'going mixed-ability', both visible form of the functional cross schooling is required to bear: a dominant technicist 'doing differentiation' drive, related in its strength and details to the efficiency of administrative systems serving existing interests and a lesser egalitarian thrust toward holding child and knowledge types together for newly-extended periods. The making different/making similar, expert/citizen, elite/communitarian tensions within the altruistic bosom of educational systems in modern industrial societies is well documented. Not even the least data-bound of our revisionist historians (see Ravitch, 1978 for comment) argues successfully either for the possible dominance to exclusion of one set of these poles or other of their historical facticity in anything like pure form. Indeed our first stage literature survey preceding stage one and adding an historic angle to the eclectic mix suggested a complex interplay between organizational states (in respect of grouping), research emphases and educational intellectual climates, viewed through a comparison of the British and American literature over a fifty-year timescale (Corbishley, 1977). What 'grouping problem' you focus on is what you fancy leaving. What the empirical findings tend to show is that a grouping change is as good as a minor attainment gain: the professional *avant garde* of easy-to-finish, graded US high school system yearned for tracking as solution to poor attainment and motivation, whereas in early everything (especially academic labelling) British bipartism (but remember as an antidote to history-as-yesterday-pushed-backwards-as-far-as-is-convenient, our hard-to-finish grade system in the public sector until the second world war which Hadow was pleased to suggest would benefit from a touch of streaming?), romance is heterogeny. The ideological innards of education discourse serve to provide topics and censor them differentially. For example, only those studies of streaming and even the bits of them which celebrate class division, de-motivation and social-loss made much trade wind from the fifties until the universal bodycheck of Black Papers, Yellow Book and Green Paper, symptomatizing in turn the public faces of a successive bipartisan hallowing of confidence in the educational system to deliver the goods giving way to loss of confidence in system performance. The other finding across the literature is that the measurable pupil attainment differences assignable to variation in grouping types/or arising from innovative change are not worth the candle in comparison with variations in other features of school organization associated with them for example like participation rates of differing social classes and genders by length of time, type of exam entry etc. that come not only as part of the grouping 'message' itself but also as part of other features of systems which share elective affinities or are planned concomitantly with or become emergent properties of mere grouping modes.

This view of things provides a useful instance of the common-place that not only is there no datum worth the name without theory but that theory alters the meaning of data. We kept on encountering the 'problem' 'Now we've got the grouping, where'll we get the teaching?'. Our theoretical ideas tuned us to hearing this either as a non-issue ('it doesn't matter how you teach') or as a new issue whose-name-we-did-not-yet-know. As the former, we could properly say of mixed ability innovation as a 'movement' that not even a well aimed bandwagon will push a fundamentally unchanged system in a different direction i.e. with school subject and evaluatory and child-type educational cultures unchanged, aims to realize equal value[16] of children's education will founder as rapidly as parity of prestige among institutions did. But such cynicisms oil seminar, staff and tap rooms while they do not much run schools. The more interesting line, it seemed to us, when school managements foisted or allowed mixed ability change, was to ask what was its effect in terms of the pedagogic word inscribed on most teachers' hearts, many of whom appeared to experience very great threat to job skills and emitted appropriate assorted distress behaviour. And this led us to the apprehension that teachers did not know what to do next because they did not know much about what they were doing now.

By the time we had proceeded through the first thirty of what were to be over seventy school visits, where we became connoisseurs of fear of the old ('sink streams come from streaming and we have too much potential in that direction') and the exigencies of the new (particularly the poorly orchestrated flow of clear pupil intelligence at secondary transfer), the methodological point that we now want to make was very clear. A local construction of particular school 'meanings' only would have provided a perfectly satisfactory tale in its place, emphasizing the idiosyncratic and contingent. The top-down system map on *its* own would have provided an explanation that rendered the interactive bits contingent, the social current all. Juxtaposing levels *via* data culled by necessarily diverse methods (after all you interrogate free dinner files and headteachers' differently) provides 'more' explanation of 'the same' events. The deeper metaphor, if you will, rests on a belief (assumption) about the necessary duality of social explanation which one would be happy to leave at large in Weberian terms or for those who see too much of the methodological individualist in those old bones, in terms of 'the essential importance of the duality of structure' (Giddens, 1978, p. 95), not that this is free of the charge of taking the person too seriously. Procedurally, as we have argued at opening, it probably makes sense to regard the competing claimants to social explanatory power as not even necessarily belonging to the same 'subject'. Maybe physics and impressionism have more in common than marxism and phenomenology. Why waste breath on an ontological energy sapper, for example, which hopes to bed ethnomethodology with materialism or symbolic interactionism with functionalism when all one needs is a pragmatic planting for light, shade and colour? Competing orthodoxies only detract when their impulse is absolutist. The synthetic project in social theory is no nearer to integration than juxtaposition. But in the end, we should not confuse the 'high' of the multi-methodologic aha! moment for a solution to our theory urges. You stick two nice explanatory modes together and you get ply or laminate. They're stronger, but that is not to say they are better for all purposes.

Life in Classrooms: Framing the MOT

Our stage two problems, though the main 'method' became paper and pencil observation, were not fundamentally different from most of those in stage one. Having gone through a repeat trauma of revised grant application with the SSRC (and a curious courtship *en route* with the quicker, more personalized but equally incoherent form of financial rejection known as Nuffield), we once more ended up planning to provide the moon for small pennies via the same research officer (Corbishley), a full-time research secretary, Catherine Kenrick (at a lower-rung officer wage) and a full-time quota award student (already an experienced teacher who had completed a full-time MA in the department), John Evans, to work in acknowledged harness with the project. We were awarded money for two years and a subsequent extension for a third, during which time the project moved with the Director's change of job, to the Centre for Science Education at Chelsea College. The complex fruits of stage one were squeezed to produce two dominant criteria for the selection of case study schools: the nature of pupil intake and motives for/amounts of mixed ability. Pragmatically simplifying the field by electing only to look at mixed comprehensives with around six forms of entry (our best guess at the 'shape' of the secondary future), we located four case study schools to start with: two with 'balanced', two with unbalanced (relatively low) ability 'intakes', cross-cut for amounts of and motives for 'going mixed ability' (less, i.e. mainly first year, 'soft' humanities curriculum and technicist *vs* most of three years, subjects and 'egalitarian') with fieldworkers full-time in two, the project Director holding the fort in the other two, to allow for swaps in the second and subsequent terms of what was to be our data collection year with the research secretary specializing in the remedials in both and available to act as hand or ear in areas/with people in relation to whom the other workers might have difficulty. The arrangement collapsed in a bout of managerial hypertension and continued only in the two schools in which Corbishley, Evans and increasingly Kenrick, were located full-time (Fridays back at the ranch).

A thoroughly-combed classroom literature told us that nothing worked: the effectiveness, measurement-oriented tradition took the scum off a pot that might have anything in it, ethnography stuck, too thrilled by the moment.[17] Both celebrated the pretty unvarnished centrality of individual actors, or even their atomized intra-person characteristics.[18] We were, equally, still as depressed about using scenes from classroom life to pin the ancedotal tail on the structuralist donkey. We were sceptical of the importance of individuals but impressed by the centrality of the importance of pedagogy — its historical rootedness, system determined nature, its relation to the teacher's head in relation to how the image of the subject was held and made active. This enabled us to see the practical problem of 'mixed ability' as an expression of teaching methods in which contents and mode of transmission (methods, teaching strategies) are lodged together. Sonorities apart, however, the literature on theories of instruction looked like a very bare cupboard. Bernsteinian Cs and Fs were obvious breeding lines: Lundgrenian and Dahllofian system-ideas-with-the-crap-discarded of 'framing' were very appealing with levels of determination of classroom acts, in principle, from nation states and their chums, corporate multinational, through LEAs and school organization to departments, being built in. But our basic confession was that we did not know what was happening in classrooms, at the working heart of the transmission. This agnostic-ism led us to the clock-following of classes, logging 'common-sensically' defined activities with sharp pencil and triple carbon paper. We homed in, more or less, on the 'most usual' class in the first, then second, then less extensively but decidedly more ex-haustedly, in the third year. Pragmatically 'contrast' teachers were located and observed too. Lengthy questionnaires for staff and students, — the former focusing on biography prefacing feelings/ practices in the present classroom and organizational contexts, the latter on a barer facesheet, with the main emphasis on self-rating and preferences in respect of class subjects. All children in years 1–3 were also NFER AH 2/3 tested and whatever was available by way of other ability/attainment measures of the children also collected. School files were largely available. Staff were systematically talked to about lessons observed and a large fraction (including senior staff) interviewed more formally. School and departmental events of all sorts (not only of the formal decision-taking kind) were observed and written up. Most talk with children occurred during or around lessons but there were some informal individual and group talks outside. A very small number of parents were talked with during open evenings attended.

The guts of our case study data is the classroom material, embedded in pretty rich knowledge of the organizational context of the school, annotated with a good deal of objective test and closed and open questionnaire material which, in the context of at least one form of each year group, we can embed in a good deal of teacher/ child conversation. Very little of the classroom material was cassette recorded but among the successive reported observations of 'the same' class and teacher, there are lessons where explicit focus was laid upon the verbal content of interactions. In contexts where a high proportion of classroom interaction revolved around the worksheet, the reasonably efficient paper and pencil record of teacher-to-whole-class transmission is possible. A good deal of time was spent at the other end of the classroom spectrum in prolonged observation of individual and group interaction, around the common thread of how the work gets done (or not).[19] What this allows us to provide is an account credibly up to the mark by recent conventional 'ethno-graphic' standards. It is clearly sub-ethnomethodologic, being nearer to the Becker canon in what we are glad to recognize as a broad qualitative method church of late, as befits the lonely single-person neophytes who mainly inhabit it. It has some of the virtues of repetition and comparison, categories grounded in repeated and refined observation that Glaser and Strauss achieve much more adequately, which can be systematically referred to the organizational locality in which the actors' lives are further known. Having test scores and construct analyses (of teachers' views, particularly of 'remedial children'), having measures of worksheets' readability, having 'mass' data on children's opinions of varying aspects of subjects, ways of working, and their general pupildom, enables analyses which are very different to the merely ethnographic and which add to/subtract/query/force new problems in a way which reminds us that purity is only its own reward. For example, work is forthcoming that uses pupil questionnaire data, drawing on their statements about their work, behaviour, interest and ability in the broad core of the curriculum (maths, science, English, humanities, modern language), subjected to log-linear analysis. In a very direct way, some features of the data are rather surprising — they simply 'aren't the same' as the messages of the observational material and raise issues both of method 'effects' and limits. Without using standard significance testing, we can use such data in harness with material based on attendance at school and departmental meetings to suggest that departmental ethos is 'lived out' in a way that has direct purchase on pupil identities. We have to address what it means when pupils in a school where attainment is clearly 'lower' than in another, assign higher performance status to themselves more generally. We have only 'got' to such an analysis via scepticism about existing 'classroom' work and having the proceedings of multi-form data collection to work with. Also on the quantitative side, we have just completed an analysis of further questionnaire data to comment on recent work on the connections between ability, age, gender and ethnicity in relation to involvement in extra-curricular activities, particularly school sports. By combining pupil and teacher material, and setting the specific data about the extra-curricular against a wider knowledge of in-classroom and other school processes, we can show little confirmation for cruder correspondence/reproductionist accounts, often of the case study only kind. We would argue that the virtues of our already published work on pastoral care systems and maths classrooms have the same character, emphasizing the nature of the relation of the specific to the successively wider set of contexts in which they are embedded.

Certainly analyses of these sorts are only possible on the basis *inter alia* of a thoroughly detailed questionnaire, encoded and tabulated in great detail. Indeed, in part two of the project, as in part one in relation to the per school grouping data, we faced crucial problems of the detail in which we wrote our coding frames and utilized the material. In both cases, in the context of project person-power and timescale, we made poor choices, that is to say, we went for options which were enormously detailed, took a great deal longer, without specialist help for routine work, than we could afford. For example, we estimate that the planning and executing of coding the pupil questionnaires took in excess of 200 work days and while all the material is available in computerized form, the extent to which it has been used is rather minimal. We even faced the paradox in writing-up classroom and associated material of going back directly to individual questionnaires for quick counts because the big scheme was running way out of time. We cannot underline too highly though that such 'hard' analyses as we do would signally lack meaning except in the knowledge of how classrooms, departments and other areas of the school 'were' in interactive terms.

Coming Apart

One should repeat that the initial aim was extremely ambitious — to provide a London-wide data base for detailed future SRU program-mes and also more specifically to provide the widest possible context for ethnographic work around a single area which we could rely upon as being highly 'legit' for entry purposes (as well as being important). Hindsight, that most ingrateful of all beasts and orifical of views, tells us what we always knew, as it were, but now in lights: that the project was under-resourced and insufficiently staffed with specialist expertise. The extreme short-run funding periods provided the seed-bed for such permanent obsessiveness over the place in the grant soup queue, that we coped by forgetting proper limits to modest endeavour. Unvarnished immersion in the field, from Director to secretary, in part was merely punctuated by frantic bouts of rescripting the application. We followed fascinating leads rather immodestly. LEA administrations which we hoped would quickly provide relevant data, became the objects of our investigation. The complexity of secondary transfer in LEAs nominally 'comprehensive' (let alone in those committed to mixed economies) revealed intriguing depths, and the system-related rationales of schools in electing their grouping patterns kept on moving the wind about the sails of the good ship Relative Autonomy in these waters. All hands on deck and the consequent equalization rather than hierarchization of project relations carried the seeds of deep difficulty for write-up productivity. Our agreed strategy was from early on that we would not be diverted into *ad interim* publishing except of a very minor kind and experience of the time demanded in writing up the pastoral systems article confirmed this. Our first stage analysis of material ran into the second and so aiming for a single omnibus report/publication became 'reasonable'. We always knew that one of the case studies 'belonged' to Evans as his PhD material and that this had its own priority. The other two fieldworkers were deemed to be separately responsible for their own accounts of the 'other' case study and remedial provision in both schools, respectively, which we worked toward via partial drafts of material discussed at Friday planning/report back. These three texts would, along with the part one data, become the basis for a single, unified write-up by the Director, both for the purposes of official report and then as the 'stuff' of articles or monograph. Egalitarian comment and joint responsibility for all written output at this second stage was always assumed. There is, of course, something deeply appealing about research egalitarianism, particularly in the context of recent sociology of education. Presumably this is partly why, in the trade at large, we have been so profoundly unproductive except in respect of mainly moral entrepreneurship of the ethnographic kind. It hasn't been easy to work for anyone else in a universe coming apart at its paradigmatic seams. Maybe when two or three are gathered together for ethnographic purposes four or no accounts emerge. Best plan stay at home (or mimic forage) and discourse on the ragged troop bearing faint news on the banners.

Eclecticism, while being the pejored name of a necessary form of life in studies of the social, needs to be kept only difficult. We made it impossible. The difficulty is quite irredeemable in the same sense that theoretical union of perspectival parts is a chimera. Juxtaposition is all, and the fundamental problems are managerial. To the difficulties intrinsic to the retrieval and use of initially processed data of one sort or another, (the field note, the lesson observation, the interview transcript etc.), now add holding them in relation to one another. Miniaturization does not work because much of the material is inherently discursive. On the other hand, what inevitably characterizes a multi-method project is alternation and specialization in aspects of it. Just as development characterizes any one enquiry process (the objects and elements alter meaning as they and their relations reveal themselves via additional informational and conceptual realignment), so it is even more the case when multiple data-lines are thrown together. The central 'problem' of the relation of the empirical bits to theoretical bigger bits still remains the exciting and frequently intractable core, only with more going on.

In our second stage, two school case studies, the fundamental individualism of the heart of ethnotechnology, compounding the multi-method problem of an eclectic design, became our overwhelming burden. You can send three workers into the field to do the 'no-preconceptions' thing and bring them back every Friday to shake them down for loose data, burgeoning inclination and unwarranted trend, you can even loosely align the ongoing collection, but we very much doubt in the nature of the observational mode, whether there is real old-fashioned meaning to 'doing the same thing' in the way in which questionnaires can be 'identically administered' or a focused interview pattered through in replicable manner (notwithstanding the long-standing caveats (or is it impossible dream?) of *Method and Measurement* (Cicourel, 1964)). Our case studies grew apart, and grew apart further and faster than we confessed (not the wrong word for once) or conceded (nor this) to one another. Evans pursued the MOT with increasing clarity and the growing light was that it is not knowledge that alienates, more likely it is living in a metalearning fog, where piloting (merely learning what you have been taught) is all, more Cerebus than cerebral Corbishley saw more about purity and danger — child purity needing clear conservation by the good, in danger of the shape of knowledge in teachers' heads, needing insulating and proofing — a populism up against the limits of the consequence of leaving the whole ability range in the British mastery classroom. The two schools provided a fascinating difference in terms of problems of classroom control that required differential diversions of researcher attention into pupil 'interest' (i.e. non work-task) behaviour. This may sound both highfalutin and febrile but the hard fact is that it led to increasingly different emphasis in the context of observations which were different again to the remedial work where Kenrick, given the task of establishing the system relation of repair work to mainstream school, was inevitably drawn toward more person-oriented categories to make sense of the small group interaction in withdrawal settings. That work has been continued for PhD submission on an SSRC quota place in two more non-mixed-ability schools because part of its emerging logic entails seeing the 'remedial' context as adjunct to a variety of 'ordinary' schools. The detailed 'comparison' of the mainstream work in the schools is not fully possible as the money disappeared before Corbishley's write-up was completed and there is no recourse (even if there were person power) to the other man's open-ended fieldnote. A full version of his case study school has never been written up in a way which matches Evans' completed thesis. In that sense, the project is a substantial failure of management, a powerful comment on how, if data collection is to be window (of a well known shape and size, gazed through quickly) on the empirical world, then multi-method collection better be a row of them open and shut even more quickly if we are to cope in the time-span life and funders allow us,[20] with the richness which nature affords our rather poor conceptual sight.

Acknowledgement

We gratefully acknowledge the assistance of the SSRC in funding the two projects: *A Preliminary Study of Unstreaming in London Secondary Schools* and *Teacher Strategies and Pupil Identities in Mixed Ability Curricula: a case study approach*, upon which this paper is based.

Notes

1 The final reports have not yet been delivered to the Council but will be later this year. Our published material to date is CORBISHLEY (1977), CORBISHLEY and EVANS (1980), CORBISHLEY, EVANS, KENRICK and DAVIES (1981), DAVIES (1977), DAVIES and EVANS (1983 and 1984), EVANS (1982 and 1985). EVANS (1982) has the best available full bibliography. We are far from finished, nearly a decade after.
2 Here we mean to refer not just to the Bernstein article in *Class Codes and Control*, 3, (1977) but the enormous impact it had on the 1970 BSA

Conference at Durham and its publication in YOUNG (1971), experienced variously as thrill and breakthrough and shock-horror.

3 By the mid 1970s, the great bulk of the sociolinguistic work of the SRU was published. *Class Codes and Control*, Vol. 1 was being revised by 1974, Vol. 2 was published in 1973: see them for further reference to the wider SRU *corpus*, which there is simply not the space to develop here. What we would underline here was the unmissable daily fact of departmental life that there was a 'hightech' expertise which drew very large sums in public funds for hotly contested work which we understood more about than most but which regularly moved ahead of our conceptual grasp. There was also no missing its very great international reputation and the enormous potency of its message.

4 That was sometimes the label hung on Keddie and several other ex- and current departmental MA students pursued it mightily. The first unequivocal successes were Sharp and Green.

5 In his Introduction, to *New Directions*, (1971).

6 Also in BERNSTEIN (1977): the Paris connection with Bourdieu's group also threatened to blossom still. There had been talk of concrete cooperation and exchange between his group and ours.

7 Research subjects are anonymous, researchers need naming. The *personae dramatis* here are the authors and well known significant others. Davies had withdrawn from registering as his personal PhD, fieldwork accomplished in 1970–73 for a case study of a new London secondary school (more than a whiff of which appears in DAVIES, 1976), whose warmth of welcome was matched only by his naivete in imagining that an amalgamation of two secondary moderns (prefaced by their deliberate run-down) would lead to anything other than a situation where the institution could hardly be seen for the persons. Peter Corbishley had been working on a PhD with Bernstein on contrasting patterns of primary PGCE initial training. While rationally justifiable on other grounds, maybe our decisions/failure not to write up these earlier individual studies boded ill for swift production in the loose contexts which we now sought.

8 And nowhere is it more mucky than in the popular methods 'text', for example, COHEN and MANION (1980).

9 Those MA dissertations rarely flowered in print but SHARP and GREEN (1975), WILLIS (1977) were in the making.

10 The iron law popped up for Davies in comparing personal and peer fates in his 'own' South Welsh grammar school taking 40 per cent of the cohort and his first job witness of the operation of a North London grammar, taking the top 5–10 per cent which duly pinpointed its ineducable child-booty by year three in the eyes of a good slice of the staffroom, from children who would, in ability terms, have lain well-up the 'A' stream pace in educogenic Carmarthenshire. Chance dictated that as Davies and Young arrived simultaneously in 1967 at the Institute, they fell upon a division of labour predicated partly upon taught Masters' thesis interests, mutually acknowledged lacks and Bernstein's injunction to plan a reformulation of the taught MA package. What clearly needed adding to opportunity, educability and occupation (class

chances in) were school and system organization and curriculum.

11 There was a sharp consciousness of the transience of school-based innovation on the part of new rational planners like the new Schools' Council as well as front-line comprehensive practitioners like Daunt and Mitchell at Thomas Bennett, Crawley, which Davies was particularly aware of both as a result of doing consultancy work for the Schools Council on Teachers' Centres and school innovation as well as working with ILEA schools via the Rachel MacMillan Centre in particular. The experience had led to his one act of academic individual infidelity which led to him coming second as a *de facto* Deputy Education Officer in a London borough. If offered, the job would certainly have been taken, partly because of a view of where the action was at and partly on a depressing judgment of what sort of shrift an ungrateful world gave to research of the eminence of Bernstein's.

12 The individual-characteristics-count bit is the deepest and most persistent theme in educational accounting, played up for more than ever by present DES policymakers. We develop this in DAVIES *et al.* (1983).

13 Moreover, we did not care then, anymore than we have since, for the protective sheath of the professional ideology of client centredness, whose silliest expression was that moment which said 'only teacher can do it' and which continues to compound the difficulty of educational research with values masquerading as facts about teacher-researcher relationships.

14 Talking about instrumentation is always a bit thin without the items: in this case the 'grid' consisted of an A4 page with years 1–5 running across and school subjects written down, accompanied by a legend which defined streaming, setting, mixed ability etc. and invited the school to complete in these terms, glossing any difficulty or unclarity and enclosing (if possible) any written material that would enable us to further our grasp of their grouping procedures. We estimated that someone fully *au fait* with timetable and grouping in the school could do it in ten to fifteen minutes. The information it generated created a very large coding, cleaning and computing task as preface to analysis.

15 Before the point of perspectively cutting, collapsing and verbally correlating they read Red Riding Hood, Godot, Faith, Hirst and Charity, Phoenix Wedding, quality control, one-band realism, mock (3 into 4 *will* go), populist, antisink, transit-camp and Lady Bountiful (or nob ob).

16 As characteristically used by DAUNT (1975).

17 The switch from 'what's in the black box?' to 'how do I get out now I'm in it?' is familiar to us all.

18 SCHLECHTY (1976) was of key importance in showing us that other people had the same problem about the classroom literature.

19 There's a straight thread in the interest back to PERROW (1967), refreshed by the Swedes and WESTBURY (1973).

20 Funders, apart from having minds which are hard to get to know, change them. What is hot issues at one point, good for money, can be stale gossip a little later *qua* substantive issues and methods. The public world is right to accept that the true test of a satisfactory performance is

finishing nicely. But it is not the cry of the impotent, more the shared thought of those who argue that fore, during and aft are not best conceived of in one-best way or neat terms, to suggest that good performance occurs in the context of trusting, open relationships not the hit and run world where it is only expected to be good the once and it's bye bye in the morning.

References

BECKER, H.S. (1971) *Sociological Work*, London, Allen Lane.
BELL, C. and NEWBY, H. (Eds.) (1977) *Doing Sociological Research*, London, Allen and Unwin.
BERNBAUM, G. (1977) *Knowledge and Ideology in the Sociology of Education*, London, Macmillan.
BERNSTEIN, B. (1973) *Class, Codes and Control*, Vol. 2, *Applied studies towards a sociology of language*, 2nd edition, London, Routledge and Kegan Paul.
BERNSTEIN, B. (1974) *Class, Codes and Control*, Vol. 1, *Theoretical studies towards a sociology of language*, 2nd edition, London, Routledge and Kegan Paul.
BERNSTEIN, B. (1977) *Class, Codes and Control*, Vol. 3, London, Routledge and Kegan Paul.
BROWN, G.W. and HARRIS, T. (1978) *The Social Origins of Depression*, London, Tavistock.
BURNS, T. and STALKER, G.M. (1961) *The Management of Innovation*, London, Tavistock.
CICOUREL, A.V. (1964) *Method and Measurement in Sociology*, New York, Free Press.
COHEN, L. and MANION, L. (1980) *Research Methods in Education*, London, Croom Helm.
CORBISHLEY, P. (1977) 'Research findings on teaching groups in secondary schools', in DAVIES, B. and CAVE, R.G. (Eds.) *Mixed Ability Teaching in the Secondary School*, London, Ward Lock.
CORBISHLEY, P. and EVANS, J. (1980) 'Teacher and pastoral care: an empirical comment', in BEST, R. et al. (Eds.) *Perspectives on Pastoral Care*, Heinemann Educational Books.
CORBISHLEY, P., EVANS, J., KENRICK, C. and DAVIES, B. (1981) 'Teacher strategies and pupil identities in mixed-ability curricula: a note on concepts and some examples from Maths' in BARTON, L. and WALKER, S. (Eds.) *Schools, Teachers and Teaching*, Lewes, Falmer Press.
DAHLLOF, U. (1981) *Ability Grouping, Content Validity and Curriculum Process Analysis*, New York, Teachers' College Press.
DAUNT, P.E. (1975) *Comprehensive Values*, London, Heinemann Educational Books.
DAVIES, B. (1976) 'Piggies in the middle — or "Who Sir? No, not me Sir"', in JONES-DAVIES, C. and CAVE, R.G. (Eds.) (1976) *The Disruptive Pupil in the Secondary School*, London, Ward Lock.

DAVIES, B. (1977) 'Meanings and motives in going mixed ability' in DAVIES, B. and CAVE, R.G. (Eds.) *Mixed Ability Teaching in the Secondary School*, London, Ward Lock.

DAVIES, B. and CAVE, R.G. (Eds.) (1977) *Mixed Ability Teaching in the Secondary School*, London, Ward Lock.

DAVIES, B. and EVANS, J. (1983) 'Bringing teachers back in: toward a repositioning of the second person on the log', paper presented to the *Teachers' Careers and Life Histories Conference*, St. Hilda's College, Oxford, 1983.

DAVIES, B. and EVANS, J. (1984) 'Mixed ability and the comprehensive school', in BALL, S.J. (Ed.) *Comprehensive Schooling: A Reader*, Lewes, Falmer Press.

DEMAINE, J. (1981) *Contemporary Theories in the Sociology of Education*, London, Macmillan.

EVANS, J. (1982) 'Teacher strategies and pupil identities in mixed ability curriculum: a case study', unpublished PhD thesis, University of London.

EVANS, J. (1985) *Teaching in Transition: the Challenge of Mixed Ability Grouping*, Milton Keynes, Open University Press.

FLEW, A. (1976) *Sociology, Equality and Education*, London, Macmillan.

GIDDENS, A. (1978) *Central Problems of Social Theory*, London, Macmillan.

GLASER, B.G. and STRAUSS, A.L. (1967) *The Discovery of Grounded Theory*, Chicago, Aldine.

GROSS, N., MASON, W.S. and McEACHERN, A.E. (1966) *Explorations in Role Analysis: Studies in the School Superintendent Role*, New York, Wiley.

LUNDGREN, U.P. (1972) *Frame Factors and the Teaching Process*, Almquist and Wiksell.

MARSH, C. (1983) *The Survey Method*, London, Allen and Unwin.

PERROW, C. (1967) 'A framework for the comparative analysis of organisations', *American Sociological Review*, 32, 2,, pp. 194–208.

RAVITCH, D. (1978) *The Revisionists Revisited: a critique of the radical attack upon schools*, New York, Basic Books.

SCHLECHTY, P.C. (1976) *Teaching and Social Behaviour*, London, Allyn and Bacon, Inc.

SEELEY, J. (1966) 'The "making" and "taking" of problems', *Social Problems*, 14.

SHARP, R. and GREEN, A.G. (1975) *Education and Social Control*, London, Routledge and Kegal Paul.

SIEBER, S.D. (1973) 'The integration of fieldwork and survey methods', *American journal of sociology*, 78, pp. 1335–59.

WESTBURY, I. (1973) 'Conventional classrooms, "open" classrooms and the technology of teaching', *Journal of Curriculum Studies*, 5, 2, pp. 99–121.

WILLIS, P. (1977) *Learning to Labour*, Farnborough, Saxon House.

YOUNG, M.F.D. (Ed.) (1971) *Knowledge and Control: New Directions for the Sociology of Education*, London, Collier-Macmillan.

A Guide to Further Reading

There is now a vast range of British and American textbooks, sets of papers and readings that focus on qualitative methodology. Some material has also been produced that relates specifically to the study of educational settings in general and to the world of schools, classrooms and curriculum projects in particular. The following annotated guide to further reading includes material drawn from sociology, social anthropology and educational studies. It is by no means exhaustive but is intended to give the reader some guidance on books which the editor has found useful.

Methodology

ADAMS, R.N. and PREISS, J.J. (Eds.) (1960) *Human Organisation Research*, Homewood, Ill, Dorsey, provides a range of papers written by sociologists and anthropologists and includes some very useful essays on the use of key informants. It is a 'classic' set of papers.

ADELMAN, C. (Ed.) (1981) *Uttering, Muttering: Collecting, Using and Reporting Talk for Social and Educational Research*, London, Grant McIntyre, contains papers written from a variety of perspectives with a focus on collecting and analyzing data on talk.

AGAR, M. (1981) *The Professional Stranger: An Informal Ethnography*, New York, Academic Press. An anthropological perspective of doing research in which the author draws on examples from his own studies.

BARNES, J.A. (1979) *Who Should Know What?* Harmondsworth, Penguin, is a useful introduction to the ethical issues that confront the investigator. It includes a good bibliography.

BECKER, H.S., GEER, B., RIESMAN, D. and WEISS, R.S. (Eds.) (1968) *Institutions and the Person: Papers Presented to Everett C. Hughes*, Chicago, Aldine. A useful set of papers that include discussions of the conduct of participant observation.

BELL, C. and NEWBY, H. (Eds.) (1977) *Doing Sociological Research*, London,

Allen and Unwin, provides a set of accounts in which sociologists reflect on their research experiences.

BELL, C. and ROBERTS, H. (Eds.) (1984) *Social Researching: Politics, Problems, Practice*, London, Routledge and Kegan Paul; contains reflections on doing research. There is an essay by Sue Scott on researching postgraduate education and some good essays from Janet Finch on interviewing and Nicky James on doing postgraduate research.

BLOCH, M. (1976) *The Historian's Craft*, Manchester, Manchester University Press. A personal account of historical method in which the author outlines the way in which he feels historical research should be practised.

BOGDAN, R. and BIKLEN, S.K. (1982) *Qualitative Research for Education: An Introduction to Theory and Methods*, Boston, Allyn and Bacon, provides a survey of the main theories and methods that can be used in conducting qualitative research on education.

BOGDAN, R. and TAYLOR, S. (1975) *Introduction to Qualitative Research Methods: A Phenomenological Approach to the Social Sciences*, New York, Wiley. A guide to participant observation, interviewing and life history methods drawing on the authors' own experiences.

BOWEN, E.S. (Laura Bohannan) (1964) *Return to Laughter*, Garden City, New York, Doubleday Anchor Books, Natural History Library. A personal account of anthropological research. Originally written in the form of a novel and under a pseudonym.

BULMER, M. (Ed.) (1982) *Social Research Ethics: An Examination of the Merits of Covert Participant Observation*, London, Macmillan, contains a guide to the main debates on ethical issues in Britain and the USA in the 1970s.

BURGESS, R.G. (Ed.) (1982) *Field Research: A Sourcebook and Field Manual*, London, Allen and Unwin, a collection of papers that discuss the main approaches to field research including history. It also contains a section on the use of different research strategies alongside each other.

BURGESS, R.G. (Ed.) (1984a) *The Research Process in Educational Settings: Ten Case Studies*, Lewes, Falmer Press, a series of autobiographical accounts of British research projects on education. It includes discussions of the study of schools, classrooms and the curriculum. Among the contributions is an essay by Lawrence Stenhouse in which he discusses projects he has conducted.

BURGESS, R.G. (1984b) *In the Field: An Introduction to Field Research*, London, Allen and Unwin. An introductory text on field research which provides guidance on data collection and data analysis. Many of the chapters include material drawn from the author's own research while studying a comprehensive school which has been published as *Experiencing Comprehensive Education*, (BURGESS, 1983).

BURGESS, R.G. (Ed.) (1985) *Field Methods in the Study of Education*, Lewes, Falmer Press, includes essays on the problems, processes and procedures involved in doing field research in education.

BURGESS, R.G. (Ed.) (1985b) *Issues in Educational Research: Qualitative Methods*, Lewes, Falmer Press, is a collection of essays that discuss key issues in qualitative research including: theory and theorizing, action research, research and social policy, research and the teacher.

CARR. E.H. (1964) *What is History?*, Harmondsworth, Penguin. A discussion of basic issues and questions about the relationship between history and social science.

COLLIER, J. (1967) *Visual Anthropology: Photography as a Research Tool*, New York, Holt, Rinehart and Winston. One of the few basic guides to photographic methods in social research.

COTTLE, T.J. (1977) *Private Lives and Public Accounts*, New York, New Viewpoints. A guide to the way in which Tom Cottle has developed the art of conversation as a research strategy in his own investigations.

DAVIES, B. (Ed.) (1981) *Educational Analysis*, 3, 1; *The State of Schooling*. A special issue devoted to sociological issues. The essay by Sara Delamont entitled 'All too familiar?' is a very good methodological discussion.

DENZIN, N. (1970a) *The Research Act*, Chicago, Aldine, (second edition published by McGraw Hill in 1978). A useful basic text that has been written from a sociological perspective. There is good guidance on qualitative methods; although readers need to consider the extent to which symbolic interactionism has influenced the way in which Denzin writes about research methods.

DENZIN, N. (Ed.) (1970b) *Sociological Methods: A Sourcebook*, London, Butterworths (second edition published in 1978 by McGraw Hill), is a collection of papers that reflect the main themes in Denzin's textbook.

DITTON, J. and WILLIAMS, R. (1981) 'The fundable vs. the doable: sweet gripes, sour grapes and the SSRC', *Background Papers 1*, University of Glasgow, Department of Sociology. A provocative paper on research funding in the social sciences in the UK. The authors are particularly interested in the way in which they claim qualitative research does (or does not) get funded.

DOUGLAS, J.D. (1970) *The Relevance of Sociology*, New York, Appleton-Century-Crofts. A useful collection of papers that contribute to the political and ethical aspect of social research.

DOUGLAS, J.D. (1976) *Investigative Social Research*, Beverly Hills, California, Sage, discusses a strategy of social research that is based on the techniques of investigative journalism. There is also a useful discussion of using mixed strategies of research and on ethics.

DOLLARD, J. (1935), *Criteria for the Life History*, New Haven, Yale University Press. A classic analysis of life history methods.

EPSTEIN, A.L. (Ed.) (1967) *The Craft of Social Anthropology*, London, Tavistock, a useful set of essays from anthropologists. The paper by Van Velsen on the extended case method is particularly useful.

FILSTEAD, W.J. (Ed.) (1970) *Qualitative Methodology: Firsthand Involvement With the Social World*, Chicago, Markham, is a useful set of essays that especially focus on participant observation and interviewing. There is also a good section that brings together American papers devoted to ethical issues in the 1960s.

FRANKENBERG, R. (Ed.) (1982) *Custom and Conflict in British Society*, Manchester, Manchester University Press. A set of essays on aspects of ethnographic research pioneered by the Manchester School of social anthropologists. The papers help to contextualize early ethnographic studies of schools by David Hargreaves, Colin Lacey and Audrey Lambart. Both Lacey and Lambart have contributed essays to this collection.

FREILICH, M. (Ed.) (1977) *Marginal Natives at Work: Anthropologists in the Field* (2nd Edition) New York, Wiley. An interesting set of reflective essays on anthropological fieldwork. The editor also has a good introduction to fieldwork culture.

GLASER, B.G. (1978) *Theoretical Sensitivity*, San Francisco, Sociology Press, advances the arguments that are included in *The Discovery of Grounded Theory* by Glaser and Strauss.

GLASER, B. and STRAUSS, A.L. (1967) *The Discovery of Grounded Theory*, London, Weidenfeld and Nicolson. A classic statement on the relationship between theory and research in qualitative investigations.

GLUCKMAN, M. (Ed.) (1964) *Closed Systems and Open Minds: the Limits of Naivete in Social Anthropology*, Edinburgh, Oliver and Boyd. A set of papers from British social anthropologists; especially useful on initial problems and on limiting a field of study.

GOLDE, P. (Ed.) (1970) *Women in the Field: Anthropological Experiences*, Chicago, Aldine, provides a set of accounts that highlight the problems which women encounter when doing fieldwork.

HABENSTEIN, R.W. (Ed.) (1970) *Pathways to Data*, Chicago, Aldine, contains reflections on ethnographic research. For those interested in education Blanche Geer's essay on 'Studying a College' is especially relevant.

HAMMERSLEY, M. (Ed.) (1983) *The Ethnography of Schooling*, Driffield, Nafferton. A collection of papers that focus on different aspects of ethnographic research on schools: participant observation, life history and interviewing. The editor focuses the essays around the notion of reflexivity.

HAMMERSLEY, M. and ATKINSON, P. (1983) *Ethnography: Principles in Practice*, London, Tavistock. An introductory text which outlines the main aspects of ethnographic research. Examples are drawn from numerous studies including some from education.

HAMMOND, P.E. (Ed.) (1964) *Sociologists at Work*, New York, Basic Books. Reflections on the research experience. The essay by Blanche Geer on initial field experiences is first rate.

HARGREAVES, D.H. (Ed.) (1980) *Educational Analysis*, 2, 2; *Classroom Studies*, provides a series of reviews on classroom research including: systematic observation, classroom language and ethnography.

JUNKER, B.H. (1960) *Field Work: An Introduction to the Social Sciences*, Chicago, University of Chicago Press. A critical discussion of fieldwork methods. The introduction by Everett Hughes is well worth consulting.

LANGNESS, L.L. (1965) *The Life History in Anthropological Science*, New York, Holt, Rinehart and Winston. A basic guide to the use of life history methods in empirical studies.

LIPSET, S.M. and HOFSTADTER, R. (Eds.) (1968) *Sociology and History: Methods*, New York, Basic Books. A collection of American essays on the relationship between sociology and history which contains useful discussions of concepts and methods.

LOFLAND, J. (1971) *Analyzing Social Settings*, Belmont, CA, Wadsworth. A book with an odd structure but nevertheless a useful practical guide to analysis.

McCALL, G.J. and SIMMONS, J.L. (Eds.) (1969) *Issues in Participant Observation*, Reading, Mass., Addison Wesley, focuses on a wide-ranging set of methodological issues that surround the use of participant observation as a research method.

McCORMICK, R. (Ed.) (1982) *Calling Education to Account*, London, Heinemann. A set of essays written on educational evaluation which includes useful discussions of methods.

MILLS, C.W. (1959) *The Sociological Imagination*, New York, Oxford University Press. A classic discussion which is worth reading and re-reading. The appendix is a critical discussion of the research craft.

NAROLL, R. and COHEN, R. (Eds.) (1973) *A Handbook of Method in Cultural Anthropology*, New York, Columbia University Press. A wide ranging methodological discussion with papers on quantitative and qualitative research.

NIXON, J. (Ed.) (1981) *A Teachers' Guide to Action Research*, London, Grant McIntyre. An interesting set of accounts of research by teachers — worth reading for the insight it provides on methodological problems.

PLATT, J. (1976) *Realities of Social Research*, London, Chatto and Windus for the University of Sussex Press. A fascinating empirical study of the way in which sociologists conduct research.

PLUMMER, K. (1983) *Documents of Life: An Introduction to the Problems and Literature of a Humanistic Method*, London, Allen and Unwin. A survey of documentary materials which includes theoretical discussion and a guide to research practice.

POPKEWITZ, T.S. and TABACHNICK, B.R. (Eds.) (1981) *The Study of Schooling: Field Based Methodologies in Educational Research and Evaluation*, New York, Praeger. A rather varied collection of essays on conducting research in education. The essay by Rachel Sharp is a useful reflection on theory and research.

ROBERTS, H. (Ed.) (1981) *Doing Feminist Research*, London, Routledge and Kegan Paul. A series of reflections on research experience from a feminist perspective. The essay by Catriona Llewellyn is fascinating.

RYNKIEWICH, M. and SPRADLEY, J. (Eds.) (1976) *Ethics and Anthropology: Dilemmas in Fieldwork*, New York, Wiley. A set of anthropological papers that highlight the ethical dimension of research practice.

SCHATZMAN, L. and STRAUSS, A.L. (1973) *Field Research: Strategies for a Natural Sociology*, Englewood Cliffs, NS, Prentice Hall. A useful guide to the conduct of field studies and the use of field methods.

SHIPMAN, M. (Ed.) (1976) *The Organization and Impact of Social Research*, London, Routledge and Kegan Paul. A set of essays whose authors reflect on their research experience. It includes an essay from Colin Lacey on conducting his study *Hightown Grammar* (LACEY, 1970)

SIMONS, H. (Ed.) (1980) *Towards a Science of the Singular*, Norwich, Centre for Applied Research in Education, Occasional Publication No. 10. is a set of essays on different dimensions of doing qualitative research. There are useful essays on documentary film making and journalism.

SPINDLER, G.D. (Ed.) (1970) *Being an Anthropologist: Fieldwork in Eleven Cultures*, New York, Holt, Rinehart and Winston. A book that provides 'the feel' of 'doing fieldwork'.

SPINDLER, G.D. (Ed.) (1982) *Doing the Ethnography of Schooling: Educational Anthropology in Action*, New York, Holt, Rinehart and Winston. A collection of American essays on the use of fieldwork methods in the study of schooling. There is a very useful essay by Spindler and Spindler on studying your own culture.

SPRADLEY, J. (1979) *The Ethnographic Interview*, New York, Holt, Rinehart and Winston and SPRADLEY, J. (1980) *Participant Observation*, New York, Holt, Rinehart and Winston. A pair of books that deal with two separate methods. The author discusses some useful strategies but there is a tendency to make research sound a bit 'mechanical'. There is also some overlap between the volumes.

SRINIVAS, M.N., SHAH, A.M. and RAMASWAMY, E.A. (Eds.) (1979) *The Fieldworker and the Field: Problems and Challenges in Sociological Investigation*, Delhi, Oxford University Press. An interesting set of essays on fieldwork experiences of Indian sociologists.

STANLEY, L. and WISE, E. (1983) *Breaking Out — Feminist Consciousness and Feminist Research*, London, Routledge and Kegan Paul. A further contribution to the debate about the conduct of feminist research.

VIDICH, A.R., BENSMAN, J. and STEIN, M. (Eds.) (1964) *Reflections on Community Studies*, New York, Harper and Row. Essays on doing research in 'community settings' including the classic account of the experiences of Whyte while researching *Street Corner Society*.

WAX, R. (1971) *Doing Fieldwork: Warnings and Advice*, Chicago, University of Chicago Press. A very good guide to the conduct of fieldwork based on the author's own experiences.

Empirical Studies

The papers in this volume discuss many different examples of empirical studies. Further references will also be found in the methodology books listed above. In addition there are many sets of papers reporting different kinds of educational research which utilize qualitative methods. References to these collections can be found in many of the studies. However, the editor considers that there is no substitute for reading full-length studies to get the flavour of how qualitative methods are used. The following list of studies covers a variety of different educational settings: schools, classrooms, free schools, institutions of higher education, teaching hospitals, courses and curriculum projects. Again, the list is by no means exhaustive but provides some studies that the editor has found useful and interesting.

ATKINSON, P. (1981) *The Clinical Experience*, Aldershot, Gower.

BALL, S.J. (1981) *Beachside Comprehensive: A Case Study of Secondary Schooling*, Cambridge, Cambridge University Press.

BECKER, H.S., GEER, B. and HUGHES, E.C. (1968) *Making the Grade*, New York, Wiley.

BECKER, H.S., GEER, B., HUGHES, E.C. and STRAUSS, A.L. (1961) *Boys in White: Student Culture in Medical School*, Chicago, University of Chicago Press.

BERLAK, A. and BERLAK, H. (1981) *Dilemmas of Schooling*, London, Methuen.

BURGESS, R.G. (1983) *Experiencing Comprehensive Education: A Study of Bishop McGregor School*, London, Methuen.

CICOUREL, A. and KITSUSE, J. (1963) *The Educational Decision-Makers*, New York, Bobbs Merrill.

CORRIGAN, P. (1979), *Schooling the Smash Street Kids*, London, Macmillan.

DINGWALL, R. (1977) *The Social Organization of Health Visitor Training*, London, Croom Helm.

EDWARDS, A.D. and FURLONG, V.J. (1978) *The Language of Teaching*, London, Heinemann.

GALTON, M. and WILLCOCKS, J. (1983) *Moving from the Primary Classroom*, Routledge and Kegan Paul.

GOODSON, I.F. (1982) *School Subjects and Curriculum Change*, London, Croom Helm.

HARGREAVES, D.H. (1967) *Social Relations in a Secondary School*, London, Routledge and Kegan Paul.

HARGREAVES, D.H., HESTER, S. and MELLOR, F. (1975) *Deviance in Classrooms*, London, Routledge and Kegan Paul.

KING, R. (1978) *All Things Bright and Beautiful? A Sociological Study of Infants' Classrooms*, London, Wiley.

LACEY, C. (1970) *Hightown Grammar* Manchester, Manchester University Press.

NASH, R. (1973) *Classrooms Observed*, London, Routledge and Kegan Paul.

SHARP, R. and GREEN, A. (1975) *Education and Social Control*, London, Routledge and Kegan Paul.

SHIPMAN, M. (1974) *Inside a Curriculum Project*, London, Methuen.

STANWORTH, M. (1981) *Gender and Schooling: A Study of Sexual Divisions in the Classroom*, London, WRRC (reprinted by Hutchinson 1983).

STENHOUSE, L., VERMA, G.K., WILD, R.D. and NIXON, J. (1982) *Teaching About Race Relations*, London, Routledge and Kegan Paul.

SWIDLER, A. (1979) *Organization Without Authority: Dilemmas of Social Control in Free Schools*, Cambridge, Mass., Harvard University Press.

WILLIS, P. (1977) *Learning to Labour*, Farnborough, Saxon House.

WOLCOTT, H. (1973) *The Man in the Principal's Office*, New York, Holt, Rinehart and Winston.

WOODS, P. (1979) *The Divided School*, London, Routledge and Kegan Paul.

Notes on Contributors

Alison Andrew is a lecturer in sociology at Nene College, Northampton. She initially gained a degree in sociology and education at the University of Warwick after which she proceeded to the University of Leicester where she is registered for a PhD in the School of Education. She has taught on a part-time basis at the universities of Warwick and Leicester and is currently also engaged in part-time work for the Open University. Her research interests include education and labour history and she has a personal and academic involvement in the feminist movement.

Stephen Ball is a lecturer in the sociology of education and course tutor for the MA in Urban Education at King's College, London. He was a lecturer in education and Director of Research in the Education Area at the University of Sussex. He is a sociologist by training and a symbolic interactionist by intellectual commitment. He maintains that his own rather chequered school experience as a pupil provided the basis and impetus for his later interest in the investigation of processes of schooling. His research focuses in particular on comprehensive schools, he is author of *Beachside Comprehensive* (1981), a participant observation case study, and editor of *Comprehensive Schooling: A Reader* (1984).

Robert Burgess is a senior lecturer in sociology at the University of Warwick. He has conducted research on aspects of social research methodology and in the field of education. His main publications include: *Experiencing Comprehensive Education* (1983), *In the Field: An Introduction to Field Research* (1984) and *Education, Schools and Schooling* (1985). He has also edited: *Teaching Research Methodology to Postgraduates: A Survey of Courses in the U.K.* (1979), *Field Research: A Sourcebook and Field Manual* (1982), *Exploring Society* (1982), *The Research Process in Educational Settings: Ten Case Studies*

(1984), *Field Methods in the Study of Education* (1984), and *Key Variables in Social Investigation* (1985). He is especially interested in the development of research methodology in the study of educational settings. He was Honorary General Secretary of the British Sociological Association between 1982 and 1984.

Peter Corbishley was a Research Officer at Chelsea College, University of London and formerly at the University of London Institute of Education between 1975 and 1980.

Brian Davies is Professor of Education at Chelsea College, University of London. He was formerly senior lecturer in sociology of education at the University of London Institute of Education and lectured at Goldsmith's College, London, after a period as a school teacher. He has written widely on the sociology of education and is the author of *Education and Social Control* (1976) and the editor of an issue of *Educational Analysis* which dealt with *The State of Schooling* (1981).

John Evans is a lecturer in the Department of Physical Education, School of Education, University of Southampton. He was formerly a PhD student at Chelsea College, University of London and at the University of London Institute of Education. He was originally in school teaching.

Ivor Goodson studied economic history at University College, London and the London School of Economics. He trained as a teacher at the Institute of Education in London where he gained a distinction. His first teaching appointment was in the newly-opened Countesthorpe College in Leicestershire where he was a specialist teacher in history and social studies. After this he went to Stantonbury Campus in Milton Keynes as Head of Humanities. Since 1979 he has been Director of the Schools Unit in the School of European Studies at the University of Sussex. He has also worked as a research consultant to the European Commission and the Centre for European Education in Brussels. He is currently editing a series of books on *Education and Training* and a second series on *Studies in Curriculum History*. He is author of *School Subjects and Curriculum Change: Case Studies in Curriculum History*, (1983) and *Essays in Curriculum History* (1984).

Stephen Hester is senior lecturer in sociology at Newcastle Polytechnic. He completed his PhD at the University of Kent. He has conducted research at the University of Manchester, and has taught at

Birmingham Polytechnic, the University of Durham, Queen's University and the Ontario Institute for Studies in Education. He has published in the fields of deviance, education and ethnomethodology, and is co-author (with David Hargreaves and Frank Mellor) of *Deviance in Classrooms* (1975). At present he is conducting research into the role of language in the social constitution of deviance in schools.

David Hustler has taught in primary and secondary schools as well as further education. He now lectures in the Department of Educational Studies, Didsbury School of Education, Manchester Polytechnic. He has published several articles including contributions to the two books co-edited by George Payne. His research interests relate to research methodologies generally and applications of conversational analysis in the areas of young children's acquisition of conversational skills, classroom talk and action research.

Catherine Kenrick was a PhD student at Chelsea College, University of London. She was formerly a Research Secretary at the College and at the University of London Institute of Education.

Lynda Measor is a Research Fellow at the Open University. She has worked there with Peter Woods on two research projects. The first project dealt with pupil transfer from primary to secondary education and was published in autumn 1984 by the Open University Press, under the title *Changing Schools — The Pupil Experience of Transfer*. The second project deals with teachers' careers, and researches teachers' experiences over the last forty years in education. This project will be published by Falmer Press.

George Payne died on 23 December, 1983. He taught in primary and secondary schools, before becoming Head of Sociology in the Department of Educational Studies, Didsbury School of Education, Manchester Polytechnic. He published several articles on education and co-edited *Perspectives in Sociology* (1979) and *Doing Teaching* (1982). His research interests focused around conversational analysis with its relevance to teacher research increasingly becoming his major concern.

June Purvis is a senior lecturer in the Faculty of Educational Studies at Oxford Polytechnic University. She has previously taught at Manchester Polytechnic, Portsmouth Polytechnic and at a college of advanced technology and the Open University. In 1978 she went to the Open University on a Social Science Research Council grant to research the education of working-class women in the nineteenth century and became a lecturer there in 1981. She has published articles on the social history of education, women's education, the sociology of teaching and the sociology of the curriculum. At the Open University she has worked on E205 *Conflict and Change in Education: a Sociological Introduction*, and was a co-editor (with Margaret Hales) of one of the set books *Achievement and Inequality in Education* (1983). She was also an organizer for the 1983 British Sociological Association conference on *Gender and Society* and a co-editor (with Eva Gamarnikow, David Morgan and Daphne Taylorson) of the two collections of readings from the conference *Gender, Class and Work* and *The Public and The Private* (both 1983).

Jean Rudduck was a senior lecturer at the Centre for Applied Research in Education at the University of East Anglia but she has recently been appointed Professor of Education at the University of Sheffield. Before joining the Centre at the University of East Anglia in 1970 she was a member of the Schools Council/Nuffield Humanities Curriculum Project team. Her main publications include: *Dissemination of Innovation: The Humanities Curriculum Project* (1976), *The Dissemination of Curriculum Development* (1976, with P. Kelly), *Learning Through Small Group Discussion* (1978), *Making the Most of the Short In-Service Course* (1981), *Teachers In Partnership: Four Studies of In-Service Collaboration* (Ed. 1982), *The Sixth Form and Libraries: Problems of Access to Knowledge* (1984, with David Hopkins), and *Research as a Basis for Teaching: The Work of Lawrence Stenhouse* (Ed. 1984, with David Hopkins).

Rene Saran has worked in industry, commerce and as an adult education lecturer. She is now principal lecturer in politics at the City of London Polytechnic, teaching decision and policy-making courses. Rene Saran's earlier policy research resulted in *Policy-Making in Secondary Education* (1973) and an Open University course unit *The Politics of Educational Policy-Making: Pressures on Central and Local Government* (1979). She is currently working on a book arising from a Social Science Research Council financed investigation into the Burnham salary negotiations since 1945.

Author Index

Subject Index

access
  and research, 11, 23–51, 55,
    56–63, 87, 95, 214
adult education
  in nineteenth-century England,
    186–99
Alexander, Lord, 214, 219, 224
American Anthropologist, The, 17n6
anonymity
  and research, 46, 62
  see also confidentiality
anthropology, 10, 79–80, 81, 123
  see also cognitive anthropology;
    social anthropology
appearance
  of researchers, 37, 58–63, 79
  of teachers, 60–1, 64, 65–6
archives, 14, 207–41
  and Burnham Project, 212–20
  and research on educational
    policy, 207–14
  see also documentary materials;
    historical research
Association for the Advancement of
  State Education, 211
Association of County Councils
  (ACC), 213, 216
Association of Education
  Committees (AEC), 213, 214, 216
audio recordings, 6
audio-visual recordings, 6

'Beachside Comprehensive'
  [school], 25, 26, 33, 80
Beloe Report, 137, 143

bias
  and research, 16, 57, 194–5, 200
  see also objectivity
biographical background
  and qualitative research, 121–51
bipartism, 309
Birmingham
  youth club in, 36

Bishop McGregor School, 80–97
boys
  as key informants, 32
Britain
  educational research in, *passim*
British Library, 103, 107, 186–7,
    195
  Research and Development
    Department of, 103
British Medical Association, 189
Burnham Committee, 212–28, 232,
    239n1
  see also Burnham Project
Burnham Project, 209–28, 231–39
  aims of, 211–12
  archives used in, 212–20
  data gathering for, 212–28
  official documents used in,
    215–20
  research methods applied to,
    231–29
  research sources for, 212–28

Cambridge, University of, 188
Carpenter, M., 191
'case data', 102

343

values
  and research, 14, 210
verification, 103–5, 110, 116n1,
  117n6
video recordings, 6, 7

Wandsworth Emergency College,
  132
'Wendy's Story', 270–6
Whitby, G., 140, 142
Wives of England, The, 195
women
  education of in
    nineteenth-century England,
    179–205
Women of England, The, 194
*Women of Ideas and What Men
  Have Done to Them*, 184
Women's Co-operative Guild, 187,
  197

working class
  and education in
    nineteenth-century England,
    153–78
  and women's education in
    nineteenth-century England,
    179–205
*Working Men's College Journal,
  The*, 194
Working Men's College Movement,
  188, 191, 194, 198, 199
Wrotham Secondary Modern
  [school], 133–6, 140
Wyggeston, 295

Yorkshire
  mechanics institutes in, 188–9,
  191, 199

Young, A., 141